WAR, CULTURE AND SOCIETY
IN RENAISSANCE VENICE

WAR, CULTURE AND SOCIETY IN RENAISSANCE VENICE

―――――

ESSAYS IN HONOUR OF JOHN HALE

EDITED BY
DAVID S. CHAMBERS, CECIL H. CLOUGH
AND MICHAEL E. MALLETT

THE HAMBLEDON PRESS
LONDON AND RIO GRANDE

Published by The Hambledon Press 1993
102 Gloucester Avenue, London NW1 8HX (U.K.)
P.O. Box 162, Rio Grande, Ohio 45674 (U.S.A.)

ISBN 1 85285 090 6

© The contributors 1993

A description of this book is available from
the British Library and from the Library of Congress

Typeset by York House Typographic Ltd
Printed on acid-free paper and bound in
Great Britain by Cambridge University Press

Contents

Acknowledgements		vii
John Hale: A Tribute upon his Seventieth Birthday		ix
J.R. Hale: A Bibliography		xiii
Illustrations		xxv
Contributors		xxix
Abbreviations		xxxi
1	Fortified Enclosures in Italian Cities under *Signori* Nicolai Rubinstein	1
2	The Cittadella of Verona John E. Law	9
3	Fortress and Fleet: The Defence of Venice's Mainland Greek Colonies in the Late Fifteenth Century Simon Pepper	29
4	Venice and the War of Ferrara, 1482-84 Michael E. Mallett	57
5	After the War of Ferrara: Relations between Venice and Ercole d'Este, 1484-1505 Trevor Dean	73
6	Love and War in the Veneto: Luigi da Porto and the True Story of *Giulietta e Romeo* Cecil H. Clough	99
7	Benedetto Agnello, Mantuan Ambassador in Venice, 1530-56 David S. Chambers	129

8	Pietro Barbo – Paul II: *Zentilhomo de Uenecia e Pontifico* Ian Robertson	147
9	Architectural Taste and Style in Early Quattrocento Venice: The Façade of the Ca' d'Oro and its Legacy Richard J. Goy	173
10	Giorgione's Pre-Venetian Beginnings: A New Proposal Terisio Pignatti	191
11	The Language of Sanudo's *Diarii* Anna Laura Lepschy	199
12	Horatio Brown, John Addington Symonds and the History of Venice Brian Pullan	213

| Index | 237 |
| Subscribers | 247 |

Acknowledgements

The editors are most grateful to the Gladys Krieble Delmas Foundation for a generous grant to meet the cost of illustrations, as they are to the Departments of Italian, History and History of Art in University College, London, and the Department of History in the University of Liverpool, for grants in aid of publication. They also wish to thank warmly their publisher Martin Sheppard for his attentive work and forbearance; the Warburg Institute and its Library for essential help and facilities; Dr Stella Fletcher for her research on the bibliography; Dr M.A. James for compiling the index; Patricia Mallett for drawing the map on p. 56; Sarah Quill for providing photographs of John Hale and Ian Jones for his skill in preparing the one selected for this book; finally they would like to thank Lady Hale for advice and for keeping the secret until the moment came to reveal it.

John Hale

(*photo: Sarah Quill*)

John Hale: A Tribute upon his Seventieth Birthday

There is much about John Hale which calls to mind *The Tempest*, of all Shakespeare's plays the one which contains most of the themes essential to the Renaissance. The setting of broad horizons, of travel, of exotic dreams; the characters, the magician and wordsmith Prospero, the mischievous spirit, Ariel, and Caliban, warning us of war and violence; even John's present (it is hoped only temporary) deprivation of speech finds resonance in the play.

John was reared in that tradition of the Italian Renaissance as the dawn of modernity in all aspects of human endeavour, which was fashionable at Oxford in the days of his mentor Cecilia Ady, before the Department of the History of Art was founded and the era of specialisation began to intrude. In that tradition he has shown himself to be as at home in intellectual and cultural history as he is in the political and military world of Machiavelli. John Hale's Renaissance has no compartments; the art of war and the art created for princes are likewise approached from the point of view of their impact on the imaginations, sensibilities and lives of ordinary people. If there is an area in which his work and expertise have made a particular impact it is the history of fortification. But even here it is fortification as art, as the product of human labour and human investment, as symbol of power, as much as fortification as military technique which has interested him. His range is universal, and the bibliography which appears in this volume reminds us of this and calls to mind the exceptional enthusiasm and style with which he tackles every topic. All of his work is tinged with that youthful verve and the fertile imagination and dramatic sense which make his contribution to Renaissance studies so special. It should be remembered that, as well as so many other arts, theatre has always been one of his strongest interests, and that in his earlier years he was acclaimed at Oxford as both actor and producer.

For more than fifteen years a Fellow of Jesus College, John inspired generations of Oxford undergraduates taking the special subject in the

Italian Renaissance. Then, in 1964, he accepted the position of founding professor of history in the University of Warwick, and from this time came to associate himself ever more closely with Venice and the Veneto. His idea of sending history undergraduates abroad to study, and particularly to study in the unique historical environment of Venice, has endured; so has his own commitment to the archives, libraries, works of art and enormous problems of survival of that city. One of his earliest concerns on arriving with the first Warwick students in 1967 was to learn for himself the art of the gondolier, and this – like his determination to take a course in surveying before he began to study military architecture – epitomises so much about John; history in all its aspects has to be experienced, not just studied.

In 1970 John was appointed to the Chair of Italian formerly held by Roberto Weiss at University College, London and in 1985 to a Chair in Italian History at the same college. This move to the capital gave new scope to his widening interests: he joined the Trustees of the National Gallery and quickly became their Chairman; he became increasingly involved in the work of the Museums and Galleries Commission. Among his many other commitments (for instance, he served as Chairman of the Society for Renaissance Studies and was London University's public orator for two years), John's concern for Venice remained paramount; his students continued to study there, he masterminded the *Genius of Venice* exhibition at the Royal Academy in 1983, and he became one of Venice's leading advocates on radio and television as well as being a most active member of the Venice in Peril committee. The honours bestowed on him, culminating in a knighthood in 1984, were received with the characteristic lack of pomposity that all who know him well would have expected.

The decision to focus this volume of essays, written in his honour, on Venice, was a natural and inevitable one. It was, however, a decision which excluded many from contributing, and for that the volume is the poorer. Similarly the editors decided that space would not allow offerings from John's numerous friends overseas, particularly many in Italy and the United States where he has been a frequent visitor, notably at Harvard, Johns Hopkins and Princeton Universities, the University of California at Berkeley and the Folger Library. The late Felix Gilbert was to have been a notable exception to this ban, but sadly his essay was not ready when he died. Thus Terisio Pignatti, one of John's most longstanding Venetian friends, and Ian Robertson (of Melbourne) are the only contributors from abroad. All the writers are friends of John – and in some cases, including each of the editors, his former students – who share his commitment to Renaissance Italy and (nearly all of us) his special attachment to Venice and the Veneto. The range of topics reflects his own diversity of interests. War, of course; culture, naturally; society inevitably; what else could be expected in a tribute to a scholar among whose recent major books have been *War and Society in Renaissance Europe, 1450-1620* and *Artists and Warfare in Renaissance Europe*?

In the popular mind the term 'Renaissance' is associated with the concept of the 'all-round man' – the universalist. In that sense John is indeed a Renaissance man. Supreme stylist and rhetorician, endowed with an encyclopaedic knowledge, he also emanates that genial nonchalance, that *sprezzata disinvoltura*, praised above all other qualities by Castiglione.

The Editors

J.R. Hale: A Bibliography

*Essays preceded by an asterisk are reprinted in *Renaissance War Studies*, 1983. Reviews and review articles are not included.

1950

Edited with Introduction, *Settlers: Being Extracts from the Journals and Letters of Early Colonists in Canada, Australia, South Africa and New Zealand* (London: Faber and Faber), 408 pp., 16 plates, 6 maps.

1951

Great Uncle Toby [a tale], with drawings by Shirley Hughes (London: Faber and Faber), 150 pp., 29 illustrations.

1954

England and the Italian Renaissance: The Growth of Interest in its History and Art (London: Faber and Faber), 216 pp.; for the revised edition see 1963.
Napoleon: The Story of his Life (London: Faber and Faber), 216 pp., 4 plates, map.

1955

'Samuel Rogers and the Italy of *Italy*: A Re-Discovered Journal', *Italian Studies*, X, pp. 43-50.

1956

Introduction and translation, Niccolò Machiavelli, *Mandragola: A Comedy* (Swinford, Eynsham, Oxfordshire: Fantasy Press), x+52 pp.
[First performance using this translation by the Merton College Floats, May 1956.]

Edited with Introduction, Samuel Rogers, *The Italian Journal: With an Account of Rogers' Life and Travel in Italy in 1814-1821* (London: Faber and Faber), 325 pp., 24 illustrations.

'The Cruel Art', *Listener*, LV, no. 1412 (April 19), pp. 454-56, 3 illustrations. Text of a broadcast on the BBC Third Programme.

1957

'International Relations in the West: Diplomacy and War, 1493-1520', *The Renaissance, 1493-1520*, ed. G.R. Potter, *New Cambridge Modern History*, I (Cambridge: Cambridge University Press), pp. 259-91.

'Cosimo and Lorenzo dei Medici: Their Reputation in England from the 16th to the 19th century', *English Miscellany*, VIII, pp. 179-94.

Contributor, *A History of Oxfordshire*, V, ed. Mary D. Lobel, *The Victoria History of the Counties of England* (Oxford: Oxford University Press, for the University of London Institute of Historical Research), pp. 267-75.

1958

'Armies, Navies and the Art of War, 1520-1559', *The Reformation, 1520-1559*, ed. G.R. Elton, *New Cambridge Modern History*, II (Cambridge: Cambridge University Press), pp. 481-509.

'Aids to Memory', *Listener*, LIX, no. 1508 (February 20). Text of a broadcast on the BBC Home Service.

Editor, *The Oxford Magazine*, LXXVI, no. 9 (23 January) to LXXVII, no. 16 (12 March 1959) (Oxford: The Oxonian Press).

1959

'Charles Lever and Italy', *English Miscellany*, X, pp. 233-47.

'In Memoriam: Cecilia M. Ady: A Bibliography of her Books and Articles on Italian Subjects', *Italian Studies*, XIV, p. 105.

1960

★'War and Public Opinion in Renaissance Italy', and 'A Bibliographical Note on Cecilia M. Ady', *Italian Renaissance Studies: A Tribute to the Late Cecilia M. Ady*, ed. E.F. Jacob (London: Faber and Faber), pp. 94-122, 484-87.

1961

The Art of War and Renaissance England, in the series of Folger Booklets on Tudor and Stuart Civilization (University Press of Virginia, for the Folger Shakespeare Library, Washington, D.C.), 59 pp., 25 plates.
Machiavelli and Renaissance Italy, in the Teach Yourself History Library (London: The English Universities Press), xii+244 pp., 2 maps; for the revised edition see 1972.
Edited and translated, Niccolò Machiavelli, *The Literary Works: Mandragola, Clizia, A Dialogue on Language, Belfagor, with Selections from the Private Correspondence*, in the Oxford Library of Italian Classics (London and Florence: Oxford University Press), xxvi+202 pp.
'A Newberry Library Supplement to the Foreign Books in M.J.D. Cockle's *A Bibliography of English Military Books up to 1642 and of Contemporary Foreign Works*', *The Papers of the Bibliographical Society of America*, LV, pp. 137-39.
'Forcing the Young into the Past', *Listener*, LXV, no. 1667 (March 9), pp. 415-16. Text of a broadcast on the BBC Home Service.
'Why did Machiavelli Write *The Prince*?' *Listener*, LXV, no. 1673 (April 20), pp. 698-99. Text of a broadcast on the BBC Third Programme.
'Pulpit and Sword in Renaissance England', *Listener*, LXVI, no. 1690 (August 17), pp. 239-41. Text of a broadcast on the BBC Third Programme.

1962

★'War and Public Opinion in the Fifteenth and Sixteenth Centuries', *Past and Present*, XXII, pp. 18-33.
'The Problem Parent' *Listener*, LXVII, no. 1732 (July 7), pp. 975-76. Text of a broadcast on the BBC Home Service.
'Bow versus Gun' *Listener*, LXVIII, no. 1741 (August 9), pp. 212-13. Text of a broadcast on the BBC Third Programme.

1963

England and the Italian Renaissance: The Growth of Interest in its History and Art, a revised edition of the 1954 publication with a New Preface (London: Arrow Books), 223 pp.

1964

Editor, *The Evolution of British Historiography: From Bacon to Namier* (Cleveland, Ohio, World Publishing Company; London and Melbourne: Macmillan, 1967), 381 pp.

Edited with Introduction, Sir John Smythe, *Certain Discourses Military*, in the series Folger Documents of Tudor and Stuart Civilization (Ithaca: Cornell University Press, for the Folger Shakespeare Library, Washington, D.C.), xcviii+120 pp.

Edited and abridged with Introduction, Francesco Guicciardini, *History of Italy and History of Florence*, in the series The Great Histories. Translated from *Storia d'Italia* and *Storia fiorentina* by Cecil Grayson (New York: Washington Square Press; London: New English Library, 1966), lii+ 378 pp.

Translation, Giordano Bruno, *The Candle Bearer,* in *The Genius of the Italian Theater*, ed. Eric Bentley (New York: The New America Library of World Literature), pp. 194-314 with appendix.

★'The Argument of Some Military Title Pages of the Renaissance', *Newberry Library Bulletin*, VI, no. 4, pp. 91-102.

★'An Anomalous Elizabethan', *Listener*, LXXII, no. 1842 (July 15), pp. 93-94. Text of a broadcast on the BBC Third Programme.

1965

Editor [with J.R.L. Highfield and B. Smalley], *Europe in the Late Middle Ages* (London: Faber and Faber), 521 pp., 42 plates, 3 maps.

★'The Early Development of the Bastion: An Italian Chronology, *c.* 1450-*c.* 1534', *Europe in the Late Middle Ages*, ed. J.R. Hale, J.R.L. Highfield and B. Smalley (London: Faber and Faber), pp. 466-94. 42 plates, 1 map.

With the Editors of Time-Life Books, *Renaissance*, in the series Great Ages of Man: A History of the World's Cultures (New York: Time Incorporated), 191 pp., 168 illustrations, 2 genealogies, 2 maps, 3 chronological charts.

1966

With the Editors of Time-Life Books, *Age of Exploration*, in the series Great Ages of Man: A History of the World's Cultures (New York: Time Incorporated), 192 pp., 116 illustrations, 19 maps, 2 chronological charts.
'What Help from Art?' [for historians], *Times Literary Supplement*, no. 3345 (April 7), pp. 292-93.
★'Gunpowder and the Renaissance: An Essay in the History of Ideas', *From the Renaissance to the Counter Reformation: Essays in Honor of Garrett Mattingly*, ed. C.H. Carter (New York: Random House; London: Jonathan Cape), pp. 133-44.

1967

'A World Elsewhere: Geographical Horizons and Mental Horizons', *The Age of the Renaissance*, ed. Denys Hay (London: Thames and Hudson; New York: McGraw Hill), pp. 317-45, 43 illustrations.

1968

Renaissance Exploration (London: British Broadcasting Corporation), 110 pp., 16 plates, map. Based on seven talks first broadcast on BBC Radio 3 in 1968.
'Armies, Navies and the Art of War, 1559-1610', *The Counter Reformation and Price Revolution, 1559-1610*, ed. R.B. Wernham, *New Cambridge Modern History*, III (Cambridge: Cambridge University Press), pp. 171-208.
★'Francesco Tensini and the Fortification of Vicenza', *Studi veneziani*, X, pp. 231-89, 5 plates.
★'The End of Florentine Liberty: The Fortezza da Basso', *Florentine Studies: Politics and Society in Renaissance Florence*, ed. Nicolai Rubinstein (London: Faber and Faber), pp. 501-32, 39 plates.

★'The True Shakespearean Blank', *Shakespeare Quarterly*, XIX, no. 1, pp. 33-40.
'Museums and the Teaching of History', *Museum*, XXI, no. 1, pp. 67-78.

1969

Advisory Editor, *Renaissance and Reformation*, text by Robert Knecht, in the series *The Hamlyn History of the World in Colour*, IX (Feltham: Hamlyn), 128 pp., 156 illustrations.

1971

Renaissance Europe, 1480-1520, in the series The Fontana History of Europe (London: Fontana), 350 pp., 5 maps. Reissued in 1972 as *Renaissance Europe: Individual and Society 1480-1520* (New York, Harper and Row).
★'Incitement to Violence? English Divines on the Theme of War, 1578 to 1631', *Florilegium Historiale: Essays Presented to Wallace K. Ferguson*, ed. J.G. Rowe and W.H. Stockdale (Toronto: University of Toronto Press), pp. 369-99.
★'Sixteenth-century Explanations of War and Violence', *Past and Present*, LI, pp. 3-26.
★'The First Fifty Years of a Venetian Magistracy: The *Provveditori alle Fortezze*', *Renaissance Studies in Honor of Hans Baron*, ed. Anthony Molho and John A. Tedeschi (Florence: Sansoni), pp. 501-29.
With Denys Hay, *The Renaissance* (Wakefield: Sussex Tapes). Sound cassette and booklet.

1972

'Violence in the Late Middle Ages: A Background', *Violence and Disorder in Italian Cities, 1200-1500*, ed. Lauro Martines (Berkeley and London: University of California Press), pp. 19-37.
'La Serenissima: Social Harmony in Renaissance Venice', *Listener*, LXXXVIII, no. 2261 (July 27), pp. 106-8. Text of a broadcast on BBC Radio 3.
Machiavelli and Renaissance Italy, revised edition of the 1961 publication (Harmondsworth: Penguin Books), xii+190 pp. 2 maps.

1973

Editor, *Renaissance Venice* (London, Faber and Faber), 483 pp., 53 plates, map, tables.
★'Military Academies on the Venetian Terraferma in the Early Sixteenth Century', *Studi veneziani*, XV, pp. 273-95.

1974

'From Peacetime Establishment to Fighting Machine: The Venetian Army in the War of Cyprus and Lepanto', *Il Mediterraneo nella seconda metà del '500 alla luce di Lepanto*, ed. Gino Benzoni (Florence: Leo S. Olschki, for the Fondazione Cini, Venice), pp. 163-84.
'The Renaissance Label', *Background to the English Renaissance*, introductory lectures with a foreword by J.B. Trapp (London: Gray-Mills Publishing), pp. 31-42.
'The Renaissance of Giorgio Vasari', *Listener*, XCII, no. 2365 (July 25), pp. 112-13. Text of a broadcast on BBC Radio 3.
'Florence: The Fifth Element', *Listener*, XCII, unnumbered (October 10), pp. 462-65, 2 illustrations. Text of a BBC Television Programme.

1975

★'Men and Weapons: The Fighting Potential of Sixteenth-Century Venetian Galleys', *War and Society: A Yearbook of Military History*, ed. Brian Bond and Ian Roy (London: Croom Helm), pp. 1-23.
★'To Fortify or not to Fortify? Machiavelli's Contribution to the Renaissance Debate', *Essays in Honour of John Humphreys Whitfield*, ed. H.C. Davis, J.M. Hatwell, D.G. Rees and G.W. Slowey (London: St. George's Press, for the Department of Italian, University of Birmingham), pp. 99-119.

1976

★'The Military Education of the Officer Class in Early Modern Europe', *Cultural Aspects of the Italian Renaissance: Essays in Honour of Paul Oskar Kristeller*, ed. Cecil H. Clough (Manchester: Manchester University Press; New York: Alfred F. Zambelli), pp. 440-61.
'Art and Audience: The Medici Venus, *c.* 1750-*c.* 1850', *Italian Studies*, XXXI, pp. 37-58.

1977

Florence and the Medici: The Pattern of Control (London: Thames and Hudson), 208 pp., 36 plates.

Italian Renaissance Painting from Masaccio to Titian (Oxford: Phaidon; New York: E.P. Dutton) 271 pp., 188 plates.

Renaissance Fortification: Art or Engineering? The Eighth Walter Neurath Memorial Lecture (London: Thames and Hudson), 64 pp., 62 illustrations.

★'Andrea Palladio, Polybius and Julius Caesar', *Journal of the Warburg and Courtauld Institutes*, XL, pp. 240-55, 14 plates.

★'Printing and the Military Culture of Renaissance Venice', *Medievalia et Humanistica*, n.s. VIII, pp. 21-62; for the revised edition in Italian see 'Industria del Libro . . .' 1980.

1978

★*On a Tudor Parade Ground: The Captain's Handbook of Henry Barrett, 1562.* Text of the Annual Lecture of the Society for Renaissance Studies, delivered at University College, London, on 13 January 1978. The Society for Renaissance Studies, Occasional Papers 5 (London: The Society for Renaissance Studies), 54 pp., 6 plates.

Editor and Translator from the Italian (with J.M.A. Lindon), Antonio de Beatis, *The Travel Journal: Germany, Switzerland, The Low Countries, France and Italy, 1517-1518*, Hakluyt Society, 2nd series CL (London: Hakluyt Society), xii+206 pp., 2 plates, genealogy, map, table.

'Renaissance Armies and Political Control: The Venetian Provveditorial System, 1509-1529', *Journal of Italian History*, II, pp. 11-31.

'Terra Ferma Fortifications in the Cinquecento', *Florence and Venice: Comparisons and Relations*, 2 vols., ed. Sergio Bertelli, Nicolai Rubinstein and Craig Hugh Smyth (Florence: La Nuova Italia, for Villa I Tatti, The Harvard Center for Italian Renaissance Studies), II, pp. 169-87.

1980

'Industria del Libro e Cultura militare nel Rinascimento', *Storia della cultura veneta: Dal primo quattrocento al concilio di Trento* (Vicenza: Neri Pozza), III, parte 2, pp. 245-88; revised edition of 'Printing and Military Culture . . .' 1977.

1981

Editor and Contributor, *A Concise Encyclopaedia of the Italian Renaissance*, The World of Art Library (London: Thames and Hudson), 360 pp., 237 illustrations, 3 maps, 11 genealogies, chronological chart.

'Castiglione's Military Career', *Italian Studies*, XXXVI, pp. 41-57. Reissued in *Castiglione: The Ideal and the Real in Renaissance Culture*, ed. Robert W. Hanning and David Rosand (London and New Haven, Conn.; Yale University Press, 1983), pp. 143-64, with the notes reduced.

Contributor, *Great Paintings*, ed. Edwin Mullins (London: British Broadcasting Corporation; New York: St. Martin's Press), pp. 74-9, 186-91, 270-5. Based on the BBC Television series '100 Great Paintings'.

1982

'Brescia and the Venetian Militia System in the Cinquecento', *Armi e cultura nel bresciano, 1420-1870* (Brescia: Ateneo di Brescia), pp. 97-120.

★'Tudor Fortifications, 1485-1558', *The History of the King's Works*, IV ed. Howard Colvin (London: H.M.S.O.), pp. 367-401, 20 illustrations.

Renaissance War Studies (London: The Hambledon Press), x+524 pp., 118 plates, figures, maps, tables; for the contents see the head of this Bibliography.

'Italian Renaissance Images of War'. The Selwyn Brinton Lecture, delivered to the Royal Society of Arts, on 25 May 1983, *Journal of the Royal Society of Arts*, CXXXII, no. 5329, pp. 61-79, 14 plates.

'Humanism and Renaissance: 1350-1527', *The Italian World: History, Art and the Genius of a People*, ed. John Julius Norwich (London: Thames and Hudson), pp. 121-46, 42 illustrations.

'Venice and its Empire', *The Genius of Venice, 1500-1600*, ed. Jane Martineau and Charles Hope. Exhibition Catalogue (London: Royal Academy of Arts in aassociation with Weidenfeld and Nicholson), pp. 11-15, 3 illustrations; also Catalogue entries H16-18, pp. 400-1.

1984

With Michael E. Mallett, *The Military Organization of a Renaissance State: Venice, c. 1400 to 1617* (Cambridge: Cambridge University Press), xiv+525 pp., 2 maps, tables, diagrams.

'Post-Renaissance Fortification: Two *Relazioni* by Francesco Tensini on the Defence of the Terraferma (1618-1632)', *Proceedings of the Conference on Fortifications* (Vicenza: Centro Andrea Palladio), pp. 11-12.

1985

War and Society in Renaissance Europe, 1450-1620, in the series Fontana History of European War and Society (London: Fontana, in association with Leicester University Press), 282 pp.
'Girolamo Maggi: A Renaissance Scholar and Military Buff', *Italian Studies*, XL, pp. 31-50, 5 plates.
'Shakespeare and Warfare', *William Shakespeare: His Work, his World and his Influence*, ed. J.F. Andrews (New York: Scribner, 2 vols.), I, pp. 85-98.
'The Soldier in Germanic Graphic Art of the Renaissance', *Journal of Interdisciplinary History*, XVII, pp. 85-114, 11 illustrations. Reissued in *Art and History: Images and Their Meaning,* ed. Robert I. Rotberg and Theodore K. Rabb (Cambridge: Cambridge University Press, 1988), pp. 85-114, 11 illustrations.

1986

'Soldiers in the Religious Art of the Renaissance', *Bulletin of the John Rylands University Library of Manchester*, LXIX, 1, pp. 166-94, 8 illustrations.

1988

'A Humanistic Visual Aid: The Military Diagram in the Renaissance', *Renaissance Studies*, II, pp. 280-98, 12 illustrations.
'Michiel and the *Tempesta*: The Soldier in a Landscape as a Motif in Venetian Painting', *Florence and Italy: Renaissance Studies in Honour of Nicolai Rubinstein*, ed. Peter Denley and Caroline Elam. Westfield Publications in Medieval History, 2 (London: Committee for Medieval Studies, Westfield College, University of London), pp. 405-18, 6 plates.
'Women and War in the Visual Arts of the Renaissance', and 'Epilogue: Experience and Artifice', *War, Literature and the Arts in Sixteenth-Century Europe*, ed. J.R. Mulryne and Margaret Shewring (London: Macmillan), pp. 43-62, 12 plates, pp. 190-96.

1989

'The Battle Scene in Italian Renaissance Art', *L'età dei Della Rovere*, 2 vols., *Atti e memorie della società savonese di storia patria*, n.s., XXV, II, pp. 171-85.

1990

Artists and Warfare in the Renaissance (New Haven, Connecticut and London: Yale University Press), ix+278 pp., 345 illustrations.

1991

'Venezia e la rivoluzione militare europea', *Crisi e rinnovamenti nell'autumno del rinascimento a Venezia*, ed. V. Branca and C. Ossola in the series Civiltà veneziana, saggi XXXVIII (Florence: Leo S. Olschki, for the Fondazione Cini, Venice), pp. 85-103.

1993

The Civilization of Europe in the Renaissance (New York and London: Harper-Collins), forthcoming.

Illustrations

John Hale (*photo: Sarah Quill*)   *facing* viii

Between Pages 88 and 89

Plate I   Giorgione, *The Preaching of John The Baptist* (*Pearl Collection, Washington DC*)

Plate II   Lazzaro Bastiani (attrib.), *The Piazzetta* (oil on panel, *c.* 1490): Doge Agostino Barbarigo meeting Duke Ercole d'Este and his son Alfonso, in Venice for the carnival, February 1488 (*Museo Correr; photo: Osvaldo Böhm, Venice*)

Between Pages 24 and 25

1   Verona, *c.* 1439 (*Biblioteca Comunale, Verona*)
2   Citadella area of Verona, *c. 1439 (detail of Fig. 1)*
3   Verona, late fifteenth century (*Biblioteca Comunale, Verona*)
4   Cittadella area of Verona, late fifteenth century (detail of *Fig. 3*)
5   Verona in 1540 (*British Library*)
6   Modon, late fifteenth-century view from E. Reuwich's engraving for Bernard von Breydenbach, *Peregrinationes in Terram Sanctam* (Mainz, E. Reuwich, 1486) (*British Library*)
7   Modon, fifteenth-century ravelin viewed from the north west (*Photo: Simon Pepper*)
8   Modon, Sea Fort viewed from the southern end of the town (*Photo: Simon Pepper*)

9 Modon, dressed-stone gunport and relieving arch in east face of fifteenth-century ravelin (*Photo: Simon Pepper*)

10 Napoli di Romania (Nauplion), Acropolis, Venetian fifteenth-century scarping to the Castle of the Franks (*Photo: Simon Pepper*)

11 Napoli di Romania (Nauplion), Acropolis, late fifteenth-century Venetian artillery tower on the most exposed north-east corner of the land front (*Photo: Simon Pepper*)

12 Coron, fifteenth-century cylindrical Venetian gun-towers (*Photo: Simon Pepper*)

13 Medallion of Lucina Savorgnan, engraved by Fra Antonio da Brescia (diameter 46 mm. unique copy. (a) Reverse: The Triumph of Chastity (?) (b) Obverse: Portrait bust (*Museo Civico, Trento; photo: C.H. Clough*)

14 Pope Paul II, marble bust by unknown Roman sculptor, *c.* 1470 (*Museo Nazionale del Palazzo Venezia, Rome; photo: C.H. Clough*)

15 The birthplace in Venice of Pietro Barbo (Paul II); façade towards the Rio della Pietà (*Photo: Jeremy Kruse*)

Between Pages 184 and 185

16 Ca'd'Oro, Venice: façade to the Grand Canal (*Photo: Richard Goy*)

17 Ca'd'Oro: detail of *loggia*, by Matteo Raverti, *c.* 1425-26 (*Photo: Richard Goy*)

18 Ca'Foscari, Venice: the eight-light window of the *piano nobile* and the windows to the top storey, derived from Raverti (*Photo: Richard Goy*)

19 Palazzo Giovanelli, Venice: principal façade towards the Rio di Noale (*Photo: Richard Goy*)

20 Palazzo Cavalli (later Franchetti), Venice: façade to the Grand Canal (*Photo: Richard Goy*)

21 Palazzo Venier Contarini, Venice: façade to the Grand Canal (detail) (*Photo: Richard Goy*)

22 Porta della Carta, Palazzo Ducale, Venice: central window by the Bon workshop (detail) (*Photo: Richard Goy*)

23 Giorgione, *Rustic Idyll* (*Museo Civico, Padua*)

24 Giorgione, *The Judgement of Solomon* (detail) (*Uffizi, Florence*)

25 Giulio Campagnola, St Jerome (engraving) (*Department of Prints and Drawings, British Museum, London*)

26 Unidentified fifteenth-century German artist, *St John the Baptist* (woodcut) (*Kupferstichkabinett, Berlin*)

27 Conrad von Megenberg, *Buch der Natur (Augsburg, 1482)* (woodcut) (*Germanisches National Museum, Nuremberg*)

28 Giorgione, *The Preaching of John the Baptist* (*Pearl Collection, Washington DC*)

29 Unidentified fifteenth-century artist, *woodcut in the anon. Plenarium* (Augsburg, 1489)

30 Lucas Cranach, *The Preaching of John the Baptist* (woodcut) (*Albertina, Vienna*)

31 Albrecht Dürer, woodcut in Sebastian Brant, *Das Narrenschiff* (Basle, 1494), fol. 22 (*Germanisches National Museum, Nuremberg*)

32 Giorgione, *The Epiphany* (*National Gallery, London*)

33 Giorgione, *The Preaching of John the Baptist* (detail) (*Pearl Collection, Washington DC*)

34 Giorgione, *The Preaching of John the Baptist* (X-ray photograph) (*Pearl Collection, Washington DC*)

35 Giorgione, *Rustic Idyll* (detail of X-ray photograph) (*Museo Civico, Padua*)

36 Giorgione, *Rustic Idyll* (detail of X-ray photograph) (*Museo Civico, Padua*)

37 *The Epiphany* (detail of X-ray photograph) (*National Gallery, London*)

38 Horatio Brown (*Bristol University Library*)

Illustrations in Text

i	Venetian Greece: the theatre of operations, 1499–1500, with inset showing Venetian colonies in southern Messenia	31
ii	Fortifications of Modon in 1500, redrawn and adapted from the survey for Francesco Grimani (1685–1715)	32
iii	Modon, sketch-plan of Venetian ravelin at the lower level and two sections	33
iv	Map illustrating the Po Valley and the War of Ferrara, 1482–84 (*Patricia Mallett*)	56
v	Ferrara, 1490 (woodcut) (*Biblioteca Estense, Modena*)	75

Contributors

David S. Chambers	Warburg Institute, University of London
Cecil H. Clough	Department of History, University of Liverpool
Trevor Dean	Department of History, Roehampton Institute, London
Richard J. Goy	London
John E. Law	Department of History, University of Wales, Cardiff
Anna Laura Lepschy	Department of Italian, University College, London
Michael Mallett	Department of History, University of Warwick
Simon Pepper	Department of History, University of Liverpool
Terisio Pignatti	Biblioteca Correr, Venice
Brian Pullan	Department of History, University of Manchester
Ian Robertson	Melbourne
Nicolai Rubinstein	Warburg Institute, University of London

Abbreviations

ASFi	Archivio di Stato, Florence
ASMa	Archivio di Stato, Mantua, Archivio Gonzaga
ASMi	Archivio di Stato, Milan, Archivio Sforzesco
ASMo	Archivio di Stato, Modena, Archivio Segreto Estense, Cancelleria
ASPar	Archivio di Stato, Parma
ASUd	Archivio di Stato, Udine
ASegVat	Archivio Segreto Vaticano (Vatican Archives)
ASV	Archivio di Stato, Venice
ASVer	Archivio di Stato, Verona
RIS	L. Muratori, *Rerum Italicarum Scriptores* (new edn. unless otherwise indicated)
Sanuto	Marino Sanuto [Marin Sanudo], *I diarii*, ed. N. Barozzi, G. Berchet, R. Fulin, and F. Stefani, 58 vols (Venice, 1879-1903)

Other abbreviations are indicated in individual essays

1

Fortified Enclosures in Italian Cities under *Signori*

Nicolai Rubinstein

When, at Naples in 1535, Florentine exiles presented to Charles V a list of complaints about the rule of Duke Alessandro de' Medici, among the evidence to prove the tyrannical nature of that rule they cited his building of a large fortress near the Porta a Faenza. The building of the Fortezza da Basso, to which John Hale has devoted the definitive study,[1] had just reached the point when it was ready to receive its first garrison.[2] The exiles argued that: 'avere edificato una fortezza, [era] cosa tutta aliena a qualunche città libera,'[3] as was shown by the example of Venice, Siena, Lucca and Genoa.[4] In his response to the exiles' complaints, Alessandro asserted that their very existence proved how necessary such a fortress was for his own and his citizens' safety.[5]

The duke's reply had, most probably, been drafted by Francesco Guicciardini, his counsellor at Naples.[6] A few years earlier, Guicciardini, when commenting on Machiavelli's statement in the *Discourses on the First Decade of Livy*, that to a prince 'nothing could be more useless than a fortress as a means to keep his citizens in check,'[7] had substituted, for Machiavelli's 'to a prince', 'to a tyrant of a city, and to every prince'.[8] In describing, in contrast

---

1 'The end of Florentine liberty: the Fortezza da Basso', in N. Rubinstein ed., *Florentine Studies. Politics and Society in Renaissance Florence* (London, 1968), pp. 501-32.
2 Ibid., p. 514: on 5 December 1535. Its foundation stone had been laid only one and a half years earlier.
3 Their grievances and demands are edited by G. Canestrini, in Francesco Guicciardini, *Opere inedite*, 10 vols., (Florence, 1857-67), IX, pp. 331-54, 375-8, 386-8, 389-92.
4 Ibid., p. 336; cf. p. 377: 'a' capi pubblici non tirannici basti al tenergli sicuri l'autorità del magistrato e benevolenza de' cittadini'. Cf. Donato Giannotti, *Republica fiorentina*, I, 1, ed. G. Silvano (Geneva, 1990), p. 75: 'al presente niuno è che non possa conoscere quale sia la intenzione di chi è padrone della presente tiran-

nide, vedendo levati i magistrati, edificare fortezze . . .' The work was completed in 1534.
5 Guicciardini, *Opere*, IX, p. 369: 'Che la deliberazione del fare la fortezza fussi bene consultata e necessaria . . . ne fanno testimonio questi medesimi che la dannano . . .'
6 See R. Ridolfi, *Vita di Francesco Guicciardini* (Rome, 1960), p. 374.
7 *Discorsi sopra la prima deca di Tito Livio*, ed. S. Bertelli (Milan, 1960), II, 24, p. 351: 'tale fortezza per tenere in freno i suoi cittadini non può essere più inutile.' Cf. *Il Principe*, c. xx.
8 *Considerazioni intorno ai Discorsi del Machiavelli sopra la prima deca di Tito Livio*, in F. Guicciardini, *Scritti politici e Ricordi*, ed. R. Palmarocchi (Bari, 1933), p. 58: 'dico che ad uno tiranno di una città, ed a ogni principe, sono utilissime le fortezze . . .'

to Machiavelli, the possession of a fortress as useful, he refers in the first place, to tyrants, and only in the second place to princes in general. Guicciardini was conforming to republican language. Ever since the early years of the signorial regime, the building of fortresses was considered to be characteristic of its tyrannical nature; indeed, it was the most visible manifestation of the power of a tyrant who, as Savonarola put it much later, 'per forza sopra tutti vuole regnare', and in particular of one 'che di cittadino è fatto tiranno',[9] as had been the case of many *signori*. In his *De institutione rei publicae*, composed between 1465 and 1471, the Sienese humanist Francesco Patrizi discusses the question whether a fortress (*arx*) is to be erected in a free city.[10] He cites Pseudo-Asconius as having most fittingly defined a fortress as a tyrant's seat, *sedem tyranni*,[11] and praises the Corinthian Timoleon for having demolished that of Syracuse[12] after having captured it from that city's tyrant. Timoleon's exemplary action, he says, 'taught that a city which is held with the help of a fortress can hardly ever exist without tyranny'.[13]

Even before the new despotic regime had taken root in northern Italy in the last decades of the thirteenth century, Ezzelino da Romano appears to have tried to impose his rule over his short-lived dominions by building castles in subject cities,[14] and during the following century *signori* such as the Este at Ferrara and the Della Scala at Verona would either build new castles in their cities or strengthen existing ones, to protect themselves against popular risings and enemy factions.[15] But castles, *rocche*, were not the only type of fortification to which the *signori* resorted to secure their safety and to enforce their absolute authority over the citizens. During the formative period of the signorial regime, when its authority was often fragile, fortified enclosures within the city walls might offer a form of

9 *Trattato circa el reggimento e governo della città di Firenze*, II, 2, in G. Savonarola, *Prediche sopra Aggeo*, ed. L. Firpo (Rome, 1965), p. 456.
10 VIII, 9 (Strasburg, 1608), pp. 338-41: 'sitne statuenda arx in urbe liberae civitatis'. On the date of composition, see F. Battaglia, *Enea Silvio Piccolomini e Francesco Patrizi: Due politici senesi del Quattrocento* (Florence, 1936), p. 101.
11 Ibid. In fact, Aristotle argues, in *Politics*, VII, 1330b, that a hill-citadel (acropolis), while suitable for an oligarchy and a monarchy, does not suit a democracy.
12 'Optime Pedianus arcem definit sedem esse tyranni'. Cf. Pseudo-Asconius [Pedianus], *In divinationem*, 18, T. Stangl ed., *Ciceronis orationum scholiastae*, ii, (Hildesheim, 1964), p. 191: 'Arx vel sedes tyranni dicitur, ut saepe alibi'. . .
13 'docuit urbem, quae arcis praesidio teneretur,

vix unquam sine tyrannide esse posse'. The source of this statement is Plutarch's *Life of Timoleon*, 22, where he narrates how Timoleon made the Syracusans destroy the citadel, 'the tyrants' bulwark'.
14 He did so in Brescia. Cf. Rolandino da Padova, *Cronica in factis et circa facta Marchie Trivixane*, ed. A. Bonardi, *RIS*, VIII, i (1905-7), p. 151: 'castra fieri fecit in civitate ad omnium detrimentum et mortem'. See *Storia di Brescia*, III (Brescia, 1964), p. 1089.
15 On Ferrara, see Ferreto de' Ferreti, *Historia rerum in Italia gestarum*, in *Opere*, ed. C. Cipolla (Rome, 1908-20), I, pp. 237, 243-4; on Verona, G. Barbetta, *Le mura e le fortificazioni di Verona* (Verona, 1978), pp. 45-8, and John Law's contribution to this volume, below pp. 9-27.

protection which could ensure military control over wider areas of the city than a *rocca*. There were precedents, though on a much smaller scale, of such enclosures in the fortified enclaves with their own piazze which in the thirteenth century magnate lineages and *consorterie* had, in a number of cities, created around their houses and towers.[16] In Genoa, one such precinct, that of the Doria, had even provided the seat of the government.[17] But while fortified enclaves such as the Genoese *contrade*[18] and the Sienese *castellari*[19] were designed to defend noble families from attacks by their enemies, and to reinforce their dominant position in their neighbourhood, the fortified enclosures erected by *signori* were to secure their control of the city by transforming part of it into a citadel.

One of the earliest examples of such fortified enclosures of *signori* is provided by Modena. In order to enjoy more securely the rule his father had established over that town, writes a near-contemporary chronicler, Azzo VIII d'Este, who had succeeded as *signore* in 1293, built within the city 'mirabile oppidum muris valloque septum', a town within the town surrounded by walls and moats, demolishing in the process a large part of the city.[20] This enclosure was destroyed by the Modenese in 1306 after they had expelled the Este.[21]

Yet Azzo's *mirabile oppidum* within the walls of Modena could have served as a model for the citadel which Castruccio Castracani built in Lucca after having been elected, in 1320, *dominus generalis* for life.[22] Giovanni Villani called it a *castello*; but like the citadel at Modena, which was in its turn

---

16 See F. Niccolai, 'I consorzi nobiliari ed il comune nell'alta e media Italia', *Rivista di storia del diritto italiano*, XIII (1940), pp. 299-300, and the following notes.

17 E. Poleggi, 'Le contrade delle consorterie nobiliari a Genova tra il XII e il XIII secolo', *Urbanistica*, XLII-XLIII (1965), p. 18.

18 Ibid., pp. 15-20 and L. Grossi Bianchi and E. Poleggi, *Una città portuale del medioevo: Genova nei secoli X-XVI* (Genoa, 1980), pp. 109-11. Cf. D. Owen Hughes, 'Urban Growth and Family Structure in Medieval Genoa', *Past and Present*, LXVI (1975), pp. 9-11.

19 One of these enclaves, that of the Ugurgieri, still exists. On enclaves owned by magnate lineages in Florence, see now C. Lansing, *The Florentine Magnates: Lineage and Faction in a Medieval Commune* (Princeton, 1991), pp.93-7, 100-1; but cf. F. Klein, 'Ceti dirigenti e controllo dello spazio urbano a Firenze: i legami di vicinato', in *I ceti dirigenti nella Toscana tardo comunale* (Florence, 1983), pp. 212-13, who considers such enclaves around a private piazza to have been exceptional in Florence.

20 Ferreto, *Historia*, I, p. 214: '. . . intra Mutine aggeres labore multo construxit, cuius ambitus magnam nobilissime urbis portionem destruxit'.

21 Ferreto calls here the enclosure which he had just described as an *oppidum*, a *castrum* ('castrumque ab Azone constructum'; see below, n. 41). In thirteenth- and fourteenth-century Italy, the word *castrum*, *castello*, was used for fortified villages and small towns, see J. Plesner, *L'émigration de la campagne à la ville libre de Florence au XIIIe siècle* (Copenhagen, 1934), ch. 1; it was clearly with this meaning that Ferreto applied it to the fortified enclosure within the city.

22 L. Green, *Castruccio Castracani: A Study on the Origins and Character of a Fourteenth-Century Italian Despotism* (Oxford, 1986), p. 81. Castruccio had been in mercenary service in northern Italy early in the century: ibid., pp. 45-7.

described as a castle, it was a fortified enclosure.[23] Thanks to Louis Green's study of this enclosure, which Castruccio called *Augusta*, we are able to trace its boundaries with considerable accuracy.[24] Ringed by a *fortissimo muro* with twenty-four towers, it included a large part, according to Villani about one fifth, of the city. Castruccio resided within this enclosure in the palace of one of his supporters, the Dal Portico; together with newly acquired buildings and with its *cortile del signore*, it formed the centre of his government and administration.[25] While, if we are to believe Ferreto de'Ferreti, Azzo VIII demolished 'a large part' of Modena to construct his citadel,[26] Castruccio appears to have limited such demolitions almost exclusively to properties that were to make place for the walls he had constructed for the *Augusta* and a space beyond them.[27] According to Villani, Castruccio decided in 1322 to build the *Augusta* because he was terrified by the assassination of Count Federico da Montefeltro in a popular uprising at Urbino,[28] and by tumults at Pisa in the same year. If this was the case, the fact that the lord of Urbino had been killed although he had sought refuge in his *rocca* may have influenced his decision to build a fortified enclosure within Lucca rather than a castle near its walls.[29]

The *Augusta* may in its turn have provided a model for the fortified enclosure which the duke of Athens, Walter of Brienne, who had been elected *signore* of Florence in 1342, was planning to create in that city before his expulsion in the following year. Described by Villani, like the Este citadel at Modena, as a *castello*,[30] it was to comprise the palace of the Signoria, now the ducal residence, and the area at its rear, with the palaces of the Captain of the People and of the Executor of the Ordinances of Justice; at the same time, the piazza in front of the Palazzo Vecchio was to be extended and its accesses secured with barriers.[31]

---

23 *Cronica*, IX, 154, ed. I. Moutier (Milan, 1848), II, p. 246: 'ordinò nella città uno maraviglioso castello'. A fourteenth-century Lucchese chronicle equally refers to the *Augusta* as to a *castello*; quoted by L. Green, 'Il problema dell'Augusta e della villa di Castruccio Castracani a Massa Pisana', *Actum Luce*, XIII-XIV (1984-5), p. 354.

24 See Green, *Castruccio Castracani*, pp. 105-11. According to R. Davidsohn, *Geschichte von Florenz*, III (Berlin, 1912), p. 600, the name *Augusta* was designed to reflect Castruccio's exalted vision of his power. The name may also have had imperial overtones: by the time of the building of the *Augusta* Castruccio had the title of imperial vicar.

25 Green, 'Il problema dell' Augusta', p. 365;

idem, *Castruccio Castracani*, pp. 110-12.

26 See above, p. 3.

27 Green, *Castruccio Castracani*, pp. 106-7.

28 Ibid.

29 *Cronica*, IX, 141 (II, pp. 237-8): the count had been 'rinchiuso e assediato dal popolo nella sua fortezza della terra' and had surrendered, 'vedendosi non guernito né da potere riparare'. See Davidsohn, *Geschichte von Florenz*, III, pp. 666-8.

30 *Cronica*, XII, 8 (IV, p. 17): 'Il detto compreso fece cominciare e fondare di grosse mura e torri e barbacani per fare col palagio insieme uno grande e forte castello . . .'

31 See my forthcoming book on the Palazzo Vecchio, 1298-1532, ch. 3.

A few years later, the *signore* of Milan, Luchino Visconti, who in 1346 had acquired Parma, had that city's Communal piazza, its *platea communis*, as well as part of the streets leading into it, enclosed with crenellated walls;[32] in Brescia, the Visconti, who had become *signori* of that city in 1337, surrounded the civic and ecclesiastical centre of the city abutting on the castle with crenellated walls; and in 1423 Filippo Maria Visconti appears to have enlarged and reinforced this citadel on the eve of the war with Venice.[33] In Parma, the central square was faced by the Communal palace and the palaces of the podestà and the captain of the people;[34] in Brescia it was faced by the Broletto, which under the Visconti became the residence of their vicars.[35] The Visconti called Parma's fortified square *Sta in pace*;[36] they evidently tried to justify the construction of a citadel within the city with the help of an argument which was used from the early fourteenth century onwards in defence of the *signoria*, that it brought peace to the faction-ridden cities. 'Civitates, in quibus ipse dominium obtinebat', affirmed one of Matteo Visconti's counsellors to the papal legates in 1317, 'pacem habebant per eius industriam'.[37]

In a more realistic vein, the decision of the Sforza governor of Parma in 1478 to have the walls surrounding the *platea communis* repaired and their gates reinforced,[38] was explained by a contemporary chronicler with the observation that: 'in the turmoils which had occurred in Parma until now, that piazza had always been captured, and whoever had done so, had remained the victor'. Consequently 'the officials whose residence was located on it and the partisans of the regime would in an emergency be safer' if the fortified enclosure of the square was reinforced,[39] one of these officials being the Sforza governor himself.[40] These words highlight one of the principal reasons why *signori* fortified the civic centre of their towns. Control of the central piazza, with the seats of government and administration around it, could in times of civic unrest be decisive for the survival of the signorial regime.

32 M. Pellegri, in V. Banzola, ed., *Parma: la città storica* (Parma, 1978), p. 134.
33 F. Odorici, *Storie bresciane*, VII (Brescia; 1857), p. 170; *Storia di Brescia*, II, pp. 4-5; III, pp. 1097-8; D. Hemsoll, 'Le piazze di Brescia nel Medioevo e Rinascimento', forthcoming in *Annali di architettura*. I am grateful to Dr Hemsoll for letting me read the manuscript of his paper.
34 J. Schulz, 'The Communal Buildings in Parma', *Mitteilungen des Kunsthistorischen Institutes in Florenz*, XXVI (1982), pp. 282ff.
35 *Storia di Brescia*, III, p. 1100.
36 See above.
37 Ed. S. Riezler, in *Vatikanische Akten zur deutschen Geschichte in der Zeit Kaiser Ludwigs des Bayern* (Innsbruck, 1891), pp. 22-39.
38 A. Pezzana, *Storia della città di Parma*, IV (Parma, 1852), pp. 104-05; Pellegri, as in n. 32.
39 *Cronica gestorum in partibus Lombardie*, ed. G. Bonazzi, RIS XXII, 3 (1904-11), p. 28: 'quod in tumultibus ortis hactenus in Parma semper platea ipsa capiebatur et capiens victor remanebat et ut officiales intra eam existentes et amici status in omni adventu forent securiores'.
40 See Schulz, 'The Communal Buildings in Parma', p. 302.

The enemies of that regime, on the other hand, regarded the *signori*'s fortified enclosures, like their castles within the city, as concrete manifestations of tyrannical rule. After the expulsion of the Este from Modena and the restoration of its republican government, the citizens demolished the town within the town which Azzo VIII had built in their city.[41] Lucca, which after Castruccio's death had been governed by a succession of imperial and royal vicars and *signori*, was in 1342 acquired by Pisa. In 1369, Emperor Charles IV restored her independence and confirmed her liberties, and in the following year, the Lucchese decided, according to a Lucchese chronicler unanimously, that Castruccio's *Augusta* be levelled to the ground, 'because owing to it, Lucca and the Lucchese had been subjected and subjugated for more than forty-eight years'.[42] After Venice had conquered Brescia from Filippo Maria Visconti in 1426, its citizens petitioned the doge to have demolished the citadel which the Visconti had created in their city.[43] The 'perversity and insolence of the tyrants', they complained, had deprived them, among other public buildings of the area enclosed, of the ancient palace of the Commune;[44] and they now appealed to the Venetians, who had given them back their liberty, to destroy the walls of that citadel, 'so that the palace which used to belong to the Commune be liberated' and could serve, 'following ancient custom', the administration of justice.[45] The petition emphasises the importance of the accessibility of the churches and public palaces: the restoration by the Venetians of Brescia's liberty will make it once more possible for the citizens who live inside and outside the citadel to get together, 'ad invicem conversari'.[46] Their city had been physically divided and disfigured by the tyrants: St Mark will reunite it and restore it to its former state.[47]

41 Ferreto, *Historia*, I, p. 219: 'populus gubernationem accepit, castrumque ab Azone constructum plebeis ministris signavit; donec illud paucis diebus solo prostratum equari iussit.'
42 Giovanni Sercambi, *Le croniche*, ed. S. Bongi (Rome, 1892), I, pp. 187-90: in 1370, 'disponendosi i ciptadini a uno volere che il castello dell'Agosta si mandasse per terra, considerato che quello era stato cagione che Luccha e Luchesi erano stati subiecti et soctoposti più di XLVIII anni'. See Green, *Castruccio Castracani*, p. 108.
43 The petition of 1427 is edited in A. Zanelli, *Delle condizioni interne di Brescia dal 1426 al 1644* . . . (Brescia, 1898), pp. 207-22.
44 Ibid., pp. 217-18: 'cum cives et comunitas Brix. supplicantes privati fuerint hactenus protervitate et insolentia tyrannorum' of the cathedral churches, the bishop's palace and the chapter houses, 'necnon de pallatio veteri [ed. veteris] comunis, in quo iura semper reddebantur ante tempus captionis do. Bernabonis, propter clausuram videlicet murorum et circuitus urbicule in quo fuerunt dicte ecclesie, domus et pallacium introcluse . . . '
45 'quod dicte ecclesie et pallatium sive pallatia olim comunis in libertate constituantur et adiri et possideri possint et a populo secundum antiquam consuetudinem visitari et iura reddi in dicto pallatio sicut semper fiebat antiquis temporibus'.
46 'Et cum per dictam etiam libertatis concessionem cives et civitatis [ed. civitates] et citadelle poterunt ad invicem conversari . . . '
47 'Et ut civitas hec vestra per truculentiam tyrannorum hactenus divisa et miserabiliter deformata per Beatis. Evangelistam Marcum et clementiam vestri ser. dominii omnimodo uniatur et ad statum pristinum reducatur . . . '

Freedom of movement within the city walls was a major aim of urban legislation in city republics such as Florence and Siena.[48] The openness of the square in front of the Communal Palace, as well as responding to aesthetic considerations, had an overriding political significance. A comparison between the central piazze at Parma and at Florence bears this out. In contrast to the fortified *platea communis* of Parma, the Piazza della Signoria in Florence lacked any permanent fortifications; on the rare occasions on which popular assemblies on the piazza or civic disturbances caused the government to control access to it, this was done by erecting improvised barriers.[49] Accordingly, when in 1491 a raised platform was constructed, apparently on Lorenzo de' Medici's initiative, between the Palazzo Vecchio and the Loggia dei Lanzi, in order to facilitate communications between the two buildings, this was criticised on the ground that it rendered circulation more difficult.[50]

The Venetian Signoria gave a non-committal reply to the petition of the Brescians: 'this is not the moment to provide what has been requested'.[51] The refusal to demolish the Visconti citadel in 1427 was probably due to initial doubts about the lasting loyalty of the Brescians to their new master.[52] Their loyalty was dramatically demonstrated during the siege of Brescia by Filippo Maria Visconti in 1438; yet when a group of citizens conspired to surrender the city to the duke of Milan, the Venetian governor, Francesco Barbaro, relied on the citadel to enforce continued resistance.[53] To city republics such as Venice, citadels had their usefulness in subject towns, however much they were condemned by republicans as tyrannical in cities ruled by *signori*.

The Florentine exiles, to whom Alessandro de' Medici's Fortezza da Basso was a self-evident symptom of his tyrannical rule, would have had no

---

48 See W. Braunfels, *Mittelalterliche Stadtbaukunst in der Toskana* (Berlin, 1953), pp. 90-2, 109, 120-1; G. Pampaloni, *Firenze al tempo di Dante: documenti sull'urbanistica fiorentina* (Rome, 1973), pp. xxiv-xxviii; D. Friedman, *Florentine New Towns: Urban Design in the Late Middle Ages* (Cambridge, Mass., and London 1988), p. 205: 'The physical city of the [Florentine] merchant commune was an open one. The uniformity of authority and jurisdiction that the government strove for was translated directly into a concept of urban space, in which every part of the town was equally accessible . . .'

49 N. Rubinstein, 'Parma e Firenze nel Quattrocento', in *Parma e l'umanesimo italiano* (Padua, 1986), pp. 3-7.

50 Luca Landucci, *Diario fiorentino*, ed. I. Del Badia (Florence, 1883), pp. 61-2: 'in modo che non potevano passarvi più nè cavagli nè altre bestie; e anche un poco incomodo agli uomini . . .'

51 Zanelli, ed., *Condizioni interne di Brescia*, pp. 207-22: 'Non est modo tempus ad hoc quod petitur providere'. On the citadel of Brescia under Venetian domination, see G. Lupo, 'Platea magna communis Brixiae (1433-1509)', in M. Tafuri ed., *La Piazza, la chiesa, il parco: saggi di storia dell' architettura (XV-XIX secolo)* (Milan, 1991), pp. 56-95 (pp. 56-60).

52 *Storia di Brescia*, II, p. 31.

53 E. Manelmi, *Commentariolum de quibusdam gestis in bello Gallico . . . seu de obsidione Brixiae anno MCCCCXXXVIII* (Brescia, 1728), p. 31. See P. Gothein, *Francesco Barbaro: Früh-Humanismus und Staatskunst in Venedig* (Berlin, 1932), p. 210.

scruples about the expediency, indeed necessity, of controlling subject cities such as Pisa with the help of fortresses.[54] When Machiavelli criticised the opinion of 'nostri savi, che Pisa e l'altre simili città si debbono tenere con le fortezze' ('that Pisa and other similar cities should be held by means of fortresses'), he did so solely on the ground that the fortresses built by republics, 'not at home but in the places which they acquire', were useless.[55] But then the Florentines, like the citizens of other republics, applied different criteria to liberty at home and in their dominions.[56]

---

54 Hale, 'The End of Florentine Liberty', p. 504.
55 Machiavelli, *Discorsi*, II, 24 (p. 349).
56 This ambivalence was not lost on the advocates of the signorial regime. Giangaleazzo Visconti's secretary, Antonio Loschi, responds, in his *Invectiva* against Florence written in 1397 during the war between the duke of Milan and the Florentines, to their assertion that the Duke was a tyrant by accusing them in their turn of oppressing their subject peoples 'sub acerbissima tyrannide'; quoted by Coluccio Salutati, *Invectiva in Antonium Luschum Vicentinum* (Florence, 1826), p. 51.

2

The Cittadella of Verona

John E. Law

A major theme running through John Hale's contributions to the military history of Renaissance Italy concerns the debates that could surround the construction of fortifications: how should they be designed; were they cost effective; how should they be paid for; where should they be located? Such issues could be discussed with particular force and urgency when fortifications were planned and built within, or across, the walls of a city and were designed to express and defend the authority of an imposed regime, republican or princely. Structures of this kind were built throughout late medieval and Renaissance Italy, and they were designated by various terms. *Castello*, *rocca* and *fortezza* are common. In central Italy, *cassero* is often found, conveying the idea of a commanding structure looking down – literally or figuratively – on a subject community. The word *cittadella* is used with the same sense; it can also convey the idea of an extensive barracks area, a fortified city within a city.[1]

The builders of such internal fortifications could look on them in a positive light, as worthy expressions of their power, wealth and authority: this was the case with the *Augusta* of Castruccio Castracane within the walls of Lucca, and with the Castel Sismondo of Sigismondo Pandolfo Malatesta in Rimini.[2] Others might view them with fear and distaste: for the destruction they caused; for the taxation and other burdens they demanded; for the threat to autonomy and political liberty they posed. As John Hale has

---

1 Perhaps the most influential as regards what follows are; J.R. Hale, 'The End of Florentine Liberty: The Fortezza da Basso', and 'To Fortify or Not to Fortify? Machiavelli's Contribution to a Renaissance Debate', in his *Renaissance War Studies* (London, 1983), pp. 31-62 and 189-210. For the terminology see UTET, *Grande Dizionario della Lingua Italiana*.

2 L. Green, 'Il problema dell'*Augusta* e della villa di Castruccio Castracane', *Actum Luce*, XIII-XIV (1984-5), pp. 353-77; Joanna Woods-Marsden, 'How Quattrocento Princes Used Art: Sigismundo Pandolfo Malatesta of Rimini and *cose militari*', *Renaissance Studies*, III (1989), pp. 387-414; idem, 'Images of Castles in the Renaissance: Symbols of *Signoria*: Symbols of Tyranny', *Art Journal*, XLVIII (1989), pp. 130-7; S. Pepper, 'The Meaning of the Renaissance Fortress', *Architectural Association Quarterly*, V (1973), pp. 19-27; and see Nicolai Rubinstein's essay in the present volume, above, pp. 1-8.

emphasised, a prominent and influential figure in the latter tradition was Niccolò Machiavelli, whose doubts about the efficacy of fortresses in general were given a particular moral and political dimension at the prospect of fortress-building within the walls of Florence.[3]

But references to fortresses in the works of Machiavelli are not always polemical. In his *History of Florence*, Book V, he describes a dramatic sequence of events in and around Verona in November 1439. This involved the *condottieri* Niccolò Piccinino and Francesco Sforza, and required Machiavelli to explain to his readers the position of the fortresses in the city of Verona, which he himself had visited in November–December 1509 during the war of the League of Cambrai.[4] The River Adige divides the city unequally 'leaving much more of the city on the side of the plain than on that of the mountains'. On high ground, on the left bank, there are two castles, the Castel San Pietro and the Castel San Felice; Machiavelli notes that these fortresses gain their strength from their dominant position rather than from their walls. On the plain, on the right bank, there are two citadels, the Old and the New. He describes them as being situated up against the walls as well as being linked together by a wall, which he likens graphically to the string to the bow provided by the 'ordinary city walls'.[5]

The 'Old Citadel' was the first fortress built within the communal walls of late-medieval Verona. It was originally known as the Castello di San Martino in Aquario, after a church on the site; it came to be called more familiarly the Castelvecchio, and the circumstances of its construction explain why it could qualify as a citadel. It was built on the orders of Cangrande II della Scala after he had crushed a revolt led by his natural brother Fregnano in February 1354. When the fortress had been largely completed in 1356 it exhibited many of the features needed to protect the regime and overawe its subjects.[6] It was defended by a wall with towers, a

---

3 The key references are: Niccolò Machiavelli, *The Prince*, chapter 20; idem, *The Discourses*, ii, chapter 24; and his letter of 2 June 1526 to Francesco Guicciardini in N. Machiavelli, *Lettere*, ed. F. Gaeta (Milan, 1961), p. 470, letter no. 219. For another telling sixteenth-century example, Judith Hook, 'Fortifications and the End of the Sienese State', *History*, LXII (1977), pp. 372-87.

4 V. Bertolini, 'Niccolò Machiavelli a Verona durante la Lega di Cambrai', *Atti e Memorie dell'Accademia di Verona*, series vi, IX (1959), pp. 273-301; I. Cervelli, *Machiavelli e la Crisi dello Stato Veneziano* (Naples, 1974), pp. 344-7.

5 N. Machiavelli, *Istorie Fiorentine*, ed. F. Gaeta (Milan, 1962), bk v, chapter 24 pp. 365-6. Gilbert translates *adosso* as 'astride'; in fact, as will be shown below, the 'old citadel' was astride one of the circuits of walls, the 'string' to Machiavelli's 'bow'. However, the 'bow' itself, the outer circuit, did not link the two citadels, Niccolò Machiavelli, *The Chief Works and Others*, ed. and trans. A.H. Gilbert (3 vols., Durham NC, 1965), pp. 1265-6.

6 For the building of the Castelvecchio, L. Simeoni, 'La ribellione di Fregnano della Scala e la politica generale italiana', *Studi Storici Veronesi*, XI (1961), pp. 5-62; B. Bresciani, *Castelli Veronesi* (Verona, 1962), pp. 44-7; M. Carrara, *Gli Scaligeri* (Varese, 1966), pp. 195-200; U.G. Tessari, *Castelvecchio* (Verona, 1965), pp. 5-10; E. Rossini, 'Verona Scaligera', in *Verona e il suo Territorio*, III, part i (Verona, 1975), pp. 47-9, 688-95.

moat, the River Adige and a canalised branch of the Adige, the Adigetto. It straddled the inner, twelfth-century, circuit of the communal walls. It dominated a populous area of the city and the Borgo di S. Zeno. It could accommodate a large garrison and, connected as it was by a fortified bridge to open country on the north bank of the Adige, it could be reinforced with less likelihood of effective interference from the urban population.[7]

Subsequently the Della Scala sought to make the castle an expression of their power in more than military terms, using it as a residence and having its apartments decorated; but the security and comfort they found within its walls were short-lived. On 17 October 1387 Antonio della Scala fled from the castle after a succession of military reverses at the hands of Francesco 'il Vecchio' da Carrara of Padua and Giangaleazzo Visconti of Milan, and in the face of the indifference or hostility of his own subjects.[8]

Antonio's fall may have persuaded Giangaleazzo Visconti, his successor, that something more secure than the Castello di San Martino was needed to defend his *signoria* in Verona. The early years of his rule saw work on the other three fortresses mentioned by Machiavelli: the castles of San Felice and Pietro north of the river, and the Cittadella on the plain.[9] When these works were actually begun is not entirely clear. The reliable G.B. Verci and most modern authorities on the basis of early sources, date the beginnings of all three to 1389-90.[10] However, one contemporary and two informed early authorities date work on San Felice and San Pietro to 1393, or even to 1395.[11]

It is not absolutely clear what prompted this building campaign. The later Della Scala are generally described as discredited and unpopular; that might

---

7   These features were present in other fourteenth-century citadels, as at Pavia (1360) and Ferrara (1385), A. Vincenti, *Castelli Viscontei e Sforzeschi* (Milan, 1981), pp. 54-65; J.E. Law, 'Popular Unrest in Ferrara in 1385', in *The Renaissance in Ferrara and its European Horizons*, ed. June Salmons and W. Moretti (Cardiff and Ravenna, 1984), pp. 51-3. For the topography of Verona in the fifteenth-century, see the Appendix to this essay.

8   J.E. Law, 'La caduta degli Scaligeri', in *Istituzioni, società e potere nella Marca Trivigiana e Veronese: sulle tracce di G.B. Verci*, ed. G. Ortalli and M. Knapton (Rome, 1988), pp. 83-98.

9   G. Barbetta, *Le mura e le fortificazioni di Verona* (Verona, 1978), pp. 50-2. The building of the Castel San Felice resulted in the Castel San Martino becoming known as the Castelvecchio.

10 P. Zagata, *Cronica della città di Verona, ampliata e suppleta da G.B. Biancolini* (2 vols., Verona, 1745-9), I, p. 122; G.B. Verci, *Storia della Marca Trivigiana e Veronese* (20 vols., Venice, 1786-91), XVII, bk 20, pp. 78-80; G. Soldi-Rondinini, *La dominazione Viscontea a Verona*, in *Verona e il suo territorio*, IV, part 1 (Verona, 1981), pp. 123-5; E. Rossini, 'La città tra basso medioevo ed età moderna', in *Una città e il suo fiume*, ed. G. Borelli (2 vols., Verona, 1977), I, pp. 189-90. Bresciani, *Castelli veronesi*, pp. 40-44, gives 1389-90, but in his *Vestigia e visioni* (Verona, 1938), pp. 39-41, he appears to suggest 1391 for the Castel San Felice and the Castel San Pietro.

11 Boninsegna de Mitocolis, 'Parva Cronica', in Verci, *Storia*, VII, p. 238, documenti; C. Cipolla, 'La relazione di Giorgio Sommariva sullo stato di Verona, e del Veronese', *Nuovo archivio veneto*, VI (1893), p. 197; G. dalla Corte, *Storia di Verona* (Verona, 1744), II, pp. 308-9, 319: Dalla Corte is a sixteenth-century source.

suggest that Giangaleazzo's principal concern was to protect the strategically-placed city of Verona against external attack, and to turn it into a strong point to help maintain his dominions in eastern Lombardy and the Veneto. But historians may well have exaggerated Veronese rejection of the della Scala; apprehension as to the activities of the exiled dynasty and its supporters, as well as doubts of the loyalty of the Veronese towards the new regime in a period of war and famine, may well have prompted Giangaleazzo to initiate these major works.[12] This hypothesis is strengthened when the siting of the three fortresses is examined. San Felice guarded the northern approaches, but it was not close to the centre of urban settlement, and little more than its foundations may have been laid in the Visconti period. The Castel San Pietro had a much more central and prominent position. It was on the site of the Roman *arx*, it dominated the quarter of Castello and a crossing of the Adige, the Ponte Pietra.[13]

The Cittadella, which was almost certainly the first of these works to be begun and completed, was situated on the plain and like the Castel San Pietro was close to one of the more populous areas of the city, the Quartiere Maggiore. In its construction, advantage was taken of existing defence works. Towards the south it was protected by the outer city wall built on the orders of Cangrande I della Scala between 1323 and 1325. This wall turned north to follow the river until it joined the twelfth-century innerring of defences at the Torre della Paglia.[14] It was this wall, on the line of the present Via Pallone, which provided the northern defence of the Cittadella. To enclose it completely, the Visconti engineers had to erect one stretch of wall, probably defended by a ditch, close to the line of the present Corso Porta Nuova.

Other measures were undertaken to strengthen the zone. The positioning of the wall-walk and the battlements on its northern side were reversed to face into the city; properties were cleared and a ditch dug further to defend that north-facing wall. The section linking the Cittadella to the Castelvecchio was strengthened to create a wall-walk protected on both sides, the 'string' to Machiavelli's 'bow'. The point where the double-wall met the Cittadella at the Porta della Bra' was defended by a pentagonal tower and a small fort referred to as the Rochetta.[15] Entry was gained to the Cittadella

12 Law, 'La caduta', cited in note 8 above.
13 Sommariva and Dalla Corte both mention the rebuilding of the Castel San Pietro, thereby implying an older structure on the site.
14 Rossini, 'Verona Scaligera', pp. 262-9. This study also provides a valuable guide to the settlement of the city in the fourteenth-century, see especially pp. 31-54.
15 I am grateful to Bernard Bishop for his advice in determining the layout of the Cittadella.

by at least two principal gates, the Porta San Antonio to the south, and the Porta Rofiolo to the north, to allow the garrison both to enter Verona and to be reinforced from outside; there was probably a third entry, the main-gate, on the new west wall giving access to the Borgo di San Zeno. What was created, therefore, was less a castle and more a fortified area which could contain a substantial number of troops, a city within a city. From its inception it was known as the Cittadella.[16]

According to the chronicle of Zagata, the purpose of the Cittadella was to hold the Veronese in check, but its construction almost certainly contributed to the build-up of resentment against Visconti rule. Moreover, the Cittadella not only posed an obvious threat to the city, it enclosed an entire urban *contrada*, that of Santa Croce. Although it was not a densely populated area – and Dalla Corte almost certainly exaggerated when he said that it contained 'infinite case, e alcuni superbi palazzi' – it affected a number of religious foundations, as well as lay inhabitants and property-owners. The monastic buildings of San Fermo in Braida were demolished; while outside the Cittadella other buildings were cleared to make room for the ditch protecting the north wall. It is true that the monks were compensated, as was the Veronese citizen, Arcolino *quondam* Alboino di Pocapoina on 16 April 1389: his properties lay in the same area. But Arcolino was exiled as a rebel the following year.[17]

It seems likely, therefore, that the enclosure of the Cittadella, together with other grievances – which possibly included work on other fortifications – contributed to a rebellion against Visconti rule on 22 June 1390. However, on that occasion the Cittadella demonstrated its worth to its builders. It repelled the rebels, and through it the Visconti *condottiere* Ugolotto Biancardo was able to introduce reinforcements into the city on 26 June, leading to the crushing of the revolt and the sack of the city, as well as the death, captivity and exile of many of its inhabitants. This, together with the strengthening of the garrison, contributed to the failure of an

---

16 Torello Sarayna calls it an *urbiculam*, *De origine et amplitudine civitatis Veronae* (Verona, Putelleti, 1540), fol. 42v. See also L. Moscardo, *Historia di Verona* (Verona, Rossi, 1668), p. 249. For a parallel in the *Augusta* of Lucca, Green, 'Il problema dell'*Augusta*'. In the case of Verona, both the fifteenth-century views show a gate in the west wall.

17 Zagata, *Cronica*, I, p. 122; Verci, *Storia*, XVII, bk. xx, pp. 79–81; L. Simeoni, *Verona guida storico-artistica* (Verona, 1909), p. 234; ibid., 'La "Cittadella" di Gian Galeazzo Visconti e le mura al Pallon', *Studi storici veronesi*, II (1949/50), pp. 236–7. On Arcolino, G.B. dalle Vacche, 'Cronica inedita veronese', Verona, Biblioteca Comunale, MS 885, fol. 180. On 25 August 1407 he was awarded Venetian citizenship, ASV, 'Senato, Misti', reg. 47, fol. 130. On 21 October 1412, he is described as a Veronese living in Venice, ASVer, 'Antico Archivio del Comune [AAC]', reg. 56, fols. 210v–211v.

attempt to retake Verona for the Della Scala in January 1391.[18] Later the Cittadella proved a point of resistance when the Carrara and the Della Scala took the city from Caterina Visconti on 8 April 1404.[19] Only on 27 April were the allies able to dislodge the garrison under Biancardo. It is hardly surprising, therefore, that thereafter the Cittadella, as a potent symbol of Visconti power, was slighted by the Veronese. Probably the west wall was demolished and the merlons on the northern walls destroyed. Properties within the Cittadella which had been acquired by the Visconti were sold.[20]

Verona surrendered on terms to a Venetian army on 23 June 1405 and subsequently sent a delegation to Venice to carry out a final act of submission before the doge on 12 July.[21] The Veronese hoped to secure the Republic's acceptance of a set of *capitula* worked out with its representatives in the field, together with some additional clauses devised in Verona after further reflection. On 12 July, Doge Michele Steno assured the Veronese that the people who had walked in darkness had seen a great light, but the two sets of petitions received a more guarded welcome in the Senate. Finally, on 16 July, that body accepted most of the initial requests but was much less generous as regards the second set, the eighth clause of which concerned the Cittadella.[22]

The Veronese asked that *de gratia* they be granted a privilege to console the present generation, and as a memorial for their heirs: that the Cittadella should never be rebuilt and no other fortress built on the site.[23] The Senate's reply was in the negative, though it was phrased to avoid giving offence. A 'public privilege' along the lines requested would prove too compromising of the Republic's honour, but Venice was anxious to reassure the Veronese that nothing would be done to prevent 'their hearts being at one with ours.'[24] The Veronese were told that their goodwill would be the citadel

---

18 On the rebellion see J.E. Law, 'The Commune of Verona under Venetian Rule, 1405-1455, (unpublished D.Phil. thesis, University of Oxford, 1974), pp. 56-8; Soldi Rondinini, 'La Dominazione Viscontea . . . ', pp. 127-131. The 'Minerbetti' chronicle gives a detailed account of events and describes the Cittadella as the *cassero*, see *Cronica Volgare di Anonimo Fiorentino già attribuita a Piero di Giovanni Minerbetti*, ed. E. Bellondi, RIS, XXVII, part ii (1918), pp. 104-5.

19 Law, 'The Commune', pp. 48-54. The most authoritative discussion of the sequence of events and the source material can be found in F. and C. Cipolla (eds.), Marzagaia, 'De modernis gestis', in *Monumenti storici della R. deputazione veneziana di storia patria*, series iii, II (Venice, 1890), especially pp. 175-7, 249-51, 303-5; see also T.M. Scarabello, 'La dominazione dei Carraresi su Verona', *Vita veronese*, VIII (1955), especially pp. 66-72, 116-7, 181-4.

20 Below p. 15-17.

21 J.E. Law, 'Verona and the Venetian State in the Fifteenth Century', in *Bulletin of the Institute of Historical Research*, LII (1979), pp. 12-14.

22 ASV, 'Senato, Secreta', reg. 2, fols. 126-8; 'Pacta, reg. 7, 3-4v; ASVer, AAC, reg. 52, fols. 1v-7v.

23 'quod numquam rehedificabitur citadela Verone nec in aliquam aliam fortiliciam reducetur pro consolatione viventium et memoriam futurorum'.

24 'quod cor eorum omnium sit unum cum nostro'.

and the security Venice desired; that being the case, the Republic's favourable disposition towards its subjects would increase daily.[25]

The presentation of the Veronese request and the phrasing of the response illustrate clearly the delicacy and importance of the matter to the Republic's new subjects. At the same time Venetian policy was not being shaped by the legal implications of a *publicum privilegium*, but rather by the need to secure its new acquisition on the *Terraferma*; after all the Veronese had accepted the *signoria* of the Carrara, while the city's surrender to Venice had been achieved only after a year's hard campaigning.[26] Moreover, in July 1405 the Carrara remained a force to be reckoned with, whereas the newfound loyalty of the Republic's subjects could not be guaranteed.

Nevertheless, the first concern of the Venetian government appears to have been less to repair the damage done to the Cittadella in 1404 and more to enhance its use as an area to billet troops.[27] On 29 April 1408 the Senate referred to the fact that there were many houses in the Cittadella owned by citizens but assigned to troops. This was a source of friction as the soldiery had reduced them to a poor condition; steps would have to be taken to avoid inconvenience to the Republic and loss to its subjects. Accordingly the Senate ordered the *capitano* of Verona to compensate all citizen-owners with equivalent properties held by the *Camera Fiscale*, and to take accommodation in the Cittadella into public ownership. In future it was to be assigned to cavalry, presumably because it was more convenient to stable and graze horses there than in the more populous areas of the city; also, these troops were to pay rent. Clearly the Senate deemed that it had arrived at a policy: its decision was to be incorporated in the commissions of future *capitani*.[28]

Almost at once, however, the policy ran into difficulty. On 6 October the *rettori* and the *camerlenghi* wrote to the doge that a survey had been carried out of those who had purchased property in the area from the Carrara, the state of repair of these properties and their potential as billets. The properties were valued at 4,500 ducats, the repairs at 1,500 ducats; over three hundred lances and many foot soldiers could be lodged in the area. The problem was that the one hundred citizens concerned could not be satisfied with the type of property still in the hands of the *Camera*. Rather than trying

---

25 'quod bona voluntas sua sit illa Citadella, sit illa securitas quam habere volumus'. The Venetian response to a similar request from Brescia in 1427 was more curt, A. Menniti Ippolito, 'La dedizione di Brescia a Milano (1420) e a Venezia (1427); *Stato, società e giustizia nella Repubblica Veneta*, ed. G. Cozzi (Rome, 1985), pp. 41-2 and Rubinstein, 'Fortified Enclosures', above pp. 1-8.

26 Law, 'The Commune', pp. 29-38, 48-54.

27 M.E. Mallett in Mallett and Hale, *The Military Organization of a Renaissance State: Venice, c. 1400 to 1617* (Cambridge, 1984), pp. 88-9, 134; Barbetta, *Le mura e le fortificazioni*, pp. 82-3.

28 ASV, 'Senato, Misti', reg. 48, fol. 2.

for property exchanges, the Republic's representatives proposed selling off the *Camera's* holdings and compensating the citizens in cash.[29]

Greater urgency was given to discussions on the Cittadella by serious threats to Venetian rule both from within and without Verona: on 2 May 1412 there was a revolt, and in January 1413 the exiled Della Scala approached the city with the military backing of Sigismund, King of the Romans.[30] On 21 November 1413 the Senate discussed advice received from the *rettori*, *provveditori*, and other Venetian nobles in Verona: if the Republic wanted to hold the city it had to have a citadel suitable for the safe quartering of troops.[31] Apparently this was also seen as a cost-effective solution: secret orders had already been given to gather timber, iron and other necessary materials, so that work could begin in December. Now the Venetian government was given the freedom to expedite matters and to dispatch the manpower needed; moreover, because of the importance of the project for the general war effort, funds could be allocated from Venetian sources. Finally the *rettori* and *provveditori* were instructed to remove any citizens who might threaten the work and Venetian security; a note in the Senate minutes observes that on 23 November the *Collegio* extended the discretion of its local officials to cover 'a number of clans', (*alique parentelle*). It seems unlikely that the Senate and the *Collegio* were referring to disgruntled property owners, but rather to those who might oppose the repair of the Cittadella on political and military grounds. Quite who they were is unclear. Certainly the Republic was alive to the threat posed by adherents of the Della Scala, and a contemporary chronicle records that in December 1413 some Veronese were hanged for telling Brunoro della Scala about work on the Cittadella.[32]

Exactly what building was undertaken is also unclear, although the numbers concerned were so large that on 7 December 1413 the Veronese Council of Twelve had to make special arrangements for legal cases involving those employed.[33] However operations do not appear to have lasted long. On 19 January 1414, the Senate referred to the diligent work being carried out in Verona by the *provveditore*, Pietro Contarini, and to the fact that the Cittadella was now in good condition, *bono termine*; the *provveditore* was given leave to return to Venice and the two *camerlenghi* were ordered to carry out the programme begun by Contarini and his

---

29 ASV, 'Senato, Lettere di Rettori', busta 1, no. 100.
30 J.E. Law, 'Venice, Verona and the Della Scala after 1405', *Atti e memorie della Accademia di Verona*, series vi, XXIX (1977-8), pp. 166-177.
31 ASV, 'Senato, Secreta', reg. 5, fol. 166v, 'necessarium est facere Citadellam in qua gentes nostri reduci possint'.
32 De Mitocolis, 'Parva cronica', p. 160.
33 ASVer., AAC, reg. 56, fol. 237v.

colleague Andrea Mocenigo.[34] On 10 February the Senate decided to take advantage of the local knowledge acquired by its representatives and co-opted them as non-voting members until the end of March.[35] The result was a series of measures for the defence of Verona and its *territorio* presented on 23 February.[36] As far as the city was concerned, the Cittadella was to be given an enhanced role. In periods of reduced tension – *in temporibus non suspectis* – it was proper to save money, *ad parsimonizandum pecuniam*.[37] The Castel S. Pietro cost over 3000 ducats a year to maintain, yet it was less effective because it was surrounded by city walls. On the other hand, the Cittadella had been newly built – *noviter edificata* – and was suited for the defence of the whole city. The garrison of the castle was to be reduced and surplus munitions transferred to the Castelvecchio and the Cittadella. However, it is also clear that improvements were still needed to the latter; the current *rettori* and their successors were ordered to raise the height of the wall on its southern side – *a parte campanee usque ad Athicem* – and to repair the ditches. Finally, a treasurer was appointed at 100 ducats a year to oversee the munitions and other materials stored in the Cittadella.[38]

In view of this activity it is hardly surprising that a Venetian chronicler of the period noted under 1414, 'at this time, the *Signoria* built a citadel in Verona'.[39] Even so, civilians were still holding property within its walls; on 5 March 1415, the Senate had to rehearse its policy of 29 April 1408, as the current *rettori* were unsure if it still applied.[40] Other difficulties also remained. On 2 July 1418, the Senate considered a long report forwarded by the *rettori* drawing its attention to the delays in building work caused by the harvest, and to the anger these delays caused the captain of the Cittadella, Fregnano da Sesso, and other soldiers resident there.[41]

Eventually the Senate had to give a new impetus to its policies towards the fortification, although Verona was no longer under immediate threat. On 16 October 1421 it rehearsed the fact that it had long been recognised by the *rettori* of Verona, as well as by *provveditori* and others sent there, that to hold Verona *sub nostro dominio et potestate* it was necessary to construct

---

34 ASV, 'Senato, Misti', reg. 50, fol. 62vi; Contarini had apparently gone about his duties 'alacriter et libenter'.
35 Ibid, fol. 70v.
36 Ibid., fol. 73v.
37 A truce had been signed with Sigismund lasting from 1413 to 1418.
38 ASV, 'Senato, Misti' reg. 50, fol. 73v.
39 'Cronachetta veneziana, 1402-1415', ed. V. Joppi, *Archivio veneto*, XVII (1879), p. 322.

40 ASV, 'Senato, Misti', reg. 51, fol. 2. From 1418, the *contrada* of Santa Croce, co-terminus with the Cittadella, was removed from the city's *estimo*; its appearance in the 1409 assessment reveals its low population. A. Tagliaferri, *L'economia veronese secondo gli estimi dal 1409 al 1635* (Milan, 1966), pp. 42, 44, 77.
41 ASV, 'Senato, Misti', reg. 52, fols 107v-108. For da Sesso see below, p. 20.

a citadel to house troops.[42] The original decision to build had been taken on 21 November 1413, and now there was a need to finish the structure. There were around 200 *pertiche* of wall to complete; once finished this would greatly fortify the city and hence the *Terraferma*.[43] Current and future *rettori* were ordered to see to the building of around thirty and forty *pertiche* during their terms of office; the stretch of wall referred to ran between the two circuits of communal wall, roughly on the line of the modern Corso Porta Nuova.[44] From the distance recorded, it is clear that most of the west wall still had to be repaired or rebuilt. A few days later the Senate passed another resolution to strengthen the city's defences. Verona was dear to the Republic because of its strategic position; its retention would ensure the conservation of all other cities of the *stato di terra*: 'conservata civitate Verona, omnes alie a parte terre conservantur'. In this instance attention was directed at the double-wall between the Cittadella and the Castelvecchio, which provided for their mutual defence. The *rettori* were ordered to spend 200 ducats on its repair.[45]

Although that Senate resolution dealt with only one aspect of Venice's defence and a relatively small sum of money, it also reveals a broader strategic understanding of the place of Verona in the conservation of the *Terraferma* state, as well as of the role of its two connected citadels. Moreover, the goals set out in October 1421 continued to be pursued, even when Verona and the *Terraferma* as a whole were not under immediate threat of attack. On 4 March 1422 the most detailed surviving *ducale* on the strengthening of the Cittadella was issued by the *Collegio*, acting on the authority of the Venetian Senate.[46] In substance it was made up of the recommendations and conditions of employment of *magistri Picini ingenarii nostri*.[47] His many proposals, it was claimed, would be for the good of Venice as well as to the benefit of its subjects. Two other masters, Stefano and Giovanni of Cremona, were placed under the direction of Picino as supervisor, *superstans*. The work was once again to the 'Corso Porta Nuova' line, suggesting that previous orders had been at most only partially

42 'In qua gentes nostri reduci et teneri possint', ASV, 'Senato, Misti', reg. 53, fol. 191.
43 'Erit magna fortificatio status nostri'. The length of a *pertica*, or perch, varied from region to region. The *Grande dizionario della lingua italiana* suggests a measure of around three metres.
44 In this period, the Porta Nuova did not exist. The wall is described as running 'versus portam a calzariis', a reference to the Porta Calzaro, closed with the refortification of Verona in the sixteenth-century. The *ducale* was dispatched on 20 October; for its receipt and registration in Verona see ASVer, AAC, reg. 9, fol. 60.
45 'ita quod castrum possit succurere citadele et citadela castro', ASV, 'Senato, Misti', reg. 53, fol. 192. The *ducale* took longer to process; it was registered on 23 December 1421, ASVer, AAC, reg. 9, fol. 66v.
46 Ibid., fol. 68r-v. This ducale was published in part by A. da Lisca, *La fortificazione di Verona dai tempi romani* (Verona, 1916), pp. 106-7.
47 He is also described as 'prothoingenarius ducalis dominii Venetorum'.

implemented. The foundations of the earlier – presumably Visconti – defences were to be followed, but the new wall was to be stronger and equipped with battlements, gunloops and arrowslits. Detailed provision was also made for the supply of materials, for payment and for the supervision of the work, which was expected to last one year from 1 March.

As before, problems were encountered. On 11 September 1425 it was decided to send a high-powered delegation of three members of the *Signoria* to Verona.[48] They were to consult with the *rettori* and such experts – 'other than Master Picino' – as they saw fit to ensure that work on the Cittadella was carried out properly. Other difficulties concerned the organisation of labour-services from *contado* communities; on 10 July 1424, a *ducale* exempted the highland vicariate of the Montagna del Carbone from the work, accepting the claim of its inhabitants that they had no carts.[49] On 24 October 1424, the Senate arrived at a further series of measures to advance the construction, to supply the Cittadella, and to improve its defences.[50] To control costs, the captain of Verona was ordered to enrol three carpenters and three masons into each company of soldiers stationed in the area; from these *maestri* the most capable was to be appointed superintendent of billets, reporting to the captain on their state of repair; although these men were expected to carry arms and attend musters, they were exempted from sentry duty and received a daily bonus. Various artillery experts were to be treated in a similar fashion and lodged in the Cittadella; blacksmiths on the Venetian payroll were to be compelled to live and work within its walls. Further provisions concerned the maintenance of adequate supplies of cut timber and fodder; as regards the latter, the abbey of Santa Trinità, which owned meadows within the walls, was allowed to use its fodder for its own horses, but had to store the surplus – presumably in case the garrison needed to buy it – selling it only at harvest time. The Senate was also alarmed at the poor condition of the sixteen cannon within the Cittadella; those not needed in the Castelvecchio were to be relocated there. Finally, the wall separating the Cittadella from the city was regarded as a point of weakness, being without merlons and turrets; the *rettori* were ordered to get the newly recruited *maestri* to work on these as soon as possible. But as was so often the case in Verona and elsewhere, the intentions of the Venetian government could be frustrated; a *ducale* of 16 July 1425 ordered the *rettori* to urge the *maestri* Stefano and Picino to press on with their work.[51]

---

48 ASV, 'Senato, Misti', reg. 54, fol. 147v.
49 ASVer, AAC, reg. 9, fol. 119v. The area is also known as the Montagna dei Tedeschi.
50 ASV, 'Senato, Misti', reg. 55, fols. 65v-66; *ducale* of 7 December 1424, ASVer, AAC, reg. 9 fol. 124-v.
51 ASVer, AAC, reg. 9, fol. 132v.

Other measures taken at about the same time underline the importance of the Cittadella, as also the abiding nature of the problems of funding, supervision and billets. On 5 February 1422, the *rettori* confirmed the appointment of a treasurer, made on 1 December 1421.[52] On 28 April the Senate released further sources of revenue for the project.[53] On 18 February 1423 the same body discussed the replacement of its captain, Fregnano da Sesso, a Veronese of proven loyalty.[54] He had been appointed in June 1417, but now he was old and ill, and it was necessary to have a man in post able to supervise the on-going work.[55] The Senate was aware of the need for tact; Fregnano was to be assured by the doge that his loyal service in such an important command was fully recognised, and though the time had come for his replacement he was to be kept on full salary of 500 ducats a year.

On 26 March, the Senate considered appointing another reliable *condottiere*, Antonio de' Roberti at 200 ducats a year,[56] but on 11 May 1423 it signalled the importance of the posting by electing a Venetian noble, Andrea Giuliano, as *provveditore* for two years at an annual salary of 400 ducats.[57] Giuliano's supervision of the Cittadella appears to have been rather spasmodic: he was granted leave for most of 1424, leaving an unnamed noble in his place.[58] On 18 June 1425 he was re-elected for another two year term, and on 5 August the Senate stressed that he, like Fregnano, was subordinate to the captain of the city; but his second tour of duty was punctuated by various diplomatic and military missions.[59]

Problems surrounding billets and properties within the Cittadella remained. On 22 October 1421 a *ducale* congratulated the *rettori* on their letter of 8 October, in which they had explained why they had rejected as baseless claims for compensation advanced by the abbot of Santa Trinità.[60] A much more sympathetic response was given to another monastic community situated within the walls. On 3 July 1423 the *rettori* were asked to comment on a petition presented to the doge and his 'pious and gracious

---

52 Ibid., fol. 67v.
53 ASV, 'Senato, Misti', reg. 54, fol. 25v.
54 Ibid., fol. 88v. J.E. Law, 'A New Frontier: Venice and the Trentino in the Early Fifteenth Century', *Atti dell'Accademia Roveretana degli Agiati*, series vi, XXVIII (1988), pp. 175-6. On 3 November 1405, the Senate had decided to offer the post to Nicolao Cavalli. He was the son of Giacomo, a Veronese *condottiere*, who had served the Republic loyally and effectively. In the campaign that had led to the fall of Verona, Nicolao had been wounded and had lost his arms and horses in Venetian service. However, it is not clear for how long – if at all – he was in command of the Cittadella, ASV, 'Senato, Secreta', reg. 2, fols. 162, 190v.
55 In the atrium of the church of Santa Trinità within the Cittadella, Fregnano had buried his daughter Antonia in a marble sarcophagus in 1421, Simeoni, *Verona guida* (cited in note 17), p. 197.
56 ASV, 'Senato, Misti', reg. 54, fol. 95v; Mallett and Hale, *Military Organization*, p. 27.
57 ASV, 'Senato, Secreta', reg. 8, p. 105; S. Troilo, *Andrea Giuliano: politico e letterato veneziano del quattrocentro* (Geneva and Florence, 1932), pp. 43-57.
58 ASV, 'Senato, Misti', reg. 55, fol. 75v.
59 Ibid., fols. 127, 154v.
60 ASVer, AAC, reg 9, fol. 60.

council' by the abbess and nuns of Sant'Antonio a Corso. It was not proper for soldiers and nuns to live so closely together, and to avoid scandal the latter had abandoned 'their beautiful and spendidly decorated church', 'their convenient and highly suitable accommodation', their gardens and fields; they had put honour and chastity before worldly wealth.[61] The community was now living in poverty, leaving behind property admirably suited to the housing of troops. For that reason they were seeking an exchange so that they could furnish themselves with a church and living quarters, allowing them to celebrate the Offices punctiliously to the honour of God and the Venetian dominion. Of course, if Venice did not come to their aid, they could be sure that Sant'Antonio would save them from 'adversity and shipwreck'; yet they prayed that God would protect and increase the Venetian state. The *rettori* had seen the petition and they had sent engineers to value the property; it was reckoned to be worth 600 ducats; the accommodation could house fifty cavalry or 150 foot; as *cossa sacra*, the church was left out of the calculations. Finally, on 17 July 1425, the Senate ordered the *rettori* to carry out the exchange.[62]

The strengthening of the Cittadella as a fortified barracks area overlapped with the first phase of the series of wars fought with Filippo Maria Visconti, leading to an extension to the Republic's frontiers westwards into Lombardy. It is hardly surprising, given the escalating costs of warfare in general and the efforts involved in developing the Cittadella in particular, that the Republic seized the opportunities brought by victory and peace to reduce troop levels and expenditure. Slight reductions in the manning of the Cittadella were among a series of cuts detailed in a *ducale* of 23 October 1427; they included the decision not to appoint another *provveditore*.[63] After the Peace of Ferrara (19 April 1428), heavier cuts were proposed in Verona, and sanctioned in *ducali* of 1 and 9 June 1428, despite some reservations on the part of the *rettori*. They included cuts in troop levels at key points in the Cittadella, the Rochetta and the Porta Rofiolo.[64]

---

61 ASVer, Archivio della Camera Fiscale' (ACF), reg. 99, fols. 8r-v, 'quia voluerunt preferre honorem atque castitatem divitiis temporalibus'. For Sant 'Antonio a Corso and other religious foundations in the area, V. Fainelli, 'Chiese in Verona esistenti e distrutte', *Madonna Verona*, IV (1910), pp. 50-66; T. Lenotti, *Chiese e conventi scomparse a destra dell' Adige* (Verona, 1953), pp. 50-68. As in the case of Santa Trinità, registers recording the rents due to Sant'Antonio – a few coming from the area of the Cittadella – are preserved in the Archivio di Stato in Verona. For the later history of Sant'Antonio, M.L. Ferrari Aprili, 'Un monastero femminile in terraferma veneta: S. Antonio del Corso di Verona', *Studi Storici Veronesi Luigi Simeoni*, XXXVIII (1988), pp. 121-51.

62 ASV, 'Senato, Misti', reg. 55, fol. 145v.

63 ASVer, ACF, reg. 99, fol. 44v.

64 ASVer, ACF, reg. 3, fols. 25-26.

There were probably strategic as well as economic reasons for a decline in the numbers stationed in the Cittadella. In neither war nor peace was the Republic likely to want to accommodate large numbers of troops on a long-term basis in the area, especially as the 'front' moved westwards towards Milan. That, taken together with the fact that its long stretches of wall were in general bereft of elaborate defences and were protected on only one side by the natural barrier of the Adige, could make it a weak point in the city's defences. According to many contemporary and later accounts it was treachery that exposed that weak point to anti-Venetian forces led by Niccolò Piccinino, Gianfrancesco Gonzaga and Alvise dal Verme on 17 November 1439, ushering in a dramatic chain of events which saw the city lost and recovered by Venice in the space of three days, events which attracted the attention of Machiavelli, among other chroniclers and historians.

Perhaps the most vivid and immediate account is that recorded in the margin of the *atti* of the councils of Verona.[65] According to this, the marquis of Mantua, Piccinino, and Dal Verme entered the Cittadella by stealth, thanks to the poor guard or to the connivance of the garrison. They used the Cittadella as Biancardo had done in 1390, entering Verona by the Porta Rofiolo to deploy through the city at will, taking all the bridges and gates, though not the Castelvecchio, the Rochetta and the castles of S. Pietro and S. Felice. Then on 20 November Francesco Sforza launched a surprise counter-attack from the north, entering the city through the Castel San Felice and driving out the enemy, *favore popoli*.

In Venice the Senate had reacted to the *dolorosam novitatem* on 19 November; the *rettori* with this news, however, also had reported that the castles were still held and had asked for speedy reinforcements.[66] Accordingly, letters were written to Giacomo Antonio Marcello, the *provveditore* with Sforza's army, urging a counter-attack through the Venetian-held positions, so as to effect the recovery of a city that represented 'a great part of our mainland state'. On 24 November the Senate was making arrangements to congratulate Sforza, to admit him to the *Maggior Consiglio*, and to award him the palace in Venice once granted to the Gonzaga as he had retaken the whole city *cum Citadella*.[67]

Similar accounts appear in non-official sources. The 'Anonimo Veronese' described the surprise attack by 3000 men on 17 November. The walls of the citadel were scaled by night and the garrison overpowered, thanks to the

---

65 ASVer, AAC, reg. 58, fol. 39v.
66 ASV, 'Senato, Secreta', reg. 14, fol. 238v.
67 Ibid., reg. 14, fols. 239v-240.

treason or neglect of one Giacomazzo of Bologna and the watch.[68] The Porta Rofiolo was taken and the noise and confusion caused the citizenry to think that the whole Visconti army had arrived. The enemy contemplated invading the Borgo San Zeno but were told that the area was poor and in any case, would be theirs once the city had fallen. Verona was overrun except for the fortresses until the lightening counter-attack from Sforza. Surprised and assailed by the citizenry, the enemy retreated via the Cittadella. The account given by the Veronese poet and military engineer Giorgio Sommariva in his *Relazione* of 1478 is fuller and yet more dramatic, in part because he ascribed a leading role in the recovery of the city to his father and uncle.[69] The 'mala guardia de un Jacomazo' and others is again blamed for allowing the walls to be scaled, and Sommariva claims that had the 'torre e rocheta de la Bra' fallen Piccinino would never have had to abandon the Cittadella; instead reinforcements reached the valiant garrison from the Castelvecchio 'per el muro doppio'.[70]

In a further report of 7 June 1478, addressed to the *capitano* Giacomo Marcello, on the condition of fortresses in Verona and the Veronese, Sommariva listed the troop strengths in the 'Rocheta di la bra' and at the gates of the Cittadella, as well as within its walls.[71] There is no evidence that the near-debâcle of 1439 lessened the importance of the place in the eyes of the Republic, even though the public records in Verona do not appear to record any further major building projects.[72] Yet difficulties in maintaining the structure remained. On 12 September 1449 the Veronese Council of Fifty objected to being asked to pay for repairs to the double-wall: the commune accepted responsibility for the walls that secured its own defence but not for these fortifications which were judged as protecting Venetian

---

68 *Parte inedita della Cronaca di Anonimo Veronese*, ed. G. Soranzo (Verona, 1955), pp. 30-1.

69 'Relazione di Giorgio Sommariva', pp. 201-3. Cipolla also published a passage from the contemporary Venetian 'Cronaca Zangoruol' which confirms this sequence of events.

70 Bartolomeo Sacchi, Platina, related that Gianfrancesco Gonzaga was told that the Cittadella was poorly guarded and took advantage of darkness and bad weather to scale the walls, *Historia inclytae urbis Mantuae*, ed. L.A. Muratori, *RIS*, XX (Milan, 1731), coll. 831-3. It is highly likely that the allies were well informed; both the marquis of Mantua and Alvise dal Verme had previously served Venice. The latter was Veronese, and the Dal Verme palace was situated close to the northern wall of the Cittadella, Law, 'Commune of Verona', p. 338.

71 'Lettere, Ducali, Opinioni, Decreti, Parti . . . a proposito del Serraglio del Veronese', Verona, Biblioteca Comunale, MS 2094, fols. 11-v, 68.

72 I have consulted the index prepared by Virgilio Zavarise to *ducali* dispatched from Venice and the deliberations of the Veronese councils, which covers much of the period 1405-99, Verona, Biblioteca Comunale, MSS 948 and 2891. Zavarise was chancellor of Verona between 1498 and 1511, G. Sancassani, 'Cancellerie e cancellieri del comune di Verona', *Atti dell'Accademia di Verona*, series vi, X (1960), pp. 293-5.

lordship.⁷³ On 19 August 1451 the Senate was still complaining about the poor condition of this important element in the city's defences.⁷⁴

The idea, expressed in July 1405 and resurfacing in 1449, that the Cittadella represented foreign rule and was not in the interests of the Veronese, finds no place in the verse description of the city composed in December 1477 by Francesco Corna da Soncino.⁷⁵ His account is long, detailed and enthusiastic. He mentions the fine arsenal where munitions are stored, and a channel – presumably the Adigetto – where river craft could be moored. He lists the strong points of the Cittadella: the Torre della Paglia, the Rochetta, the pentagonal tower, the double wall running to the Castelvecchio. Within the walls there are many fine monasteries and churches as well as open spaces: meadows, gardens, orchards.

After his visit in 1483, Marino Sanuto composed an even more detailed and enthusiastic – if not always accurate – account of the Cittadella, comparing it in size to Treviso and to Vicenza, mentioning the failure of Piccinino to take the Rochetta, as well as the double-wall and the arsenal.⁷⁶ Also noted are the billets, a gunpowder factory, a water-driven sawmill, stores and grazing for horses. As elsewhere in his *Itinerario* Sanuto was anxious to stress the strength of the place in terms of its walls, gates, towers and ditches. He called it the 'eyes of Verona': those controlling it would hold the city. He also records that it was commanded by Francesco Grassi, captain for life, with a force of 220 men; in fact, Grassi served Venice beyond Verona; just before his death in 1496 he led a detachment of infantry to the *Regno*.⁷⁷ On the analogy of what had happened in 1423, this long-serving *condottiere* probably had been replaced by Venetian noble commanders.⁷⁸

References to the Cittadella also appear in Sanuto's *Diarii*, most obviously when Verona found itself on the line of the battle-front during the War of the League of Cambrai. After the defeat at Agnadello on 14 May 1509, as the Venetian army retreated eastward, its commanders had tried to

---

73 ASVer, AAC, reg. 59, fol. 281.
74 ASV, 'Senato, Terra', reg. 2, fol. 204v.
75 Francesco Corna da Soncino, *Fioretto de le antiche croniche de Verona*, ed. G.P. Marchi and P.P. Brugnoli (Verona, 1873), pp. 36-8. The fact that Corna was not a Veronese by birth may have made him less sensitive to the implications of the Cittadella.
76 M. Sanudo, *Itinerario di Marino Sanudo per la terraferma veneziana nel 1483*, ed. Rawdon Brown (Padua, 1847), p. 100.
77 Was he related to the Grasso da Venezia recorded as Captain in 1459? A *condottiere* of that name had served Venice in 1416, ASVer, 'VIII Vari', item 28, fol. 110v; Mallett and Hale, *Military Organization*, pp. 29, 58.
78 D.S. Chambers, 'Marin Sanudo, Camerlengo of Verona', *Archivio veneto*, series v, CIX (1977), pp. 42, and below n. 81.

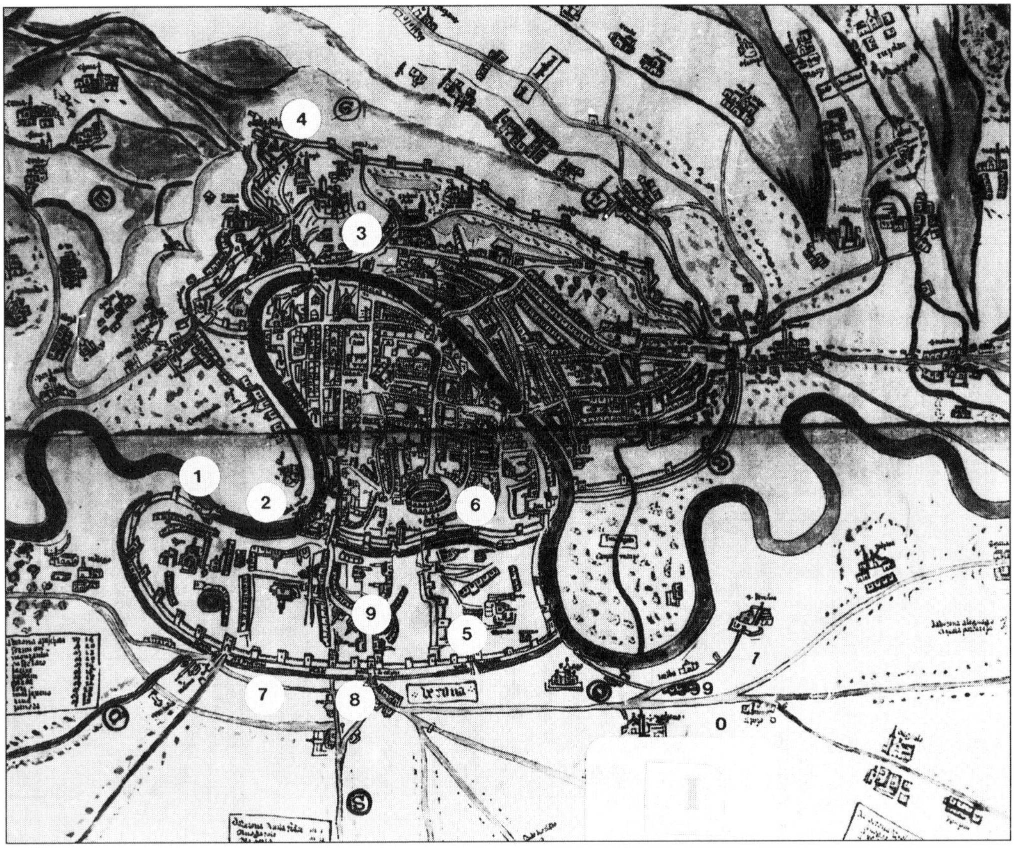

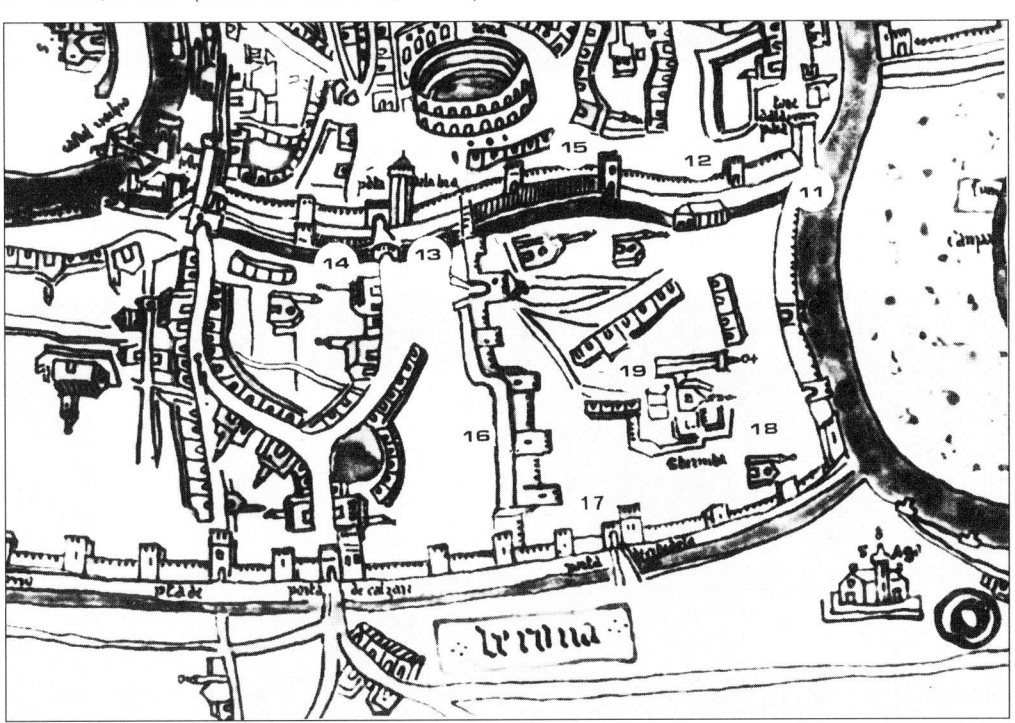

1 Verona, *c. 1439* (*Biblioteca Comunale, Verona*)

2 Cittadella area of Verona, *c. 1439* (detail of *Fig. 1*)

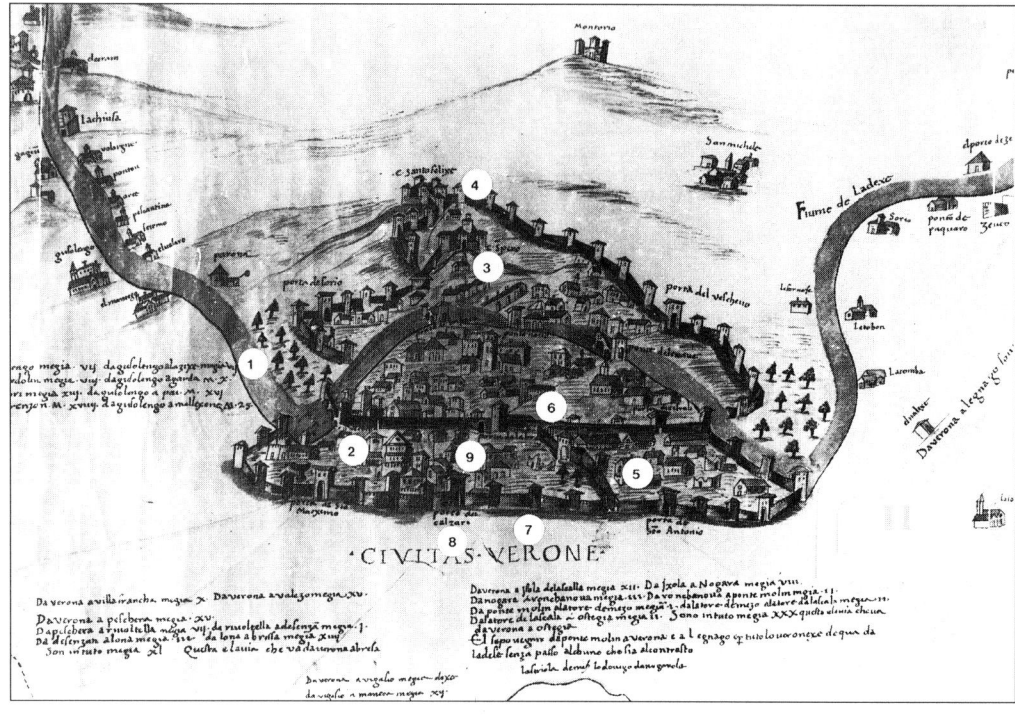

3 Verona, late fifteenth century (*Biblioteca Comunale, Verona*)

4 Cittadella area of Verona, late fifteenth century (detail of *Fig. 3*)

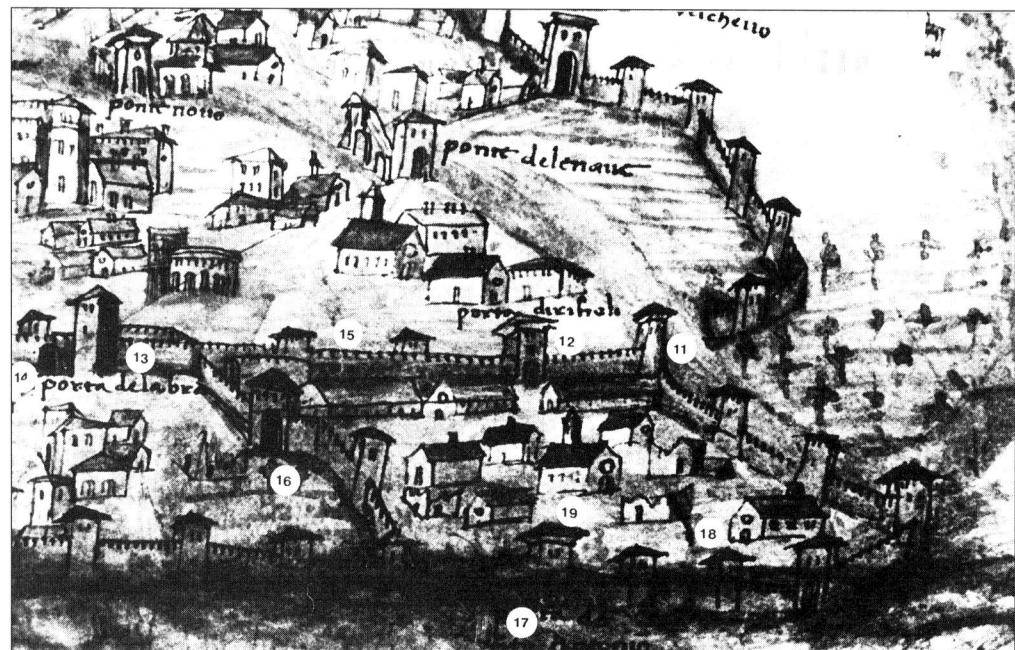

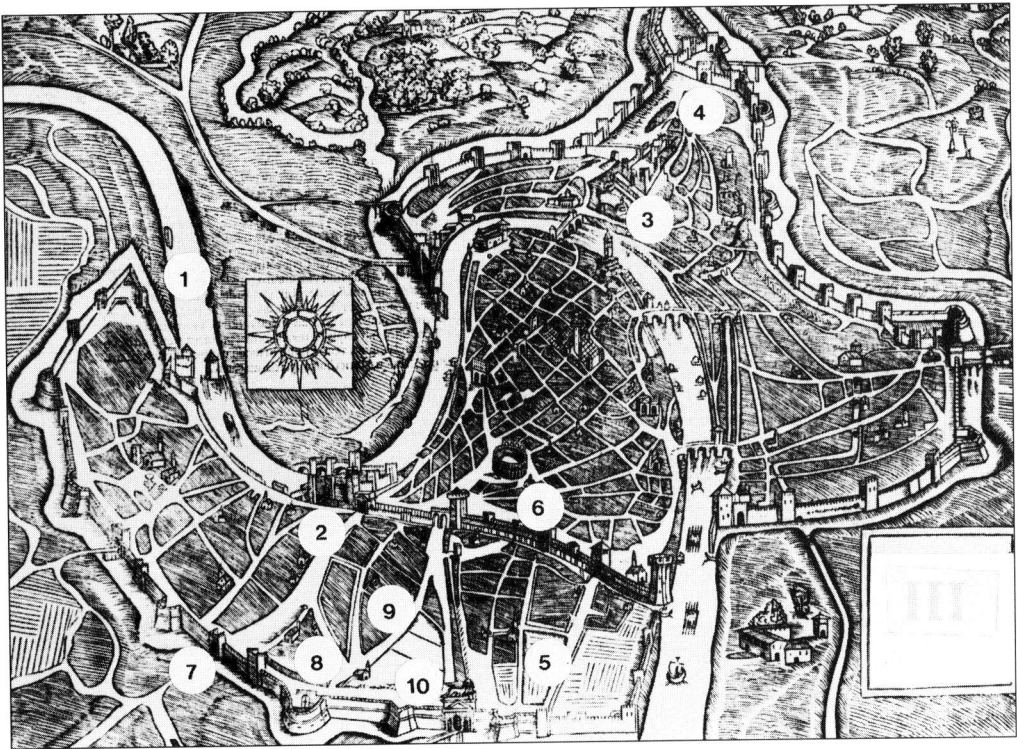

5 Verona in 1540 (from T. Sarayna, *De origine et amplitudine civitatis Veronae*) (*British Library*)

Key to general views (Figs. 1, 3, 5)

1 River Adige
2 Castello di San Martino (Castelvecchio)
3 Castello di San Pietro
4 Castello di San Felice
5 Cittadella
6 Communal walls of the twelfth and thirteenth centuries
7 Walls of Cangrande della Scala, extensively modified in the sixteenth century
8 Porta Calzaro, closed in the sixteenth century
9 Borgo di San Zeno
10 Porta Nuova, opened in the sixteenth century (*Fig. 3*)

Key to the Cittadella area (Figs. 2, 4)

11 Torre della Paglia
12 Porta Rofioli
13 Rochetta della Brà
14 Double wall and line of the Adigetto
15 North wall and line of the Adigetto and the present Via Pallone
16 Visconti-Venetian wall and line of present Corso Porta Nuova
17 Porta di Sant'Antonio, or della Cittadella
18 Sant'Antonio a Corso
19 Santa Trinità

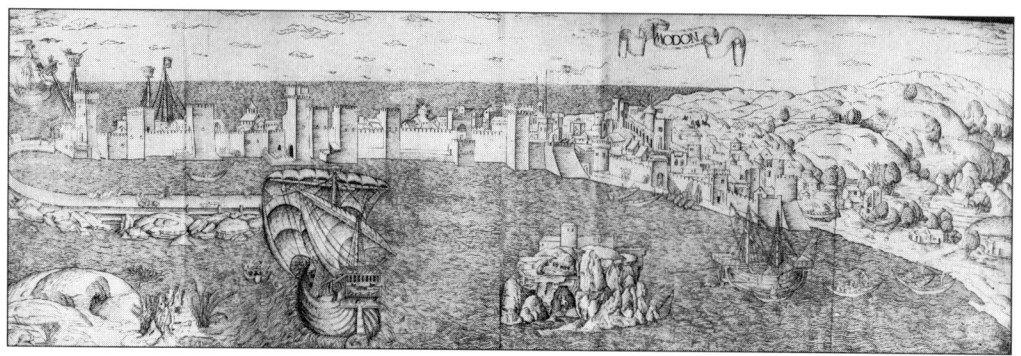

6 Bay of Modon, late fifteenth-century view copied from E. Reuwich's woodcut for Bernard von Breydenbach, *Peregrinationes in Terram Sanctam* (Mainz, E. Reuwich, 1486). The island in the foreground, with the monastery of St Mark, has been identified by Soulis (1959) as Skhiza: the land (*left-hand lower corner*) represents the island of Sapienza. The fortifications and ditches of the land front are unfortunately obscured, but heavy scarping is visible in sections of the walls fronting the beach (*right centre*) and defensive artillery can be seen in towers, on the walls (*right centre*) and on the quay (*left centre*). (*British Library*)

7 Modon, fifteenth-century ravelin viewed from the north west. Note the round projection (*left*) flanking the front of the work, and the Torre Maestra (*right rear*) overlooking the approaches. The lower enclosed casemates are located just above the natural rock foundations, below the cordon moulding. (*Photo: Simon Pepper*)

8 Modon, Sea Fort viewed from the southern end of the town. The apron battery and the upper domed section of the tower are Turkish additions to the original late fifteenth-century octagonal Venetian tower. (*Photo: Simon Pepper*)

9 Modon, dressed-stone gunport and relieving arch in east face of fifteenth-century ravelin. This is one of the ports to the enclosed casemates on the lower gallery level (port E on *Fig. iii*). (*Photo: Simon Pepper*)

10 Napoli di Romania (Nauplia), Acropolis, Venetian fifteenth-century scarping to the Castle of the Franks (*Photo: Simon Pepper*)

11 Napoli di Romania (Nauplia), Acropolis, late fifteenth-century Venetian artillery tower on the most exposed north-east corner of the land front. (The works in the foreground are late seventeenth-century Venetian additions now undergoing excavation and restoration). (*Photo: Simon Pepper*)

12 Coron, fifteenth-century cylindrical Venetian gun-towers (*Photo: Simon Pepper*)

13 Medallion of Lucina Savorgnan, engraved by Fra Antonio da Brescia (diameter 46 mm.); unique copy. (*Museo Civico, Trento; photo: C.H. Clough*)

(a) Reverse: Triumph of Chastity (?) (b) Obverse: Portrait bust

14 Pope Paul II, marble bust by unknown Roman sculptor, *c.* 1470 (*Museo Nazionale del Palazzo Venezia, Rome; photo: C.H. Clough*)

15 The birthplace in Venice of Pietro Barbo (Paul II); façade towards the Rio della Pietà (*Photo: Jeremy Kruse*)

persuade the citizens to allow their forces to occupy the citadel. Reports dated 21 and 22 May make it clear that the Veronese, ready to stress their loyalty and to explain their caution in terms of a food shortage in the city, were unwilling to accept the risks and see their city turned into a battle zone.[79] The political and military weakness of the Republic at this juncture prevented her contesting or rejecting the decision, and following the loss of Verona to imperial representatives, Sanuto recorded the names of the Veronese commanders appointed to the Cittadella.[80] Subsequently the area was used to garrison some of the troops of the League; by 1510 Maximilian's chronic shortage of cash had forced him to pawn the Cittadella to the king of France.[81] On 21 September 1510 the Venetians were contemplating attacking Verona through the citadel; it is easy to see why the contemporary military situation, as well as his own experience, stimulated Machiavelli's interest in the events of November 1439.

The war of the League of Cambrai helped spell the end of the Cittadella, even though the captain of Verona was still arguing for the importance of the Rochetta in August 1525.[82] The policy of armed neutrality, which the Republic adopted in the wake of these hostilities, led to a radical redesigning of the defences of cities like Verona to ensure they were better able to carry and resist artillery.[83] The Cittadella became seen as an anachronism which impeded internal communications as well as frustrating the spread of civilian housing and industries. In a *ducale* of 29 June 1535 the Senate announced its decision to level the wall that divided the city along the present Corso Porta Nuova; lest the land and buildings in the area ran to ruin, they were to be auctioned off and the revenue used to pay for billets near the walls.[84] The Veronese architect Michele Sanmicheli was to design a street plan to encourage purchasers, but the Adigetto was to be retained in view of its potential to power machinery. The policy had some success; reports to the Senate of 1538, 1542 and 1571 refer to the sale of properties and the rehousing of troops closer to the walls.[85] The *contrada* of Santa

---

79 Sanuto, VIII, 298, 303, 304, 324, 327, 332. The Veronese were prepared to allow the army to camp on the Campo Marzo, outside the city walls.
80 Sanudo records the escape of the Venetian noble commander Francesco Zorzi, and the loss of the position from the *rezimenti* open to Venetian nobles, Sanuto, VIII, 387, 470, 482.
81 For instance, Sanuto, X, 264, 295, 682, 726.
82 *Podestaria e capitanato di Verona*, ed. G. Borelli, *Relazioni dei rettori veneti in Terraferma*, IX (Milan, 1977), pp. 3-4.
83 Mallett and Hale, *Military Organization*, pp. 409-28.
84 E. Langensköld, *Michele Sanmicheli, the Architect of Verona* (Uppsala, 1938), pp. 268-70.
85 Ed. Borelli, *Podestaria*, pp. 7, 11, 77.

Croce reappeared in the city *estimo* in 1545; the commune of Verona itself invested in the area in 1584; there were some new religious foundations.[86]

Yet, as John Hale has pointed out, there were those among the Republic's military advisers who saw Verona as a 'suspect city' in the 1540s.[87] When Sanmicheli was asked for his opinion in 1548, he argued that Verona needed two citadels, one for each bank of the Adige, or one built near the Torre della Paglia linked by a stone bridge to the left bank of the river so as to allow for the secure movement and reinforcement of troops – rather on the model of the Castelvecchio. But his advice was apparently offered without enthusiasm, possibly because of his involvement in the demilitarisation of the Cittadella, possibly because of his own Veronese citizenship: he asked for his views to be treated in confidence. He also argued that it was unwise to build citadels in heavily fortified cities, and it was probably views of this kind that urged the development of the Castel San Felice as a citadel 'to keep enemies in fear and the population in check'.[88] With longer-range artillery and an elevated site, this fortress had acquired a much more dominating position than it had had when it was constructed; by contrast the low-lying, straggling and relatively lightly defended Cittadella probably appeared as an outdated liability. However, the area did not lose its military character entirely. In 1624 the gunpowder store in the Torre della Paglia exploded, and though most of the rest of the fortifications of the Cittadella disappeared in a less dramatic fashion, the modern visitor to the church of Santa Trinità, to the 'Tomba di Giulietta' and even to the state archives, will still notice the memorials, the barracks, the ex-servicemen's associations linked with more recent garrisons and conflicts.

---

86 ASVer, AAC, 'Processi', busta 79, filze 1787-90; busta 271, filze 3163-4; reg. 301, 'Sommaria di Materia Diverse', fols. 44v-45; Tagliaferri *L'economia veronese*, pp. 42, 44-5, 77; Simeoni, *Verona guida* (cited in note 17), pp. 182-202; Lenotti, *Chiese e conventi*, pp. 50-68.

87 Mallett and Hale, *Military Organization*, pp. 421-2.

88 Ibid., p. 422, citing Baldassare Rangoni, military commander of Verona in 1547.

The Cittadella of Verona

Appendix

The first four illustrations are taken from two fifteenth-century views or plans of Verona, the originals of which are in the Archivio di Stato in Venice. The earlier view was dated by Roberto Almagià to c. 1439 (Misc. Mapp. 1438) (*Fig. 1*); the other has been dated to the late fifteenth century (Scuola della Carità, B 36, no. 2530) (*Fig. 3*). Their present state of conservation makes their study and reproduction difficult; fortunately faithful, clear later copies made by a certain Don Trecca exist in the Biblioteca Comunale of Verona from which these photographs are taken. Neither is in the same class in terms of detail and accuracy as the famous De' Barbari view of Venice, but both clearly indicate the position of the Cittadella, whose surviving physical remains are virtually confined to the north wall on the line of the present Via Pallone (*Figs. 2, 4*). The third view is by Giovanni Caroto, and was published in the *De origine et amplitudine civitatis Veronae* (Verona, 1540) of Torello Sarayna (*Fig. 5*). It clearly show how quickly the area of the Cittadella was down-graded as a military zone.

In preparing these illustrations I would like to thank the Archivio di Stato, Venice, the Biblioteca Comunale, Verona, and the British Library. I am also most grateful for assistance to Roger Davies, the Arts Faculty photographer of University College Swansea.

For Veronese cartography, A. Bertoldi, 'Topografia Veronese', *Archivio veneto*, XXXV (1988), pp. 455-73; R. Almagià, 'Un'antica carta topografica del territorio veronese', *Rendiconti della R. Accademia Nazionale dei Lincei: classe di scienze morali*, XXXII (1923), pp. 63-82; E. Morandi Custoza. *Verona in mappa* (Verona, 1977). pp. 20-2; R. Avesani, 'Verona nel Quattrocento: La civiltà delle lettere', in *Verona e il suo territorio*, IV, part iii (Verona, 1984), p. 188; F. Cavazzana Romanelli and E. Casti Moreschi, *Laguna. lidi, fiumi; esempi di cartografia storica commentata* (Venice, n.d.), pp. 60-5.

Key to General Views (*Figs. 1, 3, 5*)

1. River Adige.
2. Castello di San Martino (Castelvecchio)
3. Castello di San Pietro
4. Castello di San Felice
5. Cittadella
6. Communal walls of the twelfth and thirteenth centuries
7. Walls of Cangrande della Scala, extensively modified in the sixteenth century
8. Porta Calzaro, closed in the sixteenth century
9. Borgo di San Zeno
10. Porta Nuova, opened in the sixteenth century

Key to the Cittadella Area (*Figs. 2, 4*)

11. Torre della Paglia
12. Porta Rofioli
13. Rochetta and Porta della Brà
14. Double wall and line of the Adigetto
15. North wall and line of the Adigetto and the present Via Pallone
16. Visconti-Venetian wall and line of the present Corso Porta Nuova
17. Porta di Sant'Antonio, or della Cittadella
18. Sant'Antonio a Corso
19. Santa Trinità

3

Fortress and Fleet: The Defence of Venice's Mainland Greek Colonies in the Late Fifteenth Century

Simon Pepper

During the second half of the fifteenth century Venice refortified her Greek colonies to face the growing Ottoman threat.[1] The fall of Constantinople had demonstrated the effectiveness of Turkish artillery fired by gunpowder, both in the destruction of the Byzantine walls and the interdiction of Venetian fleet operations in support of the besieged city. Venice's response was amongst the first programmes of refortification to counter a threat which in some parts of Italy only manifested itself with the French invasions from 1494. This in itself makes the Greek works interesting as examples of military architecture in transition from medieval to early modern bastion-and-rampart forms. The Venetian fortifications in Greece also experienced an early baptism of fire. The first Turkish War of 1463-79 cost the Republic its most prized Greek possession of Negropont in 1470, together with large numbers of smaller inland fortresses in the Morea. The Second Turkish War of 1499-1503, and in particular the disastrous years of 1499 and 1500, saw the loss of Lepanto (Naupactos) on the gulf of Corinth, together with Modon, Coron and Zonchio (old Pylos) on the Messenian peninsula. By the beginning of the sixteenth century the only mainland Greek colonies remaining in Venetian hands were Monemvasia and Napoli di Romania (Nauplia), and these had to be given up in 1540 in the negotiations which ended the Third Turkish War. Negropont, Lepanto, Modon, Coron and Zonchio represent a grim chronicle of defeat, which suggests that the Venetians had misjudged their mainland defences and siege strategy in 1470 and 1499-1500 as badly as they had handled their fleet in the same campaigns. Yet, this is too precipitate a judgement. How the Venetian military

---

1 The author gratefully acknowledges financial support from the Gladys Krieble Delmas Foundation for research in Venice and Greece in connection with the preparation of this essay.

architectural response was pitched, how effective it proved, and how the Turks themselves exploited their new artillery arm and their rising naval power in the second half of the fifteenth century, are questions which this essay sets out to address.

The Ottoman threat to Negropont was recognised immediately after the fall of Constantinople in May 1453. As early as August the engineer, Bartolomeo Suligo, was commissioned to fortify the fortresses of the city and island, which for all practical purposes formed part of mainland Greece.[2] Delays still caused concern in 1459;[3] in 1461, as Venice drifted toward the First Turkish War, instructions became more strident. It was important, stated the Ten, that the city and fortress of Negropont be 'non solamente forte ma fortissima . . . ' Buildings close to the walls or ditches were to be demolished to clear fields of fire, together with other clearances on the approaches.[4] Few details are known of the walls and towers that faced the Turks in 1470, but accounts of the siege emphasise the depth and width of the wet ditch. Although nothing of it now remains, when visited in the eighteenth and early nineteenth centuries the ditch was the most notable feature of the surviving works and was then said to be twenty feet deep and one hundred wide.[5]

The dry rock-cut ditch is still the most dominant feature of Modon's defensive system. Modon was the most advanced of Venice's mainland Greek fortifications and, despite subsequent Turkish, Venetian and French additions it is still possible to identify most of the fifteenth-century features. With the other fortresses of the Morea, Modon was resurveyed by the Venetians during the early stages of Morosini's seventeenth-century re-occupation, and the drawings were published by Andrews.[6] The early volumes of Sanuto's *Diarii* provide a wealth of detail relating to the siege and the events immediately preceding it,[7] while Sathas published many of the key documents from the Venetian State archives,[8] and Donado da Lezze incorporated into his *Historia Turchesca* the little-used account of the siege by

---

2 F. Thiriet,*Délibérations des assemblées Vénitiennes concernant la Romanie*, II, *1364-1463* (Paris, 1971), p. 197, Doc. 1484, (24 August 1453).
3 Ibid., p. 217 (21 January 1459).
4 Ibid., p. 231, Doc. 1604, (9 December 1461).
5 Kevin Andrews, *The Castles of the Morea* (Princeton, NJ, 1953), p. 188.
6 Ibid., pp. 242-56 for catalogue of the plans drawn from surveys for Francesco Grimani, a Venetian soldier and magistrate active in the Venetian conquest and occupation of the Peloponnese, 1685-1715.
7 Marino Sanuto, *I diarii*, ed. N. Barozzi, G. Berchet, R. Fulin and F. Stefani (58 vols. Venice, 1879-1903). Hereafter, Sanuto.
8 C.N. Sathas, *Documents inédits relatifs à l'histoire de la Grèce au moyen age* (9 vols., Paris, 1880-90). Hereafter, Sathas.

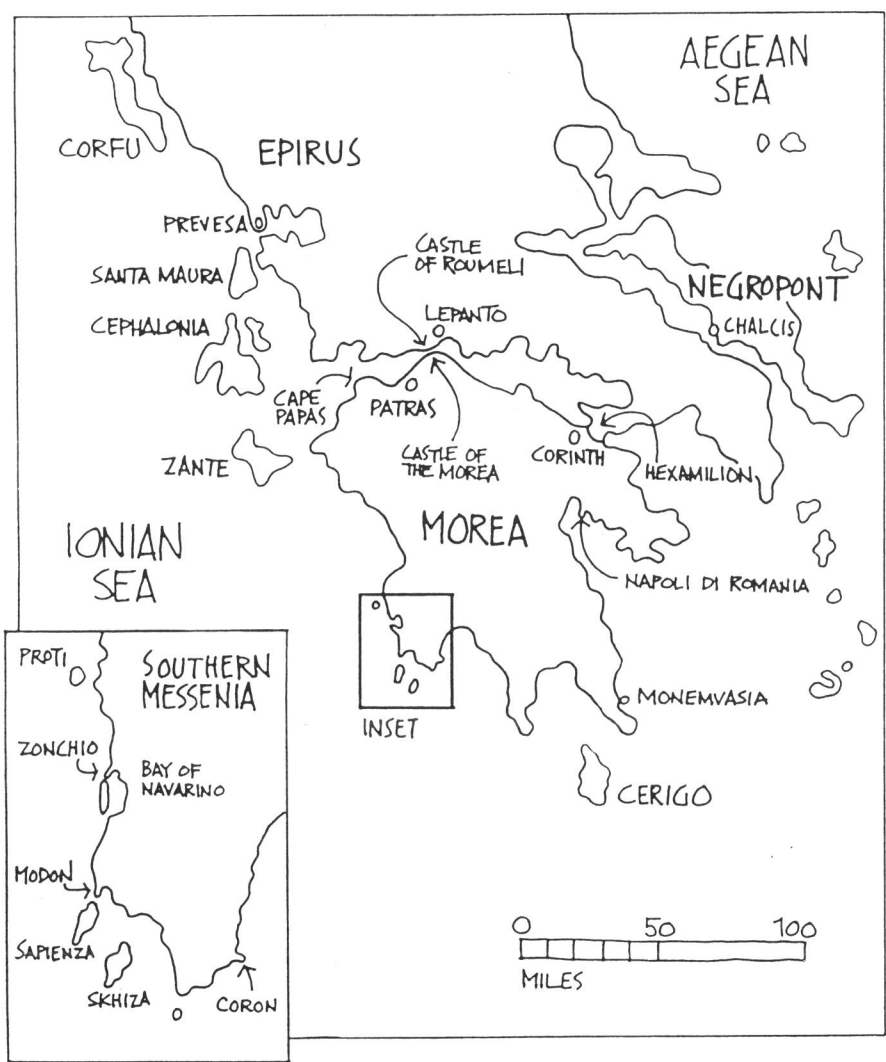

Fig. 1 Venetian Greece: the theatre of operations, 1499–1500, with inset showing Venetian colonies in southern Messenia

32 *War, Culture and Society in Renaissance Venice*

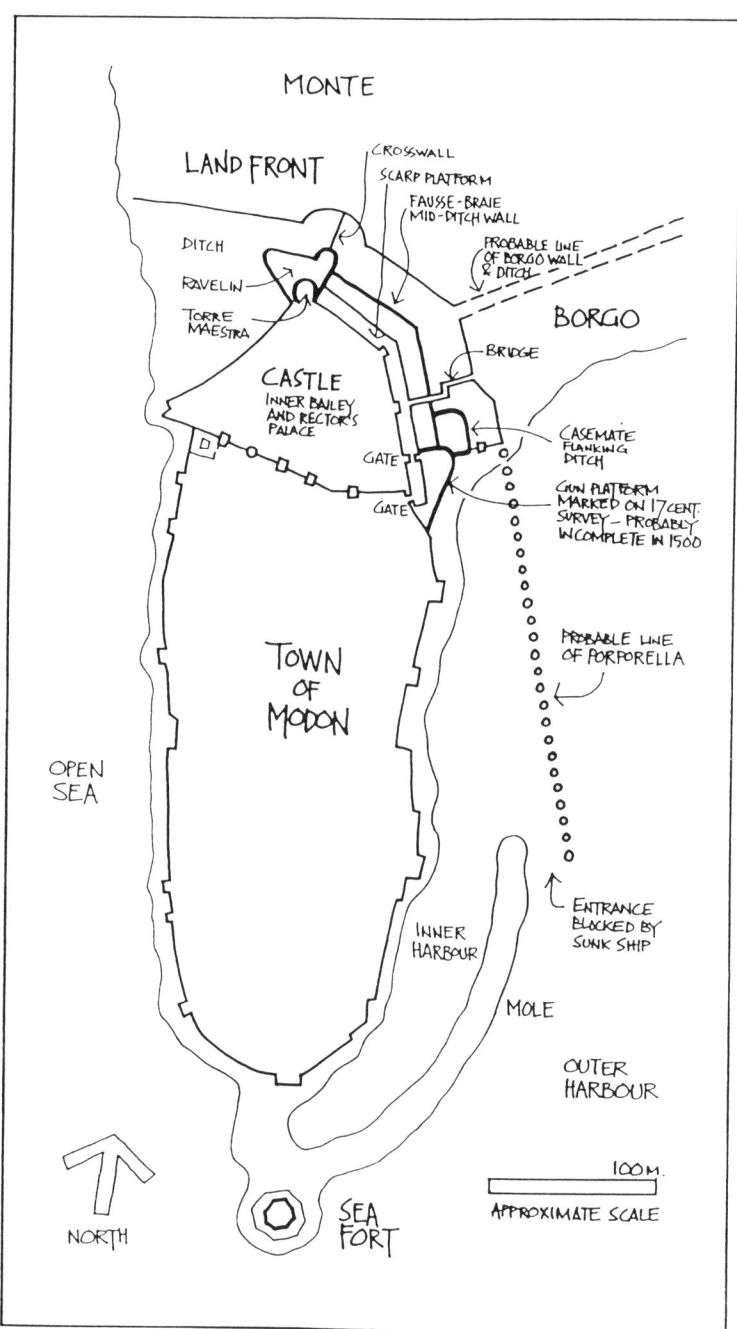

Fig. ii Fortifications of Modon in 1500, redrawn and adapted from the survey for Francesco Grimani (1685–1715) published by Andrews, *Castles of the Morea* (Plate XVI). The line of the Borgo wall and ditch is conjectural, as is the suggested line of the Porporella (sea obstacle). The line of the cranked bridge between the Borgo and the scarp platform is as marked on the Grimani survey drawing; it is much closer to the eastern defensive works than the extant stone bridge.

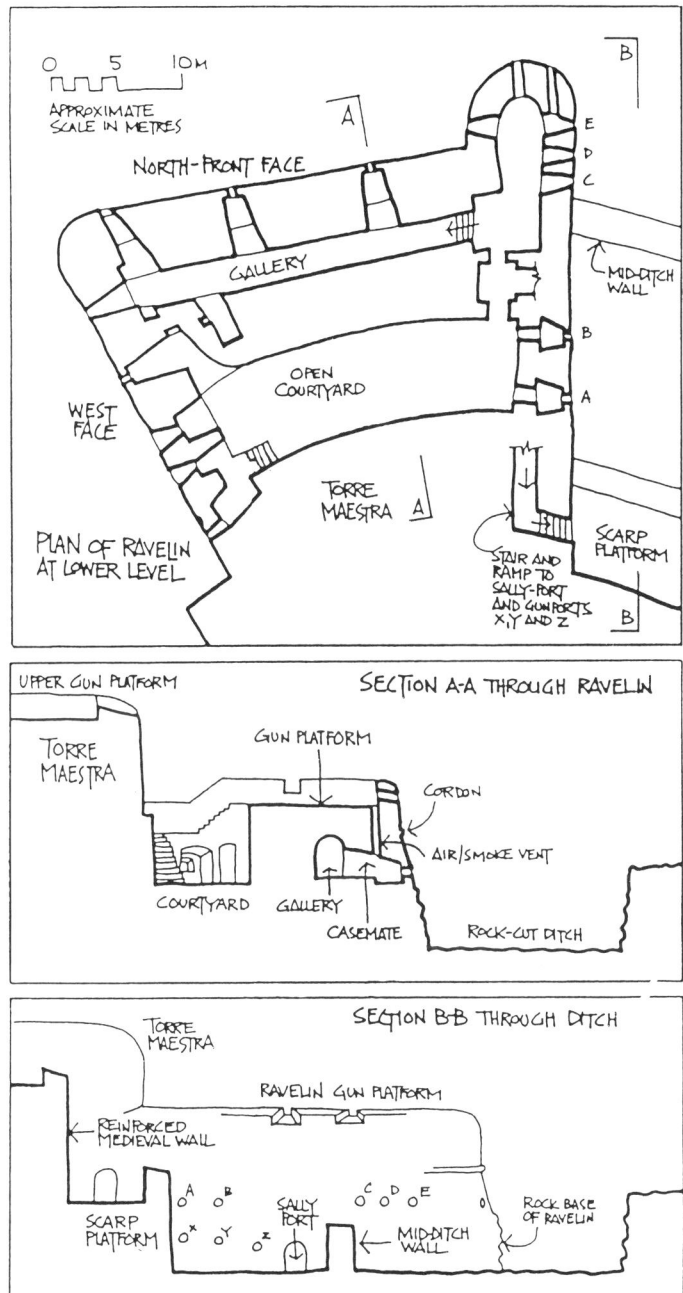

Fig. iii Modon, sketch-plan of Venetian ravelin at the lower level, showing the gallery serving enclosed gun casemates, with sections (A-A) through ravelin, and (B-B) through medieval wall, scarp platform and ditch. These are sketches based on a rough survey in 1991 and should be treated only as indicative of the arrangements. The location of the sally port and its relationship with the mid-ditch wall shown in section B-B is conjectural, since all of this section is buried beneath seventeenth-century works.

Andrea Balastro, *camerlengo* of Modon.⁹ Modon's early fortifications are sufficiently interesting to repay detailed description.

In March 1462 the *savii* of the *Terraferma* wrote to the Rectors of Modon, instructing them, on the advice of the *strenuo* Piero Palmier, to have a ditch made around the place, scarping – that is, thickening – the lower parts of the medieval walls on the town side for greater strength. Warehouses and houses which had been built near the ditch in the *borgo* – the suburb outside the town – were to be demolished after careful valuations had been prepared, and a *piazza*, or cleared space twenty to thirty paces wide, established to enable the defensive use of bombards and spingards against an enemy who would enter by force. The ditch of the *borgo* was to be excavated on the landward side to make it twelve paces wide, and as deep as possible down to the solid rock, the earth to be used both to reinforce the walls and to build up the outer bank.¹⁰ These instructions followed earlier orders dated June 1461, authorising the expenditure of 1,000 ducats on Modon's fortifications, and the employment of the crews of two galleys, together with various skilled building tradesmen culled from the rest of the fleet.¹¹

The ditch of Modon's *borgo* was evidently a new undertaking, designed in 1462 to protect a suburb outside the walls of the Venetian town housing a cosmopolitan society of Greek pig traders and Jewish silk-workers described as 'the Port Said of Frankish Greece'.¹² Gypsies had settled the high ground outside the *borgo*, where they were considered a security risk.¹³ The *borgo* can be seen in a well-known late fifteenth-century illustration (*Fig. 6*) extending along the shoreline to the right of the main walls, with the gypsy huts behind on the *monte* overlooking the city.

Venetian Modon proper was contained within its early fourteenth-century walls.¹⁴ It occupied a promontory extending south to form the

---

9 Andrea Balastro, 'Progressi seguiti di tempo in tempo delle cose aricordate et fatte per cagione dell'infelice obsidione della città di Modone et miserandi pupilli', in Donado da Lezze (or Leze), *Historia Turchesca, 1300-1514*, ed. I. Ursu (Bucharest, 1909), pp. 241-62. Hereafter, Balastro/Lezze.
10 Sathas, I. Doc. 159 (26 March 1462).
11 Sathas, I. Doc. 158 (23 June 1461).
12 William Miller, *The Latins in the Levant: A History of Frankish Greece, 1204-1566*, (London, 1908), p. 495.
13 Arnold Von Harff, *The Pilgrimage of Arnold Von Harff, Knight . . . in the Years 1496 to 1499*, trans. M. Letts, Hakluyt Society (London, 1946), p. 82: ' . . . they have become vagabonds and spy out the land'.

14 For the history of Venice's colonies in Messenia, see Christine A. Hodgetts, 'The Colonies of Coron and Modon under Venetian Administration, 1204-1400' (Unpublished Ph.D. thesis University of London, 1974) and for brief general coverage: Nikos A. Bees, 'Modon' in *Encyclopedia of Islam*, ed. M.Th. Houtsma et al. (Leiden and London, 1936), III, pp. 546-9, pp. 566-77 (Morea); pp. 882-3 (Navarino) and 'Koron'; new edition, ed. C.E. Bosworth et al, (London, 1986), V, pp. 270-1; Stephen B. Luce, 'Modon: A Venetian Station in Mediaeval Greece', in Leslie W. Jones, ed., *Classical and Mediaeval Studies in Honor of Edward Kennard Rand* (New York, 1938), pp. 195-208; G.C. Soulis, 'Notes on Venetian Modon,' *Peloponnesiaka*, III (1959), pp. 267-75.

protected bay, making it into the most important staging post between Corfu and Crete, and it was the obligatory port of call for all Venice-bound shipping from the Levant.[15] An inner bailey accommodated the small garrison and formed a strong point at the vulnerable landward end. A mole had been constructed in the late fourteenth century to enclose a small harbour with a two-galley arsenal for ship repairs.[16] Each of the three gates onto the quays was protected by a tower and portcullis, and strict rules governed the number of foreign ships permitted in the inner harbour, as well as access to the town at night. Since the early years of the fifteenth century harsh measures had been enforced to make the Venetian town secure against Turks who had already settled the hinterland of the Morea.[17] Towards the end of the fifteenth century an octagonal tower had been built on rocks in the sea to the south of the promontory (*Fig. 7*). This tower formed the nucleus of what was later to be elaborated by the Turks as the sea fort.[18]

Modon's main defences were concentrated along the ditch which ran some 200 yards across the narrow neck of land joining the promontory to the mainland. This ditch had been started in 1358.[19] It was cut through solid rock and was probably originally intended to connect with the sea at each end. However, this proved too ambitious and the ditch floor remained well above sea level. Besides the new ditch of the *borgo*, the documents of 1461 and 1462 almost certainly refer to a widening of the original rock-cut ditch to accommodate what Von Harff, who visited Modon in 1494 as a pilgrim, described as 'a rampart against the wall on which stood many fine cannon . . .'[20] This was the 20–30 foot wide platform and its parapet wall which still forms the centre of Modon's land front. Built in front of the medieval

15 Even while Modon was under siege in the summer of 1500 the Senate insisted that Venice-bound ships call at the port, presumably in this case to maintain the flow of information. ASV, 'Senato Mar', reg. 15, fol. 62 (19 March 1500/01) cancelled the standing order, substituting Zante or Corfu, months after Modon's fall.
16 Sathas, III, Doc. 635 (20 December 1414) orders stone for the mole which is then 'almost finished'. Hodgetts, *Colonies*, p. 149, records construction of an inner harbour in 1358, and first mention of a mole in 1372.
17 ASV, 'Senato, Lettere dei Rettori', busta 1, no. 65 (1 April 1397), Antonio Bembo and Marino Caravello from Modon and Coron, respectively, notify Doge Antonio Venier of the local advance of the Turks; one of the earliest notices on record. Sathas, IV, pp. 94, 96, 102, 103 and 107, prints documents recording security measures at Modon and penalties for non-compliance.
18 Nicolaos Lianos, 'Il castello da mare di Methoni', in Giovanni Carbonara and Franca Pietrafitta, ed., *Dieci tesi di restauro (1982-1985)* (Rome, 1987), pp. 61-74 and Samuel Tamari, 'The Venetian-Ottoman fort-castel da Mare in Modon', *Atti dell'Accademia Nazionale dei Lincei, rend. morali*, series viii, XXXIII (1978), pp. 7-12, 527-52.
19 Hodgetts, *Colonies*, p. 145.
20 Von Harff, *Pilgrimage*, p. 81.

curtain, it was a characteristic fifteenth-century solution to the twin problems posed by the advent of effective gunpowder artillery: the reinforcement of older walls against the impact of cannon balls, and the achievement of a broad, stable platform upon which large numbers of defensive artillery could be mounted.[21]

What the extended platform did not provide was flanking fire along the ditch. At the most exposed point of the land front another artillery fortification was built projecting into the ditch with a wedge-shaped plan (*Fig. 8*). An inscription high up on the flank wall provides a date of 1494 for its completion, during the rectorate of Pietro Bembo. This work, which Andrews called the Bembo bastion but which was known to contemporaries as the *Revellino*, or Ravelin, was placed where the ditch turned a corner, so that the two long diverging sides of the bastion housed flank batteries pointing directly down the two branches of the ditch.[22] The front face was set roughly parallel to the centre-line of the ditch, with its gun embrasures firing straight out at the most threatening sector of the approaches, the rising ground of the *monte* occupied in peacetime by the gypsies. These locational factors explain what – even in the late fifteenth century – was an unusual plan form for a bastion or ravelin, most of which were then still being built on circular or semi-circular plans if they were not already beginning to employ the triangular pointed footprints which would eventually become standard. The fully developed sixteenth-century bastion derived its triangular plan from the need to eliminate any potential 'blind spots' which could not be swept by defensive fire. At Modon the unknown designer of the Bembo bastion ensured that *almost* all of the vulnerable front face was swept by guns firing from a small round turret projecting from the north-east corner.

The upper works and parapets of the Bembo bastion are now largely of Turkish masonry, rebuilt following extensive damage to these exposed parts during the siege of 1500. The interior of the Bembo bastion, however, is close to its original form. A lower tier of gun galleries provided additional gun positions in casemates which were completely shielded by thick masonry from the fierce enemy fire that could be expected in this advanced work. Five enclosed casemates can be seen today on each of the three faces of the main internal level (*Fig. 8*). At least four additional casemates – possibly more – were provided at a lower level on the east flank, where they are now blocked by seventeenth-century additions (*Fig. 9*).

---

21 For similar works in Italy and France, S. Pepper and N. Adams, *Firearms and Fortifications* (Chicago etc., 1986) pp. 18–21 and fig. 11.

22 Andrews, *Castles of the Morea*, p. 70 for the Bembo bastion and Balastro/Lezze, pp. 250 and 253-4 for Revellino.

Above the Bembo bastion or ravelin rose a work known in the fifteenth century as the Torre Maestra.[23] A solid tower with a facetted front, it formed a high-level gun platform overlooking the approaches. In consequence of its prominence the Torre Maestra was to suffer heavily during the siege of 1500, its ruins forming a slope up which the Turks eventually entered the inner bailey and town. The existing tower behind the Bembo bastion must have been extensively reconstructed, but probably incorporates the original foundations.

Today no trace is to be seen of another defensive work, described by Modon's *camerlengo* as the 'bastione revelin di sotto alle due porte'.[24] This was evidently under construction in June 1500 – just before the siege – and is probably the irregular work marked on the seventeenth-century plan just outside the two gates which formed the main entrance to the inner town. A fortification here would have flanked the eastern branch of the main ditch, as well as the beach which led to the much less heavily fortified medieval east curtain. Any remains have been obliterated by the much larger extant seventeenth-century Venetian bastion. The Venetians of 1500 recognised this zone as a weak spot in the defensive system, however, and perhaps because the *bastione revelin* was not going to be finished constructed a beach and sea obstacle known as the *porporella*.[25] This was a pallisade of piles driven into the beach and the water out to the mole, with a small gap left in it to allow the passage of a single galley.[26] A similar obstacle surrounded the sea-fort at Napoli di Romania which, as a small and isolated work, would otherwise have been vulnerable to a determined amphibious assault.[27]

Von Harff's description of Modon mentions three ditches, and it is likely that two of his three were formed by the subdivision of the main ditch into two halves by a bank, or wall, similar to the later *fausse-braie* which is still to be seen.[28] The third would have been the new *borgo* ditch. Besides the *fausse-braie*, there were probably casemates (or pill-boxes) on the floor of the ditch

---

23 Balastro/Lezze, pp. 253-4.
24 Ibid., p. 246.
25 Sanuto, III, 574: 'Hanno fatto la porporella a torno, retenuto una nave e una maran per afondar su la bocha.' Andrea Balastro's account of his escape mentions that from the two gates, whence he had been dragged, he climbed onto 'un riparo principiato' (but not evidently finished) and from there jumped down into the ditch. (Balastro/Lezze, p. 255.)
26 Bembo, *Della historia vinitiana volgarmente scritta Libri XII* (Venice, 1570), p. 317: ' . . . Essi Modonei . . . fecero nel mare uno argine, dal quale le navi de' nimici si ritenessero, che pie vicino alle mura gir non potessero: e tanto aperto solamente vi lasciarono, quanto bastasse ad entrarvi una nave . . . '
27 Andrews, *Castles of the Morea*, plate XXI.
28 Seventeenth-century documents refer to 'L'antico antemurale, che dividenda la larghezza del Fosso s'estende dal Fianco del mezzo Baloardo sudetto sino alla Piattaforma S. Maria (previously the Bembo bastion) e abbassato al seno, che fu creduto necessario . . . La vecchia falsabraga . . . ', quoted by Andrews, *Castles of the Morea*, p. 65, n. 26.

which were still under construction during the 1490s when orders were given to complete them 'lest they provide steps' into the fortress.[29]

Elsewhere in mainland Greece the Venetians relied heavily on towers as artillery platforms. Sometimes these were medieval towers which had been reinforced by the addition of massive external scarps. Napoli di Romania had its second line of defence on the acropolis treated in this way, so that the slender perpendicular towers and curtains of the so-called Castle of the Franks were completely encased by a massive sloping scarp, or thallus, with an angle of about 45 degrees.[30] The extent of this modification can be seen in a section where the scarp masonry has fallen away (*Fig. 10*).

New towers were also built during the late fifteenth century specifically as artillery platforms. Those still to be seen at Napoli di Romania (*Fig. 11*) and Lepanto were low and squat in their general proportions, with pronounced scarped bases spreading skirt-like beneath the high cordon moulding. The interiors of these works were solid, save for the passages leading to sally-ports. The guns were placed on the upper platforms, protected by massive parapets which are curved to deflect incoming shot.

At Coron a different type of artillery tower was used. These were much taller in their general proportions, cylindrical in form, and without scarped bases. They provided gun positions at two levels: on the open upper platforms, and at low level inside the tall vaulted casemates. On steeply sloping sites it made good sense to stack guns vertically, rather than to embark upon the massive foundations and earth-fill implied by low, spreading works. Two such tall gun-towers were placed on the steep slope running from the medieval walls down to the harbour, in a position which allowed their artillery to sweep the eastern walls and the barbican outside the main gate, as well as to cover the harbour (*Fig. 12*). Two more were built on the southern approach to the walls, overlooking the unoccupied plateau at the end of the peninsula which could have been used by an enemy attacking from the sea. The two southern towers flanked a long raised platform overlooking the plateau, similar to that on the land-front at Modon.

Andrews identifies the two towers overlooking the harbour as Venetian in origin. On the basis of their poorer quality masonry and lack of a cordon moulding beneath the parapet embrasures, he attributes the other pair to the

---

29 Sathas, I, Doc. 205 (8 October 1499).
30 For Napoli di Romania see Andrews, *Castles of the Morea*, pp.90-105 and G. Gerola, 'Le fortificazioni di Napoli di Romania,' in *Annuario della Regia Scuola di Archeologia di Atene*, XIII-XIV (1930-31), pp. 347-410.

Turkish occupation after 1500.[31] Neither set of towers is like other contemporary late fifteenth-century Venetian works in mainland Greece, but both sets bear a strong resemblance to the cylindrical towers employed by the Ottomans in their fortresses on the sea approaches to Constantinople and the Fortress of the Morea (near Patras), which the Turks began to build in 1500 following their capture of Lepanto.[32] Without better documentary evidence it is difficult to say whether Andrews's split attribution of the Coron towers is sustainable. However, tall cylindrical gun towers were widely used in the fifteenth and early sixteenth centuries in France, Italy, Spain, Germany and central Europe and there is no reason to see in them distinctive Venetian or Turkish characteristics. Fifteenth-century artillery fortification took numerous forms as designers experimented with the new technology. Low towers, tall towers, extensive ditchworks and proto-bastions are all represented in the mainland Greek colonies of the Venetian Republic. Somewhat surprisingly, the only type of work which is not to be found anywhere in this region in this period is an early triangular bastion.

The First Turkish War of 1463-79 inspired a final attempt to secure the entire Peloponnese with a wall across the isthmus. The ancient Hexamilion, or *Semili* to the Venetians, had been raised by the Peloponnesians against the Persians, restored by Valerian against the Goths, and rebuilt by Justinian against the Huns and Slavs. The most recent reconstruction by the Emperor Manuel II had been carried out in 1415 in only twenty-five days, leaving a wall about six miles long, strengthened by 153 towers and a ditch.[33] Sultan Murad II's invasion of 1446 made short work of Manuel's wall: Constantine's Peloponnesian army of 60,000 men, defended it for four days before being overwhelmed by the Janissaries.[34] Despite this unpromising recent precedent, Venice attempted to seize and refortify the Hexamilion in 1463, only to be frustrated by protracted Turkish resistance on the Acrocorinth which forced the Republic to abandon the enterprise after much of the building had been completed.[35] Contemporary and even later Venetian plans to defend the Isonzo frontier in the Friuli with much longer 'permanent field fortifications', suggest that this Maginot Line philosophy was a consistent theme.[36] However, what might be defended in mainland Italy

---

31 Andrews, *Castles of the Morea*, pp. 17-20.
32 Sidney Toy, 'The Castles of the Bosporus', *Archaeologia*, LXXX (1930), pp. 215-28; Hans Hogg, *Turkenburgen an Bosporus und Hellespont* (Dresden, 1932); Albert Gabriel, *Les Châteaux Turcs du Bosphore* (Paris, 1943). The Fortress of the Morea awaits a proper description because Andrews was unable to gain access.
33 Miller, *Latins*, p. 377.
34 Ibid., pp. 412-13.
35 R. Lopez, 'Il principio della guerra veneta-turca nel 1463', *Archivio veneto*, XV (1934), pp. 45-131.
36 Mallett and Hale, *Military Organization*, pp. 91-4 for the 15th century schemes.

could not necessarily be defended by Venice in Greece, where manpower was limited, and where the wall could so easily be circumvented by a force with ships in support. A strongly sited coastal fortress in the vicinity of the Isthmus would have been an effective threat to the lines of communication of any invader, and defensible by a small fraction of the men needed to garrison the Hexamilion.

This was in fact the pattern adopted for the principal Venetian possessions elsewhere in mainland Greece. The fifteenth-century acquisitions of Lepanto, Napoli di Romania, and Monemvasia, together with the much older colonies of Coron, Modon and Zonchio at the southern end of the Messenian peninsula all enjoyed strong sea-side sites. All except for Lepanto were located on peninsulas, surrounded on three sides by water. All of them relied heavily on naval support in the event of serious attack. Indeed, the defensive campaigns in Venice's eastern empire show a close relationship between fortifications and fleet.

Initially the principal Venetian colonies in Greece relied exclusively on naval defence. Modon and Coron were the first ports to be occupied following the 1204 partition of the Eastern Empire. Both were maintained for many years purely as naval stations, with their older walls slighted to prevent their potential use by the Genoese or Pisan 'pirates' who managed from time to time briefly to occupy them. Only after 1261 – when Michael VIII retook Constantinople and threatened the entire Latin position in Greece – did Venice begin seriously to fortify Coron, which was then regarded as the more important port. Modon's walls were started even later, in 1292-93, during the period of tension preceding the War of Curzola.[37] In the time it would have taken to assemble a force and assault their narrow land fronts using medieval siege techniques, Venice would have been able to bring in reinforcements, land a force to threaten the besiegers' communications or, in the worst case, evacuate non-combatants and survivors.

Venetian reliance on naval defence, however, became increasingly misguided as Ottoman naval and artillery strength improved dramatically in the second half of the fifteenth century. New shipyards and arsenals were established on the Sea of Marmora and the Black Sea after 1453, protected by Mohammed II's new forts on both shores of the Dardanelles and the Bosphorus, which were now armed with guns capable of firing clear across the channels.[38] The *odjaklik* system was introduced by Sultan Mohammed,

---

37 Hodgetts, *Colonies*, p. 143.
38 Article on Kanak-Kale Boghazi in *Encyclopedia of Islam* (new edition, 1965), pp. 11-12 and references under note 32 above.

whereby a region or community was given responsibility for supplying an arsenal with one particular ship-building commodity or skill, a measure which raised productivity to a level which would eventually rival that of Venice's arsenal. Turkish sea-power, moreover, permitted the Ottomans to deploy their new artillery arm against accessible coastal sites in ways that were often denied them in overland European campaigns. Venetian naval defence of coastal fortresses was challenged by an Ottoman offensive potential; a fundamental change in the strategic balance of eastern Mediterranean siege warfare which should have been evident after the disastrous loss of Negropont in 1470.

Although bravely held against an overwhelming Turkish force for almost three weeks, the city of Negropont was on the point of collapse when the Venetian fleet under the captain-general, Niccolò da Canale, attempted to raise the siege. The Venetian fleet approached the doomed city from the northern Atalante channel – the narrower southern approach was denied them – but failed to press home an immediate attack against the galley boom that had been constructed by the Ottomans precisely with this in mind. The boom was probably covered by coastal batteries, which had been used so effectively against the Venetian ships at the siege of Constantinople. At least Canale feared such guns. While the Venetian captain-general hesitated, the Turks stormed the breach and Negropont was lost in a memorable bloodbath. Canale was disgraced and imprisoned for his failure to snatch victory from defeat.[39] Venetians found it easier to explain the disaster in terms of weakness on the part of the commander than to consider the predicament of their captain-general. Canale could have thrown his fleet against boom and batteries, and might – with luck – have been able to reinforce the place or evacuate some survivors. He was unable to attack the Ottoman fleet which, in greatly superior numbers, was safely beached to the south, behind the narrows of the Euripos channel, well protected by guns on both shores. Geography weighed decisively against Venice at Negropont. In the confined waters between the island and the Greek mainland, far from its Cretan or Peloponnesian bases, operating against an increasingly well armed and numerous opponent, the Venetian fleet could

---

39 L. Fincati, 'La perdita di Negroponte (luglio 1470)', *Archivio veneto*, n.s. XXXII (1886), pp. 265-307 gives the most detailed account; Polidori, ed., 'Due ritmi e una narrazione in prosa di autori contemporanei intorno alla presa di Negroponte fatta dai Turchi a danno dei Veneziani nel MCCCCLXX', *Archivio storico italiano*, Appendice, IX (1853), pp. 403-40 includes the eyewitness account of Fra Jacopo della Castellana, one of very few survivors to be spared after the surrender of the castle of Euripos; Miller, *Latins*, pp. 471-7 gives a vivid account and mentions another survivor's account, that of Paolo Andreozzo.

no longer be expected to deliver the support which had helped to sustain Constantinople for so long.

These strategic circumstances were reversed in the gulf of Corinth, where Lepanto had been acquired by Venice in 1407 by enforced purchase.[40] The famous 'triple tiara' of walls rising on a steep hill behind the port were described by one patriot as 'the strongest bulwark of the Christian peoples' but, in truth, Lepanto's fortifications still suffered from age and unrepaired earthquake damage when in 1477 a large Turkish force threatened the place for three months.[41] The wall of the lower town had been breached, when the timely arrival of Antonio Loredano's fleet forced the Turks to raise their siege.[42] Here the Turks were fighting at the end of extended lines of communication through mountainous terrain. Despite the terrifying numbers of lightly-armed fighters supporting their offensive Balkan campaigns in the 1460s and 1470s, the Ottomans were unable in these waters to use their fleet to support land forces with the heavy equipment increasingly necessary for siege warfare.

An unusual example of the defensive role of naval forces was the operation mounted in 1474 by Piero Mocenigo and Triadano Gritti in support of Scutari (old Scodra, modern Shkader in Albania). A squadron of Venetian galleys equipped with additional overhead timber shields fought their way fourteen miles up the Bhogana river – through defended narrows, though not against artillery – to within five miles of the besieged city, with which communications were maintained by signal fires and blockade runners.[43] River fleets made a significant contribution to Venetian strategy in northern Italy during the fifteenth century, but by the end of the War of Ferrara in 1484 it was clear that river warships were highly vulnerable to gunfire from the banks.[44] In the absence of coastal batteries, however, the ability to use ships to move men and material quickly into besieged or threatened places was an enormous advantage which Venice customarily enjoyed in her own Adriatic or Ionian waters. Without this facility and with difficult Balkan country to cross, the Turks had been forced to assemble a camel train – one account mentions 12,000 beasts – to transport gun-metal

---

40 Miller, *Latins*, p. 363.
41 Ibid., p. 459, D. Malipiero, *Annali veneti dall' anno 1477 al 1500*, ed. T. Gar and A. Sagredo, *Archivio storico italiano*, series i, VII (1843), p. 114: 'ha le mure quasi tutte in terra, per vecchiezza e per terremoti . . .' (probably a slight exaggeration, but they were clearly not in good condition).
42 Miller, p. 480; Malipiero, p. 114.
43 Barletius, *Dell'assedio di Scutari . . . libri III*, in Francesco Sansovino, *Dell'historia universale dell' origine et imperio de' Turchi* (Venice, 'F. Sansovino compagni', 1560-1), fols. 69v-90 and a memoir of one of Mocenigo's galley captains, Coriolano Cippico, 'Incursion des Strathiotes en Asie Mineure sous Pierre Mocenigo (1472-1474), in Sathas, VII, pp. 262-302.
44 Mallett and Hale, *Military Organization*, pp. 96-100.

to Scutari, where it was cast *in situ* into great guns. After each of the two sieges of Scutari had been abandoned, the Turks broke up their guns and hauled the metal away in manageable loads.[45] If gunpowder artillery was a significant new factor in fifteenth-century siege warfare, the ability to transport guns over the long distances involved in Balkan or eastern Mediterranean campaigns was almost equally significant. Sea power was to prove a vital element when Venice next faced the Turk in battle in 1499.

By the late 1490s it was becoming clear that the Turkish truce was almost at an end. Sultan Bayezid II had long felt threatened by the widely flaunted French promises to launch another crusade from Naples and had lived for years in fear of western plans to use his exiled younger brother, Prince Djem, as the nucleus for revolt.[46] Djem's death in 1495 relieved Bayezid of this fear, while the disordered state of war-torn Italy offered an opportunity for a renewed offensive. Venice, it seemed, was occupied with the defence of her newly-acquired ports in the heel of Italy, as well as by campaigns against Florence (in support of rebellious Pisa) and Milan (in alliance with France). Florentine and Milanese agents were active at the Ottoman court encouraging the Turks to move against Venice. Besides the usual piracy, raids and reprisals, Venice also became involved in a number of incidents which provided the Turks with grievances. In Albania, Venice favoured Giorgio Czernovic against the sultan in a boundary dispute. In Greece, Venice rejoiced too blatantly in the successful ambush and massacre of some 500 Turks by its *stradiotti* from Napoli di Romania. In June 1497 the Republic's galley *Sappho* carrying treasure and pilgrims to the Holy Land exchanged shots with the 'pirates' Enrichi and Barbeta off Cerigo: both sides claiming the other had fired first after a failure to return signs of friendship, both governments taking too much satisfaction in the performance of their commanders for this to be dismissed as a pirate skirmish.[47]

---

45 Knolles, *Generall Historie of the Turkes* . . . (London, 1603), pp. 413-26 for the second siege of Scutari in 1479-80.

46 Djem survived the succession struggle of 1481 and found asylum with the Knights in Rhodes in 1482. They sent him for safety in France, accepting an annual 'fee' of 45,000 ducats from Bayezid. Djem and the subsidy were then passed to Pope Innocent VIII, who had just surrendered him to Charles VIII in 1494, when the prince died. V.J. Parry, 'The Ottoman Empire, 1481-1520', *The New Cambridge Modern History* (Cambridge, 1957), pp. 396-8; Sydney Nettleton Fisher, *The Foreign Relations of Turkey, 1481-1512* (Urbana, 1948), pp. 28-50 and L. Thuasne, *Djem: sultan, fils de Mohammed II, frère de Bayezid II (1459-1495)* (Paris, 1892).

47 These were the key grievances of the Turks, according to the report of Andrea Gritti who was in Constantinople at the time and later, after internment, was released to negotiate peace: 'Relazione di Andrea Gritti oratore straordinario a Bajazid II, letta in Senato 1i 2 Dicembre 1503', in Eugenio Alberi ed., *Le relazioni degli Ambasciatori Veneti al senato durante il secolo decimosesto*, series iii, III (Florence, 1855), pp. 21-3. See also Fisher, *Foreign Relations*, pp. 51-66 who argues that the Venetian alliance with France drove Bayezid to arms.

When it became known in October 1498 that the Knights' representative to the Porte had been refused an audience with the sultan, the apparent threat to Rhodes added to the tension throughout the region.[48]

Reports of large-scale ship-building activity in Gallipoli and Constantinople began to circulate at the same time, and were taken seriously enough for the Venetians to review their own naval situation. In December 1498 the *Collegio* heard the *proveditor* of the Arsenal list the Republic's assets: nine galleys on station in the Levant, and four with Domenico Malipiero off Pisa, two *barze* at Pola, ten galleys at Candia, two at Corfu, three in Dalmatia, and four in Puglia (where the Venetians garrisoned Brindisi following the Republic's role in the removal of the French after their retreat from Naples in 1495). In the Arsenal there were twenty-five hulls of *galie grosse* and fifty-two *sotili*, of which twenty were in good order, waiting only to be rigged. The cost of necessary works was a frightening 51,000 ducats, of which only 20,000 was available.[49]

Venice took its fleet 'out of mothballs' with impressive speed.[50] By the summer of 1499 the newly-appointed captain general of the sea, Antonio Grimani, commanded the most powerful Venetian naval force ever to put to sea: forty-four light galleys and twelve great galleys, together with twenty-eight armed roundships, *navi* or *barze*, including four very large ships of at least 1,200 tons burden, with crews of more than 300, armed with much heavier weights of broadside artillery – the shape of things to come in naval warfare.[51] Despite complaints of undermanning, this was a floating army of some 20,000 to 25,000 men.[52] The fleet could go wherever it was needed, and had been mobilised with great efficiency by the mass-production factory techniques of the Arsenal.[53]

Fortifications, on the other hand, responded poorly to eleventh-hour emergency programmes. The centralisation of Venice's governmental system was ill-fitted to cope with the differing topographical and political situations in the Republic's far-flung colonies. Where the Arsenal concentrated the talents of Venice's naval architects, overseas colonies generally

---

48 Sanuto, II, 128: 'siche quel gran maestro facea provision . . .'
49 Sanuto, II, 224-5.
50 Orders to arm thirty galleys, of which ten were to be armed in Venice itself, in ASV, 'Senato Mar', reg. 14, fol. 172v. (31 January 1498/99).
51 Frederic Lane, 'Naval Actions and Fleet Organisation, 1499-1502,' in J.R. Hale ed., *Renaissance Venice* (London, 1973), p. 149.
52 Ibid., pp. 149, 162.
53 The techniques are interesting. In January it was resolved to arm the city's galleys two-by-two until they were all finished: concentrating on getting some to sea as soon as possible. ASV, 'Senato, Mar', reg. 14, fol. 173 (31 January 1498/99). Generally the priority was for big ships. These were hired on the open market whenever possible and, after Zonchio, 4,000 ducats a month was voted to replace the two big roundships lost in the battle. ASV, 'Senato, Mar', reg. 14, fol. 195 (8 September 1499).

begged vainly for the services of one of a handful of experienced military engineers.[54] Unskilled labour was in short supply for the digging and filling that dominated fortification projects. Venice's Greek colonies had been losing population for much of the fifteenth century, prompting efforts to stem the flow by means of tax cuts and concessions permitting Orthodox bishoprics within city walls, as well as the importation of the Albanian colonists from whom the *stradiotti* were recruited.[55] Venice had assumed the existing feudal rights in Greece and, with her customary administrative zeal, had codified these rights so rigidly that it was difficult to extract more than the customary day-labour from the local Greek peasants – even in the face of danger. Hence the occasional recourse to the fleet as a floating labour pool, which could be transported to threatened sites in times of emergency. The two galleys ordered to Modon in 1461 provided about 400 oarsmen labourers, while the authority to extract building tradesmen from the rest of the fleet gave access to the pool of skills of a major city. For the same reason the crews of four galleys were drafted into last-minute work at Modon in the early phases of the siege of 1500.[56] Building materials were also in short supply.[57] Although Greece offered plentiful stone, local timber was largely exhausted and the Republic was compelled to ship in sawn planks from the Arsenal for bridges, as well as the heavy oak and elm timbers needed to construct the *porporelle* obstructing the beaches at Modon and Napoli di Romania.[58] The Turks had a similar problem, and *bastioni di legno* were amongst the military stores carried on Ottoman transports for the expedition of 1499.[59] Shortages of building materials, and lack of

54 Jacomo Coltrin had worked at Gradisca and Antivari before being posted to Corfu in September 1499, and was probably the most experienced Venetian engineer in Greece. He was much in demand, but allowed only fleeting visits elsewhere. See, ASV 'Senato, Mar', reg. 14, fol. 173 (31 January 1498/99), fol. 197 (19 September 1499) and reg. 15, fol. 45v (13 November 1500) for authority to visit Napoli di Romania to 'confer with the rectors, organise the most important building and to return to Corfu with the same galley'. Local decisions were overturned: Maestro Giovan'Antonio da Rapallo, an engineer sacked for 'insufficiency' by the Captain of Cyprus was reinstated as *sufficientissimo* by Venice; ibid., fol. 41 (26 October 1500). The lack of proper engineers was a persistent complaint from Modon.

55 Andrews, *Castles of the Morea*, pp. 14–15 and 186. This was evidently a local phenomenon of outward migration which runs counter to the general increase of population throughout the Mediterranean basin in the fifteenth century. William H. McNeill, *Venice: The Hinge of Europe 1081-1797* (Chicago and London, 1974), pp. 144–5 and 287-8, n. 46.

56 Balastro/Lezze, p. 248. They appear to have remained behind to fight in the siege together with the regular *provvisionati*, and the Albanian *stradiotti*. The locals did not evidently play much part in the defence of Modon.

57 For shortage of wood for construction and fuel, McNeill, *Venice*, pp. 145–6.

58 Sathas, I, Doc. 159. Hodgetts, *Colonies*, p. 148 reports timber was sent from Venice as early as 1362-65. This was evidently not a new problem. 2000 planks were despatched to Napoli di Romania in 1500: Sathas, I, Doc. 208.

59 'Bastioni di legno' are mentioned frequently in Sanuto, and are probably the timber shuttering often used by the Turks in place of basketwork gabions for their siege batteries and other field fortifications.

construction skills may well explain why the great majority of the many colonial fortification projects initiated in the emergency of 1499-1500 took the form simply of ditch cleaning. In addition to problems that probably surrounded any substantial possession of overseas fortresses, it was not yet absolutely certain that Venetian colonies were the objective of Turkish preparations, nor was it easy to guess where any blow might fall. Venice did the only sensible thing, concentrating her major fortification efforts on the critical positions of Corfu and Crete, and doing as much as she could elsewhere.

The Turks naturally sought to conceal their military preparations and plans. Intelligence played an important role in the crisis of the late 1490s, with Venice as the focus of an extensive network of spies and informants. The most valuable of these was the future doge, Andrea Gritti, whose many years as a successful merchant in Constantinople had brought him valuable contacts and friendships in the sultan's court, as well as unrivalled opportunities to observe shipping movements and ship-building activity at the heart of the Ottoman empire.[60]

Efforts were evidently made by the Turks to minimise *visible* activity in the shipyards. Work at Constantinople was most likely to be observed, and this was kept to a modest level: 'le cosse di qui piutosto se incalma che altramente', reported Gritti from Pera in November 1498.[61] Activity had been dispersed to other yards at Gallipoli and Nicodemia. Gritti was not deceived, however, and emphasised the seriousness of the Turkish construction programme in terms his merchant compatriots could appreciate. Money was being disbursed without having been requested: 'e il danar vien disborsato senza esser richiesto, ch'è gran signal . . .'[62] Bayezid claimed that the warships were being prepared for a campaign to clear the seas of pirates. The scale of naval construction was too vast for this story to be convincing, but there does seem to have been a deliberate attempt to confuse agents and ambassadors by encouraging Venetian hopes that the Knights of St John might be about to be revisited; or was it to be Apulia this time, or Syria, or the Venetian colonies in Greece? Gritti wrote: 'Dove la vadi, chi dice per Rodi, chi per Puja, chi per Soria, chi per i lochi nostri di la Morea, per esser el Signor intestado da quelli dil paese suo, che'l si destruze per esser Modon, Coron, Napoli e Lapanto di la Signoria nostra.'[63]

In the spring of 1499 the Ottoman land forces were ostentatiously assembled on the Asian side of the Bosphorus, towards Bursa, where the sultan

---

60 On Gritti see, James C. Davis, 'Shipping and Spying in the Early Career of a Venetian Doge, 1496-1502', *Studi veneziani*, XVI (1974), pp. 97-108.
61 Sanuto, II, 372.
62 Ibid.
63 Ibid.

himself joined them amidst speculation that the army would soon move south to Tarsus. Tarsus suggested either Rhodes – the Venetians seemed almost happy to believe this – or a campaign to snuff out the embers of rebellion still smouldering in the southern Anatolian mountains of Caraman.[64]

As late as May 1499 informants passed on information which suggested that Rhodes was indeed the objective. From Cattaro the rector wrote on 31 May, with news from an informant who had left Constantinople a month earlier. Elements of the fleet had by then moved to the mouth of the Dardanelles, and the army was concentrating at Chipsala, near Gallipoli, from where they could oppose incursions from Hungary, or go to Anatolia, or move to Greece, 'ed si dice publice va a Rhodi'.[65]

By the early summer of 1499, however, the continued movement of troops to the European side of the Dardanelles indicated a probable attack somewhere in Venetian Greece. Lepanto, Modon and Corfu were all considered potential targets and defensive preparations were increased in these places, with Corfu as the priority site. In April intelligence was received from Andrea Zanchani, the Republic's special ambassador to the Sublime Porte, who reported in code on 2 March 1499 what he had seen on his way through the Dardanelles into Constantinople: 'about 100 galleys, and some 200 sail in total . . . 17,000 oarsmen have been summoned for all of these ships. The Signoria should prepare for the fleet to sail at the end of May'.[66] Confirmation came from Corfu by hand of Fra Francesco da Legnago, who had left Constantinople on 20 April bearing a confidential letter written three days earlier by Andrea Gritti. The Turkish fleet numbered 300 sail, with 100 galleys and 200 other vessels, including a number of large transports. It was expected to sail at the end of May, or by 10 June after a festival. The sultan was now with the army which had all crossed to Greece (i.e. the European side). He also confirmed recent rumours of Turkish plans against Lepanto and mentioned items of cargo which clearly indicated that the fleet would support major siege operations. The transports carried '12 bombarde grosse, oltri bastioni di legno, et faceva far una cadena do mia lontan da Constantinople secreta, che era una gran cossa . . .' The great chain was presumably meant to boom off one of the harbours. Fra Francesco was sworn to secrecy, and lodged discreetly in San Zane Polo. Despite these security precautions, Sanuto notes: '*tamen* tutta la terra era piena di la venuta di tal frate'.[67]

---

64 Sanuto, II, 677, 685, 710.
65 Sanuto, II, 821, 31 May 1499, received by the *Collegio* 14 June 1499.
66 Sanuto, II, 598-99.
67 Sanuto, II, 740.

The Turkish fleet left the Dardanelles on 30 June 1499 and worked its way slowly down the eastern shores of Greece, through the straits of Cerigo, reaching the vicinity of Coron and Modon by the end of July. There they occupied the island of Sapienza and its harbour of Porto Longo, whilst waiting their opportunity to slip past Grimani's Venetian fleet which was manoeuvring aggressively off Modon, attempting to bring the invaders to battle.[68]

At this stage of the war, Venice could have won a victory simply by denying the Ottomans passage to the Gulf of Corinth, where Lepanto was already under siege by the army which had marched overland without its artillery. Sanuto reported to Grimani from off Sapienza: 'dice si'l campo va senza a Nepanto nulla fara, perho che le bombarde de' turchi sono su l'armada, et quelli di Nepanto si difendera virilmente . . . e in Nepanto persone 3500, zoe homeni da fati.'[69] Without their artillery, the Turks were in no position to take Lepanto. Frederic Lane drew a parallel between the Ottoman objectives in 1499 and those of the Spanish Armada of 1588.[70] Despite their numerical superiority, the Turkish fleet needed to avoid battle to be sure of getting the guns to Lepanto. Venice needed to fight.

Changeable weather and well-judged Turkish prudence denied Grimani his battle until 12 August when the Turks, hugging the coast northbound past Zonchio, were confronted by the Venetian fleet apparently ideally positioned for a decisive engagement. The 'deplorable battle of Zonchio' has been seen as a turning-point in Venetian naval history, for the day was marked by serious failures in discipline amongst the few who fought, and, amongst the many who held back. It revealed stresses in morale, weaknesses in the centrally- appointed command system, and lack of clarity in the tactics employed by the Republic's mixed fleet of roundships and galleys which have been so clearly expounded by Lane. Whether through cowardice or confusion in planning and command, only two of the Venetian roundships closed with the Turks and engaged their largest roundship. Grappling irons chained the ships together and, after a four hour struggle in which incendiaries were employed by the Turks, a fire took hold which destroyed all three vessels with heavy loss of life. The rest of the Venetian fleet took virtually no part in the action. The failure of the officers commanding the great galleys – the pride of Venice – even to close with the enemy, provoked cries of 'Hang them, hang them' from the oarsmens' benches; while the lighter and more manoeuvrable war galleys notably

---

68 See Lane, 'Naval Actions'; also L. Fincati, 'La deplorabile battaglia del Zonchio (1499)', *Rivista marittima* (1883), pp. 185ff. Ceccheti's review of Fincati in *Archivio veneto*, XXV (1883), p. 415ff, and G. Cogo, 'La guerra di Venezia contro i Turchi, 1499-1501', *Nuovo archivio veneto*, XVIII (1899), pp. 5-76, 388-421; XIX (1900), documents.

69 Sanuto, II, 1141-2.

70 Lane, 'Naval Actions', p. 149.

failed to pick up survivors. Although the losses were understandably light in the Venetian fleet as a whole, the best opportunity to break up the Turkish fleet had been lost. After further inconclusive engagements south of Zante (20 and 22 August) and off Cape Papas (25 August) the Turks sailed, damaged but unbroken, into the safety of the Gulf of Corinth. Four days later Lepanto surrendered.[71]

Shortly afterwards, the Turks established shore batteries on both sides of the narrow entrance to the gulf and proceeded to repair their fleet on the beaches of Lepanto for the next year's campaign.[72] Grimani was recalled in disgrace to Venice to face imprisonment, a humiliating trial and years of exile before his eventual restitution and election to the dogeship. Trevisan assumed command for a miserable winter campaign as the demoralised, diseased and under-strength Venetian fleet remained on station in the Ionian sea facing the prospect of a renewed Turkish offensive in 1500 from a secure base in the Gulf of Corinth.

Throughout the winter of 1499-1500 the build-up of Turkish pressure on the outlying defences of Modon and Coron made it increasingly certain that the next blow was to fall in Messenia. On 30 January 2,000 Turkish horse and 1,000 foot was engaged near Modon, while in February the 200 locally trained *schioppettieri*[73] had only to sortie four miles from the fortress to skirmish with Turkish raiders.[74] In April the nearby castle at Merona was lost, and those at Moline and Legena (each held by only twenty-five *stradioti*) were threatened by the approach of 7,000 Turkish horse.[75] By June Turkish light troops were in frequent contact with the 500 *provvisionati* commanded by Antonio da Fabri,[76] who had arrived at the end of May to stiffen the

71 The Turkish historian Khalifeh suggests that this was a surrender 'by appointment', i.e. prior agreement to give up the place if relief did not arrive. *Maritime Wars of the Turks*, p. 21: 'When they reached the fortress the heroes went out to blockade it; but the besieged, according to their former promise, sent out the keys to Mustaffa Pasha, and in the following year evacuated it'. Malipiero, *Annali*, p. 180: 'I Albanesi de Lepanto, vedendo no haver soccorso dall'armada, a'29 d'Agosto ha patteggiato co'l Turco, e ghe ha da la città, salvo l'haver e le persone'.

72 Sanuto, III, 54: 'se intese li dardanelli esser compiti al colfo, et turchi haver posto do passavolenti, era in Lepanto, quali anonzevano, adeo sara dificile intrar . . . ' Andrews, *Castles of the Morea*, p. 130 reports that the two forts known as the Castles of Roumeli (north bank) and Morea (south) were completed in three months in 1499 (presumably after the capture of Lepanto).

73 Infantry armed with firearms of the arquebus/ musket type. It is not clear whether 200 *schiopettieri* means 200 guns plus pikemen, or a mixed gun and pike force (as elsewhere in Europe), or whether we are dealing with units made up wholly or largely of men armed with guns.

74 Sanuto, III, 183, report from Marco Gabriel, Modon, 18 February 1499/1500 and Balastro/ Lezze, p. 243.

75 Sanuto, III, 230. Balastro/Lezze, p. 244 describes the capture of the Castello del Grisso, called Merodana, with the loss of 400 people, and the capture of the Castello della Zena and the mills (*moline*). I have been unable to locate these positions.

76 Originally raised in the 1470s as militia units known as the *Provvisionati di San Marco*, by 1500 the term seems to denote regular infantry (including foreigners as well as Venetian subjects). For their origins see, Mallett and Hale, *Military Organization*, pp. 78-9, 150-1.

locally trained levies and *stradioti* who still formed the bulk of Modon's garrison.[77] At the end of June reports from both Coron and Modon put the Turkish strength in the immediate vicinity of Modon at about 12,000,[78] with large numbers of reinforcements on their way, together with four great bombards which were being hauled to the southern Morea: two from Negropont, two from the 'Dardanelles of Lepanto'.[79] By 8 July some 60,000 Turks invested Modon, and the bombardment began from two bombards 'conduto da Patras' – presumably the two from the Dardanelles of Lepanto.[80]

As in 1499, most of the Ottoman siege artillery was to come from their fleet. If Modon was to be saved in 1500, Venice's fleet not only had to prevent the Turks landing heavy siege weapons, but to maintain the supply into Modon of ammunition, money and key reinforcements, especially the gunners and *provvisionati* were needed, as they seemed to be taking the brunt of the casualties. Girolamo Contarini, who had just taken command of the fleet following the death of the exhausted Trevisan, found himself in a more difficult situation than that faced by Grimani the previous year. Outnumbered and with understrength crews, he faced an enemy with secure local bases at Lepanto and Prevesa, from which the Turks could emerge to threaten Corfu to the north, or Modon to the south. With the mainland of Epirus and the Morea as well the islands of Cephalonia and Santa Maura in Turkish hands, Contarini was forced to station his fleet further to the south west where Zante offered anchorages and water supplies. Galley crews consumed prodigious quantities of drinking water, necessitating frequent rewatering stops which prevented the sustained long-range blockades which were to become possible for the sail-powered round warships just beginning to come into Venetian service in the Mediterranean.[81] Contarini was unable to keep sufficient galleys at sea off Patras to prevent the Turks emerging from the Gulf of Corinth and moving south to Navarino Bay and Sapienza, which they reached on the 17 and 18 July.[82] Contarini gave chase, however, and on 24 July 1500, attempted to bring the Turkish galleys at Navarino (south of Zonchio) to battle.[83] Although only a handful of Venetians failed to do their duty at the Second Battle of Zonchio, the action was broken off when two of Venice's great galleys were overwhelmed by

---

77 Sanuto, III, 445 and 481, letters from Marco Gabriel and Antonio Zantani, Rectors, 29 May and 3, 8 and 16 June 1500.

78 Sanuto, III, 518 and 526, letters dated 25, 27 and 28 June 1500.

79 Sanuto, III, 499–500.

80 Sanuto, III, 602–3, from Marco Gabriel and Antonio Zantani, Rectors, 8 July 1500.

81 John Francis Guilmartin, *Gunpowder and Galleys: Changing Technology and Mediterranean Warfare at Sea in the Sixteenth Century* (Cambridge, 1974), pp. 62–3.

82 Sanuto, III, 620–22, from Marco Gabriel and Antonio Zantani in Modon, 23 July 1500.

83 Lane, 'Naval Actions', p. 164.

the Turks and when Contarini's galley, leading a counter-attack, was almost sunk by a single cannon ball. The Turkish fleet remained in its secure anchorages north and south of Modon, while the Venetians retired to Zante to recharge their water casks.[84]

The Turks took immediate advantage of the withdrawal of Contarini's fleet to land nine bombards and two mortars at Modon on 25 July. Until then perhaps as few as three big bombards had been in action against Modon's fortifications, one of which had been knocked out by the defenders.[85] The additional heavy artillery – it is not clear whether these guns had been brought on transports, or were 'borrowed' from warships – gave the Turks a substantial supplement to their siege battery and probably marks the point at which serious damage was inflicted on Modon's fortifications. Before this, however, intense pressure had come from the reckless courage with which the lightly armed Turks had thrown themselves against the land front.

Andrea Balastro's account of the siege, together with a handful of despatches to come out of Modon from the two senior officers, Marco Gabriel and Antonio Zantani, gives a vivid impression of the fighting during July and August. The enemy build-up had been marked by fierce skirmishing on the approaches, with high Turkish casualties and heavy expense of the defenders' ammunition. The bombardment from the first Turkish guns to arrive began on the 8 July. Three days later Gabriel and Zantani reported Turkish *ripari soto la terra* (no doubt saps in the ditch, rather than mines) and their estimate of ten days supply of powder and six of arrows remaining. According to Balastro, the early attacks were concentrated on the *borgo* which had not previously been cleared of houses and now had to be defended and cleared under fire, pending the inevitable retreat to the main defensive line.[86]

At this stage of the siege the Venetians were still able to provide naval support. On 9 July the galleys commanded by Valerio Marcello and [Battista?] Polani arrived from Crete carrying pay for the *provvisionati* who had mutinied the previous month.[87] 12 July saw the arrival of Girolamo Pisani, *proveditor* of the fleet, with ten galleys, four of which were detached from the squadron to support the defenders. The crews of these four

---

84 ASV, 'Senato, Mar', reg. 15, fol. 28, 13 August 1500, records belated arrangements to provide two caravelles of 300 *botti* burthen to supply the fleet with water.

85 Sanuto, III, 729, information from Francesco Zigogna, Proveditor-General of the Morea, in Coron, despatched on 7 August 1500, just before the fall of Modon.

86 Balastro/Lezze, p. 248. Balastro tells of fierce arguments about the clearance of the Borgo, and blames Gabriel for delay, although Sanuto, III, 371 records Gabriel's plans for clearance in a letter dated 30 April.

87 Balastro/Lezze, p. 248; for the mutiny, p. 246.

galleys, plus those of Marcello and Pisani who also seem to have remained at Modon, probably added about 1,200 men to the force clearing the *borgo*, which was finally abandoned on 16 July.[88]

With the arrival of the sultan by land on 17 July, and the Turkish fleet on 18 July, Ottoman strength was estimated at between 90,000 and 100,000. On 16 July – following the loss of the *borgo* – two bombards were brought forward to the edge of the main ditch, supported by a variety of smaller calibre weapons. By 23 July the two commanders estimated that between one-third and a half of the *provvisionati* were already dead or wounded, together with many from the town. The Turks were now throwing in mass attacks. At dawn on 19 July a major assault was pressed for four hours on the western end of the land front; then it was switched to San Bernardino; that night to Lambi; next morning back to San Bernardino again. Towards the end of July the bombardment became continuous, day and night. Balastro identified twenty-two Turkish artillery pieces (implicitly big guns) plus two mortars. The heavy guns fired between 130 and 150 rounds a day between them, while the mortars lobbed twenty-five to thirty rounds daily into the town.[89] Balastro's figures are confirmed by Antonio Remer, *comito* to Girolamo Pisani, who took his *gondola* into Modon on 8 August to brief the defenders on the planned relief and managed to escape the following night.[90] Gabriel and Zantani in their despatch of 23 July estimated that as many as 500 pieces of artillery were in action (most of them no doubt very small guns which must have been discounted by Balastro), as well as *schioppettieri*, crossbowmen, archers and stone slingers. 'We do not have to tell you of our necessities', they wrote in what proved to be the final appeal for relief, 'gunners, powder, masons, carpenters . . . but time is not on our side. We have done and will do more than is possible, but we have around us . . . an infinite number of men who do not value their lives . . .'[91] The defenders were being worn down by continuous pressure from an overwhelmingly numerous enemy, with no respite from the day and night bombardment, which included random fire into the town from the mortars.

---

88 Ibid., pp. 248-9.
89 Ibid., p. 250. Balastro dates the opening of the heavy bombardment to 20 July and specifies seven Turkish batteries, but the Turkish landing of guns following Second Zonchio makes it likely that 25 or 26 July was the real beginning of heavy artillery fire.
90 Precise rank equivalents are often difficult. Remer as *comito* was second in command, or sailing master, to Pisani who, besides serving as *proveditor* of the fleet (commodore of a squadron), was *sopracomito* or commander of his own galley. Remer managed to get his small boat and a dozen passengers out of the city on the night of the fall, and reported what Gabriel had shown him of the defences. Gabriel pointed out twenty-two Turkish bombards (Balastro's figure), together with other artillery, and said that more than 5,000 rounds had been fired into the town. Sanuto, III, 774-5.
91 Sanuto, III, 602-3, despatches of 7, 8 and 12 July, and 620-22, 23 July 1500.

Modon was running out of troops, powder and arrows faster than the food or water which had earlier concerned the fortress commanders.

Under the aggressive leadership of Contarini the rewatered fleet made final desperate plans to relieve Modon. Five of the best galleys were loaded with almost 400 additional soldiers, plus eight or nine gunners, five ships carpenters, 400 barrels of powder and fifteen cases of arrows. On the night of 9-10 August four of the five relief galleys succeeded in penetrating the Turkish screen off Modon and beached their vessels on the mole. Many of the defenders came out to help get the supplies into the fortress, leaving the fortifications so weakly held that an assault by the Janissaries succeeded in establishing a lodgement on the land front, where the depleted defenders were overwhelmed. The fighting went on for most of the night through the castle and town, which was fired by the defenders as they retreated to the sea fort to make a last stand. Smoke from the fires, it was said, could be seen from Zante.

Many of Modon's non-combatants had already been evacuated to Crete or Zante before the siege, leaving relatively few wives and children for the slave markets.[92] However, orders from the sultan to give no quarter to adult male survivors resulted in a massacre to rival that of Negropont in its frightfulness. About a dozen of the senior officers were taken prisoner and later ransomed, in most cases after many years in the Castello del Mar Mazor, outside Constantinople.[93] Most of those who survived the assault – about 800 to 1,000 men according to Balastro – were killed in cold blood after the town's capture. Some of Modon's defenders died on the impaling stakes or at the flaying posts, or lived long enough to see their viscera eaten by dogs.[94] Antonio Zantani died in the fighting. Marco Gabriel was taken prisoner to Constantinople, where he was executed a year later, apparently for killing a Turk.[95] The most vivid accounts of the fall of Modon came from the handful of escapers who got back to Venice whilst their story was still news. These concentrated almost exclusively on the drama of the

---

92 Balastro, however, criticises the rectors for postponing evacuation in September 1499 and again in February 1500, Balastro/Lezze, pp. 243-4.

93 Sanuto, VII, 649 and 663 records that the biggest group of captives was released in 1508, after years of haggling over the ransom payments. Valerio Marcello raised his own ransom and reached home early in 1501. Ibid., III, 1554-5. With the help of the state, Andrea Balastro paid his 700 ducats and was home, via Genoa, in the autumn of 1501. ASV, 'Senato Mar', reg. 15, fols. 62v-63 and Sanuto, III, 1625 and 1634.

94 ASV, 'Senato Mar', reg. 15, fol. 34v (19 September 1500) for the official formula. Balastro, p. 254, writes of the horrors and cruelties of the night of the fall, but describes (p. 258) only the beheading of between 800 and 1,000 survivors in a killing field beneath the Monte di Pigadulgia on 10 August, watched for about two hours by the sultan and his court. This was an organised mass execution, involving none of the elaborate tortures described in other Venetian sources.

95 Sanuto, IV, 145, 172.

attempted relief which, because it represented a credible hard-luck story, quickly became established as the official explanation for the fall of the fortress, the stubborn defence of which contrasted so markedly with the naval set-backs and the poor resistance offered elsewhere on land.

Coron and Zonchio were shamefully surrendered following the massacre at Modon. The effectiveness of their defensive systems escaped the test of battle on this occasion, although when Morosini recaptured the Morea for Venice in 1685 the fortifications of Coron were essentially unchanged and put up a creditable defence against their former masters.[96] Napoli di Romania successfully defied what seems to have been a somewhat half-hearted Turkish attack in the late summer of 1500.[97] Venice made much of this solitary success as the Republic attempted to rally international support in the aftermath of Modon's capture.[98]

If the Venetian fleet performed feebly in 1499-1500, the transitional system of fortifications at Modon did as well as could be expected. Although badly damaged, Modon resisted bombardment for four weeks, of which two weeks can be properly regarded – by contemporary standards – as an exceptionally heavy bombardment from an unusually large number of heavy guns. Here I accept Balastro's confirmed figure of twenty-two heavy pieces plus two mortars, and his rates of fire. Gabriel and Zantani's figure of 500 guns is sometimes quoted but clearly does not help our understanding of the Ottoman siege-battery potential, although a large number of smaller firearms may well account for the heavy casualties amongst defenders. Certainly there was no hint of the collapse suffered by many traditional Italian fortifications when bombarded by the French artillery train in 1494. The deep ditches, the scarped gun platform, and perhaps flanking fire from the primitive bastion-cum-ravelin, presented a serious obstacle to the Turks and allowed Modon's defenders to extract a heavy price in enemy casualties for the loss of the town. Contemporary criticism focused on the shortages of guns, gunners, trained infantry and ammunition, as well as the inability of the Venetian fleet to resupply the besieged fortress in time to save it. So it would be a mistake to see the loss of Modon as the penalty for any backwardness in adopting modern systems of fortification in the Republic's overseas colonies.[99]

The wider lesson of 1499-1500, of course, was a painful reminder of the

---

96 Andrews, *Castles of the Morea*, pp. 11-13.
97 Lane, 'Naval Actions', p. 165.
98 Sathas, I, doc. 207.
99 Guilmartin, *Gunpowder and Galleys*, pp. 260-3 takes such a view. He was misled in this particu-
lar respect, I believe, by the figure of 500 Turkish guns and by accounts of the sudden final collapse. The rest of his strategic analysis is not damaged by a revaluation of Modon.

limitations on Venetian military power. Large island bases such as Cyprus, Crete or Corfu would still be defended by the well-tried combination of fortress and fleet, for here the Ottomans – with their enormous manpower – faced even greater logistical problems than those of Venice. Inside the Adriatic Venice still enjoyed her traditional naval superiority. Mainland positions in Greece, however, were highly vulnerable to an Ottoman challenge which combined large, locally reinforced armies and increasingly effective naval support. To meet this challenge successfully without substantial backing from powerful allies, and to fight a mainland Italian war on two fronts, was now beyond the capacity of the Republic.[100]

There are still uncertainties surrounding the loss of Modon. The tragic collapse may not have been entirely the result of confusion or lack of discipline amongst the defenders on the night of the relief. Balastro was not himself an eye-witness of the break-in, but did have the opportunity to speak with his Turkish captors and fellow prisoners. He tells us that the defenders had been deliberately thinned on the land front to provide a screening force of all the available *schioppettieri*, supported by twenty guns, to cover the expected relief. There may well have been indiscipline amongst those few defending the land front who left their posts in excitement to support the landing, and it is possible that exhausted sentries were asleep – as Balastro reports – when the first Janissaries got in. Balastro tells us, however, that the Turks who first broke into the bastion-ravelin had to climb only about six feet up from the pile of rocks and timber thrown into the ditch, and that a wall which crossed the ditch prevented a sight of the Turkish ascent, and had made it impossible for the defenders to prevent the Turks blocking the ditch. Once inside the ravelin, the Turkish storming party was able to climb onto the Torre Maestra and into the inner bailey up a heap of masonry which 'formed stairs for the enemy' but which could not be cleared because of the bombardment.[101] From this information it seems that a ditchwork – perhaps a caponier, or a wall running parallel to the main defences on the line of the extant *fausse-braie*, or even a cross-wall segmenting the ditch – obstructed the defenders' sight-lines and fields of fire, making it easier for the Turks to bridge the ditch at its narrowest point. Such design mistakes were common enough in the learning phase of the new military architecture. Sometimes they had serious consequences.

---

100 France did, of course, provide a small supporting squadron in 1499 (which was withdrawn following first Zonchio), while Spain provided some troops in 1500 following the loss of Modon. However, for all practical purposes, Venice fought the war in the east on her own.

101 Balastro/Lezze, pp. 253-4.

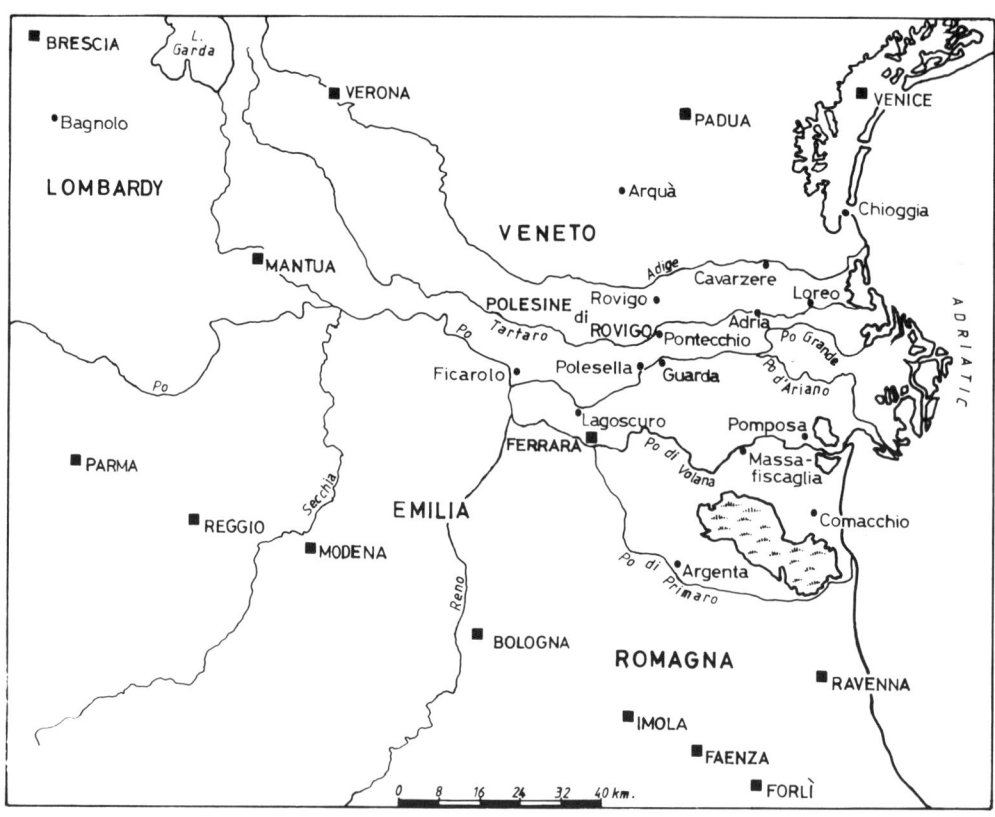

Fig. iv Map illustrating the Po Valley and the War of Ferrara, 1482–84

4

Venice and the War of Ferrara, 1482-84

Michael E. Mallett

The War of Ferrara (1482-4) has been seen both as a 'brush fire' war, a relatively unimportant martial episode which only slightly marred the constructive serenity of post-Lodi balance of power politics, and as an outstanding example of Venetian hegemonic aspirations and of long-term imperialist planning in the fifteenth century.[1] Part of the purpose of this essay is to investigate these contrasting views, to give some dimensions to the scale of the war, particularly on the Venetian side, and to analyse attitudes towards it in Venice at official, popular and individual levels. During the course of the discussion it will also be possible to draw out the relevance of this episode to some other much debated themes, such as the commitment of the Venetian patriciate to state interests and the changing relationship between the Council of Ten and the Senate.

The immediate background to the War of Ferrara was a period of realignment and tension in the Italian political system following the Pazzi War (1478-80). During that war Venice had been allied with Milan and Florence, and therefore involved, somewhat reluctantly, in the defence of

---

1 These attitudes towards the War of Ferrara roughly correspond to the sides in the debate about 'the balance of power' in post-1454 Italian politics; see, for summary of this debate and the bibliography on it, G. Pillinini, *Il sistema degli stati italiani, 1454-94* (Venice, 1970) and M.E. Mallett, 'Diplomacy and War in Later Fifteenth-Century Italy', *Proceedings of the British Academy*, 1xvii (1981), pp. 267-88; republished in *Lorenzo de' Medici: Studi*, ed. Gian Carlo Garfagnini (Florence, 1992), pp. 233-56. Of particular importance for an assessment of attitudes towards Venice in this period is N. Rubinstein, 'Italian Reactions to *Terraferma* Expansion in the Fifteenth Century', in J.R. Hale (ed.), *Renaissance Venice* (London, 1973), pp. 197-217. For accounts of the war itself, see E. Piva, *La Guerra di Ferrara* (2 vols., Padua, 1893-4) and R. Cessi, 'Per la storia delle guerra di Ferrara,

1482-3', *Notizie degli Archivi di Stato*, VIII (1948). The forthcoming vol. VII of the *Lettere di Lorenzo de' Medici*, ed. M.E. Mallett (Florence, 1994) will also cover the war in considerable detail. The main narrative sources for these accounts are also used in this essay: D. Malipiero, *Annali veneti dall'anno 1477 al 1500*, ed. T. Gar and A. Sagredo, *ASI*, ser.I, VII, 1(1843); M. Sanuto, *Vite de'duchi di Venezia*, RIS, xxii (Milan, 1723), with a new edition of the part relating to this period in *Marin Sanudo il giovane: le vite dei dogi (1474-94)*, I, ed. Angela Caracciolo Aricò (Padua, 1989); M. Sanuto, *Commentarii della guerra di Ferrara tra li veneziani e il duca Ercole d'Este nel 1482* (Venice, 1829).

(These sources are referred to hereinafter as Malipiero, *Annali*, Aricò, *Sanudo* and Sanuto, *Commentarii* respectively).

Florence against the assault of papal, Neapolitan and Sienese armies led by Alfonso, duke of Calabria and Federico da Montefeltro, duke of Urbino. The captain general of the league of northern states was Ercole d'Este, duke of Ferrara; this appointment had not pleased Venice, but the Republic had not had an alternative to offer at the time as its own long-standing captain general, Bartolomeo Colleoni had died in 1476 and not been replaced. The Pazzi War had gone badly for the northern league, and particularly Florence, and the decision to seek peace was taken in haste in December 1479 by Milan and Florence without consultation with Venice. This was the context of Lorenzo de' Medici's famous journey to Naples; it is clear that the decision to act without properly involving Venice was in part dictated by King Ferrante of Naples who was anxious to break up the opposing league and isolate Venice. There were also suggestions that Ercole d'Este was behind it.[2] The desired effect was achieved; the Venetians were considerably offended and moved towards an understanding with the pope, Sixtus IV, who also felt betrayed by Ferrante's acceptance of Milan and Florence's pleas for peace. An alliance was agreed on 15 April, 1480 and the period of cold war between 1480 and 1482 became dominated by the opposing alliances of Venice and the pope on the one side and Milan, Florence, Naples and Ferrara on the other. The latter league was cemented by an agreement signed in Naples on 25 July, 1480 which included a secret clause guaranteeing to Ercole d'Este the support of the League if he was attacked by Venice.[3]

The tensions between Venice and Ferrara went back a very long way. Traditionally, Venetians living in and trading in the Ferrarese state enjoyed immunity from a wide range of impositions and customs duties, while trade to and from Ferrara via the Adriatic had to pass through Venetian hands. The responsibility for ensuring that these traditional *patti* were observed and for investigating and pursuing smugglers lay with the Venetian *visdomino*, a noble appointed normally for one or two years, whose authority and jurisdictional powers went far beyond those of a normal ambassador. For Ercole d'Este and his subjects the immunities and restraints were hard to bear, particularly as the number of groups who could be identified as 'Venetians' had expanded considerably since the early fourteenth century when the *patti* had been formally restated. Furthermore, as a result of Niccolò d'Este's abortive attempt to help the Carraresi against Venice in

---

[2] For the most recent discussion of the ending of this war, see *Lettere de Lorenzo de' Medici* (hereinafter referred to as *Lettere*), IV, ed. N. Rubinstein (Florence, 1981), pp. 249-351, and 391-400.

[3] *Lettere*, V. ed. M.E. Mallett (Florence, 1990), pp. 40- 54 and 317-25.

1405, Venetian salt monopolies had been extended to Ferrara, denying to the Este the right to use the Comacchio salt pans.[4]

A further cause of friction lay in the territorial status of the Polesine di Rovigo. This area had been conceded to Venice in 1393 by the Este as security for a loan of 50,000 ducats, and subsequently restored in 1438 as a token of Venetian gratitude for Niccolò d'Este's help in the war against Milan. There were many in Venice who regarded the Polesine as rightfully Venetian, particularly those who had acquired lands there during the Venetian occupation. Frontier and jurisdictional disputes abounded and a permanent atmosphere of tension existed along this border.[5]

However, what gave particular urgency to these traditional tensions in the early 1480s was Ercole d'Este's perception of his improving political status, as a result of close links with Milan during the regency of Duchess Bona, his marriage with Eleanora d'Aragona in 1473 and his new military and political standing in the League of 1480. His confidence and willingness to press issues with Venice a good deal further than his predecessors were prepared to do stemmed also from a realisation that Venice was weakened and still distracted by the long war with the Turks.

For much of 1481, as tensions rose between the two states, there was little unanimity in Venice. Doge Giovanni Mocenigo and most of the senior politicians were extremely reluctant to risk war with the League over Ferrara. They were not immediately attracted by the possibility of papal support due to a widespread distrust of Girolamo Riario and his Romagna ambitions.[6] On the other hand, there were a number of younger and vociferous politicians, some of whom had personal interests in Ferrara and the Ferrarese, who were actively fomenting hostility towards Ercole d'Este. Prominent among these were Benedetto Trevisan and Gianvettore Contarini who had experience of Ercole's attitudes at first hand because they had both been *visdomini*, and had lands and interests in the Ferrarese. Contarini was indeed the current *visdomino*, who in the summer of 1481 was forced to leave Ferrara, having been excommunicated by the vicar of the bishop of Ferrara for arresting a priest and publicly striking the vicar's messenger sent

---

4 For recent discussions of the background to the war of Ferrara and the long-term disputes between Ferrara and Venice, see *Lettere*, VI, excursus, pp. 345-61; T. Dean, 'Venetian Economic Hegemony: The Case of Ferrara, 1220-1500', *Studi veneziani*, n.s., XII (1986), pp. 45-98; see also reference to the issues in Trevor Dean's essay, below pp. 73-98, and the map on p. 56; G. Cozzi and M. Knapton, *Storia della Repubblica di Venezia: dalla guerra di Chioggia alla riconquista della Terraferma* (Turin, 1986), pp. 65-70. Piva, *Guerra di Ferrara*, I, pp. 9ff. remains also a useful account.

5 *Lettere*, VI, p. 346 and P.G. Bassan, *Il dominio veneto nel basso Polesine* (2 vols., Abano Terme, 1972), I, pp. 100-1.

6 For a refutation of Piva's view that the visit of Girolamo Riario to Venice in September 1481 was the crucial turning point, see *Lettere*, VI, pp. 35-6, 354-5.

to secure the priest's release. Alongside these two key figures were other influential members of the Trevisan and Contarini families, and also the most vehement and influential of all Ercole d'Este's critics in Venice, Francesco Michiel. Michiel also knew Ercole personally, having been *provveditore* in Tuscany during the Pazzi War, and he seemed to be particularly sensitive to the implications of the duke's rising political standing. From July 1481 he was one of the *savi di terraferma* and therefore in a position in the College (*Collegio*) to press a consistently anti-Ferrarese attitude. Alongside him in the College were two other supporters among the young politicians, Marco di Ca' Pesaro and Giovan Antonio Minio.[7] Among the more senior of Venice's political leaders who showed deep antagonism towards Ercole d'Este was Giovanni Capello, who publicly threatened the Ferrarese ambassador in the ante-room of the Senate.[8]

It was consistent pressure exerted by these men over a series of relatively minor incidents, salt smuggling, the excommunication of the *visdomino*, border disputes, together with a new determination on Ercole d'Este's part not to be bullied and indeed to seek opportunities to limit his dependence on Venice, which produced a gradual escalation of tension. In late September 1481 the Venetian Senate agreed to a proposal to erect three wooden forts between Loreo and Cavarzere to prevent cross-border incursions and mark clearly the frontiers.[9] With the forts went inevitably military garrisons, and equally inevitably protests from Ferrara that the forts were actually being placed within Ferrarese territory. The large majority in the Senate in favour of this proposal and the fact that the majority was now led by Bernardo Giustinian, one of the most powerful and influential politicians in Venice, indicated a changing atmosphere. But it was an atmosphere of determination to make Ercole d'Este climb down rather than any acceptance of a military solution at this stage. In November the Doge and a majority of the College were still urging that the siting of the prefabricated forts be delayed pending further negotiations, but by a two-to-one majority the Senate voted to go ahead.[10] On 27 November the Senate agreed by ninety-nine votes to seventy to a proposal of Francesco Michiel to send an ultimatum to Ercole calling for complete acceptance of the *patti*.[11] Ercole d'Este's response was something less than a complete acceptance, and in a further

---

7 Malipiero, *Annali*, pp. 255-6 and *Lettere*, VI, pp. 347-58. The reports of Alberto Cortesi in which the activities of the anti-Ferrarese nobles are described are to be found in Archivio di Stato di Modena, Archivio Segreto Estense, carteggio degli ambasciatori, Venezia, *busta* 2.
8 Alberto Cortese to Ercole d'Este, 23 January 1481, ibid.
9 ASV, 'Senato, Segreto', reg. 30, fol. 42v, 24 September 1481.
10 Ibid., fol. 40v, 7 November 1481; *Lettere*, VI, pp. 355-6.
11 Ibid., fol. 41r-v, 27 November 1481.

vigorous debate on 17/18 December the conservatives only just held the line against a complete breach with Ferrara.[12] By 4 January 1482 that resistance had crumbled and authorisation was given for the beginning of large scale mobilisation.[13] By this time considerable popular support in Venice for a war was emerging and Alberto Cortese, the Ferrarese ambassador, left Venice in fear of his life at the end of the month. Before leaving he reported that certain nobles had been stirring up popular feeling in the *campi*.[14] Subsequent votes in the Senate on preparations for war became overwhelming; the corporate identity had begun to assert itself and opposition to the war, or even doubts about the war, could no longer be expressed easily. Malipiero commented that with the announcement of war 'se ha visto un contento si grande nel populo che mai è sta tolto a far guerra de tanto consentimiento'.[15]

The military machine which Venice was able to call into action in the early months of 1482 was a substantial one. Some 8000 heavy cavalry were in billets stretched across central Lombardy and the Veneto, and the numbers could be increased quickly by authorising the captains to expand their companies. Large contingents of these troops had seen service in Tuscany and against the Turks in Friuli in the late 1470s. The number of professional infantry under arms was substantially lower, but Venice did have an elite group of infantry constables on long service contracts, who could quickly recruit and mobilise large bodies of infantry. The first mobilisation proposal of 4 January 1482 authorised the dispatch of 1500 cavalry, and 300 infantry under the veteran Carlino di Novello, to garrison the new forts on the frontier.[16]

Three issues had to be resolved before a full mobilisation could go ahead. First, there was the question of military leadership. Since the death of Bartolomeo Colleoni in 1476 Venice had been hesitant about the appointment of a new captain general. The obvious possibilities were Federico da Montefeltro and Roberto da Sanseverino; but Federico seemed to be firmly attached to the pope and Naples until the last months before the war when he finally accepted a *condotta* with the League, and Roberto was closely

12 Ibid., fol. 53-v, 17/18 December 1481; *Lettere*, VI, pp. 357-8. This was probably the debate at which Michiel delivered the tirade reported by Malipiero, *Annali*, pp. 255-6; see also Cozzi and Knapton, *Storia della Reppubblica di Venezia*, p. 67.
13 Ibid., fol. 46v, 4 January 1482.
14 Alberto Cortese to Ercole d'Este, 12 and 25 January 1482 (see note 7 above).
15 Malipiero, *Annali*, p. 257; *Lettere*, VI, pp. 358ff; Piva, *Guerra di Ferrara*, I, pp. 69ff.
16 ASV, 'Senato, Segreto', reg. 30, fol. 46v, 4 January 1482. For discussion of Venetian military potential and organisation at this stage, see M.E. Mallett and J.R. Hale, *The Military Organization of a Renaissance State: Venice, c. 1400 to 1617* (Cambridge, 1984), pp. 50-3 and 77-8.

linked to Ludovico Sforza and had joined him in taking over control of Milan in late 1480. A decision had finally been made in late 1479 to give the post to Roberto Malatesta, a considerable soldier but one who was always somewhat preoccupied with the protection of his own base in Rimini.[17] It was perhaps this factor that made the Senate reluctant now to offer command of a major campaign north of the Po to Malatesta, and anxious to secure the services of the more prestigious and more ambitious Roberto da Sanseverino for this enterprise. It was clear that much depended on this and on Roberto's growing alienation from the Sforza regime in late 1481 and January 1482. When he finally fled from Castelnuovo, his fief in Lombardy, on 7 February 1482, Venice breathed a sigh of relief and immediately made arrangements to employ and welcome him as lieutenant general and leader of the main assault on Ferrara.[18]

The second restraint which affected Venetian preparations was uncertainty about the Turks. Negotiations for peace to end the war which had been preoccupying Venice since 1463 had been underway for months, but without a secure peace in the East no major commitment to war in Italy could be undertaken. News that the peace had finally been signed in Constantinople reached Venice on 26 February.[19]

Once these two problems had been resolved, then the third essential preliminary could be addressed – money. The collection of four new *decime* was authorised for February and March, and on 5 March three leading patricians were elected to take charge of raising money for the war.[20] In April 240,000 ducats were taken from the special war chest created by the will of Bartolomeo Colleoni and a *monte nuovo* was set up, paying interest of 5 per cent.[21] With these massive funds, advances were paid to the standing troops, 5,000 ducats were sent to Pier Maria Rossi to subsidise his rebellion against the Sforza regime, preparation of a huge river fleet got under way, 3000 infantry were recruited in Corfu and an additional 1000 professional infantry and 1000 handgunners were hired in Italy.[22] In addition to all this expenditure the money for the new *condotta* signed with Roberto da

---

17 *Lettere*, IV, p. 328. It also needs to be remembered that Roberto Malatesta was the son-in-law of Federico da Montefeltro; for this and other important recent discussion of Federico, see C.H. Clough, 'Federico da Montefeltro and the Kings of Naples: A study in Fifteenth-Century Survival', *Renaissance Studies*, VI, 2 (1992), pp. 113-72.

18 For extended discussion of the gradual alienation of Roberto da Sanseverino from Ludovico Sforza and his reception in Venice, see *Lettere*, VI, *ad indicem*. Roberto's condotta was for 60,000 ducats in wartime and 40,000 in time of peace; Aricò, *Sanudo*, p. 236.

19 *Lettere*, VI, p. 358.

20 Piva, *Guerra di Ferrara*, I, pp. 69-73; Malipiero, *Annali*, p. 253.

21 Ibid., and Aricò, *Sanudo*, pp. 239 and 241. Sanuto commented that because of the availability of the Colleoni funds 'li danari abondava per tutto, e si spendeva gaiardamente'.

22 ASV, 'Senato, Segreto', reg. 30, fols. 62v and 69v.

Sanseverino on 3 April had to be found, and 10,000 ducats were sent to Girolamo Riario for his recent military contract with Venice.

Perhaps even more significant than the commitment of money to the war was the commitment of Venetian personnel. Large numbers of patricians were appointed to posts as *provveditore* and in various lesser administrative capacities with the army. Antonio Loredan, the hero of the defence of Scutari (1478), became *provveditore generale*, and Francesco Michiel, 'principal author della guerra di Ferrara', and Giacomo da Mezzo were other prominent commissaries.[23] Damiano Moro, patron of the arsenal, took command of the main river fleet of over 400 craft with large numbers of patricians as commanders of galleys and flotillas of smaller boats. More than 10,000 Venetians must have been involved in the manning of this fleet, which was in addition to the main war fleet in the Adriatic of 25-30 galleys led by the captain general of the sea, Vettore Soranzo.[24]

There can be no doubting Venice's intention to launch a massive assault which would knock out Ferrara before effective help could arrive from its allies. To what extent there was an intention permanently to occupy the entire Ferrarese state is not clear. Sixtus IV had certainly cleared the way for this by formally transferring the vicariate of Ferrara to Venice in April, but hard-headed Venetian politicians, aware of the long-term problems that occupation of Ferrara itself might create, were probably thinking only of recovery of the Polesine and effective reinstatement of the *patti* and of economic hegemony.[25] But either way, a speedy, coordinated assault was essential, and on 2 May Roberto da Sanseverino began to cross the marshes between the Adige and the Tartaro to launch his attack from the north west, while a few days later Moro with his river fleet entered the Po and began to force his way up towards Ferrara. A third prong of the attack was to be Roberto Malatesta's army coming up from the Romagna, but this seemed to be less well prepared. Meanwhile an ambassador, Andrea Bragadin, was sent with further funds and promises to encourage the Rossi, whose rebellion against Ludovico Sforza's regency was an essential part of the Venetian plan, and the Adriatic fleet began to threaten the coast of Apulia in order to tie down Neapolitan forces in the south.

---

23 Piva, *Guerra di Ferrara*, I, p. 70; Malipiero, *Annali*, p. 285 (for reference to Francesco Michiel).

24 Aricò, *Sanudo*, p. 240 and Mallett and Hale, *Military Organization*, p. 99. For further details of this fleet, see below note 28.

25 E. Piva, 'La cessione di Ferrara fatta da Sisto IV alla Republica di Venezia (1482)', *Nuovo archivio veneto*, n.s. XIX (1907), pp. 396-426. For the sources for, and further discussion of, what follows, see *Lettere*, VII (forthcoming) and Piva, *Guerra di Ferrara*, I, pp. 74-86.

The plan was a good one and Venice had certainly assembled sufficient resources to sustain it for a few months. That this knock-out blow did not succeed and that the war deteriorated into a confused stalemate was the result of a number of factors. In military terms the able defensive manoeuvres of Federico da Montefeltro with outnumbered forces, and above all the unexpected resistance of Ficarolo for a full month to the battering by Roberto da Sanseverino's guns and the insidious machinations of the Council of Ten, prevented a quick break-through for the main land army.[26] The river fleet had more success but could always play only a subsidiary role. Malatesta's attack never really got started before he was ordered to go south to help protect Rome from the advance of the Neapolitan army. This was a crucial, and probably mistaken, decision by Venice, taken to mollify the pope and preserve an alliance which was of little positive help. It is doubtful whether Alfonso of Calabria would have risked an attack on Rome, and while Malatesta was able to gain a notable victory at Campomorto his absence from the assault on Ferrara was a severe handicap; anyway neither his presence nor his victory prevented Sixtus IV from abandoning the Venetians in December. The other key, and again probably mistaken, decision taken at this moment was to allow Roberto da Sanseverino, having finally taken Ficarolo, to turn northwards to occupy the Polesine rather than marching straight on Ferrara. Again the presence of Federico da Montefeltro's covering force was a factor here, with the end of the possibility of combining with Malatesta, and a sense in Venice that the Polesine was really the main target. All this led to a great opportunity being missed for a swift and successful conclusion of the war in 1482.

By 1483 Venice was isolated; the pope had joined the League and Neapolitan forces had arrived in Ferrara to join the defence. Ludovico Sforza gradually overcame the resistance of the Rossi and was able to turn his attention not just to the defence of Ferrara but also to opening up a campaign in Lombardy to recover lands and cities lost to Venice earlier in the century. That Venice was able to resist the combined pressure of the four other states and even mount a new and substantial threat to Ferrara, is evidence of the resources still available and of the determination of the Venetians. But it is also evidence of the relative inefficiency and inadequacy of the planning and preparation of the League. Federico da Montefeltro had died in September 1482 and there was no obvious commander to replace him. Disputes and differences of objectives among the powers of the League, unwillingness, and indeed inability, to spend on the scale that

---

26 Sanuto, *Commentarii*, pp. 23-29; Aricò, *Sanudo*, pp. 250-69.

Venice was willing to spend, and a general lack of commitment (except perhaps in Ferrara itself) were the main factors here.

While Venice still had opportunities in 1483 to complete the subjugation of Ferrara, the focus of the fighting gradually shifted to Lombardy. Roberto da Sanseverino was moved to that theatre in June 1483 and replaced in the Ferrarese by the duke of Lorraine and his French troops. The ineffectiveness of the duke and his men in this campaign gives the lie to the assumption of a natural superiority of French arms in this period; it certainly marked the end of a serious threat to Ferrara itself.[27]

By mid 1483 the fighting in the Ferrarese had revealed a number of distinctive charactistics. While river fleets, and the collaboration between them and land forces, had always been a special feature of Venetian warfare on the Italian mainland, the extent to which they were used in this war was exceptional.[28] Control of the Po and the Adige, and of their tributaries, gave the Venetians an enormous advantage; troops could be moved round quickly, territory occupied by companies disembarking from the river craft, mobility denied to the enemy by the presence of the fleets at the river crossings, and sieges aided by bombardment from water as well as land. Great floating bridges were built in the Arsenal in Venice and ferried up the Po to facilitate the crossing of the river by Roberto da Sanseverino's army.[29] A good deal of the provisioning of the army could take place by water. Attempts by the League to contest Venetian control of the rivers do not seem to have been very successful. Even though galleons, one of the standard types of fighting river craft, were built in Milan and Mantua, and a river fleet created which was intended to move down the Po and threaten both the Venetian fleet and the crossing points for the army, the League's fleet never reached a size equivalent in any way to those of Venice.[30]

There was, however, another way to deal with river fleets and this was by the use of well-sited guns on the banks of the rivers. To some extent there

---

27 For the duke of Lorraine's complaints to Venice about lack of support and supplies when berated by the Senate for his inaction, see 'Senato Secreto', reg. 31, fols. 77v-8v, 26 August 1483.

28 For a discussion of Venetian river warfare, see Mallett and Hale, *Military Organization*, pp. 96-100. The Venetian river fleet in 1482 consisted of 200 *barche*, each with a crew of 16, 100 *rede-guardi lunghi* with crews of 24 each, 16 small galleys (*fuste*), and 70 large galleons (Malipiero, *Annali*, p. 253). There was also at least one full-size long galley carrying two of the most fearsome cannons in Venice's arsenal, known as 'la Ruina' and 'Non più parole' (Aricò, *Sanudo*, pp. 261-2).

29 Aricò, *Sanudo*, pp. 286 and 307.

30 For comments on the preparation of a fleet of 12 galleons in April 1483, see Jacopo Guicciardini to Dieci di Balia, 9 April 1483, ASFi, 'Dieci di Balia, Legazioni e Commissarie', 5, fols. 213v-15v. The effectiveness of the fleet was derided by Florence in instructions given to Guicciardini, when he was sent to Milan in December 1483 to attend the Diet of leaders of the League (ibid., 24, fols. 40v-45v, 19 December 1483).

was clearly an established system of river defence on the Po, and Damiano Moro's fleet in May 1482 had to fight its way up the river past forts and gun positions sited to prevent such a move. The bastion at Lagoscuro, on the Po just north of Ferrara, was the key to the defence of the city because its guns dominated the river and made it very difficult for Venetian fleets to move westwards past it, or combine effectively with the army seeking to cross at this point. Venetian fleets sustained heavy losses of ships and men in these confrontations, and to some extent the declining effectiveness of these fleets was a part of the gradual stalemate which developed.[31]

Another particular feature of this war was the use which Venice made of the Albanian and Greek stradiots. These light cavalry troops had been used in the Morea and eventually in Friuli against the Turks with considerable success.[32] There was a fierce edge to their fighting; a morale developed from family relationships and dependences within the companies, which made them on occasions extremely effective. Early in the war Venice began to bring over large numbers of these troops to strengthen its armies and they were also embarked on the Adriatic fleet for use in Apulia to carry out terrorising raids across the countryside.[33] This was the first time the stradiots had been used in Italian warfare and initially the impact was considerable. As more were employed problems of leadership, organisation and discipline began to emerge; they fretted at long absence from their homes, and at the periods of inaction which began to characterise the war. Interestingly enough the arrival of the duke of Calabria in January 1483 with his squadrons of Turkish cavalry, captured and reemployed at the fall of Otranto, gave a new dimension and edge to this light cavalry warfare. But it seems that most of the Turks quickly deserted the side of the League and joined the Venetians.[34]

Almost the most interesting feature was the degree of commitment displayed by Venetians at all levels. The large number of patrician officials sent out at the beginning of the war has already been referred to, and this practice continued throughout the war. Each new offensive, like those in September 1482 and May 1483, was accompanied by more *provveditori* taking over to stiffen the resolve of the troops.[35] In the late summer of 1483

---

31 For description of the damage done to the Venetian fleet by bombardment from the river bank, see Aricò, *Sanudo*, p. 279. A similar fate overtook a Venetian river fleet at the hands of the Ferrarese in 1509; see R. Finlay, 'Venice, the Po Expedition and the End of the League of Cambrai, 1509-10' *Studies in Modern European History and Culture*, II (1976), pp. 37-72.

32 For discussion of the Venetian use of stradiots, see Mallett and Hale, *Military Organization*, pp. 71-4.

33 Malipiero, *Annali*, p. 263; Aricò, *Sanudo*, p. 240. It was said to be Francesco Zivran who suggested to Francesco Sanuto, one of the leading figures in the College, that stradiots should be brought over for the war.

34 *Diario Ferrarese dall'anno 1409 sino al 1502*, ed. G. Pardi, *RIS*, XXIV, vii, (1933), p. 107.

35 ASV, 'Senato, Segreto', reg. 31, fols. 16v–23v; Aricò, *Sanudo*, p. 297.

when the war in Lombardy was going badly, the Venetian response was to send patrician *provveditori* to every small town threatened by the advance of the League's army.[36] Some of those who had played a part in pushing Venice towards the war now took their places in the front line. Gianvettore Contarini, resident in Arquà, intrigued incessantly amongst his contacts within the Ferrarese nobility and sought to bring about a coup in Ferrara.[37] Francesco Michiel was constantly active as a *provveditore*, particularly in the Romagna, until his death in the field in the summer of 1483.[38]

A number of Venice's leading politicians died or became seriously ill whilst serving in this war. Both Antonio Loredan and Damiano Moro were dead from marsh fever before the end of the campaign of 1482.[39] Giacomo da Mezzo and Francesco Sanuto died in the field in 1483 and Giacomo Marcello was killed in 1484 whilst leading the attack on the Apulian coast.[40] The families of these men received substantial pensions and support from the state as did those of soldiers who died in the war.[41]

As we have seen, very large numbers of ordinary Venetians also became involved. Malipiero reported in his *Annali* that 'in 1482 molti del populo senza stipendio sequita l'esercito e l'armada, per terra e per aqua; parte mossi da speranza de guadagno, parte dall'odio che i porta a la cità de Ferrara'.[42] In the autumn of that year when a new offensive was being organised large numbers were recruited from the *traghetti* and the *Scuole* to serve in the river fleets.[43] Popular enthusiasm was clearly running high in Venice in the early stages of the war; the biggest crowds ever seen in the city attended the celebrations to mark the fall of Ficarolo in early July 1482.[44] Huge crowds were again reported in August when a group of prisoners captured at Lagoscuro were sent back to Venice.[45]

There was, inevitably, another side to this picture. We are accustomed to reports of negligence and treachery from the armies of this period, and the Venetian armies in this war provided their fair share of them. The presence

---

36 ASV, 'Senato, Terra', 9, fols. 56v and 92v, 16 February and 10 July 1484.
37 ASV, 'Consiglio di Dieci, Misti', 21, fol. 15v, 29 January 1483.
38 Malipiero, *Annali*, p. 285.
39 Ibid., pp. 265-5.
40 Ibid., pp. 288 and 293-4; Piva, *Guerra di Ferrara*, I, p. 121.
41 The Senate voted a grant of 200 ducats to the families of soldiers killed at the taking of Ficarolo ('Senato, Terra', 8, fol. 158r, 1 July 1482) and 600 ducats to the wife and children of Antonio Loredan, the *provveditore generale* who died in the field in August (ibid., fol. 165v, 13 August 1482). There are many other examples of grants during the war. For a general discussion of such rewards in Venetian practice, see Mallett and Hale, *Military Organization*, pp. 194-7.
42 Malipiero, *Annali*, p. 257. On this phenomenon of a 'popular war', see also Cozzi and Knapton, *Storia della Repubblica di Venezia*, pp. 67-8.
43 Malipiero, *Annali*, p. 266; W.B. Wurthmann, 'The Council of Ten and the Scuole Grandi in Early Renaissance Venice', *Studi Veneziani*, n.s., XVIII (1989), pp. 62-3.
44 Ibid., p. 261; Sanuto, *Commentarii*, p. 28.
45 Malipiero, *Annali*, p. 266.

of Roberto da Sanseverino and his sons in the high command made some contact with their ex-colleagues amongst the Milanese captains almost inevitable, and there is plenty of evidence of fraternisation and intrigue.[46] In Venice itself there were also signs of less than total commitment. This is scarcely surprising considering the opposition to the war which had been apparent up to the last moment. Alberto Cortese had pro-Ferrarese contacts within the Venetian patriciate and it was from this circle that Dolfino Dolfin came; he was charged and exiled in January 1483 for passing state secrets to Ferrara.[47] Later that year there was a row in the Senate over contractors and merchants misusing the customs concessions offered to those who supplied the army; they were diverting the supplies to Venice and selling on the open market.[48] Great efforts had also to be made to stop Venetians conducting private negotiations and deals with the military captains.[49] By midsummer 1483 there was a growing reluctance on the part of members of the patriciate to accept appointment to posts with the army. This was no doubt as much due to the increased number of such posts as of any growing reluctance to fill them, but it created an atmosphere of detachment and lack of enthusiasm that was self-sustaining.[50]

One of the factors that may have contributed to this apparent decline in commitment amongst the rank and file patricians was the extent to which discussion and direction of the war became more confined to closed groups, particularly the Council of Ten. It is interesting that the great debate in the later months of 1481 and early 1482 about Ferrara was conducted in the Senate. There is no evidence of preliminary discussions in the Ten, or of any particular sensitivity which would have justified a resort to the closed doors of that committee. However, once preparations for war had started the role of the Ten became more apparent. Certain aspects of military preparation, stockpiling of provisions, control of artillery, espionage and fifth-column

---

46 For an example of this problem, see Mallett and Hale, *Military Organization*, pp. 183-5. The reports of Jacopo Guicciardini, Florentine commissary and orator with the army of the League in Ferrara in the spring of 1483, commented at length on meetings and discussions between the duke of Calabria and some of his leading captains and the sons of Roberto da Sanseverino; ASFi, 'Archivio Mediceo avanti il Principato', filza XLVIII, 315, 316, 317, 301, 303; see *Lettere*, VII, forthcoming.

47 ASV, 'Consiglio di Dieci, Misti', 21, fol. 11v, *c.* 16 January 1483. On Cortese's role in creating a clientele of Venetian patricians, see *Lettere*, VI, excursus, pp. 345-61 and Trevor Dean's essay in this volume below, pp. 81-2.

48 ASV, 'Senato, Terra', 9, fol. 10r, 23 June 1483.

49 Ibid., 8, fol. 144, 1 April 1482; Aricò, *Sanudo*, p. 238.

50 Fines of 2,000 ducats were imposed on those who refused posts as *provveditori* in September 1483 ('Senato Terra', 9, fol. 25r, 9 September 1483), and in the following months the length of service required was reduced to a maximum of two months in the hope of persuading nobles to accept the posts (ibid., fol. 33r, 17 October 1483). For discussion of evasion of public responsibility as a long-term characteristic of the Venetian patrician ethic, see D.B. Queller, *The Venetian Patriciate* (Urbana and Chicago, 1986), pp. 113-171.

activities, were already firmly within the purview of that committee. The funds available to the Ten were used extensively in those fields in April 1482.[51]

With the outbreak of war itself the Ten became heavily involved in receiving reports from *provveditori* and in the 'secret war', the conspiracies to subvert enemy captains and destabilise rival states, and the countering of such conspiracies devised by the League. While one undoubtedly gets an impression of a certain growth in the authority, and even in minor ways of the competence, of the Ten in this period, it has to be said that the key decisions in matters of policy and implementation of policy, such as recruiting, movement of troops and raising of money, continued to be taken in the Senate. The secret peace negotiations with Lorenzo de' Medici, with Ludovico Sforza, with Girolamo Riario, at various moments in 1483, whilst they tended to emerge initially in the Ten, were always passed at a certain point to the Senate for consideration and action.[52] It was the College and the Senate which received the reports from the negotiators at Bagnolo and which approved the terms of the peace.[53] Yet inevitably the executive role of the College and the Savi increased in war time, and it is clear that this steering committee of the Senate and the Council of Ten were acting in close collaboration as a sort of inner group controlling the war.

In 1502 Doge Loredan remarked to the Ferrarese ambassador that the War of Ferrara was a war that should never have happened and 'that there never was a worse enterprise undertaken by this state'.[54] This was not just hindsight or indeed kind words for the Ferrarese; it was a feeling that grew in Venice during the war. A prime factor in the onset of disillusionment was

---

51 ASV, 'Consiglio di Dieci, Misti', 20, fol. 157r, 15 April 1482. For the Dieci providing handguns for new recruits from its own armoury, see ibid., fol. 173v, 4 June 1482, and for the beginning of intensive fifth-column activities, see ibid., fol. 108r, 20 March 1483 and Piva, *Guerra di Ferrara*, I, pp. 75-6. For the broader debate on the role of the Dieci in the fifteenth century, see Cozzi and Knapton, *Storia della Repubblica di Venezia*, pp. 110-13; Mallett and Hale, *Military Organisation*, pp. 163-8; G. Cozzi, 'Authority and the Law in Renaissance Venice', in J.R. Hale ed., *Renaissance Venice* (London, 1973), pp. 304-5; M. Knapton, 'Il Consiglio dei Dieci nel governo della Terraferma', in A. Tagliaferri ed., *Atti del convegno Venezia e la Terraferma attraverso le relazioni dei rettori* (Milan, 1981), pp. 237-60.

52 G. Dalla Santa, 'Benedetto Soranzo, patrizio veneto, archivescovo di Cipro, e Girolamo Riario', *Nuovo archivio veneto*, ser. 2, XIV (1914), pp. 308-87, discusses the secret negotiations that went on between Venice and Girolamo Riario through Benedetto Soranzo. The first indication of the negotiation with Lorenzo de' Medici through Giovanni Lanfredini and Niccolo di Ca' Pesaro as intermediaries comes in, ASV, 'Consiglio di Dieci, Misti, 20, fols. 194r-v, 22 December 1482, and of that with Ludovico Sforza in ibid., 21, fol. 33v, 2 April 1483. Both these *pratiche* will be discussed at length in *Lettere*, VII.

53 ASV, 'Senato, Lettere di Rettori e Altre Cariche', II, fol. 27. On 7 July 1484 the Dieci invited the Savi to join in discussion of those dispatches ('Dieci, Misti', 22, fol. 76r) and from that point forward there was open discussion in the Senate.

54 See below pp. 80-81.

the sheer cost of the operation. 400,000 ducats were spent in April 1482 alone on preparations; the total cost of the war was estimated at 2,000,000 ducats.[55] In addition to loans raised from the banks, from individual patricians and from the Jews, the pay of public officials was suspended for long periods, and provincial administrative posts were sold and ecclesiastical revenues seized after the placing of the Interdict in May 1483.[56] The main impact of these costs, however, lay in rapidly rising taxation, in the ruthless pruning of other government expenditure and in the inspection of accounts. An increasingly severe financial regime inevitably had its effect on public opinion and indeed on the war effort as a whole. Malipiero commented on rising discontent at the taxes and high prices by late 1483,[57] and in the army and in the fleets mutinies and desertion became common. As early as March 1483 a mutiny in the Po river fleet led to new demands on the banks in Venice;[58] by mid 1484 the situation was critical. The crews of the river fleet were deserting in droves and the *provveditori* in the camp in Lombardy reported that no military action was possible unless money could be found for the troops.[59] By this time the phenomenon already described of patricians refusing to serve in the field was widespread. When Francesco Michiel died in the late summer of 1483, Malipiero commented: 'tuttavia se maledise per tutta la Terra chi ha persuaso questa guerra'.[60]

These tensions and pressures were only the background to an increasing political awareness that the war had outlived its usefulness and should be ended on the best terms possible. Crucial to this realisation was the abandonment of Venice by Sixtus IV and the eventual Interdict which he imposed on Venice in late May 1483. Venice put a brave face on the Interdict; it banned its publication in Venice, threatened clergy who accepted it, recalled its prelates from Rome and sent ambassadors to all the courts of Europe denouncing the pope's action and appealing to the verdict of a General Council.[61] But already before the publication of the Interdict – in March and April 1483 – secret negotiations for peace were underway in a number of directions. Venice was prepared for an honourable peace by

---

55 For the costs of the war, see Malipiero, *Annali*, pp. 263-4 and 296 (for the estimate of 2,000,000 ducats as the total cost); Piva, I, pp. 69-73; F. Ferrara, 'Documenti per servire alla storia dei banchi veneziani', *Archivio veneto*, I, ii, pp. 841-4.
56 Aricò, *Sanudo*, pp. 271-2; Malipiero, *Annali*, pp. 279-84.
57 Ibid., p. 285.
58 Ibid., pp. 278-9.
59 ASV, 'Senato, Terra', 9, fols, 88r and 90v, 4 and 6 July 1484.
60 Malipiero, *Annali*, p. 285.
61 For the Interdict as a turning point in Venetian attitudes towards the war, see Piva, *Guerra di Ferrara*, II, pp. 44-6; Cozzi and Knapton, *Storia della Reppubblica di Venezia*, pp. 69-70; Malipiero, *Annali*, pp. 281-4; G. Dalla Santa, 'Le appellazioni della Repubblica di Venezia dalle scomuniche di Sisto IV e Giulio II', *Nuovo archivio veneto*, XVII, 2 (1899), pp. 217ff.

which it meant retention of the Polesine di Rovigo, reinstatement of the traditional *patti* and recovery by the Rossi of their Milanese lands.⁶² The move in this direction was strengthened by the departure of the duke of Lorraine in the autumn of 1483, following the death of Louis XI, and by a growing distrust of Roberto da Sanseverino. However, early in 1484, the Senate authorised a renewed offensive; fresh rewards were offered to Roberto to retain his loyalty for a little longer and dramatic increases in *condotte* for the cavalry captains were announced.⁶³ It is likely that the eyes of Venetian leaders were now on winning the peace, rather than the war, by these demonstrations of aggressive intentions, because the military outcome of the new preparations was slight.

At this point, in the spring and early summer of 1484, the factors of revised political intentions, a rising tide of public opinion and a draining of financial resources, came together. Malipiero commented:

> Adesso se considera che la guerra de Ferrara ha causato tutti questi inconvenienti. E stà tolto 128,000 ducati dell'una per cento, deputati a pagar el pro de Monte Nuovo; è stà cresciuto un terzo tutti i dacii; è stà impegnato tutte le volte de Rialto a rason de 28 per cento a l'anno; è stà pagato in Zeca i argenti de particulari sie ducati la marca; è stà tolto le cadenele d'oro che le donne portava al collo, e messe in comun. Se fa i Officii e Rezimenti con la metà e un terzo manco de salario. Oltra tante decime, è stà messo tanse a la Terra; le entrate de la Terra e quelle de la Terra ferma è calade; se ha perso molte nave e galie; se ha tolti homeni della guerra nudi e rotti, perchè no se ha possuto far altro; se ha evacuato l'Arsenal che altre volte ha fatto tremar el mondo; avemo fame e peste; mendicheremo la pace, e ghe restituiremo el tolto; se ha speso un milion e dusentomila ducati; et è morti tanti homeni da ben.⁶⁴

This is not the place to consider how it was that despite this situation Venice was able to gain most of its aims in the peace except for the restoration of the Rossi. The answer to that question lies mainly in the distractions of and disunity amongst the powers of the League. It is no doubt true that accounts of Venice's exhaustion were exaggerated and further efforts could have been made if necessary; it is certainly true that the leaders of the League did not see Venice as so weakened as to be forced into

---

62 The first open indication of Venice's willingness to make peace on honourable terms came in approaches made by the Venetian cardinals to the pope in March 1483 (Pier Filippo Pandolfini to Dieci di Balìa, 26 March 1483, ASFi, 'Dieci di Balìa, Responsive', 27, fols. 186-7).

63 ASV, 'Senato, Segreto', reg. 31, fol. 120v, 5 January 1484; Malipiero, *Annali*, pp. 288-9.

64 Ibid., pp. 289-90. These comments were written in the autumn of 1483 by which time 1,200,000 ducats had been spent on the war.

peace. But it was their own problems which obsessed those leaders and led to the end of the war.[65]

The War of Ferrara was no 'brush fire' war, although no doubt Venice had hoped that it would be a good deal quicker and less costly than it was. It was opportunistic and limited in intention. Nevertheless, it revealed the capacity which Venice had for large-scale mobilisation of men, resources and commitment. It also revealed, yet again, the broader problems of disunity, distrust and inertia in the Italian political world which were to bear their fruit ten years later, in 1494.

---

[65] R. Cessi, 'La Pace di Bagnolo dell'agosto 1484', *Annali triestini di diritto, economia e politica*, XII (1941), pp. 277-356; Piva, *Guerra di Ferrara*, II, pp. 51-4. For further full discussion, see *Lettere*, VII, forthcoming.

5

After the War of Ferrara: Relations between Venice and Ercole d'Este, 1484-1505

Trevor Dean

Did the War of Ferrara settle anything? For over two years (1482-84), the war consumed the political and military energies of the major Italian states, mostly ranged against Venice. It also deployed against each other the leading military commanders of the day. Yet the war also strained to breaking-point both the Venetian and anti-Venetian alliances, and ended in a peace treaty in which the interests of Ferrara were sacrificed to those of its allies. The original issues of the conflict – of a purely economic and commercial nature, but masking deeper political amibitions and friction – were hardly addressed in a treaty that essentially restored the status quo. So how did relations between Ferrara and Venice develop in the decades that followed? How was defeat in war and loss of territory dealt with in the Renaissance principality?

The costs of the war were certainly high for Ferrara: apart from loss of important territory, the social and economic damage was grave. One chronicler tells of the ruin caused by 'this cursed war' to the rural houses and palaces of Ferrarese citizens, of the impossibility of cultivation for three successive years in half of the Ferrarese *contado*, and of the immense financial cost to Ferrara for imported foodstuffs alone.[1] Another diarist wrote of the shortage of rural labour after the war and of the many deserted and devastated places.[2] Sanuto's account of his tour of the Venetian *Terraferma* in 1483 also recorded along the Po the burned-out houses, the flooded fields, the deserted villages.[3] The bishop of Adria lost all his revenues for the

---

1 *Corpus chronicorum bononiensium*, ed. A. Sorbelli, *RIS*, XVIII, pt 1, iv (2nd edition, Bologna, 1924-40), p. 470.
2 Ugo Caleffini, 'Cronica di Ferrara', Vatican Library, MS Chigi, I.I.4, fol. 241v (old numeration).
3 *Itinerario di Marin Sanuto per la terraferma veneziana*, ed. Rawdon Brown (Padua, 1847), pp. 48, 49, 50-51. 56. See for general reference the map on p. 56 above.

duration of the war and by 1485 had nothing on which to live.[4] Description of the estates of the abbey of Pomposa estimated a 30 per cent reduction in income between 1482 and 1485, with much of the property war-damaged: woodland had been burned, there was a lack of oxen, a whole area had been flooded, and property everywhere had been usurped.[5]

To uncertain (and expensive) food-supplies in the post-war period, was probably added the problem of inflation: the value of the *lira ferrarese* fell dramatically against the ducat during the war and did not recover.[6] Ercole's finances seem to have been forced into a permanent state of weakness. Gabelle-yields fell.[7] Ercole was in unending debt (at thousands of ducats) to the Venetian salt office for supplies of salt.[8] He had jewels in pawn in Venice, as well as other creditors there.[9] Venetian observers noted his lack of funds and his difficulty in raising credit in either Venice or Florence.[10] In 1499 the Venetian *visdomino* (consul) in Ferrara reckoned Ercole's overall debt at 140,000 ducats; and at 200,000 only four months later.[11] Such difficulties explain Ferrarese sensitivity to Venetian tax exemptions, as we shall see. But the war had also affected the other cities ruled by the duke of Ferrara: Modena during the war suffered from food shortages, emigration, disorder, disease and factional strife.[12] Increasing lawlessness throughout the state led to the appointment of notoriously severe 'captains of justice' and special commissioners.[13]

Against this background, the war also marked a turning-point in Ercole's involvement in both internal government and Italian politics. Ercole's personal interests – in the theatre, music, architecture, religious devotion, fishing and travel – now absorbed more of his time and resources, leaving Ferrara as perhaps an undergoverned state, certainly one with disorderly

---

4   ASMo, 'Ambasciatori, Venezia', busta 5, 15 January 1485.
5   T. Dean, *Land and Power in Late Medieval Ferrara: The Rule of the Este, 1350-1450* (Cambridge, 1987), pp. 187-88; A. Samaritani, 'Presenza economico-politica di Pomposa a Venezia in contrada di S. Maria Formosa nei secoli XIII-XVI', *Ravennatensia*, VI (1977), p. 378.
6   V. Bellini, *Delle monete di Ferrara* (Ferrara, 1761), pp. 161-66.
7   R.G. Brown, 'The Politics of Magnificence in Ferrara, 1450-1505' (unpublished Ph.D. thesis, University of Edinburgh, 1982), pp. 186-87, 474-77.
8   ASMo, 'Ambasciatori, Venezia', busta 7, 20 May, 28 May, 4 June, 11 June, 12 June, 1 July, 7 July, 16 July 1489 etc, for frequent complaints by the Ferrarese ambassador in these matters.
9   Ibid., busta 7, 13 June, 1 July, 3 July 1489; busta 10, 22 December 1491; busta 11, 1 February, 6 April 1502.
10 Sanuto, II, 823, 1014.
11 Ibid., II, 1194; III, 1336.
12 *Cronaca modenese di Jacopino de' Bianchi detto de' Lancellotti*, ed. C. Borghi, Monumenti di storia patria delle provincie modenesi, Cronache (Parma, 1861), pp. 67-103.
13 *Diario ferrarese dall'anno 1409 sino al 1502*, ed. G. Pardi, RIS XXIV, vii (Bologna, 1928-33), pp. 183-84; Bernardino Zambotti, *Diario ferrarese*, ed. G. Pardi, RIS, XXIV, vii (Bologna, 1934-37), p. 282.

After the War of Ferrara

Fig. v Ferrara, 1490. Woodcut (Biblioteca Estense, Modena)

conflicts among the ruling family.[14] The war was also responsible, it seems, for Ercole's desire for non-involvement, or avoidance of commitment, in the subsequent Italian warfare of the 1480s and 1490s. During the 1470s he had turned away from Venice – his sole supporter at his accession in 1471 – and towards Milan, arranging Sforza marriages for two of his children, Beatrice and Alfonso. The peace treaty of 1484, in which Milan had allowed Venice to retain conquered Ferrarese territory, soured Ferrarese faith in the Sforza;[15] nevertheless, Ercole was a close political associate of Lodovico Sforza in the 1490s, reluctantly joining his short-lived alliance with Venice and the pope, although always maintaining close contact with King Ferrante of Naples. Unlike Sforza, on the one hand, Ercole did not commit himself to the French cause on the arrival of Charles VIII in 1494, though he

---

14 *Diario ferrarese*, pp. 208, 211, 215, 220, 223, 224 etc. For the general outline that follows, see A. Frizzi, *Memorie per la storia di Ferrara*, 2nd edition, (5 vols., Ferrara, 1846-50), IV, pp. 150-217; P. Negri, 'Le missioni di Pandolfo Collenuccio a papa Alessandro VI (1494-1498)', *Archivio della società romana di storia patria*, XXXIII (1910); idem, 'Milano, Ferrara e Impero durante l'impresa di Carlo VIII', *Archivio storico lombardo*, series v, IV (1917); idem, 'Studi sulla crisi italiana alla fine del secolo XV', *Archivio storico lombardo*, series vi, L (1923) and LI (1924).

15 ASMo, 'Ambasciatori, Venezia', busta 7, 11 June 1490.

made no secret of his pro-French sympathies and allowed the open expression of such feelings in Ferrara. On the other hand, in 1495 Ercole declared a neutral stance that he thenceforth sought to preserve: as the French ambassador was told, 'he was staying neutral and attending to the affairs of his own state, not wanting in any way to be troubled by what was going on at the moment, being now of an age that he seeks rest more than anything else and also because he is a friend and well-wisher of his majesty the king and of the duke of Milan . . . and likewise of the Venetians'.[16] A Ferrarese diarist was more acid in his comment, perhaps indicating a difference of attitude and interest between the Este and their subjects that we shall encounter again: 'he attends to his own pleasure . . . and leaves the war to whoever wants to fight'.[17]

In accordance with his personal non-alignment, one of Ercole's sons (Ferrante) took military service with Charles VIII, while another (Alfonso) entered that of the Italian League. In 1495 custody of the *Castelletto di Genova* was entrusted to Ercole as a neutral party, as a pledge of Sforza's fulfilment of the peace terms with Charles. Ercole's acceptance of this role incurred the suspicion and hatred of Venice, which began to press on Ercole's borders in the Romagna. As a result, when Charles failed to return to Italy, Ercole recognised that 'it has been necessary to resweeten ourselves with the *Signoria* of Venice'. This 'resweetening' involved declaring his devotion to Venice, paying honour to the *visdomino*, banning French dress in Ferrara, recalling Ferrante from France and placing him in Venetian service, and visiting Venice himself (November 1497), something that Ercole had refused to do while acting as custodian in Genoa. Despite these signs of greater commitment, however, Ercole remained uninvolved in the Pisan war, and when he did intervene, in late 1498, it was to mediate a settlement. Although all sides accepted Ercole's arbitration, he was encouraged especially by Lodovico Sforza, and Venice was so suspicious that it insisted on him making some secret preliminary undertakings; but the pressure on Ercole from Milan was intense to reach a settlement acceptable to Florence so as to allow it to enter the League. Consequently, when Ercole's award was more favourable to Florence and only partly fulfilled Venetian demands, the *Signoria* was furious, forcing Ercole to make some amendments and dismissing Ferrante from the Republic's service, while

---

16 A. Cappelli, 'Fra Girolamo Savonarola e notizie intorno il suo tempo', *Atti e Memorie della Deputazione di storia patria per le provincie modenesi e parmensi*, IV (1867), p. 349.
17 *Diario ferrarese*, p. 231.

Venetian crowds hooted Ercole out of the city.[18] Back in Ferrara, Ercole recognised that his relations with Venice were at a low ebb.[19]

On Louis XII's invasion in 1499, Ercole again met the French king, placed Ferrante in his service and gave passage to French troops. But he declined to become more involved in Louis' campaigns, as he also declined to assist Lodovico Sforza in his brief recovery of Milan in 1500, thus avoiding the French retribution meted out to his neighbours among the Pio, Pico and da Correggio families. French protection, formally accorded to Ercole in 1499 was followed, as it became less effective, by the marriage of Ercole's eldest son to Lucrezia Borgia in 1502, thus removing from Ercole the threat of Cesare Borgia's campaigns in the papal states. Although Ercole was in 1503 drawn into more active military support of France, after French set-backs in both Milan and Naples, his non-alignment and customary personal interests (theatre, pilgrimage, fishing) continued to prevail until his death in 1505. Thus, in the perilous decade of French invasions and Borgia aggrandisement, Ercole had managed to avoid direct involvement in warfare and to preserve a fragile neutrality that averted damage to his state. This was achieved despite his connections by marriage to both Milan and Naples, despite his pro-French sympathies and despite his obvious vulnerability to Venetian or papal pressure. But what was the legacy of the War of Ferrara in Ercole's conduct?

As might be expected, anti-Venetian feeling ran high in Ferrara throughout the period. The bitterness of the loss of the Polesine di Rovigo in 1484 can be gauged in the chronicle of Ugo Caleffini, who recorded every year, and several times in some years, that Venice continued to occupy this conquered territory.[20] Caleffini also relished any subsequent Venetian set-backs and, like the anonymous *Diario ferrarese*, noted with satisfaction the heavy losses that Venice had sustained in the war itself.[21] Later, in 1500, Sanuto records reports of laughter and celebration in Ferrara at the Venetian loss of Modon (though Ercole sent his condolences and offered to pray for the Republic).[22] There was frequent talk of renewed war with Venice in these years too,[23] and it is not surprising that Ercole allied with Venice only

---

18 Sanuto, III, 589-94, 601-6, 635-6, 716. An earlier visit, in 1488, is illustrated in Plate II.
19 Domenico Malipiero, 'Annali veneti dall'anno 1457 al 1500', *Archivio storico italiano*, VII (1843-4), p. 554.
20 Caleffini, 'Cronica', fols. 236v, 237, 241v, 245v, 246, 249v, 256.
21 Ibid., fols. 240, 255-6; *Diario ferrarese*, pp. 120-1, 190.

22 Sanuto, III, 645, 684, 707, 757, 784. See also the essay by Simon Pepper, above, pp. 49-54.
23 Caleffini, 'Cronica', fols. 237, 237v, 247-v, 278v, 280, 284v, 300-v, 301; Sanuto, V, 269; ASMo, 'Ambasciatori, Venezia', busta 7, 29 May 1490 (the ambassador reports: 'Imo il principe me ha dicto expresse che vostro Illustrissimo Signore tene tuti li modi quali la tenne anchora quando principio la guerra').

rarely and reluctantly. When the *visdomino*, who had left Ferrara for the duration of the war, returned in November 1484, his presence sparked off some vehement reactions. Caleffini recorded that the *visdomino* arrived with 'greater pomp and haughtiness than ever before'.[24] Monks and priests refused to say mass in his presence and it needed the threat of expulsion from Ercole to bring them into line.[25] The Ferrarese arbiters, required under the old commercial treaties between the two cities for the settling of trade disputes, at first refused to swear the oath of office and then proved slow and obstructive.[26] In the following years, numerous offensive acts were directed against the *visdomino* and other Venetians in and around Ferrara. In 1491 Giovanni Querini was wounded in the street.[27] In October of the same year, some Venetian coastguards were killed by wine-smugglers at Comacchio.[28] In 1493, on the eve of the *visdomino's* customary St Mark's day procession, in disrespect the duke of Milan's coat-of-arms was affixed to the church of San Marco in Ferrara and a tall tree outside was cut down.[29] In 1495 a butcher of Pontelagoscuro was killed by Venetian troops as they passed, for telling them that they were going to their deaths going to fight the French.[30] In the following year, the law-rector of the university of Ferrara drew a sword on the *visdomino* in the street.[31] In February 1500 news that Lodovico Sforza had recovered Milan caused day-long celebration, out of hatred of Venice, with 'Moro, Moro' being shouted outside the *visdomino*'s office.[32] In 1502 the Venetian guardhouse at Volano was destroyed.[33] Such feeling seems to have been reciprocated: the *Diario ferrarese* records the constant insulting of Ercole and of Ferraresi by Venetians, and notes the Venetian song 'O guerra o non guerra, Ferrara andarà per terra'.[34] According to the Venetian diarist Malipiero, Ercole lived in almost constant fear of Venetian hostility and attack.[35] In 1496 Malipiero records that the returning *visdomino* was stopped from making the usual *relazione* to the Senate for fear of the reactions there to his reports of Ferrarese animosity towards Venice.[36]

24 Caleffini, 'Cronica', fol. 238.
25 Ibid., fol. 238v; ASMo, 'Ambasciatori, Venezia', busta 5, 25 November and 15 December, 1484.
26 ASV, 'Materie Miste Notabili', 112, fols. 83v-84, 87v-88, 99-99v. On the office of arbiters: T. Dean, 'Venetian Economic Hegemony: The Case of Ferrara, 1200-1500', *Studi veneziani*, n.s., XII (1986), pp. 56-57.
27 Caleffini, 'Cronica', fol. 289.
28 Ibid., fol. 291.
29 Ibid., fol. 307v.
30 *Diario ferrarese*, p. 155.
31 Ibid., p. 189; Zambotti, *Diario*, pp. 226-27; Sanuto, I, 370. For earlier incidents, Dean, 'Venetian Economic Hegemony', p. 51.
32 *Diario ferrarese*, p. 243; Frizzi, *Memorie*, IV, p. 198; and note Sanuto's comment regarding anti-Venetian feeling in Ferrara; 'di ogni nostro danno hanno piacer' (III, 684).
33 Ibid., IV, 456; and for background see Dean, 'Venetian Economic Hegemony', p. 65.
34 *Diario ferrarese*, pp. 152, 156, 161, 164, 194; Malipiero, 'Annali', p. 495.
35 Ibid., pp. 398, 406, 418, 432, 497, 554, 562.
36 Ibid., p. 431.

Against Ferrarese efforts to accord the *visdomino* as little respect as possible, successive *visdomini* sought to take what they were not given: claiming precedence over the Milanese ambassador in processions and receptions,[37] refusing to give way in the street,[38] enriching and amplifying the St Mark's day procession in Ferrara. Participation in this procession by nobles in and of Ferrara was slowly expanded.[39] A standard of crimson sendal, bearing a large gilt figure of St Mark, is first mentioned in 1492;[40] in 1493 it was carried on a horse and preceded by trumpets and pipers.[41] After the ceremony that year too, the *visdomino* gave dinner to twenty-two Ferrarese noblemen, held open house all day, and there were bonfires in the piazza morning and evening.[42] In 1500 the *visdomino* expanded celebrations further, to include a race for girls, in obvious extension of the usual St George's day races held in the same week.[43]

Although some *visdomini* reported well of Ercole (for example, Giovanni Mocenigo),[44] others notably did not. Even Mocenigo reported that Ferrara was poor and, without its trade with Venice, the Ferrarese would be 'disfati dil mondo'.[45] Girolamo Donà drew a picture of financial weakness, heavy taxation (25 per cent of income, he alleged) and popular discontent, of Ercole's fears of France and of Cesare Borgia, and his difficulties with his sons, especially Alfonso, whom Donà portrays as conversing only with innkeepers, as unpopular, and as damaging all his father's works.[46] Debts, popular discontent at taxation, and princely unconcern when natural disaster struck feature too in the reports of Cristoforo Moro and Marco Zorzi.[47] As Girolamo Donà concluded, 'this city is as under tyrants'.[48] But was Donà only telling Venice what it wanted to hear?

It is clear that there was mutual incomprehension between the two regimes. Federico Corner, in a private conversation with the Ferrarese ambassador to Venice, thought that Ercole 'should not take advice from anyone except himself', which hardly accorded with the best princely practice.[49] When Ercole asked for Venetian legal procedures to be bypassed in order to settle a dispute, the doge replied 'that the laws of this *Serenissima Signoria* are not such that can be derogated as would be done by a prince of the sort of your Excellency'.[50] To Ferrarese complaints about Venetian

37 Brown, 'Magnificence', pp. 385-86, 526.
38 Sanuto, I, 370.
39 Zambotti, pp. 164, 206; *Diario ferrarese*, pp. 177, 200, 227, 251, 269; Caleffini, 'Cronica', fols. 246v, 273v, 285v, 297, 307v-8.
40 Ibid., fol. 297.
41 Ibid., fols. 307v-8.
42 Ibid.
43 *Diario ferrarese*, p. 251; Sanuto, III, 261.
44 Ibid., I, 706.
45 Ibid.
46 Ibid., II, 1194; III, 314, 1449.
47 Ibid., III, 1336, 1567; V, 126.
48 Ibid., IV, 1449.
49 ASMo, 'Ambasciatori, Venezia', busta 7, 22 June 1489.
50 Ibid., 17 August 1489.

bandits congregating at Cologna, and requests for action against them as enemies and rebels because 'by common law, they lose the privilege of citizenship', the doge insisted that outlawed Venetians, no matter how serious their crimes, did not by Venetian law lose their citizenship.[51] The Ferrarese ambassador, Aldrovandino Guidoni, while negotiating in Venice over Venetian trading immunities in Ferrara, was surprised by the unity of Venetian collective response: 'Whoever said that Venetians are pigs was not mistaken, as this is their nature: when they see someone speaking against one of them or against their immunities . . . they all take it as affecting each one personally and rise up, like pigs, united against whoever opposes them'.[52] Venice thus seemed to have a picture of princely government that involved the ability to ignore advisers, to dispense with law, to remove the privileges of citizenship, and expected the prince to act in this way, showing irritation when Ercole insisted on honouring his subjects' rights and interests.[53] On the other hand, the Ferrarese were surprised at the closed and solid nature of Venetian public life, which, as we shall see, they could penetrate only through the exercise of illegal patronage.

Yet at the level of formal diplomatic exchanges, the familiar tone that had previously existed between the two regimes had immediately been reasserted after the war. The new *visdomino*, in his first audience with Ercole, said that Venice 'wanted him as a good son and that he should not look back at what had passed, because fathers and sons often come to blows, and the father gives the son a good beating, but then the son reconciles himself with his father, who receives him as a son and pardons him'.[54] Ercole too took up the old father-son imagery and declared his intention of being a good son.[55] But few probably were deceived by such declarations of filial or paternal affection. Sanuto in 1509 commented that it was all 'idle talk and trickery, as is well-known in this city'.[56] Similar scepticism was shown by the Ferrarese ambassador in 1502 in an audience with the new doge, Leonardo Loredan:

> the doge said much in commendation of your Excellency and told me that, if he had been doge at the time of the War of Ferrara, it would never have happened and that there never was a worse enterprise undertaken by this state. And I said

---

51 Ibid., 21 September 1489.
52 Ibid., 9 March 1491.
53 For example, in the dispute over the Contarini estates at Massafiscaglia, Ercole repeatedly claimed that he could not ignore his subjects' demand for justice, nor allow Venice to impose a settlement: ibid., 24 May, 12 June, 22 June 1489.
54 Caleffini, 'Cronica', fol. 238v; and see the comments of the Ferrarese ambassador immediately after conclusion of peace: M. Sanuto, *Commentarii della guerra di Ferrara* (Venice, 1829), p. 141. For previous use of this image, see Dean, 'Venetian Economic Hegemony', pp. 52-53.
55 Sanuto, *Commentarii*, pp. 148-49; ASMo, 'Ambasciatori, Venezia', busta 5, 25 November 1484.
56 Sanuto, IX, 271.

that, however it might have turned out, my lord is in all things a good son to his Serenity and the state . . . The doge replied that it was true and he knew it. But that everything was for the best and that quarrels happen between father and son, and between friends, and even within himself a man varies, now good, now bad, and that virtue lay in knowing moderation. I opened my mouth to say that the war had indeed been good for this state [Venice] as it had won the Polesine di Rovigo but I stayed quiet.[57]

Noticeable too is how the vocabulary of warfare invaded diplomatic reports of argument between the two cities: talk of 'skirmishing', 'gunpowder', 'battle' and 'coming to the battlefield' recur in Ferrarese diplomats' reports of discussions with the Venetian government. In Ferrarese eyes, the cities were still at war.

However, Ercole did find individual friends and allies among Venetian patricians, most surprisingly perhaps among former *visdomini*. In 1492 Giovanni da Canal (*visdomino* 1470-72), on leaving Venice as captain of the Barbary galleys, offered to make purchases for Ercole in Tunis.[58] On the death of Bartolomeo Vitturi (*visdomino* 1491-93), the Ferrarese ambassador recalled that he 'was a great friend and partisan of your Excellency'.[59] Giovanni Mocenigo (*visdomino* 1496), a 'true partisan of your Excellency', on his appointment as captain of Verona in 1501, recommended himself to Ercole; he and his brother Francesco were described as 'thorough-going friends and servants' in 1502.[60] When, for a friend of Francesco's, Ercole wrote some letters of recommendation to Giovanni Bentivoglio and Cesare Borgia, Francesco was reported to 'thank your Excellency countless times', and the Mocenigo were noted to be 'as dedicated and well-wishing towards your Highness as any other family here'.[61] The circle of Este friends in Venice even extended beyond the patriciate: for example, the Agostini were described by one ambassador as 'friends of your Excellency'.[62]

Such 'friendship' could be a synonym for secret agency in high political places. The Ferrarese ambassador in the mid 1480s, Alberto Cortese, had associations with two unnamed friends, one in the *Collegio* ('lo amico nostro primo') and one in the Ten ('lo amico secundo'), who provided information and extensive reports of debates. Disclosure of this sort was of course illegal and attracted official investigation on several occasions in this period.[63]

---

57 ASMo, 'Ambasciatori, Venezia', busta 11, 3 April 1502.
58 Ibid., busta 7, 14 June 1491.
59 Ibid., busta 11, 8 February 1501.
60 Ibid., busta 11, 20 December 1501, 18 May 1502. See also Dean, 'Venetian Economic Hegemony', p. 75.
61 ASMo, 'Ambasciatori, Venezia', busta 11, 15 September and 4 October 1502.
62 Ibid., busta 7, 11 September 1490.
63 Malipiero, 'Annali', p. 406; D. Queller, *The Venetian Patriciate* (Urbana and Chicago, 1986), pp. 212-24.

Considerable lengths were taken by Cortese to retain and protect his two informers: letters in code, secret meetings, cash gifts, calming their nerves when they feared discovery.[64] But even these precautions were not entirely successful: Malipiero records a rumour that Ercole had sent, as a gift to 'a great man', a brace of capons full of ducats.[65] When Cortese's successor, Guidoni, first arrived in Venice in 1489, he found information hard to come by,[6] but by 1491 he too had a ring of informers, including 'one of those noblemen who had an understanding (*intelligentia*) with Messer Alberto Cortese', and another in the Ten. From these or other sources, Guidoni received copies of Venetian government papers and correspondence.[67] 'Lo amico' who provided information from the Senate, and his relative on the Ten, both reappear in ambassadorial reports in 1497.[68]

Guidoni also sought to win friends by distributing favours. When Marco da Pesaro and Alvise Vendramin asked that Ercole spare the life of a Venetian criminal convicted in Ferrara, Guidoni advised that 'it cannot but be good to accede' to Pesaro's request, 'because he is a nobleman of great authority, which could be useful', and that both Alvise Vendramin and his father, the former doge, had been good friends to Ercole in the past.[69] For other Venetian patricians, Guidoni secured hunting licences in Este territory and summary justice against their debtors.[70] By such means the ambassador built up a block of support; and though it was the duke of Milan, not the duke of Ferrara, who was said to have at his disposal sixty votes in the Senate,[71] it was presumably support of this kind that the ambassador Bartolomeo Cartari tried to mobilise in 1501 for the election of a new *visdomino*: 'we need to have a *visdomino* who will be a *homo da bene* and suitable. I have already spoken about this with some of our men here, so that this comes about.'[72] That the ambassador influenced the election of other *visdomini* would also be suggested by his reporting of electoral outcomes: in 1489 for example, the ambassador was very pleased at the election of Antonio Erizzo, describing him as 'a *zentilhomo da bene*, all

---

64 ASMo, 'Ambasciatori, Venezia', busta 5, 2, 21, 23 January, 24 February, 13 March 1486. On Cortese, see *Dizionario biografico degli Italiani* (Rome, 1960-), XXIX, pp. 714-15. On the recurrent problem of the disclosure of state information to *signori* of the *Terraferma*: Dean, 'Venetian Economic Hegemony', p. 84.
65 Malipiero, 'Annali', p. 389.
66 'Io comprehendo che in questa terra sia male modo per potere intendere le fazende quale se tractano qua, perche pare le cosse se siane molto restrecte': ASMo, 'Ambasciatori, Venezia', busta 7, 2 May 1489.
67 Ibid., 1, 5 December 1489, 4, 9 June, 6, 12 July 1491.
68 Queller, *Venetian Patriciate*, pp. 216, 219.
69 ASMo, 'Ambasciatori, Venezia', busta 7, 7, 27 September 1489.
70 Ibid., 25 June, 2, 8 July 1491.
71 Queller, *Venetian Patriciate*, p. 219.
72 ASMo, 'Ambasciatori, Venezia', busta 11, 25 March 1501.

sweetness and humanity, and I believe your Excellency will be satisfied with him' (though in the event this confidence proved unfounded).[73] Of the varying power and number of friends there is little indication, but there was also a network of enemies as revealed by the sobering comment of Guidoni on the death of Niccolò Foscari: 'he was one of those who always attacked your Excellency's interests on any occasion and, though he was no friend, there is no cause for excessive celebration, as there remain many more of his sort'.[74]

Ferrarese animosity towards Venice was all the greater for the disappointing terms of the Peace of Bagnolo, which ended the war in August 1484. The extent of Ferrarese hopes and ambitions, nourished by the progress of the war, can be seen in briefing papers prepared by an Este official for the eventual negotiation of peace.[75] Three of these papers survive[76]: their subject is Venetian tax immunities in Ferrara and the powers there of the *visdomino*. Both of these issues, in which the war had originated, had, since the first establishment of Venetian 'economic hegemony' over Ferrara in the thirteenth century, provided frequent crises and conflicts between the two cities.[77] One of the three briefing papers was a collection or compendium of all the original treaties (*patti*) and their subsequent clarification and amendment. The other two were masterly pieces of tendentious, legal-historical analysis, aiming, in one case, to deny that the *visdomino* had any legal authority, and, in the other, to show how the Venetians had during the fifteenth century greatly abused and expanded their exemptions in Ferrara. All three papers show high standards of historical enquiry, both in the collection of documents and in the construction of arguments on the basis of their close scrutiny and frequent quotation. In approaching the substantive issues disputed between the two cities in this period, it is useful to start with these wartime position-papers, which were to be disappointed in their optimism, but confirmed in their more realistic predictions.

The longer of the two papers takes as its starting point the thirteenth-century wording of Venetian immunity as confirmed and enshrined in the

---

73   Ibid., busta 7, 14 September 1489. It was Erizzo who in March 1491 submitted to Venice a ten-page report claiming that the pacts were not being observed and using 'the most inflamed and angered words it is possible to use': ibid., 9 March 1491.

74   Ibid., busta 7, 24 December 1490. For an example of Foscari's animosity, see L.A. Muratori, *Delle antichità estensi ed italiane* (2 vols., Modena, 1717-40), II, 251.

75   Was the author Pellegrino Prisciani, who was known in Venice to be 'informatissimo' on issues between the two cities and who had in his study documents and registers relating to them (ASMo, 'Ambasciatori, Venezia', busta 7, 12, 13, 21 September 1489)? On Prisciani, archivist, historian and diplomat, see A. Rotondò, 'Pellegrino Prisciani', *Rinascimento*, XI (1960).

76   ASMo, 'Casa e stato', cassetta 58, nos. 3, 24, 31.

77   Dean, 'Venetian Economic Hegemony'.

papal bull of 1313, which had put an end to the first Venetian War of Ferrara and which the author wished to see reinstated as the Magna Carta of Venetian-Ferrarese relations.[78] As stated there,

> all men of Venice and its district are to be safe and secure in their persons and property in the city of Ferrara and its district, going, staying, coming or returning, not paying any *datium* or toll [*toloneum*] or maltolt [*male ablatum*] at Ferrara or at Ficarolo or in any other place in the Ferrarese district . . . except for 3d. only for the ship's mooring at Ferrara [pro fundo navis].[79]

As perceived in Ferrara in the 1480s, this clause was vague and unsatisfactory. The problems with its wording were essentially two: in the first place, the assumptions of its authors about the nature and pattern of trade between the two cities had been lost and the clause had never been updated to take account of economic and political changes (for example, Venetian mainland expansion);[80] secondly, Venice had wilfully set about exploiting vagueness in the clause to amplify its exemption, claiming it not just for native Venetians on commercial trips to Ferrara, but for all Venetian subjects, even 'Albanians, Slavonians and all others of their lands', for all residents at Ferrara who obtained Venetian citizenship, and for 'Venetians' moving goods across north-east Italy, for example from Bologna to Mantua, rather than simply between Ferrara and Venice.[81] The author lists thirty-one declarations and agreements by which the Venetians during the fifteenth century 'have sought to go on increasing their liberties [*loro franchisia*], defining them in their own way and to our detriment . . . wanting to be free like lords. And note how they call it servitude, not being free in their own way'.[82] Arguing instead a restrictive interpretation, the author attempts a historical reconstruction of trading patterns in the thirteenth century, which shares something with the nostalgic simplifications of the *buon tempo antico*:

> at the time of the pacts, Venetians would come to Ferrara with their own boats and with various goods and merchandise, for example salt, oil, cheese, spices etc, and these they would sell or barter in Ferrara and its district, and then they would buy our goods and leave . . . and this was because it was not the noblemen of Venice, but men of the people, of low condition, who came to buy and sell in Ferrara . . . , but nowadays it is not commoners, but noblemen who

---

78 ASMo, 'Casa e stato', 58/31, fol. 1.
79 Ibid., and see B. Ghetti, *I patti tra Venezia e Ferrara dal 1191 al 1313* (Rome, 1907); G. Soranzo, *La guerra fra Venezia e la S. Sede per il dominio di Ferrara (1308-1313)* (Città di Castello,
1905), pp. 207-30.
80 ASMo, 'Casa e stato', 58/31, fols. 3v, 4v.
81 Ibid., fol. 4v.
82 Ibid., fols. 2v-3v.

want to trade wholesale, not in things which they bring or send to sell or barter in Ferrara . . . and where their exemption should be only for the goods which they sell, barter or buy in Ferrara and its district, they want to be free and exempt for the merchandise they send to Bologna, Mantua, Milan etc, and conversely for that which they have brought from Bologna or Mantua or Milan to Venice and, what is worse, for that which they send from Bologna to Mantua or between similar places neither going to nor coming from Venice.[83]

This early piece of economic history was supported by Venetian documents found in Ferrara by the author and by arguments extrapolated from other sections of the pacts. The author concludes his paper with what amounts to a series of negotiating demands based on the assumption that 'all the pacts and customs made and observed' since 1313 'be annulled'.[84] First, 'all Venetians who at present have property in Ferrara or its district should be obliged to sell it to Ferraresi . . . so as to remove the many disputes and differences which arise every day'; secondly, the exemption enjoyed by Venetians in Ferrara should be stripped of its now-customary over-interpretation, 'because they should only be exempt from *dazi*'; thirdly, 'the Venetians who have lived . . . in Ferrara or the Ferrarese district for twelve years . . . should no longer be treated as Venetians, but as Ferrarese and should sustain the real and personal burdens that other citizens do, because according to our statutes after twelve years they become citizens'; fourthly, the author would like removed, 'if possible', the clause in the treaty of 1240 forbidding Ferrara from importing goods direct from the Adriatic, as 'it is this clause which deprived the city of Ferrara of two fine fairs which used to be held every year . . . to which merchandise came from the Marche and many other places, as it did not go to Venice', 'such that Ferrara, Lombardy and Tuscany supplied themselves at these fairs without going to Venice . . . If this pact is not annulled, we shall always be in dispute and conflict'; and lastly, if the clauses regarding Venetian immunity and Ferrarese sea-borne trade are 'corrected', 'the reason for keeping the *visdomino* here would cease, as he is here only for these two principal reasons, but I do not believe that Venice would ever consent to this'. In connection with the last two points, the author goes into another historical excursus on Venetian rights and powers over the sea and seaports: 'by the *ius gentium* they cannot occupy the sea as their own, which is common property', nor do the treaties give them any right 'to put the *visdomino* in Ferrara, nor the *podestarino* at Goro, nor

---

83 Ibid., fols. 3v, 4v. For criticism of this 'myth of Ferrara', see Dean, 'Venetian Economic Hegemony', pp. 49-50.

84 ASMo, 'Casa e stato', 58/31, fols. 8-9v.

armed boats in our ports'. They should all be removed 'because they are there by Venice's absolute power, contrary to the terms of the treaties'.[85]

A second paper, on the *visdomino*, is much shorter, but has the same legalistic, historical precision in its use of documents, coming to more accurate conclusions on the development of this office than many later historians.[86] Finding nothing about the *visdomino* in the thirteenth-century treaties, the author infers 'that he could not have existed at the time when the treaties were made'. By 1280 there is certain reference to the *visdomino* in Ferrara, but as his powers are not described in the 1313 papal bull, the author argues that 'the *visdomino* did not reside in Ferrara with any dignity, authority, *arbitrio* or jurisdiction, but he was there only as a simple envoy and lobbyist [*sollicitadore*]'. Nor is he given any authority in any subsequent agreement, except the new treaty of 1455, by which he had some authority to proceed against smuggling. So the *visdomino* had no jurisdiction deriving from any public treaty. It was only the Venetian administrative text of his oath of office which established his functions, and even there he was attributed with only two main tasks: 'first, to discover if there was any smuggling' and to report it to the Ferrarese authorities for them to act; secondly, 'to go to the courts of the *podestà*, factors and other officials to expedite Venetian matters there'.

> Thus we see clearly that the *visdomino* did not have and should not have the dignity, authority, *arbitrio* and jurisdiction that he has taken for himself from time to time . . . by the consent of Venice which has urged him on through its letters . . . And so, little by little, the *visdomino* has gone on enlarging his office, interfering in things where he ought not to, according to the terms of the treaties, as in giving judgement against Venetians . . . , in discovering and proceeding against smugglers . . . , in taking an oath from the incoming *podestà*.

In the Peace of Bagnolo, such hopes of removing the *visdomino*, of reopening Ferrara's trade with the Adriatic, and of reducing Venetian exemptions, were bitterly disappointed. For not only were the *visdomino* and all the exemptions reinstated, but Venice retained the territory to the north of Ferrara that had been conquered during the war. This added a new set of problems to all the old grievances, which rapidly resurfaced. As the author had predicted, without corrections to the treaties, 'we shall always be in dispute and conflict'. The intensity and frequency of dispute obviously

---

85 Ibid., fol. 9: 'de sua absoluta potentia contra la forma di pacti'. An early example of the words 'absolute power'?

86 ASMo, 'Casa e stato', 58/24; cf. Dean, 'Venetian Economic Hegemony', p. 74, n. 107.

varied, not least according to Venice's relations with other Italian powers. In 1490, for example, Guidoni was of the opinion that Venetian intransigence towards Ercole arose 'because they [the Venetians] see and know well on what terms they stand with the state of Milan and with the other powers of Italy', and so 'they do what they like against your Excellency because they know that there is noone to challenge them'.[87]

However, the balance of power did not always favour Venice, and Ferrara did gain some ground towards the goals of the wartime papers. This can be seen first of all in the longstanding problem of Venetian landownership in Ferrarese territory.[88] One dispute here, over the Contarini estate at Massafiscaglia, to the east of Ferrara, took up many hours of ambassadorial time and eventually provoked the doge to angered and wearied annoyance. The lands in question were those of Gian Vittore Contarini, last *visdomino* before the outbreak of the war in 1482. Given his role in the movement towards war,[89] it is perhaps unsurprising that Ercole 'could never hear his name without having his spirits convulsed',[90] refused fully to restore his lands and gave support to his own subjects at Massa demanding that Gian Vittore shoulder a fair share of the local tax burden.[91] The Ferrarese ambassador was more circumspect, reminding Ercole that Gian Vittore was 'a dangerous man with a bold tongue and not lacking in support, for he has many relatives [*parenti*]'.[92] Ercole seems to have determined to draw the dispute out as long as possible: an agreement in principle in 1489 was disavowed, provoking vehement reaction from the doge ('never has the Senate been more deceived . . .')[93]; the debate was shifted from the substantive issue to that of the *visdomino's* competence to settle it; each side took up and repeated an intransigent interpretation of the treaties.[94] Ercole's tactics disturbed his ambassador: 'I greatly fear . . . that this case . . . will give birth to some disorder and serious injury . . . I fear that such a small thing will damage your Highness in much greater things, and indeed the common people say that it is a poor *soldo* that ruins a ducat.'[95] This view was also expressed, with

---

87 ASMo, 'Ambasciatori, Venezia', busta 7, 29 May 1490.
88 Dean, 'Venetian Economic Hegemony'.
89 E. Piva, *La guerra di Ferrara del 1482. Periodo primo: L'alleanza dei veneziani con Sisto IV* (Padua, 1893), pp. 18-23.
90 ASMo, 'Ambasciatori, Venezia', busta 7, 13 September 1489.
91 The problem of the Contarini share of the local tax burden was itself an old one: Dean, 'Venetian Economic Hegemony', p. 86, n. 151; dispute over Venetian estates at Massafiscaglia was even older: ibid., pp. 60-61.

92 ASMo, 'Ambasciatori, Venezia', busta 7, 23 May 1489.
93 Ibid., 24 May 1489. Although the previous envoys, Armanno Nobili and Niccolo Roberti, had (according to Venice) agreed a settlement, they had reported otherwise to Ercole: ibid.; the *visdomino* had registered the doge's letter detailing the settlement: ASV, 'Materie', 111, fols. 102-v.
94 ASMo, 'Ambasciatori, Venezia', busta 7, 24 May, 12, 22 June, 29 July, 5, 17 August, 12 September 1489.
95 Ibid., 4 June 1489.

more menace, by Gian Vittore's uncle in a private conversation with the ambassador: 'many times it happens that a splinter enters a man's foot and makes him lame for ever'. The ambassador certainly picked up the message: 'although they will not declare war, they will do so much harm without warfare that will seem excessive'.[96] Instead, the ambassador advised 'that it would be good to seem to make a gift to the *Serenissima* of what in the end it will be necessary to give them by force'.[97] Ercole was eventually persuaded of the benefits of settling this dispute (and a parallel one involving the Capello and Loredan families)[98] on terms that pleased the doge and *Signoria*.[99] But in fact, during the 1490s, Ercole acquired Gian Vittore's lands, thus moving some way towards the reduction of Venetian landholding within his borders.[100]

An even more persistent problem was that of 'contraband'. Although the treaty of 1240 had forbidden Ferrara from receiving merchandise direct from the sea, authority to act against such trade had not been clearly apportioned. According to the Ferrarese interpretation of the treaties, the *visdomino*'s responsibility was limited to discovering contraband, gathering testimony and reporting the fact to the Ferrarese authorities. Since Venice claimed that, by agreement as well as by custom, the *visdomino* had power to seize contraband,[101] there was resistance to his efforts to make seizures and arrests.[102] At first, however, with Ercole returning to filial loyalty, the *visdomino* had his support and scored some conspicuous successes. Caleffini records an 'enormity' that took place in August 1485: the *visdomino*, 'with the aid of the captain of the piazza and his men, seized salt from many merchants who were selling it in Ferrara, and had it thrown into the Po, saying that it was not salt that had come from Venice'.[103] According to the *visdomino*'s own register, the salt had come from Cervia, the *visdomino* acted properly as instigator of action by the Ferrarese officials, and the disposal of the salt took three days' constant work – testimony to the scale of 'contraband' trade between Ferrara and the sea.[104] In 1486, again with the consent

---

96 Ibid., 22 June 1489.
97 Ibid., 12 June 1489.
98 The dispute lay between Domenico Capello and Tommaso Loredan, on the one hand, and the Mantovani family, on the other, over a piece of land that lay across the border. Capello was prepared to make a compromise, but the Ferrarese ambassador feared that Venice would not let him, because of its claim to territorial jurisdiction: ibid., 13 July and 14 September 1489.
99 Ibid., 2 October and 1 December 1489, 10 January 1490.
100 Ibid., busta 11, 6 April 1502.

101 Ibid., busta 7, 19 March 1491. On 'contraband' in Ferrara, see Dean, 'Venetian Economic Hegemony', pp. 65-67.
102 *Diario ferrarese*, p. 252; *I Libri Commemoriali della Repubblica di Venezia*, ed. R. Predelli, Deputazione di storia veneta: Monumenti storici (5 vols, Venice, 1876-1901), V, pp. 299-300.
103 Caleffini, 'Cronica', fol. 243. On the Venetian salt monopoly, see Dean, 'Venetian Economic Hegemony', pp. 58-59.
104 ASV, 'Materie', 112, fols. 85-v; and see his report to the doge in *Libri Commemoriali*, V, p. 299.

Plate I Giorgione, The Preaching of John the Baptist (*Pearl Collection, Washington DC*)

Plate II Lazzaro Bastiani (attrib.), *The Piazzetta* (oil on panel, *c.* 1490): Doge Agostino Barbarigo meeting Duke Ercole d'Este and his son Alfonso, in Venice for the carnival, February 1488 (*Museo Correr; photo: Osvaldo Böhm, Venice*)

of Ercole, and with that of the bishop of Ferrara, the *visdomino* searched the nunnery of San Silvestro for contraband salt said to have been unloaded at night from a boat on the Po. Seven sacks were discovered and seized.[105] In the 1490s Venice also made seizures at Comacchio, arrested Comacchiesi for alleged salt-smuggling and complained of salt-making at Comacchio itself.[106] According to Guidoni, 'of all the subjects that your Excellency has, the worst regarded and treated at Venice are these wretches from Comacchio'.[107]

The Ferrarese authorities did not long continue to act as Venetian customsmen. Ferrara's own gabelle officials sequestered contraband claimed by the *visdomino*.[108] More often, their attempts to collect gabelles and *dazi* from 'Venetians' raised complaints of infringement of the Venetian immunity. Among the abuses complained of were Ferrarese *daziari* frightening off the customers of Venetian traders, and Venetians being forced either to pay *dazi* or to leave deposits pending proof of their Venetian status.[109] A particular difficulty arose regarding 'Venetians' living in Ferrara. A diplomatic instruction from the period outlines a representative problem:

> The case concerns a Venetian living in the city of Ferrara who exercises the trade of making bacon, sausages, cheese and candles . . . buying pigs in the piazza, from which he makes sausages and bacon, cheese [sic] and candles and suchlike, and on his purchases he refuses to pay any gabelle, nor on his sale of bacon, cheese, sausages and candles will he pay any *dazio*, claiming that he is exempt . . . because of the treaties. And the Ferrarese *daziari* deny that he is immune.[110]

The briefing papers on this and related problems present the Ferrarese arguments: that the treaties did not cover and had not envisaged Venetians continuously living in Ferrara; that Venetian immunity was not total, for they were subject to *dazi* on goods brought to Ferrara from places other than Venice; and that individuals could only enter a trade by taking Ferrarese citizenship and, *ipso facto*, losing their privileges as 'Venetians'.[111] In this last argument, the Ferrarese advisers seem to have stumbled on a

---

105 ASV, 'Materie', 112, fols. 90v-91.
106 ASMo, 'Ambasciatori, Venezia', busta 7, 6 July 1491; busta 10, 29 November 1491; busta 11, 8 October 1502; Sanuto, II, 110, 329, 772; III, 592, 627.
107 ASMo, 'Ambasciatori, Venezia', busta 7, 27 January 1491.
108 A shipload of pomegranates, two bails of leather, 9000 almonds and some pitch: ASV, 'Materie', 112, fols. 91-v, 98v-99.
109 Ibid., fols. 84-85, 86v-87, 97v; ASMo, 'Ambasciatori, Venezia', busta 7, 13 June and 9 November 1489, 9 March 1491.
110 ASMo, 'Casa e stato', 58/20 (though undated, the document refers to the term as *visdomino* of Luca Zeno and is therefore to be dated after 1487).
111 Ibid., and 58/32.

powerful weapon that was put to use in the following years, as revealed by Venetian complaint of their subjects being forced to renounce their privileges in order to continue trading.[112] Equally difficult was the problem of taxing goods in transit. Time and again the Ferrarese ambassador or special envoy had to argue the case that Venetian exemption covered only goods originating from or bound for Venice.[113] Battle was closely joined on this issue again in 1502, over Venetian salt cargoes to Cremona, for which Ferrara claimed 1660 ducats in unpaid tax. 'I am certain that they know they are wrong', reported the Ferrarese ambassador, as the doge tried to evade his argument that the treaties between Ferrara and Venice did not allow for Venice's acquisition of Cremona (in the partition of the duchy of Milan with the king of France in 1499).[114]

The expansion of Venetian exemption was seen in Ferrara as a defrauding of Ercole's revenues. It was a similar fiscal concern that led Ferrara to attack the issue of Venetian citizenship granted by the *visdomino* to peasants of the Ferrarese *contado*. The Estensi had long protested at the abusive proliferation of such grants (*cartoline*).[115] In 1491, according to Caleffini, 'the duke was seeking to impose taxes on all *contadini* . . . and because every day he came into conflict with the *Signoria* over *contadini*, at least one third of whom were exempt from everything having procured *cartoline* as Venetians from past *visdomini*', he issued a decree, ordering all such *contadini* to present themselves for amnesty and to register for the future, on pain of branding and loss of all property.[116] 'Many, countless numbers arrived every day.' This action, which had Venice's consent, had been prepared over the past two years, originating in a special mission to Venice by Pellegrino Prisciani to discuss this and other problems. At first the doge had offered to take action only if Ferrara provided the names of '*contadini* fraudulently created Venetians', but Prisciani gradually extracted greater concessions on this point: that the *visdomino* would consult Ercole's *conservator iurium* (i.e. Prisciani himself) before issuing *cartoline* in future, and that all improper creations

---

112 In a debate in the *Signoria* on the *visdomino*'s report 'chel non e observati li pacti loro, imo chel si fa omni perforzo per rompergelli tuto il giorno et per discazar la natione veneciana da Ferrara', Niccolo Trevisan, a former *visdomino*, claimed that 'se faceano tante trame et bagatelle contra veneciani che lo era forza renunciasseno a loro privilegi et disse de uno Francesco de Diano speciale quale sta a San Zorzo che era 200 anni li suoi erano veneciano et se lo havea volluto stare a Ferrara li era stato forza renunciare et similiter quelli de Morello': ASMo, 'Ambasciatori, Venezia', busta, 7, 9 March 1491.

113 Ibid., 21 September and 2 October 1489, 9 March 1491.

114 Ibid., busta 11, 9, 12 and 29 November 1502; Sanuto, IV, 497, 514, 552, 576, 687, 712, 727, 734; V, 611, 639, 773.

115 Dean, 'Venetian Economic Hegemony', pp. 90-92.

116 Caleffini, 'Cronica', fol. 289v.

would be revoked by the new *visdomino*.[117] But, having agreed to a process of cancellation, Venice then took up complaints, referred by the *visdomino*, of 'perhaps forty *contadini* who, he claims, have been forced by jailings, poindings, beatings, threats, and by making them renounce in prison their Venetian privileges, so that they have to do dyke-work'.[118] The Ferrarese ambassador was held in a three-hour discussion of this and other issues, being reminded, in a subsequent audience, 'that the past war arose from these same matters'.[119] When in 1493 Ercole complained again of Venetian citizens fraudulently created, 'out of the fault and greed of the secretaries of the various *visdomini*', the doge again ordered the *visdomino* to cancel them.[120] Yet problems still arose when Ferrarese officials distrained the goods of some *contadini* for their refusal to work on repairs to the river-dykes or to pay poll-tax (*boccatico*).[121] But the success of the Ferrarese purge seems clear from the *visdomino*'s claim that 'of the 600 families of Venetians which . . . used to live in the Ferrarese, there are now no more than 100, and this has all come from these poor men being badly treated'.[122]

Just as Ferrarese officials felt that Venetians were defrauding their gabelles, so too they felt that Venice was not honouring Ferrara's tax privileges in Venice. The thirteenth-century treaties were unclear as to precisely what these were, but they did limit taxes there to 'ancient custom' and precluded imposition of any 'novelty'.[123] Inequality in fiscal treatment was noted during the war: 'they want to be exempt in Ferrara for the merchandise and goods that come from the Levant and from all parts of the world and are brought to Ferrara by Venetians; and we want to be exempt in Venice only for the goods which are grown or produced in Ferrara, and if a Ferrarese takes to Venice goods neither grown nor produced in Ferrara, they make him pay the *dazio*'.[124] After the war, however, Venice was taxing *all* Ferrarese goods. This formed one of the issues raised in the Venetian *Collegio* by Prisciani in 1489. It was difficult, however, to get the *Collegio* even to start thinking about it: 'as it is an old matter, it needs greater chewing', was all the doge would comment at first.[125] It was only after many weeks that the *savi grandi*, to whom the matter had been referred, reported back, accepting the Ferrarese case.[126] However, the clerks garbled

117 ASMo, 'Ambasciatori, Venezia', busta 7, 18 September, 2 and 14 October, 9 and 30 November 1489.
118 Ibid., 9 March 1491. By the terms of the 1455 pacts, 'Venetian' *contadini* were obliged to work on the dykes: Dean, 'Venetian Economic Hegemony', p. 92.
119 ASMo, 'Ambasciatori, Venezia', busta 7, 19 July 1491.
120 ASV, 'Materie', 112, fol. 101.
121 Ibid., 111, fols. 103v-104; 112, fols. 101-v.
122 ASMo, 'Ambasciatori, Venezia', busta 7, 9 March 1491.
123 ASMo, 'Casa e stato', 58/31, fols. 5v-6.
124 Ibid., fol. 6.
125 ASMo, 'Ambasciatori, Venezia', busta 7, 2 October 1489.
126 Ibid., 14 October, 3 and 9 November 1489.

the resulting ordinance and released it to only one of the two Venetian customs boards.[127] After much lobbying, the ambassador corrected their mistake and had in his hand a copy of the full immunity: 'it is a fine immunity . . . , it will be of some profit and, beyond that, there is also the honour of being reintegrated in the old privileges', and 'with time I do not doubt that the profit will grow greater, because the immunity is free and does not except anything'.[128] He was swiftly disillusioned: when he tried to sell some pigs that he had brought from Ferrera, he found that the officials at the meatmarket insisted on his paying the *dazio*. He immediately complained to the *Signoria*, asking them 'if the exemption was granted so that it be observed or so that it be not observed at all, because it seems to me that such an immunity and nothing are the same thing, because there is no office that will observe it'.[129] Although the doge at first agreed to instruct all officials to respect Ferrara's restored privilege, the debate became heated and took a different turn when Antonio Grimani, *savio grande*, insisted that the immunity did not cover pigs or cheese, and when the doge asserted that it was too costly to allow any Ferrarese produce to enter duty-free, 'because, passing as Ferrarese goods, all the goods of Lombardy would rush in', though he did agree to consider establishing a system of inspection and certification.[130] But when the ambassador tried a few weeks later to return to the topic, the doge silenced him, replying 'with so much annoyance and revulsion . . . that it seems to me certain that they do not want their heads troubled with this matter any more'.[131]

To all these tensions was added the difficulty of now having Venice as a neighbour along the Po. Border disputes flared up repeatedly: first over whether Pontecchio, Castelguglielmo, Polesella and Villamarzana were or were not part of the Polesine, which Venice occupied by virtue of the peace treaty (1484-85); then over jurisdiction on the border at Guarda and Guardazola (1490-92); over a customs-barrier erected at Trecenta (1490); also over dykes there (1502).[132] For the most part, the official Ferrarese attitude seems to have been to contain these disputes, to settle each one on an individual basis and to avoid comprehensive definition of the border, in the certain knowledge that it would be disadvantageous, while asserting at opportune moments that the border ran along Ercole's own bed in his palace in Ferrara, thus reviving the fiction that between father and son there

127 Ibid., 14 and 17 November 1489.
128 Ibid., 17 November 1489.
129 Ibid., 5 January 1490.
130 Ibid.
131 Ibid., 28 January 1490.

132 Caleffini, 'Cronica', fols. 235v, 236v, 237v; *Diario ferrarese*, p. 286; Sanuto, *Commentarii*, pp. 155-56; Frizzi, *Memorie*, IV, pp. 151, 153; Muratori, *Antichità estensi*, II, pp. 250-51.

could be no border.¹³³ 'It is throwing away words to argue of anything belonging to the jurisdiction of this *Signoria*, as they will not concede to your Excellency one drachma, rather I think their hearts would break had they not taken and held in the peace what they have at present . . . What is the point of fighting and losing?'.¹³⁴

Venetian occupation of the Polesine also created problems for Ferrara in other ways. The area had been closely tied to Ferrara politically, socially and economically, and Venetian efforts to cut those ties generated much resentment. In 1485 Venice acted to halt the emigration of *contadini* from the Polesine to Ferrarese territory;¹³⁵ and in 1486-87 to stop recourse to the Ferrarese courts and the export of crops to Ferrara;¹³⁶ presumably to the same end in 1488 a tax-free market was opened in Rovigo (though Caleffini thought it was calculated to damage Ercole's tax-revenues).¹³⁷ Ferrarese clerics and landowners with benefices or estates in the Polesine were harassed.¹³⁸ The Venetian captain in Rovigo was the source of recurrent dispute along the border.¹³⁹

Given all these issues, keen sources of conflict, it is surprising that Venice and Ferrara did not in fact find themselves again at war in this period. Venice certainly had its grievances and opportunities: yet the *Signoria* punished rather than pursued a plot in 1489 to seize the Castel Vecchio in Ferrara;¹⁴⁰ and it rejected French offers of the city in 1500.¹⁴¹ The Venetians were not averse, when the circumstances were right, to further mainland acquisition (for example, in Cremona); but with Ercole protected by the king of France and in the knowledge, drawn from experience, that an attack on Ferrara would bring the pope against them, they perhaps reckoned that the risks were too great. At the same time, Venice fended off Borgia notions of recovering Ferrara for the papacy.¹⁴² The Este made better neighbours. Popes were less inclined to feel honoured by Venetian favours and were unlikely to accept the doge as a father.¹⁴³ All that the Este had to do was wait for the grand coalition of 1509 that eventually attacked the Venetian *Terraferma* and allowed the permanent removal of the *visdomino*.

---

133 ASMo, 'Ambasciatori, Venezia', busta 7, 14 September and 9 October 1489.
134 Ibid., 29 May 1490.
135 Caleffini, 'Cronica', fols. 241v.
136 Ibid., fols. 247-v, 256v-57.
137 Ibid., fol. 264; Zambotti, *Diario*, p. 201.
138 ASMo, 'Ambasciatori, Venezia', busta 5, 15 January 1485, 4 February 1486; busta 7, 11 January 1490, 3 June 1491.
139 Ibid., 3 November 1489, 5 May 1490, 7 December 1492; busta 10, 17 January 1492.
140 Ibid., busta 7, 30 May 1489.
141 *Petri Delphini annalium venetorum*, ed. R. Cessi and P. Sambin (Venice, 1943), p. 41; cf. Sanuto, III, 116, 235, 246, 249, 255.
142 Malipiero, 'Annali', p. 564.
143 See Pius II's comment, quoted in Dean, 'Venetian Economic Hegemony', p. 79.

Appendix

Lists of the *visdomini* in Ferrara during Ercole's reign are provided in ASV, 'Segretario alle Voci', Mista [hereafter, Seg. Voci], regs. 4, 5, 6 and 9; in Biblioteca Marciana, MSS Ital., Cl. VII, 198, 'Reggimenti'; and (with errors) in L.N. Cittadella, *Notizie relative a Ferrara per la maggior parte inedita* (Ferrara, 1864) p. 456. It was thought useful to publish the list in full, with notes on each individual's office holding carreer. The dates given are those of entering office ('intravit vicedominatum die . . . '), not of election.

23 November 1470   Giovanni di Girolamo da Canal
He had served among the *Judices Crete*, 1450; as an official *super foleo auri*, 1451; among the *officiales armamenti*, 1455 and the *Justiciarii veteres*, 1468. Later, he was castellan of Peschiera, 1486-89, and count of Sebenico, 1494. He died in 1496. (Seg. Voci, reg. 4, fols. 19, 37, 81; reg. 6, fols. 17, 48).

22 February 1472   Francesco di Paolo Contarini
He had served as an official *super Ternaria*, 1442; as *podestà* of Valle, 1452; as castellan of Corfu, 1453, and of Jadra, 1455; as one of the *officiali di notte*, 1466; as *podestà* of Parenzo, 1467-68; and in the office *super Doana maris*, 1469. (Seg. Voci, reg. 4, fols, 67, 70, 74; reg. 6, fols. 2v, 29v, 62v).

10 June 1475   Girolamo di Bernardo Zane
He had been one of the *collaterales*, 1465, and in the *Catavere* office, 1471. (Seg. Voci., reg. 6, fols. 4, 89v). He was prosecuted for revealing secret information to the Ferrarese ambassador in 1482 (Queller, *Venetian Patriciate*, p. 215) and was fined and disqualified for breaking electoral rules in 1508 (Sanuto, *Diarii*, VII, 495-96).

13 March 1477   Antonio di Andrea Venier
He had been in the *Catavere* office, 1471, and among the *Provisores communis*, 1474. He later served *super imprestitis*, 1480. (Seg. Voci, reg. 6, fols. 4, 39v, 50).

5 October 1478   Benedetto di Pangrazio Giustinian
He had served among the *Auditores veteres*, 1477, and was later to serve among the *Provisores salis*, 1491; as one of the Ten, 1496; as ambassador to France, 1499; as a *savio* regarding the *Terraferma*, 1500; and as one of the forty-one electors of Doge Leonardo Loredan, 1501. (Seg. Voci, reg. 6, fols. 8, 138; reg. 9, fols. 10v-11; Sanuto, *Diarii*, III, 10, 29, 73, 853, 1156, 1247).

28 November 1479   Gianvettore di Giovanni Contarini
He had served among the *Advocatores per omnes curias*, 1471 and 1476, and among the *Judices publicorum*, 1474. (Seg. Voci, reg. 6, fols. 5, 25-v).

10 November 1484   Luca di Marco Zeno
He had served among the *Collaterales*, 1465, the *Auditores veteres*, 1468, and the *Officiales rationum novarum*, 1472; then as captain of Crete, 1472, and among the *Provisores bladorum*,

1480, and the *Avogadori di comun*, 1483; later he served as *savio del consiglio*, 1497 and 1500-3; as captain of Padua, 1498-99; and as one of the electors of Doge Loredan, 1501; before being elected *Procuratore di San Marco*, 1503. 'A poor, old man' by 1510, he was excluded from the Senate because of his tax-debts from 1511 to 1513; he refused appointment to the *zonta* to the Ten, because 'he was old in years and could not stay up late'. He died in 1516, aged eighty-five, 'of old age, without illness'. (Seg. Voci, reg. 6, fols. 6, 8, 37v, 80, 89v, 112, 115v, 130v, 141; Sanuto, *Diarii*, III, 37, 178, 1011; IV, 54, 132, 459; V, 52, 61, 80, 164; VI, 88; VII, 602, 734; XI, 533, 789; XII, 402, 462; XIII, 461, 487; XIV, 639; XV, 330, 372).

5 April 1487   Pietro di Lorenzo Donà
He had served as a member of the office *super Ternaria*, 1449; of the *Quarantia*, 1454; of the *Tabula introitus*, 1455; and among the *officiales rationum veterum*, 1469. Later he was *podestà* of Brescia, 1489-91 and a member of the Ten, 1494 and 1496, before his death in the latter year. (Seg. Voci, reg. 4, fols. 14, 43v, 44v; reg. 6, fols. 35v, 91, 109v, 141; reg. 9, fols. 6, 10v).

21 August 1488   Vinciguerra di Marco Dandolo
He appears among the *judices mobilium*, 1450, and the *advocatores per omnes curias*, 1453, and the *officiales rationum novarum*, 1467; he then served as *podestà* of Belluno, 1477-79, one of the *provisores salis*, 1483, and one of the *Avogadori di comun*, 1486. After his period as *visdomino*, he was captain of Brescia, 1490-92, but was exiled for two years and disqualified from office for ten, 'per haver fomentà le parti in Bressa' (Malipiero, 'Annali', p. 690). Returning to Venice in 1502, he was reappointed *avogadore di comun*, but as such, along with the other *avogadori*, was publicly criticised by the doge following the discovery of fraud in the *Fondaco dei Tedeschi* ('the city was ruined . . . because these present *avogadori* were worthless'). After recovering from this, he served again as *avogadore* in 1508-9, was elected to the *zonta* of the Ten several times between 1510 and 1513, and served as *governatore delle entrate*, 1512-13. By 1514, 'because he has become blind, he no longer leaves his house', and he died in 1517: 'era savio patricio', Sanudo comments. (Seg. Voci, reg. 4, fols. 8v, 65v; reg. 6, fols. 37v, 43, 91, 109v, 112; Sanuto, *Diarii*, IV, 491, 618; V, 345, 670; VI, 46; VII, 601, 733; VIII, 11: X, 601; XI, 232; XIII, 10, 503; XIV, 201; XVII, 116; XVIII, 311, 392; XIX, 96; XXIV, 148).

26 January 1489 (i.e. 1490)[1]   Antonio di Marco Erizzo
It is not clear whether the office-holding records throughout this period refer to two individuals of the same name; one is certainly distinguished as Antonio Erizzo *maior* in 1441. The following list may therefore conflate two careers. Erizzo is found among the *officiali di notte* in 1443, the *judices forinsecorum*, 1443, the *judices publicorum*, 1444, the *judices mobilium*, 1446, then as *podestà* of Torcello, 1448-49, and among the *judices examinatorum*, 1450, before becoming 'councillor' of Modone, 1455, *podestà* of Chioggia, 1462, and a *patronus arsenatus*, 1467. He was one of the *avogadori di comun*, 1470, captain of the Alexandrian galleys, 1471, *podestà* of Verona, 1472-73, and of Padua, 1474-75. Was it the elder Erizzo who then took office as *procuratore* 'de citra', 1476-83? While his namesake went on to become *podestà* of Bergamo, 1484-86, *auditor officii supragastaldionum*, 1486,

---

1   1490 is meant. He was said to be leaving Venice for Ferrara, 19 January 1490: ASM, Ambasciatori, Venezia, busta 7.

avogadore di comun and *visdomino*, 1489? (Seg. Voci, regs. 4, fols. 2v, 6, 9, 10, 11, 24, 50, 65v, 75v; reg. 5, fol. 3; reg. 6, fols. 6, 7, 16v, 19, 30v, 35v, 50v, 83, 86v, 103, 115v, 132).

25 August 1491   Bartolomeo di Matteo Vitturi
Here there is an apparent contradiction between the electoral registers, which record Vitturi as captain of Jadra, 1483-5, and one of the Ten, 1494, but with the annotation 'obiit' against the latter entry, and Sanudo, who records him as one of the Ten, 1498, 1499 and 1500, as *consier*, 1496, 1499 and 1501, as ill in 1500 and dead by February 1501. (Seg. Voci, reg. 6, fol. 69; reg. 9, fol. 6; Sanuto, *Diarii*, II, 21, 73, 439, 566, 595, 1361, 1431).

11 May 1493   Pietro di Luca Duodo
He was appointed among the *officiales armamenti*, 1467, as a galley captain, 1482, as *avogadore di comun*, 1497, *provveditore* in Pisa, 1498-99, and *savio* for the *Terraferma*, 1500. As ducal *consier*, he was one of the forty-one electors of Doge Loredan in 1501, and then served on the Ten, 1501 and 1505, as *savio del consiglio*, 1501-3, 1506-8, as ambassador to Pope Julius II, 1503 and captain of Cremona, 1503-4. He is frequently to be found taking a leading role in debates in the *Collegio*, for example, he was one of a small group involved in a *gran disputation* regarding relations with Germany in 1507. There are numerous references to his quarrels with colleagues and to ill-feeling against him. As *provveditore*-elect in 1498, his row with his colleague delayed his departure, but he had too many supporters in the *Collegio* for anything to be done about it. He gathered the largest number of negative votes in a ballot for the post of *procuratore di San Marco* in 1501 and he succeeded in few of his many candidatures for election. Eventually elected *provveditore* in Verona in 1509, he arrived only a few weeks before the rebellion, whereupon he fled to Treviso and was relieved a few months later, 'because . . . sier Pietro Duodo behaved badly at Treviso; no one praised him; he stayed at home all the time and took little action'. However, he was soon back in office in Venice: *savio del consiglio*, 1510, and on a *zonta* to the Ten, 1510-11, before being appointed *podestà* of Padua, 1512, where he died of *ponta*. (Seg. Voci, reg. 6 fols. 26v, 83v; Sanuto, *Diarii*, I, 667, 807, 996, 1102; II, 8, 716-17; III, 429, 467, 576-77, 793, 1035, 1053; IV, 132, 148, 185, 235, 294; V, 32, 297, 499, 1067; VI, 242, 267, 277-79, 332, 340, 342; VII, 95, 107, 113, 156, 602, 676; VIII, 270, 295, 335, 425; IX, 11, 27-28, 191, 216, 418, 438, 537; X, 248, 835; XI, 23, 352, 483; XII, 164, 607; XIII, 11, 502-3; XIV, 263; XV, 179; XVI, 172).

25 October 1494   Gianfrancesco di Alvise Pasqualigo
He was *podestà* of Feltre, 1485, 'count' of Jadra, 1487, *avogadore di comun*, 1493 and 1498, *savio* for the *Terraferma*, 1496, captain of Brescia, 1498-99, *savio del consiglio*, 1500, and, though now *gotoso* and reluctant to serve, a *capo* of the Ten, 1503. (Seg. Voci, reg. 6, fols. 41, 68v, 91, 132; Sanuto, *Diarii*, I, 383, 852, 1025; II, 29, 1346; III, 99, IV, 867; V, 81).

10 March 1496   Giovanni di Pietro Mocenigo
He is found among the *consules mercatorum*, 1471, as consul in Damascus, 1485-87, captain of Bergamo, 1493, and a member of the Ten, 1495. Later, he was *governatore delle entrate*, 1498, captain of Verona, 1502-3, and again on the Ten, 1504, though replaced because 'ill at home'. He was then elected *consier di San Marco* and acted as vice-doge. He was captain of Cremona, 1506, and of Padua, 1508-9, but was replaced in the crisis of 1509 because he was thought to have provoked, by his own action, the panic of Venetian flight from that city.

Returning to Venice, 'old and full of gout, he cannot move', and he failed numerous ballots for office, 1509-11. He remained a friend of the Ferrarese diplomat, Zuan Alberto della Pigna. (Seg. Voci, reg. 6, fols. 19v, 33v, 94, 133v, 147v; reg. 9, fol. 8; Sanuto, *Diarii*, III, 1267, 1483; IV, 265, 876; V, 17, 327, 469, 1059; VI, 6, 26, 30, 86; VII, 495; VIII, 314, 327, 338, 466; IX, 90, 271, 312).

12 July 1497   Bernardo di Niccolò Bembo
Born in 1433, he graduated in law at the University of Padua and then began a long and distinguished career in Venetian political and diplomatic life, from his first embassies to Castile, 1468, and Burgundy, 1471-74, to his last, to Rome, 1505. He also served as *podestà* of Ravenna, 1481-83, of Bergamo, 1489-90, and of Verona, 1502-3, and held some of the most important posts within Venice (*avogadore di comun*, 1485, 1494, 1504-5, 1509, 1512-13; on the Ten, 1496, 1500, 1505, 1511, 1513; *governatore delle entrate*, 1500; one of the forty-one electors of Doge Loredan, 1501). A protagonist in the events of 1509, he was *consigliere ducale*, 1510-11. Retiring from public life in 1514, he died in 1519. (A. Ventura, Bembo, Bernardo, *Dizionario biografico degli italiani*, VIII, 103-8)

16 July 1499   Girolamo di Antonio Donà
He was among the *auditores veteres*, 1483, and the *avogadori di comun*, 1494, was *podestà* of Ravenna, 1492-93, and of Brescia, 1495-96, *savio* for the *Terraferma*, 1497, and then ambassador to Rome, 1497-99. After his period as *visdomino*, he was ambassador to the emperor, 1501, and to the king of France, 1501-2. He was among the forty-one electors of Doge Loredan, before becoming *podestà* of Cremona, 1502-4, *savio del consiglio*, 1504, and ambassador once more to Rome, 1505. Having served as 'duke' in Candia (Crete), 1506-8, he was *provveditore* in Padua, 1509 (where his long speech to the Paduan council urging defence failed to prevent the loss of the city two days later), and ambassador to Rome, 1509-11 (he had to deal with Julius II's angry outbursts against Venice), where he died. (Seg. Voci, reg. 6, fols. 22v, 91, 105, 131, 132; Sanuto *Diarii*, I, 180, 209, 267, 401, 503, 667, 808; II, 11, 800; III, 1581; IV, 5, 83, 87, 102, 132, 174, 321, 615; V, 18, 585, 634, 691, 1067; VI, 64, 138, 163, 199, 207, 301, 323-24, 503; VII, 55, 656; VIII, 292, 327, 340, 354, 370, 510-11; IX, 414, 477; XI, 6; XIII, 86, 175-77).

19 February 1500 (i.e. 1501)[2]   Cristoforo di Lorenzo Moro
According to his own revealing apologia in 1511, he was one of the long-serving and long-suffering members of the Venetian gerontocracy. He is found as *visdomino* of the *Fondaco dei Tedeschi*, 1468, a captain of galleys, 1481 and 1484, then *podestà* of Ravenna, 1496-98, on the Ten, 1499, and *provveditore* in the Veronese and then at Lodi, 1499-1500. After his period as *visdomino*, he was *provveditore* in Faenza, 1504, but was replaced because of illness. Back in Venice, he was on the Ten and *consier*, 1504, before being appointed lieutenant in Cyprus, 1506-8. He then refused the captaincy Candia, but was *provveditore* in Brescia in 1509, falling back during the crisis of that year on Treviso and Vicenza. Ill, old and reluctant, he was appointed *podestà* of Padua, 1510-11; but when he was elected *provveditore* in Padua, 1511, he tried to refuse, 'saying he could not serve at present, given

---

2 1501 is meant. According to Sanuto, he was elected 9 November 1500 (*Diarii*, III, 1044), was still in Venice at Christmas (III, 1219), but in post by February 1501 (III, 1464).

his bad leg', and 'because of the burdens he had suffered for the state, he could serve no more, nor could he ride'. His excuses were rejected and he was welcomed in Padua, but was recalled the same year to become *consier*, but was again elected *provveditore generale in campo* (Lombardy) in 1512. The post overburdened his years and he returned to Venice, feverish and unable to move. Nevertheless, he was elected *savio del consiglio*, 1513-16, and offered to go to Padua once more, and at his own expense, when it was threatened again. He was on a *zonta* to the Ten, 1515-16, and was elected captain of Verona, 1517 (he replied that he wanted to get better first, and then go). *Consier* and vice-doge in 1517, he died in 1518 aged seventy-five, of *ponta* and in debt. (Seg. Voci, reg. 6, fols. 22v, 32v, 84, 85v, 109v; Sanuto, *Diarii*, I, 423, 963; II, 1006; III, 36, 53; VI, 23, 42, 45, 69, 97, 102, 284, 549; VII, 469, 548, 654, 662, 733; VIII, 263, 303, 400, 439; IX, 6, 84, 94, 97, 326, 459, 543; X, 14, 672; XI, 313, 668; XII, 85, 158, 174, 205, 218-19, 222, 224-5, 396, 423; XIII, 47; XIV, 66, 398, 461, 471, 540; XV, 183, 339, 341, 427, 544; XVI, 423; XVII, 103, 111; XVIII, 79, 120; XIX, 48, 106; XX, 131; XXI, 156; XXII, 65, 666; XXIII, 6, 129, 295-96, 531, 543; XXIV, 228, 708; XXV, 12, 63, 238).

October 1503   Marco di Bertuccio Zorzi
He had served as captain of Bergamo, 1496-97 (from where deputed *provveditore* in the Milanese and envoy to Savoy), *savio* for the *Terraferma*, 1496, 1498-99 and 1500-1, ambassador to France, 1499. After his period as *visdomino*, he was *provveditore* at Faenza, 1506-7, and on the Ten, 1509, 1511-12, 1513-14. (Sanuto, *Diarii*, I, 145, 220, 475, 535, 987; II, 5, 398, 420, 554, 643, 1297; VI, 301, 480; VII, 23, 40; VIII, 516; X, 46, XIII, 54, 503; XIV, 256; XVII, 327, 365, 431, 576; XVIII, 5, 475; XIX, 73; XX, 125).

August, 1504   Alvise da Mula
Podestà of Capodistria, 1499-1500, and of Crema, 1502, and a member of the Ten, 1504 and 1507, he was *podestà* of Cremona, 1508-9, where he was captured by the French, and he died later in France. (Sanuto, *Diarii*, II, 360, 1372; III, 28, 466, 600; IV, 288, 507; V, 1062).

6

Love and War in the Veneto: Luigi da Porto and the True Story of *Giulietta e Romeo*

Cecil H. Clough

On 12 November 1509 the main Venetian strike-force under Count Niccolò Orsini, the captain general, together with Andrea Gritti, the *provveditore generale*, and Girolamo Savorgnan, since December 1508 the collateral-general, moved from its encampment near Padua to Camisano, just within the territory of Vicenza. In torrential rain the following day a light cavalry advance-force captured Torri di Quartesolo, and thereafter the main force advanced to the walls of the city of Vicenza. After a bombardment and the capture of a gate, attack was halted for the night. At about *ore* 7 that same night a deputation from Vicenza reached the main Venetian encampment to negotiate the city's surrender. Terms were agreed and on 14 November the Venetians once more controlled Vicenza.[1] Some individuals of the noble Da Porto family of Vicenza had been instrumental in promoting the venture, and in contributing to an outcome satisfactory both for Venice and Vicenza. Luigi – or Alvise, the common contemporary form of his name – had been with the Venetian strike-force, while previously he had made

---

1 A letter from Vicenza dated 14 November 1509 of Girolamo Savorgnan, who was with the main Venetian force, provides full details, in Sanuto, IX, 319-21.

This essay originated with my D. Phil. thesis, presented at Oxford University in 1960. A version was given as a lecture to the Dante Society of Toronto in February 1962, and as a paper at the Southeastern Renaissance Conference of April 1962, Columbia, South Carolina; this was published in *Renaissance Papers 1962* (Durham, NC, 1963), pp. 45-52. An extended version was given as a paper at the Conference of the Society for Italian Studies of April 1977, Swansea. It was rewritten in Italian for a lecture given in the Accademia Olimpica, Vicenza, 3 May 1985, to commemorate the 500th anniversary of Luigi da Porto's birth. This study is a further revision; I am indebted to the Gladys Krieble Delmas Foundation for financial assistance to further my researches.

Over the forty years the study has matured I have benefitted from much help, many suggestions and criticisms. Here I wish to signal particular gratitude for information generously provided by Signorina Maria Gigli of Rome, Professor Edward Muir of Baton Rouge, Louisiana, Dottor Armando Mucchino of Udine, Professor Giuseppe Velli of Berkeley, Professoressa Anna Maria Vizzini Ravelli of Brescia.

A very different interpretation of the circumstances of Da Porto's life is provided in G. Guarda, '*Montorso mio dolce e ameno*' (Montorso, 1985), particularly pp. 37-9, 199, 202-10.

several secret missions from imperial Vicenza to the Venetian military authorities near Padua.[2] Presumably on these missions he acted as agent for those of his native city who had become disillusioned with imperial government. Significantly as testimony of his 'poetic' tendency, he appears to have indicated to the Venetians that a much weaker imperial force held the city than was the case: most likely this was consciously done to encourage the Venetians to make a recovery attempt.[3] Cavaliere Simone da Porto, Luigi's uncle, was chosen among others by the city's *Consiglio Maggiore* to agree terms with the Venetians on the night of 13 November.[4]

The Da Porto was a family to be reckoned with in Vicenza, anxious to preserve standing in the face of the thrusting Trissino, favoured by the imperial authorities. In 1510 the family was to hold twelve of the Council's 150 seats, though some Da Porto were to remain pro-imperial, either because of marriage ties, or out of prudence to maintain the family's interests.[5] Naturally enough the city fathers were apprehensive on 13 November 1509, as on the previous 3 June the Venetian *rettori* had left the city in the face of a supposed imperial army's approach and the consequent

2 Luigi's account of the part played by his family is in L. da Porto, *Lettere storiche*, ed. B. Bressan (Florence, 1857), pp. 142-3. As it is in print I generally cite this edition, very seriously flawed though it is; in those instances where Bressan's text is entirely misleading I cite my unpublished edition, quoted unitalicised, which is an Oxford University D. Phil. thesis, 1960, on deposit in the Bodleian Library, Oxford. Andrea Gritti in his dispatch of 18 November 1509, cited in note 7 below, referred to the fact that Luigi 'piu volte per queste prattiche di Vicentia vene a Padoa'. Luigi mentioned accompanying the main force in his *Lettere storiche*, p. 144, so presumably was at the encampment near Padua about 11 November. He may have made one secret visit, or more, on 3, 5 and 9 November, cf. Sanuto, IX, 290, under 3 November, mentioned some unspecified Vicentine nobles treating with the Venetian authorities; IX, 291, under 5 November, mentioned a report that envoys were being sent from Vicenza; IX, 290, 293, at the same time, seemingly independently, the Venetian authorities were in contact with some imperial captains in Vicenza; IX, 301, on 9 November, the Venetians heard news that their spies in Vicenza had been detected and hanged, but the Venetians were still expecting 'quella notte uno homo da qualche conto, quale lo refareria cosse verissime'.

3 Da Porto, *Lettere storiche*, p. 147, mentioned the *provveditori generali* as astonished at the strength of the garrison, which Savorgnan's letter cited in note 1 above, probably with exaggeration, put at 500 cavalry and 8,000 infantry. If one accepts that the force was more than the Venetians had expected, Da Porto, who was in a position to know the strength, was the most likely source for the misinformation.

4 Da Porto, *Lettere storiche*, pp. 145-8. Savorgnan's letter, cited in note 1, names three envoys sent to come to terms with the Venetians, who were encamped for the night at Torri di Quartesolo: Simone da Porto, Bernardino Sesso and Giacomo Thiene; G. Zugliano, 'Annali, 1509-1512', MS 189, Biblioteca del Seminario, Padua, fols. 39v-40 lists four envoys, two correspond with the first two names above, but in place of Thiene is provided Niccolò Chieregato, and Ludovico da Schio is added. The envoys reached camp at about *ore* 7 on 13 November, see Savorgnan's letter, Zugliano, fols. 39v-40, *Cronaca ad memoriam praeteriti temporis praesentis atque futuri [1237-1524] (Per Nozze Malvezzi-Chielin)*, ed. G. Marcello (Vicenza, 1884), p. 82: 'et a hore 5 di note il detto popolo [of Vicenza] mandò le chiavi della detta Città a soprascritti Provveditori Veneziani che erano a S. Giuliano . . .'.

5 In 1510 the Da Porto held twelve seats, see copy of the lost 'Libro N', in B. Bressan, 'Studi sulla genealogia della famiglia Loschi', Biblioteca Bertoliana, Vicenza, MS, Gonzati 26.8.9, fols. 2v, 3, 9, 13, 34v, 37v, 53v, 57v, 58v, 62, 71v.

opposition to Venetian authority on the part of the city's council. At their departure the imperial standard had been hoisted and the city was decreed by its Council to be a free commune under the emperor-elect. Simone da Porto, with the other two members of the delegation, had to ensure acceptable terms from the Venetians for the citizens of Vicenza, as well as negotiate the safe departure of the imperial force under Prince Rudolf of Hainnhalt-Bernberg, which had been garrisoning it on behalf of Maximilian.[6]

Five days after the surrender of Vicenza Simone da Porto went to Padua, seeking a personal interview with Gritti in order to petition that Luigi be granted a military command in the Venetian army. Late that same night Gritti reported the interview in his dispatch to the Venetian government. He wrote that he had suggested Simone and his nephew should apply directly to the Venetian government, adding that he had indicated to Simone the likelihood of a favourable response. Gritti intimated that a Venetian expression of gratitude for services rendered would be appropriate in the form of a *condotta* of twenty-five light horse.[7] On 28 November Simone and Luigi duly presented themselves in Venice and, on the evidence of the minute of the *Senato Segreto* of that day, after due deliberation it was agreed that Luigi be given a *condotta* of twenty-five light horse because of his past services, his military aptitude, and in the light of Gritti's commendation.[8] The next day the two Da Porto, on being told the decision, protested that such a negligible command was incompatible with the family's standing – in short, acceptance would result in the family losing 'face' in Vicenza. Again the Senate deliberated in closed session, whereon it was agreed that the size of Luigi's force should be doubled to fifty light horse.[9]

What was meant by Luigi's military aptitude? Gritti's dispatch to his government makes it evident that Luigi had not previously served under any military captain, otherwise this would have been mentioned. In fact little formal training was expected of a military captain, beyond tilting and cross-bow practice. In his *Lettere storiche* Da Porto recalled playing in his youth 'Prisoner's Base', a game in favour with soldiers as it fostered

---

6 For the departure of the *rettori*, see Zugliano, 'Annali', fol. 12, and Sanuto, VIII, 342, 348, 355; for the hoisting of the temporary imperial standard see ibid., 374; its cost was detailed in the city's 'Libro dei Provvisioni', I (it commences 1 June 1509), fol. 2, under 4 June, Archivio di Stato, Vicenza. The San Marco symbol was destroyed on 6 June, and on 14 July a permanent imperial standard replaced it, see *Cronaca ad memoriam*, p.75, and 'Libro dei Provvisioni', I, fol. 34v, under 13 July. For the embassy from Vicenza see note 4; details of the terms of surrender and of the departure of the imperial forces are in the letter of Savorgnan, cited in note 1, Sanuto, IX, 311, 318, Zugliano, 'Annali', fols. 39v-40, and *Cronaca ad memoriam*, p.82.

7 ASV, 'Dispacci, Provv. Gen. Terraferma e Mar', filza 26, fol. 151v.

8 ASV, 'Senato Secreta', reg. 42, fol. 88; cf. Sanuto, IX, 354.

9 Ibid., fol. 88v; cf. Sanuto, IX, 356.

corporal dexterity. No doubt Da Porto had the equestrian skill expected of a nobleman – he certainly owned a Barbery horse that ran in the *palio* – and was likely to have hunted.[10] Aged twenty-four and three months at the time of his visit to Venice, it is interesting to compare the reality of Luigi's *condotta* with his account in his *Lettere storiche*:[11]

> The Imperial force having been seen out of Vicenza proceeding in the direction of Verona in a thin line, the Venetian *provveditori* told me that I should go to Venice, as they believed I was to be given a Venetian *condotta*. On arrival there I was most graciously welcomed by the authorities, who urged me to form a force of light horse. Though its number seemed small to me, when I took into account my age – scarcely twenty-three – I accepted.

The passage is in what purports to be essentially an authentic letter which Luigi in his preface claimed to be one of a self-edited compilation of his correspondence, written to relatives and friends. The work covered the opening phases of the war that commenced with the League of Cambrai early in 1509, and continued to early 1513. Probably it was written mainly

---

10 For little formal training required see M.E. Mallett, 'Part 1, *c*.1400 to 1508', in M.E. Mallett and J.R. Hale, *The Military Organization of a Renaissance State: Venice, c.1400 to 1617* (Cambridge, 1984), pp. 142-3; for prisoner's base see Da Porto, *Lettere storiche*, p. 196; for his interest in the *palio* at Udine see ibid., pp. 25-6; in a race each horse usually carried a *fantino*, who required considerable equestrian skill. The best account of the history of the *palio* remains W. Heywood, *Palio and Ponte* (London, 1904). Girolamo da Porto in his biographical sketch of Da Porto, published in L. da Porto, *Rime e prosa*, ed. M.A. Zorzi (Vicenza, 1731), p. 10, claimed that Luigi had 'servito ne' suoi più teneri anni sotto la disciplina di . . . Guido Ubaldo Duca d'Urbino . . . ' (the original manuscript of Girolamo's text existed in the Bertoliana Library, Vicenza, until about a century ago, but now cannot be traced). There is no substance to Girolamo's claim, see C.H. Clough, 'Pietro Bembo, Luigi da Porto, and the Court of Urbino in the Early Sixteenth Century', in C.H. Clough, *The Duchy of Urbino in the Renaissance* (London, 1981), item XVII. Da Porto, *Lettere storiche*, pp. 34-43, indicates that he was in Venice, seemingly in March-April 1509, in contact with Bartolomeo d'Alviano. He possibly sought a *condotta*, and was refused, which may explain Da Porto's hostility to d'Alviano, evident in his work. Da Porto, *Lettere storiche*, p.105, indicates Luigi had been to Milan, perhaps in July 1509, and again the object may have been a *condotta*, on that occasion with the French. Gritti's commendation did not mention prior service; an individual such as Lorenzo Manzino of the noble family of Rome, who had experience was mentioned with 'qual intender ben il mestier di le arme', see Sanuto, XII, 365, 410.

11 Clough, ed. L. da Porto, 'Lettere storiche', cited in note 2 above, II, pp. 164-5: 'che io la compagnia dei cavalli leggieri facessi . . . '; Bressan, ed. *Lettere storiche*, p. 148, re-ordered the words and added the number 50: 'ch'io facessi la compagnia di 50 cavalli leggieri'.

Da Porto was born about 10 August 1485 on the evidence of the note, probably by Pietro Bembo, prefacing L. da Porto, *Rime e prosa* (Venice, Francesco Marcolini, 1539), fol. aii verso: 'Visse M. Luigi anni 43 e mesi 9, e morì . . . il 10 maggio 1529' (for this ed. see note 69 below). G. Brognoligo, *Studi di storia letteraria* (Rome-Milan, 1903), p. 5, on the basis of the note believed the date could be precisely calculated by subtracting the life-span indicated from his date of death, but Bembo's note gives no days, perhaps by chance. Luigi's parents appear to have married in 1484, see Luigi Frangipane, 'Registri Savorgnan', (in 8 cartolari), IV, Udine, Biblioteca Comunale, MS 1502, under 26 April 1484.

Da Porto was wounded on 20 June 1511 (see note 42 below), and in his letter that describes the action he provided his age correctly as 'non anche a' ventisei anni è giunta', see Bressan,

in 1522, and really is a history in the form of letters. Though based on some genuine letters the editing of any such was so heavy that its authenticity as a letter-collection is entirely lost.[12] The literary fiction of a letter, though, enabled Luigi to spotlight subtly his own sentiments and actions. His work can be seen as justifying the pro-Venetian stance that he and some of his family took in consequence of imperial control of Vicenza in the summer of 1509. It should be recalled that early in the 1520s, when Luigi was writing his history, Vicenza remained scarred by the family factions that the war had stimulated; a few former citizens were still in exile.[13] Further, one may suspect that Luigi hoped the history might stimulate the Venetian authorities to reward him for loyal service: he had been left partially paralysed in consequence of a wound received in battle.[14] Certainly his work was written with hindsight, inspired by classical models. Indeed the author's very concept of history was classical, with poetry and truth intermingled for effect. Hence autobiographical details in particular, as has already been seen, require critical evaluation against independent evidence.[15]

No source, other than Da Porto's own *Lettere storiche*, mentions his part in the fighting on the Veronese front from late December 1509 until early March 1510. Even so his participation there can be accepted. Following the recovery of Vicenza, Gritti and Count Pitigliano were in command on this front. It is possible that Luigi initially was posted where his military capacity and his loyalty could be evaluated, especially by Gritti. One can accept that Luigi was one of the bearers of the count's coffin on 27 January, after the count's demise the previous night.[16] Da Porto wrote that he had been with the camp at Lonigo for two days when news arrived – most likely on 24 December 1509 – of the Venetian defeat on the Po.[17] The first

Lettere storiche, p. 246.

12 Clough, 'Lettere storiche', I, chapter vi, pp. clxxv- ccxxxiv.

13 For the situation in the autumn of 1509 in Vicenza cf. Da Porto, *Lettere storiche*, p. 148. For Vicentine nobles in exile see G.C. (sic), 'I fuorusciti veneziani dalla battaglia di Agnadello al Congresso di Bologna', in *Archivio trentino*, XIV (1898), pp. 1-19, and A. Bonardi, 'I padovani ribelli alla Repubblica di Venezia (anno 1509-1530)', in *Miscellanea di Storia Veneta*, series ii, VIII (1902), pp. 459, 472, for the exiled Vicentine nobles. Cf. G.G. Trissino complained that the privileges granted by the Venetians to the Da Porto caused further divisions, see B. Morsolin, *Giangiorgio Trissino* (2nd ed., Florence, 1894), pp. 98-101.

14 See below at note 43.

15 See above at note 12. For Italian Renaissance concepts of history see Beatrice Reynolds, 'Shifting Currents in Historical Criticism', *Renaissance Essays*, ed. P.O. Kristeller and P.P. Wiener (New York, 1968), pp. 115-36.

16 For Da Porto under Gritti's eye see Da Porto, *Lettere storiche*, p. 173. For the advance towards Verona with Gritti see Sanuto, IX, 321, Da Porto, *Lettere storiche*, p. 155. For the death of Count Pitigliano at *ore* 3, 26 January 1510, see ASV, 'Dispacci, Provv. Gen. Terraferma e Mar', filza 26, fol. 257, cf. Sanuto, IX, 496, Zugliano, 'Annali', fol. 3, Da Porto, *Lettere storiche*, p. 169. No source other than Da Porto mentions the names of the pall-bearers at Lonigo.

17 Lonigo was recovered by an advance Venetian force on 17 November 1509, see Sanuto, IX, 323, 324; the main Venetian army arrived there the following day, see Sanuto, IX, 326. For news of the Po defeat reaching Venice at *ore* 8, 22 December, see Sanuto, IX, 405; Gritti would

payment credited to him as captain with 50 *balestrieri* was on 28 January 1510, so it is likely that then he had been in service about a month; typically the record does not indicate where he was posted.[18] The *Lettere storiche* contain accurate details of the fighting near Lonigo, Mason and Villanova, including information regarding the encampment at Lonigo before the reorganisation of mid January 1510. Only Luigi records the camp's standing orders, for example the firing of a cannon in Soave as a call to arms,[19] but his account of a skirmish near Villanova is echoed in a dispatch sent at *ore* 8, 6 January by Pietro Marcello, the other Venetian *provveditore generale* with Gritti.[20]

Gritti's letter of recommendation to the Venetian Senate of 18 November had indicated that Luigi should be urged to enlist his force quickly. That he achieved it in some three weeks is possible. The value of light cavalry was well known. On 20 January 1509, when urgent preparations were underway to counter the threat posed by the adherents of the League of Cambrai, it was agreed in Senate that five companies of light horse, each of 100 to 130 men, were to be established, there being at least thirty in each company with handguns. All the company was armed with the cross-bow, and equipped with a short lance that could be hurled as a javelin.[21] Da Porto's force was to swell this complement. In his *Lettere storiche* Da Porto mentioned a tactic he had adopted. He had short 'carbines' made in Cividale; these, tied to the trappings in front of the saddle, appeared to the enemy from a distance to be maces, so that Da Porto's light horse could approach close, as the enemy was unaware that the Venetians carried small arms.[22] He named three of his force. There was Martin Gradani from Albania, who, shortly after Da Porto was seriously wounded, and hence being without a captain, took service with the French.[23] A certain Peregrino of Verona was introduced as the individual who recounted the story of 'Giulietta e

have been informed at the latest by 24 December. Da Porto, *Lettere storiche*, p. 155, puts his arrival with his force at Lonigo as 'l'altr' ieri' before the news of the defeat came, which suggests about 22 December.

18 Sanuto, X, 235; cf. a pay parade for the light cavalry on 3 February 1510, see ibid., IX, 512.
19 For the reorganisation of mid January 1510 see Sanuto, IX, 456, 463, 466, 477; for the 'Standing Orders', only mentioned by Da Porto, see Da Porto, *Lettere storiche*, pp. 170-1.
20 Da Porto, *Lettere storiche*, pp. 169-72; ASV, 'Dispacci, Provv. Gen. Terraferma e Mar', filza 26, fol. 230v, and synopsis in Sanuto, IX, 449.
21 Mallett and Hale, *Military Organization*, pp. 71-2.
22 Da Porto, *Lettere storiche*, p. 193: 'alcuni piccoli schioppi, ch' io a Cividale avea fatto fare di tre spanne da portare legati alle coperte de' cavalli dinanzi agli arcioni, con i quali avvicinandosi alla squadra nemica senza che si accorgesse di schioppo alcuno, si potea tirando a tempo e luogo farle gran danno; perciocchè non ischioppi, ma più presto mazze di ferro parea che d'innanzi s'avesse legate . . .'; Da Porto went on to say that he had fifteen such. For similar 'disguised' carbines, presumably wheellock firearms, see J.F. Hayward, *The Art of the Gunmaker* (2nd ed., London, 1962), I (*1500-1600*), pp. 44-8, plates 4a, 4b, and H.W. Lewerken, *Kombinations Waffen des 15. -19. Jahrhunderts* (Berlin, 1989); I am indebted to Mr. C. Blair for this latter reference.
23 Da Porto, *Lettere storiche*, pp. 267-8.

Romeo'.[24] By April 1510 Da Porto had in his force Pietro d'Osmo of the Friuli, who was in the Venetian garrison at the abbey of Rosatto when it fell to imperial forces in July 1509.[25] Initial recruitment was the responsibility of the captain, just as he had to ensure his force remained at full strength.[26] On the evidence of the *Lettere storiche* Da Porto was enrolling men in early December. For this an agent with a tambourine might be sent round the towns and local communities. Venetian *capi di guerra*, as well as other captains, were likely to know of displaced men eager to serve.[27] Each man initially was expected to provide his horse, harness and weapons, while the captain had to ensure each man was capable and fit for service, just as he was responsible for the discipline of his force and for paying it.[28]

In the case of cavalry, Venetian officials with the army provided fodder-straw for the horses as well as wood and bedding-straw for the men.[29] The captain could obtain cloth in part-payment of his *condotta*, and this cloth could be distributed to troops in partial lieu of their monthly wage.[30] When billeted in Venetian territory troops were required to pay for what they took as food, but they were allowed to appropriate what provisions they could acquire from enemy territory.[31] Venetian provisioners sold food to the captain, who deducted a messing charge from his troop's pay.[32] There is evidence that, initially at least, Luigi was allocated monthly payments, at the end of each month's service; one can suppose that usually he received

---

24 [L. da Porto], *Hystoria novellamente ritrovata di due nobili amanti* (Venice, Benedetto Bendoni, n.d. [1530?]), fol. aiii; copy at shelf-number C.106.a.4, British Library, London, and shelf-number 17579, John Rylands University Library of Manchester.

25 Da Porto, *Lettere storiche*, p. 184.

26 For the initial muster and for periodic inspections by Venetian authorities see Mallett and Hale, *Military Organization*, pp. 117-21.

27 Da Porto, *Lettere storiche*, p. 153, claims that Luigi was an eye-witness of the execution of the four Paduan nobles in Venice, which was on 1 December, see Sanuto, IX, 359. Da Porto was in Venice on 28 and 29 November (see notes 8 and 9 above). One can suppose Luigi began recruiting while in Venice; his letter relating to the execution of the Paduans states: 'non fo altro che pormi in punto per andarmene in campo' (p. 148), which presumably referred to this. He claimed that his *condotta* was doubled on his posting to Friuli (see note 36 below) and in his *Lettere storiche*, pp. 176-7, falsely claimed that then: 'mi preparo all'andata; alla quale ora niun' altra cosa mi tarda, che il provvedere il numero di que' cavalli che mi venne accresciuto, cavalli ch' io spero più agevolmente di trovar in questo campo [Villanova] ed in questi paesi, che in Friuli, ch' è quasi fuori della conversazione degl' italiani soldati; ove pochi ne càpitano, se a bella posta non vi vanno.' It appears possible that Da Porto brought his force to the strength of fifty, as required, when he first arrived at Lonigo, towards the end of December, see note 17 above. For the use of the tambourine see Sanuto, XIII, 15, concerning Malfatto's recruitment of infantry: 'cussì il tamburlini andò atorno la terra suonando . . .'. For the Venetian authorities' awareness of men suitable for service see Mallett and Hale, *Military Organization*, pp. 145-6.

28 For initial provision of horse, harness and weapons see ibid., pp. 117-18, and cf. p. 143 for prisoners being dispoiled to necessitate their re-equipment and provide resources for the victors; for horses being replaced in certain circumstances, see pp. 138-40; for discipline, see pp. 121-2.

29 Ibid., pp. 136-7.

30 Ibid., pp. 127, 141.

31 Ibid., p. 140.

32 Ibid., p. 127.

them monthly – it could be advantageous, if the state was unsure of a captain's loyalty, to make him wait as long as possible for pay.[33] On 28 January 1510 Da Porto's pay was 216 ducats for the month. It is likely, though not certain, that most individuals of his force received the same basic wage, perhaps four ducats a month. On the Veronese front Luigi, as a captain, was directly under the command of the Venetian *provveditori generali*, and it was to them that he would have made any of the required administrative returns.[34] The *provveditori generali* communicated with the *Consiglio dei Dieci*, or war council, and only in very exceptional circumstances would a captain of Luigi's status have written direct to the authorities in Venice; no such letter is known.

On 16 February 1510 Luigi's uncle, Antonio Savorgnan, arrived in Venice from Udine for a long interview with the *Capi dei Dieci*. Antonio, who was consistently accused by the faction opposed to him in the Friuli of acting as though *signore* of Udine, held from the Venetian authorities the life-appointment as *colonello* of the *Adunanza* of Friuli, a part-time force of some 4,000 men. In Venice Savorgnan, who feared an imperial attack in the spring, sought urgent military reinforcements. It was agreed to send him Baldassare Scipione with his fifty light cavalry, and another force of like strength, whose captain is not now recorded in Venetian records.[35] Certainly the latter captain was Luigi da Porto, who in his *Lettere storiche* implied that Antonio had asked specifically for his nephew to be sent. This can be accepted, but Luigi also falsely indicated that on being posted to the Friuli his force was doubled.[36] What he did in his history was retime the

---

33 Ibid., pp. 127–8.
   The only known evidence for Da Porto is of the payment of 28 January 1510, for which see note 18 above.

34 For the 28 January 1510 payment to Da Porto see note 18 above. Mallett and Hale, *Military Organization*, p. 126, indicates that in the late fifteenth century pay for each *stradiotto* was indeed 4 ducats a month and two sacks of corn; for the *caposaldo* of a captain see p. 123; for Da Porto apparently directly under the *provveditori generali* see notes 16 and 40.

35 For Savorgnan's visit to Venice in February see Sanuto, IX, 537, which indicates Scipione 'et uno altro capi di balestrieri con . . . [sic]'. Da Porto, *Lettere storiche*, p. 188, put the early 1510 *Adunanza* at about 6,000; for Antonio Savorgnan's authority in the Friuli see ibid., pp. 188, 276–7. Liliana Cargnelutti, 'Antonio Savorgnan e l'insurrezione del 1511', in *I Savorgnan e la Patria del Friuli dal XIII al XVIII secolo* (Exhibition catalogue) (Udine, 1984), p. 121, indicates that Antonio succeeded his father Niccolò as *colonello* for life, and p. 122 puts the strength of the force at 2,000 to 4,000 men. The *Adunanza* was a semi-feudal force that gave power to its *colonello*. In 1510 the Venetian authorities had sought to form it into a force called the *Ordinanza marchesca*, on a footing with the *Ordinanza*, or *Cernide*, comprising the *provvisionati*, or territorials, raised elsewhere on the Terraferma, see Mallett and Hale, *Military Organization*, p. 352.

36 For Antonio's supposed specified request for Luigi see Da Porto, *Lettere storiche*, p. 196; for Luigi's claim that his force was doubled, p. 176 (which Bressan at note 1 wrongly indicated as giving Luigi command of 100 light horse), see the original *condotta* of 28 November, doubled to fifty the following day, indicated in notes 9 and 11. The payments to Luigi for his force were consistently for a maximum of 50 men, see also note 37.

initial doubling of his *condotta*, a circumstance not mentioned previously in his work. Payments allocated to him in April, as subsequently, mention him as captain of fifty *balestrieri*, as in the *condotta* of 29 November 1509.[37]

The date of Luigi's arrival in Cividale can be deduced as about 8 March 1510.[38] At first he was subordinate to Teodoro dal Borgo, whose *condotta* was for 100 light horse; hence the two captains together were responsible for a company of 150.[39] On 20 April Luigi had a long session with the *Collegio* in Venice, for unspecified reasons; the following September Da Porto went to Venice to petition the *Capi dei Dieci* that he be detached from the company and that he be given command directly under the *provveditore*, as had been the case when he was on the Veronese front. This request was granted.[40] In March 1511, after a year based at Cividale, Luigi was posted to the garrison town of Gradisca, which was very close to the imperial frontier.[41] On the afternoon of 20 June an imperial raiding party of light horse, returning with booty to its base at Cormons, was encountered by a Venetian force from Gradisca that included Luigi. In the ensuing fight Luigi was wounded by the point of a spear entering his neck and touching his spinal cord. Found lying on the ground by a medical doctor of Udine,

---

37 For April 1510, see note 34; for June, see Sanuto, X, 589; for 30 September 1510, see Sanuto, XI, 339 (duplicated at 474); under 31 July 1511 Luigi's force was indicated to be reduced in strength to 42, see Sanuto, 318.

38 Scipione reached Udine on 10 March 1510, when Luigi was already in Cividale, see Sanuto, X, 36, 37; Da Porto, *Lettere storiche*, p. 188, indicates that when Da Porto arrived the Venetian *provveditore generale* of the Friuli, Luigi Dolfin, and some infantry captains were at Cividale; these latter had arrived there by 4 March, when a faction fight broke out in Udine, see two letters of 5 March from Antonio Savorgnan in ASV, 'Lettere dei Consiglio dei Dieci, Capi di Guerra', busta 308. Hence Da Porto appears to have reached Cividale between 4 and 10 March. He may have travelled with his force from Villanova to Venice and there taken ship to Marano, thence by road to Cividale; this would have been quicker and easier for the horses than crossing the *Terraferma* by way of Treviso and Pordenone, cf. Da Porto, *Lettere storiche*, p. 178. For Luigi and Scipione engaged with the enemy on 16 March, see a dispatch of that date in Sanuto, X, 50.

39 In June 1510 the two captains and their forces were bracketed together in Sanuto, X, 589, and see note 40. For a company comprising some 100 to 130 men or so see the text above, p. 104.

40 For the visit on 20 April see Sanuto, X, 167; Da Porto may have protested then at being subordinate to Dal Borgo. Under 10 September 1510 Sanuto recorded Luigi attending the Senate in Venice: 'dicendo è fedelissimo et voria conducta per sè, per poter far facende et mostrar la fede et animo suo. Fu commesso a li savi di terra ferma', Sanuto, XI, 319. The implication is that Luigi was subject to Dal Borgo, who commanded 100 *balestrieri*, despite the latter being stationed in Gradisca and Luigi in Cividale, clearly an unsatisfactory arrangement. Brognoligo, *Studi* (cited in note 11), p. 12, seemingly misunderstood the situation, and thought that Luigi visited Venice in September to renew his *condotta*.

41 Da Porto, *Lettere storiche*, p. 237 alone specifies the posting from Cividale to Gradisca, without a verifiable date. On the evidence of a letter of 12 November 1510 Luigi was still at Cividale, see Sanuto, XI, 642-4, as he was in late February 1511 at the time of the disturbances in the Friuli, see below at note 62; in mid March he may have been summoned to Venice for the Inquiry regarding the disturbances, see note 63 below. At the end of March a German offensive directed at Gradisca was anticipated, see Sanuto, XII, 108, and Da Porto may have been posted to Gradisca in consequence; moreover, in view of the disturbances centred in Udine and rumours regarding Luigi's part (see the text at note 60) the Venetian authorities may have deemed his posting expedient. For the permanent garrison

Marco Lazara, presumably at the scene looking for custom, he was transported to Udine.[42] There, thanks to Dr Lazara's ministrations, Da Porto made a partial recovery, and though paralysed on his left side, eventually was able to hobble with the aid of a metal crutch.[43] The Venetian lieutenant general of the Friuli, while not present at Luigi's last military engagement, informed the Venetian government of Da Porto's serious injury in a dispatch, commending him as an effective and brave captain.[44]

On the evidence of Luigi's *Lettere storiche*, his attitude to fighting was consistently chivalric. He stated categorically that he preferred fighting a hundred against a hundred, for then individual prowess could be discerned.[45] He himself sought to fight where his actions could be witnessed by his superiors and by those in authority.[46] He expressed pleasure in seeing open combat between a few, where he himself could view skill and courage, and he praised for these qualities friend and foe alike.[47] He admired the French men-at-arms on the Verona front, one of whom verbally sought man-to-man combat with a similarly armed enemy. He deemed this voluntary combat in cold blood of higher courage than that required to advance in mass into battle when ordered.[48] Such sentiments are reminiscent of the Marquis Ludovico Gonzaga of Mantua, who took inspiration from the romances of Arthur: there is testimony in Gonzaga's authentic letter of 1453 addressed to his wife, where the issue was struggle to the death

---

in Gradisca see Mallett and Hale, *Military Organization*, pp. 134-5.

42 Da Porto, *Lettere storiche*, pp. 245-6. Brognoligo, *Studi di storia letteraria*, pp. 46-7, calculated the date of the engagement as 18 June; Girolamo da Porto (see note 10 above) as 'XI Cal. Luglio', on the basis of the biographical note attributed to Bembo, see note 11 above. The evidence of the authentic letters cited in note 44 below is that the engagement took place on 21 June 1511.

43 A now lost document written within a decade of Luigi being wounded recorded: 'Alvise da Porto de lo anno 1511 era capitanio de cavalli legieri de questa Ill [ustrissi] ma Signoria, et fu mandato in Friuli . . . combatendo da valente homo. Hebe da inimici molte ferite, et fu lassato per morto, et restato tuto strupiato che apena puote andar cum una ferla et de presenti qui in Venetia. Et ogni dì è in corte de palazzo, et tutti puono sapere, et vedere, et che modo fuse trattato et sia condicionato, per la sua fidelitate et servitù.' This document is in Eugenio Masucci, 'Luigi da Porto' (Tesi di laurea, 1926, la Segreteria, Università degli Studi, Rome), p. 1. Masucci stated that it was 'contrassegnato dal numero 14, esistente nell'Archivio Porto-Colleoni a Thiene (secondo communicate e trascrizione favorita di là dal Sig. D. Rizieri Zanocca, archivista)'. In 1958 I was unable to trace this document when I was permitted access to the Archivio in the Castello di Thiene. It is to be noted that G. Marzari, *La historia di Vicenza* (Venice, G. Angelieri, 1591, colophon date 1590), p. 159 indicates Luigi was 'ferito di una lanzata, rimase della manca parte storpiato a fatto . . .'

44 Dispatch dated 21 June 1511 from Luigi Gradenigo, Lieutenant General of the Friuli, paraphrase in Sanuto, XII, 255; cf. letter dated 22 June from Antonio Savorgnan, in full, in ibid., 261, referring to Luigi's part: 'Lo magnifico proveditor fece da uno heroe; certo è homo che vale'; letter dated 23 June from Baldassare Scipione, paraphrase in ibid., 256.

45 Da Porto, *Lettere storiche*, p. 214.
46 Ibid., p. 194.
47 For open combat, ibid., pp. 164-5; for praise of friend and foe, p. 182.
48 Ibid., pp. 164, 173-5.

with his brother Carlo for control of the state. The marquis' letter gives emphasis to the glorious battle that he watched from a hill-top.[49] Seventy years on Castiglione's *Book of the Courtier* sought to instil much the same chivalric ideals.[50] Seemingly Da Porto did not know French, but one can assume that he was steeped in those Italian versions of French romances that were popular in the *Quattrocento* at the courts on the Italian peninsula, and which had inspired Castiglione no less than the Marquis Ludovico.[51] Certainly Luigi judged the man-at-arms of the French heavy cavalry as the flower of chivalry.[52] Chaumont's debauchery in his quarters on the Ferrarese front during the spring of 1510 was strongly condemned by Da Porto, not least since it failed to accord with the highest standard of chivalry that he expected from the French.[53]

Da Porto claimed in his *Lettere storiche* that he much regretted being posted to the Friuli. It was on the Veronese front that the French were fighting, and one can speculate that he had specifically sought to be sent there on first obtaining his *condotta*.[54] Moreover the political situation in Udine was to result in his name becoming besmirched, with rumours circulating that he was a foul murderer; his uncle Antonio certainly became a traitor to Venice, and delivered most of the province of Friuli to the imperial forces.[55] Most likely one of Luigi's motives in writing his history was to dissociate himself from his uncle's actions of 1511. The letter-form, with its apparent spontaneity, was the best possible means for asserting Luigi's innocence, as it appeared to preclude hindsight and special pleading.

The Venetian Republic became mistress of the Friuli in 1420 through the support of Tristano, head of the Savorgnan family. By the time of Luigi's

---

49 C.H. Clough, 'Chivalry and Magnificence in the Golden Age of the Italian Renaissance', in *Chivalry in the Renaissance*, ed., S. Anglo (Woodbridge, 1990), pp. 41-2, and the sources cited there.

50 B. Castiglione, *Il Libro del Cortegiano* (Venice, 'Nelle case d'Aldo Romano e d'Andrea d'Asola', 1528); work on it matured over a decade at least from sometime before 1514, see C.H. Clough, 'Francis I and the Courtiers of Castiglione's *Courtier*', in Clough, *The Duchy of Urbino in the Renaissance*, item XVI, pp. 24-6. Castiglione's stress was on fighting in public spectacles, see B. Castiglione, *Il Libro del cortegiano*, ed. B. Maier (3rd ed. rev., Turin, 1981), see pp. 112-4, I, xvii; 119, I, xxi-xxii. Cf. J.R. Hale, 'Castiglione's Military Career', in *Italian Studies*, XXXVI (1981), pp. 54-7.

51 Da Porto, *Lettere storiche*, p. 173, mentioned a Frenchman as speaking to him in Latin, the implication being that if Da Porto had known French the conversation would have been in that language. For romance literature in the Italian courts see the admirable survey in Joanna Woods-Marsden, *The Gonzaga of Mantua and Pisanello's Arthurian Frescoes* (Princeton, NJ, 1988), pp. 22-6.

52 Da Porto, *Lettere storiche*, p. 173; the same is implied by Castiglione, ed. cited in note 50, pp. 121, I, xxii, 161-3, I, xlii.

53 Da Porto, *Lettere storiche*, pp. 206-7.

54 For Da Porto's regret at his posting to the Friuli because he preferred the nature of the fighting on the Veronese front see ibid., pp. 176-7, 196; at the first of these references Da Porto also remarked on the debilitating consequence of being garrisoned, for which cf. Mallett and Hale, *Military Organization*, pp. 135-6.

55 See below at notes 60 and 64.

posting to Cividale the family was divided into two main rival branches: that headed by Luigi's uncle, Antonio, which was known as Della Torre; and that headed by Girolamo, known as Del Monte. Antonio's father, Niccolò, was the son of Urbano, whose father was Tristano. Girolamo was of the cadet branch, being the son of Tristano's youngest son, Pagano.[56] In the second half of the fifteenth century Niccolò, backed by Venice, had established the dominance of his branch when he became *colonello* of the *Adunanza* of the Friuli, an office that passed on his death to Antonio.[57] As already mentioned, Antonio had become virtually *signore* of Udine. His ascendancy was viewed with suspicion and jealousy by the Del Monte branch of the Savorgnan. There is a further complication exacerbated by party names. Antonio had built up for his support a party, or faction, that of the *Zambarlani*, consisting of pro-Venetian nobility and the *popolo minuto* of Udine, as well as the *contadini* of the province. An opposed faction had developed known as the *Strumieri*, or *Torriani* (nothing to do with the Della Torre branch of the Savorgnan, but so-called because they held *torri*, or castles). This party, often referred to as that of the *Castellani*, comprised the old nobility of the Friuli, and most of the noble families of Udine itself, including the Della Torre family.[58] In disputes Girolamo Savorgnan, whose first wife had been a Della Torre, tended to favour the *Strumieri*, above all because of his hatred of Antonio; however sometimes he appears to have dissociated himself from both factions, probably in a bid to win favour with Venice — his last three wives were of the Venetian patriciate.[59]

Da Porto's posting to the Friuli at his uncle's behest inevitably linked him to his uncle's party. Cergnocco, a virulent Udinese partisan of the *Strumieri*,

---

56 Liliana Cargnelutti, 'Tristano Savorgnan (1377-1440) nella crisi del Patriarcato', in *I Savorgnan e la Patria del Friuli*, cited in note 35, pp. 113-8, and the sources cited there, for the importance of Tristano and his part in ensuring that the Friuli passed under Venetian control. Marco Barbaro 'Arbori di patrizi veneti' ASV, MS 3002 (6 volumes), VI, fol. 581 (for Savorgnan); 'Genealogia [della famiglia Savorgnan]', with notarial documents cited in testimony, ASUd, Archivio Savorgnan, MS 2382, busta 89, fols. 181-99.

57 See note 35 above.

58 Cargnelutti, 'Antonio Savorgnan e l'insurrezione del 1511', p. 121; for Antonio's authority see also note 35 above. There has now appeared E. Muir, *Mad Blood Stirring: Vendetta and Factions in the Friuli during the Renaissance* (Baltimore, 1993), which focuses on such rivalry.

59 Animosity that amounted to hatred existed between Antonio and Girolamo Savorgnan; for example, on 25 June 1510 the latter wrote to Doge Loredan: 'Questo avversario mio, dico Messer Antonio Savorgnan, il quale sempre veglia alla ruina mia; e sa Vostra Serenità, quanta riputazione Ella vuole che egli abbia ed in questa patria ha gran mezzi per li quali è atto a turbare ogni buona impresa. E se al tempo del fatto primo di Cadore [1508], che gli teneva inimicizia ed odio suo occulto, operò sì che la caccia mia, le mie fatiche ed i disagi miei mi furono rotti e tolti di mano; è da pensare che ora che egli mostra gli odii palesi contro di me, sia per fare peggio assai . . . ', see G. Savorgnan, *Lettere storiche dall'anno 1508 al 1528*, ed. V. Joppi (Udine, 1896), pp. 11-12, letter no. VI. Girolamo's wives were: Maddalena Della Torre (married 13 July 1491, died 1495); Felicità Tron, widow of Mattia Tiepolo (married 1496, died 1501); Bianca Malipiero, widow of Marco Tiepolo (married 1502, died 1507); Orsina Canal, widow of Marcantonio Marcello (married 1508, died 1556).

writing some twenty years after the event, stated that Luigi's serious wound was divine retribution for his part in the faction fighting in Udine on the day of the Carnival, *la zobbia grassa*, 27 February 1511. What Cergnocco echoed was the rumour that Luigi with his light cavalry had approached Udine feigning to be imperial attackers, thereby providing his uncle Antonio with the excuse to arm his followers, who were then turned against the *Strumieri*. Cergnocco claimed that Luigi himself actively participated in the slaughter, throwing his victims' bodies down a well.[60] Certainly a very serious faction fight occurred in Udine, with individuals killed, property looted and destroyed, and rioting quickly spread to the countryside.[61] Luigi does not appear to have been engaged in it, though it is possible that he was called upon by the Venetian Lieutenant to assist in ending the disorder.[62] The following month, when a court of inquiry into the disturbance was held in Venice, Da Porto perhaps may have been summoned as a witness. At this inquiry Antonio's conduct was investigated and he was exonerated; as far as is known Da Porto was not the subject of the inquiry.[63] Yet in the summer

60 G.B. Cergnocco (or Cergneu), *Cronaca delle guerre dei Friuliani contro i Germani dal 1507 al 1524* (Udine, 1895), p. 49, and also Gregorio Amaseo, 'Historia della crudel zobbia grassa', in L. and G. Amaseo and G.A. Azio, *Diarii udinesi dall'anno 1508 al 1541*, ed. A. Ceruti (Venice, 1884), pp. 507, 518-19; the latter was clearly the source for P. degli Olivi, *Historie del Friuli* (Udine, 1660), p. 105.

61 The fighting in the Friuli in 1509 had stimulated factional divisions, and in December Antonio claimed that it was necessary in consequence to keep the *Adunanza* on stand-by. As a result of this the *Castellani* summoned their partisans to Udine (cf. Sanuto, IX, 554). The following March 1510 fighting between the two factions broke out in Udine (see note 38 above), and the Venetian government ordered an inquiry. Representatives of both factions were summoned to Venice and a reconciliation agreed, see letters of A. Giustinian dated 3, 4, 9, 11, March, and one of Antonio Savorgnan, 5 March, 1510, in ASV, 'Lettere del Consiglio dei Dieci, Capi di Guerra', busta 308, for which see also G. Baldissera, *Il contegno del famigerato Antonio Savorgnan all'espugnazione de' castelli di Vilpulzano e S. Martino di Quisca nel 1510 (Per Nozze Del Bianco-Nussi)* (Venice, 1513); a copy is in the Biblioteca Comunale, Udine, shelfnumber: Miscell. 1130.8. The situation deteriorated until there was the serious disturbance of late February 1511. For this latter see Da Porto, *Lettere storiche*, pp. 276-81; the most coherent contemporary account, in part eye-witness, is the letter of Antonio Badoer to his father, dated from Udine 28 February 1511, in Sanuto, XII, 17-19; see also his letter of 2 March in ibid., XII, 26. For rioting in the countryside see Laura Casella, 'I Savorgnan, o delle piccole corti', in *'Familia' del principe e famiglia aristocratica*, ed. C. Mozzarelli (2 vols., Rome, 1988), II, pp. 395-6, and the sources cited there.

62 It is possible that Luigi was at the dance given by Maria Savorgnan on the evening of 26 February, see note 92 below; in such circumstances it is entirely unlikely that he would have had his force of light horse with him. The lieutenant general of the Friuli on the night of 27 February wrote to Gradisca (not Cividale, where Luigi was stationed) for help to quell the disturbance; Amaseo, mentioned Da Porto's presence with his force in his 'Historia della crudel zobbia grassa', cited in note 60 above. Luigi indicates in his *Lettere storiche*, cited in note 61, that he was an eye-witness of some of the disturbance; he may have arrived on 27 February, called from Cividale, but been unable to deal with the deteriorating situation, and hence the lieutenant turned to Gradisca for more assistance. My supposition is that Luigi and his force arrived at Udine from Cividale because he had been ordered to do so by the Venetian authorities.

Antonio Belloni, a notary of Udine, who was in the city at the time of the disturbances and wrote an account shortly afterwards as 'De clade Turriana', ASUd, MS in busta 5448, and see Biblioteca Comunale, Udine, MSS 561 and 690; this work does not mention Da Porto.

63 For the trial see in the ASV, 'Consiglio dei

of 1511 Antonio secretly negotiated with imperial authorities, coming to terms with them in September.⁶⁴ According to Luigi's *Lettere storiche*, his uncle was driven to treachery because he feared his enemies in the Friuli – one can suppose Girolamo above all – and those among the Venetian patriciate who were intent on his downfall, and who were seeking what amounted to his retrial.⁶⁵ It seems to me possible that the Venetians, who promoted a 'divide and rule' policy on the *Terraferma*, as Machiavelli remarked in his *Prince*, believed that Antonio was too powerful in the Friuli, hence a threat to their authority, and were indeed plotting his downfall.⁶⁶ The consequence was that Girolamo and the Del Monte branch came to the fore; Girolamo acquired much of the property, many of the privileges, as well as some of the authority with the *Zambarlani* faction, that Antonio had enjoyed.⁶⁷ These circumstances were to have an important consequence for Luigi, as hinted in his *Giulietta e Romeo*, and it is the story behind this famous *novella* that I now wish to examine.

Dieci, Criminali', reg. 1, fols. 168v (for which see also note 96 below), 172v, 179, 185; reg. 2, fols. 16, 36, 37, 52v; 'Consiglio dei Dieci, Misti', reg. 35, fols. 31v, 70, 80-v; 'Capi del Consiglio dei Dieci: Lettere dei rettori', busta 169 (Udine), fols. 78, 80, 81, 96, 102, 104. Some of the above documents are partially printed in P. de Musset, 'Recherches sur le Conseil des Dix', in *Revue de Paris*, n.s., V (1848), p. 164, but with errors regarding the background circumstances.

64 Da Porto, *Lettere storiche*, pp. 280-2. On 3 August 1511 an imperial offensive began on the Veronese front and, after the fall of Vicenza, thrusts were made at Treviso and Padua. Since both these cities were heavily defended the imperial army moved on 12 September towards the Piave. By 8 September Antonio Savorgnan with a force of the *Adunanza* reached Sacile, see Sanuto, XII, 488. The imperial army advanced, taking Oderzo on 14 September, see Sanuto, XII, 527. Sacile was abandoned on 16 September, a withdrawal that Savorgnan justified, stating to the Venetian authorities that he had no regular troops and no artillery in the face of a considerable imperial force, see XII, 530, 535-6. Savorgnan appears to have decided to come to terms with the enemy on 18 September, and he agreed them the following day, see Sanuto, XII, 544, and the letter of Girolamo Savorgnan, dated 19 September 1511, cited in note 93 below; see also the imperial decree, dated 15 October 1511, cited in ibid.

65 Da Porto, *Lettere storiche*, pp. 280-1. On 30 May 1511 the *Consiglio dei Dieci* concluded that various individuals, including some of Antonio Savorgnan's servants, were to be arrested for their part in the disturbances, see ASV, 'Consiglio dei Dieci, Criminali', reg. 1, fol. 168v; some were arrested, taken to prison and eventually executed, see the editor's note in Amaseo, *Diarii udinesi* p. 531 n.1. On 21 June a letter sent from the Venetian government to the Lieutenant of the Friuli ordered him to warn Savorgnan 'di continuare nella via intrapresa di non favorire nessun partito, ma piutosto di procurare che cessino le novità . . .', see P. Antonini, *I baroni di Walsee* (Florence, 1877), pp. 84-8. It is highly likely that a body of Venetian patricians was eager to see Antonio's downfall, including those of the patriciate associated with Girolamo Savorgnan through marriages. It is evident, too, that after the disturbances of March 1510 in Udine (see note 38 above) the Venetians were guilty of duplicity in their treatment of Antonio, and he became aware of this.

66 N. Machiavelli, *Il principe*, chap. XX, cf. ed. and trans. of Q. Skinner and Russell Price (Cambridge, 1988), p. 72.

67 Cf. F. Nani Mocenigo, 'Girolamo Savorgnan', in *Ateneo veneto*, XXVII (1904), pp. 17-25. Even so the Venetian government was concerned that Girolamo should not become too powerful. On 3 November 1511 the newly elected *provveditore generale* in the Friuli was cautioned by the *Consiglio dei Dieci*: 'Sopra tuto advertirete de non sublevar né far capo o superior, né el dito Hieronymo Savorgnan, né alcun altro de loro: ma tenerli tuti equali, et sotto la debita regola et obedientia verso la Signoria nostra, per non incorrer neli errori preteriti: che el tropo auctorizar et favorir Antonio Savorgnan ha producti mille mali et inconvenienti, sì come la experientia molte volte, et maxime ultimamente, ha

The literary sources for the *novella* have been identified as including Ovid's *Metamorphoses* and *Art of Love*, as well as the twelfth-century 'Piramus et Tisbé' most likely in a version in Latin or Italian, Dante's *Divine Comedy*, early commentators on this latter, Boccaccio's writings, the *Refugio de' miseri*, *Lionora e Ippolito*, and the *novella* of *Giannozza e Mariotto* by Tomaso Guardati, better known as Masuccio of Salerno.[68] Yet what inspired Da Porto to write has received little attention, despite the work's dedication to Lucina Savorgnan, and the *novella's* concluding harsh remarks that compared unfavourably the women of his day with Giulietta's love, faithful unto death. The issue should be examined on the basis of a text that reliably reflects the author's intentions, and to anticipate my conclusion the one printed by Marcolini of Venice in 1539 is not that.[69] The Marcolini version appears to have been edited by Pietro Bembo for publication, probably at the behest of Bernardino da Porto, Luigi's younger brother, who had inherited Luigi's literary papers with the rest of the latter's estate. Significantly Bembo omitted the concluding remarks on women in his – the second – edition.[70] The first edition was printed by Benedetto Bendoni of Venice, almost certainly without authorisation by Bernardino da Porto, as one can conclude from the absence of the author's name. On the basis of existing evidence this first edition, which bears no date, was printed late in

dimostrato', quoted in Casella, 'I Savorgnan', cited in note 61, p. 396. Cf. also ASV, 'Indice 140: Feudi', for privileges and investitures conceded to Girolamo Savorgnan from 22 September 1511.

68 For Ovid see O.H. Moore, *The Legend of Romeo and Juliet* (Columbus, Ohio, 1950), pp. 48-57, note 86 below, and A.H. Diverres, 'The Pyramus and Thisbe Story and its Contribution to the Romeo and Juliet Legend', in *The Classical Tradition in French Literature: Essays Presented to R.C. Knight*, ed. H.T. Barnwell, A.H. Diverres, G.F. Evans, F.W.A. George and Vivienne Mylne (London, 1977), pp. 9-22; for Dante and his commentators see Moore, *Legend of Romeo and Juliet*, pp. 13-20; for Boccaccio's writings, notably *Il filostrato* and *Il filocolo*, but with echoes from *Il decamerone*, see ibid., pp. 21-7 and R.A. Saner, 'Da Porto, Boccaccio and the Romeo Legend', in *Romance Notes*, VII, ii (1968), pp. 1-5 of the offprint; for *Il refugio*, see G.H. Bumgardner, intro. to *Novelle cinque: Tales from the Veneto* (Barre, MA, 1974), pp. 22-8, where the link between 'Giulia e Pruneo' and Luigi's title is noted (p. 23); for Masuccio see Moore, *Legend of Romeo and Juliet*, pp. 35-48.

69 Two copies are in the British Library, London, shelfnumbers G.10638 and 241.d.13; a copy is in the John Rylands University Library of Manchester. For this edition see S. Casali, *Gli annali della tipografia veneziana di Francesco Marcolini*, ed. A. Gerace (Bologna, 1953), pp. 94-9.

70 A. Torri, *Giulietta e Romeo: novella storica di Luigi da Porto di Vicenza* (Pisa, 1831), pp. 16-48, indicates the major Marcolini (1539) variants at the foot of each page of Bendoni's text [1530?], and see p. 46 for the omission of the concluding paragraph by Marcolini. From ibid., pp. 49-52, the linguistic variants are discernible. In 1753 Giuseppe Gennari had made the case for Bembo being responsible for the variants in the 1539 edition, ibid., pp. 52-3 (where Gennari's case is reprinted). Certainly the linguistic changes conform to Bembo's *Prose della volgar lingua* (Padua, 1525), while Marcolini dedicated the work to Bembo (reprinted by Torri, p. 53), which suggests that the printer was indebted to Bembo for the text. In 1529 Bernardino had inherited the estate of his brother, Luigi, see B. Morsolin, 'Luigi da Porto, storico della Lega di Cambrai e autore della Giulietta e Romeo: appunti e rettificazioni', in *Archivio veneto*, XXXVII (1889), pp. 118-19 for Luigi's will, dated 9 May 1529. Torri, *Giulietta e Romeo*, p. 49, argued that the textual variants were the work of Bernardino, but since the latter surrendered his brother's literary papers to Bembo in 1531 (see note 73 below), a circumstance

1530.[71] Five years later Bendoni issued a reprint, with some of the original printing's typographical errors corrected, and the author's name provided. This revised first edition has the colophon date of '10 June 1535'.[72] Which of these two editions is that most faithful to Luigi's intentions, that edited by his friend Bembo, or that apparently published clandestinely?

To help resolve this problem it is necessary to examine Luigi's literary activity, and the vicissitudes of his literary manuscripts. From Bembo's letter-collection it is known that on 18 February 1531 he wrote to Bernardino about Luigi's literary papers, which he believed Bernardino had given him permission to study at his Paduan *palazzo*. He bemoaned the fact that the material had not been consigned to his relative, Agostino Angiolello, then residing in Vicenza, who had gone to collect these papers.[73] In September 1530 Bembo had been appointed official historian of Venice, and one work he sought to read in this capacity was Da Porto's 'Lettere storiche', which existed only in manuscript, probably at that time in a unique fair copy.[74] Since Bembo did incorporate passages from Da Porto's work in his *Historia Viniziana*, as printed in 1552, one can assume that Bernardino eventually did consign the 'Lettere storiche' to him.[75] Bembo appears to have retained the manuscript of this history, as all the late

unknown to Torri, I find this supposition unacceptable.

71 Benedetto Bendoni was printing in Venice on his own account from at least 1532 to 1541, see Ester Pastorello, *Tipografi, editori, librai a Venezia nel secolo XVI* (Florence, 1924), p. 10; he had begun printing about 1524 in association with his brother Agostino, but may have printed on his own at least from 1530. The dated printing of 1535 (see note 72) is subsequent to the undated one on the evidence of the corrections to the typographical errors, and the addition of the author's name; cf. Torri, 'Catalogo bibliografico', in his *Giulietta e Romeo*, p. I. Note that A. Torri, *Bibliografia della novella di Giulietta e Romeo di Luigi da Porto* (Florence, 1961) is merely a reprint of Torri's 'Catalogo bibliografico', and since essential cross-references are not included, the text does not always make sense. The 1535 Bendoni printing has the same type as that in use in 1524 and the colophon device of that year and subsequently; both its type and device are like those of the undated printing, attributed to 1530? There is no evidence that Bendoni had a licence to print, which may support the supposition that publication was not authorised by Luigi's heir. What substantiates the date of 1530? is the evident interest in the *Giulietta* on Landi's part by early March 1531; this may suggest that he had seen in circulation the printed text, which is to be associated with Bendoni's first printing (see the text at note 79 below).

72 A copy is in the British Library, London, shelf-number G.9882; cf. Torri, 'Catalogo bibliografico', p. II.

73 P. Bembo, *Delle lettere* (Venice, Gualtiero Scoto, 1552), III, pp. 231-2, for the letter of 18 February 1531; for Bembo referring to Angiolello as *cugino*, see ibid., p. 60. Angiolello was in Vicenza *c.* 13 February 1529, probably in residence there, see C.H. Clough, 'A Portion of Pietro Bembo's "Epistolario"', in *Bodleian Library Record*, VIII, i (1967), p. 34.

74 C.H. Clough, 'Le "Lettere Storiche" fonte della *Historia Viniziana* di Pietro Bembo' in *Archivio veneto*, series v, LXXIII (1963), pp. 5-15. For the manuscript tradition see Clough, 'Lettere storiche', I, chapter I, pp. viii-xviii, chapter III, pp. xlviii-lxviii.

75 Clough, 'Lettere storiche', cited in note 74. In a letter to Bernardino da Porto dated 31 December 1532, Bembo mentioned his indebtedness, which may refer to Bernardino having consigned to him Luigi's literary papers, see Bembo, *Delle lettere*, III, p. 232.

sixteenth-century transcripts are to be linked to copies originating in Bembo's library. Bembo appears to have recovered at least four original letters which previously he had sent to Luigi; perhaps they too were sent with Luigi's literary papers.[76] Thirdly, as already mentioned, it seems that Bembo edited for publication Da Porto's 'Giulietta e Romeo', and it is likely that he had received from Bernardino Da Porto's own copy of this work. One can postulate that Bembo made his corrections directly on this copy which was destroyed as printer's copy after its printing by Marcolini. In any event the original manuscript is not known, and appears not to have been transcribed in Bembo's library, as was the case with the 'Lettere storiche'. Marcolini's edition of 1539 included a selection of Da Porto's poetry, which presumably also was with the literary papers that Bembo received.

Early in 1531 the literary world of northern Italy was showing interest in Da Porto's 'Giulietta', and hence probably Bembo had sought this *novella* when he wrote to Bernardino on 18 February. The following 13 March Bembo replied to a now lost letter from Count Marc' Antonio Landi stating that neither he, nor his secretary Cola Bruno, had the 'Giulietta'.[77] From Bembo's reply to Landi one can deduce that the latter was eager to trace Luigi's text, and supposed Bembo to have the manuscript. Landi's interest may have been sparked because Bendoni's edition was already circulating, though alternatively he may merely have anticipated that Bembo had received Luigi's literary papers from Bernardino da Porto.[78] A possibility associated with either of these suppositions is that Landi had knowledge of

---

76 For the manuscript of the 'Lettere storiche' see Clough, cited in note 74. The four original letters sent from Bembo to Luigi are of: 25 May 1506, Vatican Library, MS Chigiano L.VIII.304, fol. 1; 15 December 1506, Vatican Library, MS Barb. lat. 5692, fols. 74-75v; 11 September 1525, Vatican Library, MS Chigiano L.VIII, 304, fol. 8; 11 July 1528, ibid., fol. 16. Both MSS consist of original letters written by Bembo and collected together by his literary executor, Carlo Gualteruzzi. While it is possible that the latter recovered them from Bernardino only after Bembo's death in 1547, it remains more likely that they were among Da Porto's literary papers that were consigned to Bembo about 1531.

77 Original letter sent in ASPar, 'Epistolario scelto', busta 2 (BA-BEN), lettera n.3, printed from this by A. Ronchini, *Lettere d'uomini illustri conservate in Parma* (Parma, 1853), I (all printed), pp. 21-2. The letter ends: 'State sano. La Gilietta [sic] io non ho, né credo M[esser] Cola l'habbia.' It appears Count Marc' Antonio died at about the very time the letter was written, and the *Giulietta* is not mentioned in the subsequent existing correspondence to his wife, Costanza, and to his son, Agostino, who was Bembo's godson, see also note 78 below.

78 For the likely date of the publication of Bendoni's first printing of the *Giulietta* see note 71. In about 1510 Costanza Fregoso, niece of Duke Guidobaldo da Montefeltro, married Landi, and their first child, Agostino, was born about 1511. Bembo promoted Agostino's studies and remained in contact with Agostino's parents, see V. Cian, 'Dizionarietto biografico' to his ed. of B. Castiglione, *Il libro del cortegiano* (4th edition, Florence, 1947), p. 513. In various letters of 1528-9 Cola Bruno kept Marc' Antonio Landi informed regarding Luigi da Porto, see Ronchini, *Lettere d'uomini illustri*, pp. 22-8. Bembo himself wrote to Landi with the news of Luigi's death.

the work from it having been sent previously to Bembo, for comment, by the author. That Da Porto had sent some of his literary work to Bembo for his criticism is evident from the latter's letter to Luigi of 9 June 1524.[79] It has been assumed that the unspecified work mentioned in the letter of that date was the 'Giulietta', and the other work, likewise unspecified, mentioned flatteringly was perhaps his 'Lettere storiche'.[80] However Giacomo Marzari, a notary of Vicenza, who appears to have owned a transcript of the 'Lettere storiche' which was made while the original was in the library of Bembo in Padua in the late *Cinquecento*, seems to have been aware of an accumulation of Luigi's literary papers, almost certainly in the Bembo library, which included poetry as well as some *novelle* written in the style of Boccaccio.[81] I believe a *novella* other than the 'Giulietta' can be identified as Luigi's, as will be considered shortly.[82] In these circumstances Bembo's letter of 9 June 1524 may not refer to the 'Giulietta' nor imply that it had but recently been completed, as hitherto has been accepted. I suggest that the 'Giulietta' was written for the wedding in 1517 of Lucina Savorgnan, to whom the work was dedicated.[83] Moreover it is likely that Da Porto circulated in manuscript his 'Giulietta' for, as has been seen, it was known to Bembo before he received Luigi's literary papers, and apparently was known also to his secretary. Hence there are at least two possible sources for the copy utilised by Bendoni for his printing of the first edition of late 1530. It could have been from the dedication copy presented to Lucina or, more likely, from a transcript made when Da Porto was circulating the text to critics. Two sixteenth-century manuscripts of the 'Giulietta' are extant, each independent of the other and both closely corresponding to Bendoni's printed text but not deriving from it.[84]

Points of importance for the present essay that result from a reconstruction of the lost original based on the early manuscript tradition and Bendoni's revised printing of 1535 are: first, the language and the style of writing are in accord with Da Porto's 'Lettere storiche'; secondly, in the edition of Marcolini the revealing autobiographical allusions in the dedication to Lucina have been somewhat modified, and the concluding personal

---

79 Bembo, *Delle lettere*, III, p. 123.
80 This has been accepted since G. Milan-Massari, *Notizie intorno alla vita e agli scritti di Luigi da Porto (Per Nozze Da Porto)* (Padua, 1830), p. 22: 'la qual novella, per quanto ci fa conoscere una lettera del Bembo [9 giugno 1524], compose egli nel 1524, e . . . offerse in dono alla . . . Lucina.'
81 Marzari, *La historia di Vicenza*, pp. 158-9. A transcript now lost of Da Porto's 'Lettere storiche' existed in the late sixteenth century, and the hypothesis is that it belonged to Marzari, see Clough, 'Lettere storiche', cited in note 74.
82 See the text below at note 107.
83 For her wedding in 1517 see note 101 below.
84 I have for publication an edition of the 'Giulietta' on the basis of the two early manuscript copies and Bendoni's printings; I remain much indebted to Professor Velli for bringing the manuscripts to my attention many years ago.

comments on women entirely removed.[85] The opening words of the dedication make it clear that Lucina was to receive the presentation copy, and it follows that the work was intended by Da Porto to have a particular significance for her. Autobiographical details in the dedication confirm that Da Porto was the author – this despite the anonymity of the first Bendoni printing. Interestingly the two early manuscript copies are not only without a title but lack the author's name, which explains why they have remained unknown.

In the dedication Lucina was told:[86]

> And I address it to you in order that . . . you in reading it may see more clearly to what risk, to what rash steps, to what a very cruel death poor unhappy lovers are very often led by love . . . and having decided that this will be my last *novella*, I send it to you . . . so that my foolish romanticising may end with you. And as you are a worthy harbour of beauty, and gracefulness, be such too, I beg, to the little boat of my genius (which, loaded with much ignorance, impelled by love, has run across the less-deep sea of poetry) that on reaching you, perceiving its great mistake, may surrender helm, oars and sails to others, who with more skill and a brighter star sail the same sea of poetry, and may thus unimpeded make itself fast safely to your shore. Therefore accept it, my lady, decked out as it is, and read it readily, both for its subject which seems to me very beautiful and moving, as for the close bonds of relationship and sweet friendship that exist between yourself and the person who wrote it: who always, and with all reverence, commends himself to you.

Both the syntax and the metaphor render this passage somewhat obscure, perhaps by design. The opening sentence (likewise echoed at the commencement of the *novella* itself) presents the medieval image of the prison of

---

85 For the modification to the dedication see note 86 below; for the concluding paragraph regarding the fickleness of women see note 70 above.

86 Bendoni printings [1530?], cited in note 24, fol. aii-aii verso. The allusion to a boat reaching harbour in this context could have sexual implications, cf. Masuccio, *novella* XXX, which relates how a young man found the 'vaga damigella di soavi odori ripiena con le braccia aperte e con gran festa il ricevette, e dapoi infiniti baci dati e ricevuti al signore, montati in barca, racconciato il timone, e fatta vela, ancora che nell'arte marinaresca non fosse molto esperta, pur quanto dal tempo loro fu concesso per lo mare d'amore nivigaro; e al debito termine al porto con piacere condotti . . . '; see Masuccio Salernitano, *Il novellino*, ed. L. Settembrini (Naples, 1874), p. 330. Hence the dedication letter of Luigi may be alluding to him having had sexual relations with the dedicatee, Lucina. This passage was somewhat modified in the Marcolini edition, see Torri, *Giulietta e Romeo*, p. 18.

The sexual connotation derives from Ovid's *Art of Love*, cf. from the Italian trans., Publio Ovidio Nasone, *L'Arte d'Amore*, ed. E. Barelli (Milan, 1982), Lib. I, p. 43 line 4, p. 45 lines 74-7, p. 62 lines 611-4, p. 75 line 1101, p. 76 concluding three lines; Lib. II, p. 77 lines 13-5, p. 91 lines 503-7, p. 143 lines 117-9. The issue is complicated in that the imagery is also in Petrarch's poetry as echoed by Da Porto, cf. L. da Porto, *Rime*, ed. G. Gorni and Giovanna Brianti (Vicenza, 1983), p. 5, Sonnet V, and see the note at pp. 48-9.

love, and appears to derive from 'Piramus et Tisbé.' Leaving that aside, though, at the most obvious level it appears as though Da Porto, the author, in accordance with the convention of his day, was depreciating his work as inadequate. There seems also to be a meaning that was hidden save to those who could read it. The passage suggests that Da Porto was impelled by love to write the story and to send it to Lucina. That the *novella* was a pastiche of classical and near-contemporary literary works in no way precludes this supposition. Moreover Da Porto told Lucina that this was his last *novella* (probably a fiction), while previously he had written her poetry, as had others more skilled and more fortunate than he; it was to these latter that he bowed out. The passage appears consciously to take words and ideas found in Dante (for instance: *Paradiso*, II, 1-17) and almost parallels Petrarch's sonnet on the death of Laura (CCCIV); there Petrarch deemed writing further poetry pointless, it being too late because of his love's death (this did not stop him doing it, though). Hence the dedication to Lucina Savorgnan suggested that the author's literary effusions had ended as Lucina was unattainable, presumably on her marriage. That Lucina was familiar with Petrarch seems to be confirmed by the reverse of her medallion portrait, which appears to portray Petrarch's 'Triumph of Chastity' (*Fig. 13b*).[87] Da Porto told Lucina to read the story for its moral too. In effect Luigi was telling her in terms that she would have understood, that he appreciated that she was lost to him, and that his unhappy love affair with her had echoes in the story of 'Giulietta e Romeo'. The concluding tirade against the women of his day for their faithlessness – modified from one of his literary sources – seems directed at Lucina, a point to which I will return.

Before considering autobiographical details within Luigi's *novella*, what is known of Lucina? Her medallion has been mentioned. It was engraved by Fra Antonio da Brescia (active 1485-1515), with her head and shoulders in profile on the obverse; the only known example is so badly oxidized that the finer points of her features cannot be distinguished (*Fig. 13a*). What appears to be 'The Triumph of Chastity' on the reverse suggests the medallion was engraved prior to her wedding of 1517. Fra Antonio, a Minorite, may have resided for some time in the friary associated with the Church of San Francesco, which was very near to the Savorgnan *palazzo* in Udine, where Lucina lived.[88] She was born at least by 1496, the daughter of Giacomo

---

87 See note 88 below.
88 George F. Hill, *A Corpus of Italian Medals of the Renaissance before Cellini* (2 vols., London, 1930), I, p. 313, no. 1333 and II, plate 201. The medallion is signed 'F.A.B.'; Hill does not identify the female figure in the two-wheeled-cart. For Lucina's wedding in 1517 see note 101 below. For the Savorgnan *palazzo* see note 92.

Savorgnan of the Del Monte branch, and she died in 1543. Giacomo was a younger brother of Girolamo, already mentioned, who died in November 1498 fighting at Pisa, serving Venice as a captain.[89] Three years later his young widow, Maria, became the mistress of Pietro Bembo.[90] Hence the story of 'Giulietta' dedicated to the daughter of his erstwhile mistress was not without memories for Bembo himself. Maria, probably married at the age of fourteen or so in 1487, was the daughter of Matteo Griffoni of Sant' Angelo in Vado, a condottiere who had served Venice for over twenty years before his death in 1473.[91]

89 Lucina had two brothers and a sister, Giulia; in 1498 the two brothers were described as *putini*, the girls as *fie picole* (see notes 91 and 113 below). One can conclude Lucina was born at least by 1496, since she was referred to as *Madonna* in 1511 when she sang; *Madonna* indicates she was then a woman, so at least fourteen (see notes 91 and 92 below). She died on 16 January 1543 according to the 'Genealogia Savorgnan d'Osoppo', MS owned by Count Bonati Savorgnan d'Osoppo of Padua. For the four children see ASUd, 'Genealogia [della famiglia Savorgnan]', fols. 196-9, cited in note 56, and 'Memoriale di Urbano e di Niccolò figlio di Urbano [Savorgnan e continuato] fino al 1547', though this has a space left for the age of each; I am indebted to Signorina Gigli for this latter reference. The two males only are indicated by Barbaro, 'Arbori di patrizi veneti', cited in note 56. For Giacomo Savorgnan see note 90 below; for Girolamo see the genealogies cited above and for his defence of Osoppo see Matilde E. Brambilla, *Gerolamo Savorgnan e la difesa di Osoppo* (Udine, 1906). For Antonio's treachery see the text above at note 64.

90 For Giacomo, son of Pagano, see Barbaro, 'Arbori di patrizi veneti' cited in note 56, where his marriage to Maria Griffoni is given as being in 1487'; the 'Genealogia [della famiglia Savorgnan]', fol. 184, cited in note 56; according to the 'Genealogia Savorgnan d'Osoppo', cited in note 89, he was born in 1464; the 'Memoriale', cited in note 89, states that he died on 18 November 1498.

For his widow, Maria, as Bembo's mistress, see Maria Savorgnan and Pietro Bembo, *Carteggio d'amore (1500-1501)*, ed. C. Dionisotti (Florence, 1950). The editor's suggestion (p. xx n.1) that the Bernardino mentioned in the correspondence was probably, but not certainly, Maria's husband can be clarified; from 18 January 1500 Maria and her children lodged in Venice in the *palazzo* of Bernardino Sbrojavacca of Udine, and it is Sbrojavacca who is to be identified as the Bernardino of the letters, see the 'Memoriale'; I am indebted to Signorina Gigli for this reference.

91 Maria, also called Agnesina, was the daughter of Matteo, son of Biagio Griffoni of Sant' Angelo in Vado. Matteo served under Count Federico da Montefeltro, 1440-1, see V. Lanciarini, *Il Tiferno Mataurense e la provincia di Massa Trabaria: memorie storiche* (revised edition, 2 vols., Sant' Angelo in Vado, 1988), I, pp. 392-4; II, 808. Thereafter he commanded a company of infantry in Venetian service, from 1455 residing in Crema, becoming a citizen of that city, where he died on 26 September 1473, see P. Terni, 'Storia di Crema', Crema, MS Palazzo Terni, fol. 98, Mallett and Hale, *Military Organization*, pp. 76-7, 80-1 and F. Sforza Benvenuti, *Dizionario biografico cremasco* (Crema, 1888), pp. 162-4. His wife, Leonarda, daughter of the conte di Carpegna, died in 1482. Their son, Angelo Francesco, was born 8 May 1468, and he married Maria, daughter of the conte dei Collalto of the Friuli; like his father he served as a Venetian captain, see Terni, fol. 100, Sforza Benvenuti, pp. 165-5. On the evidence of Maria's marriage in 1487 (see note 90), one can suppose she was born shortly before her father's death; the marriageable age of a girl was fourteen, see C.H. Clough, 'Federico da Montefeltro and the Kings of Naples', *Renaissance Studies*, VI (1992), p. 136, n.94, and W. Heywood, *The 'Ensample' of Fra Filippo: A Study of Medieval Siena* (Siena, 1901), p. 119. Maria, having learnt of her husband's death, on 22 December 1498 accompanied 'con do putini et do fie picole, belissime creature, et suo fratello d. Anzolo Francesco', went to the Collegio to petition a pension, though seemingly received none, see Sanuto, II, 245 (ASV, 'Senato Terra', reg. 13, makes no mention of the visit under 22 December). The date of her death is not known, but she was still alive *c.* January 1515, when she held the castle of Ariis in the Friuli, see Sanuto, XIX, 385; other references to her are in the 'Geneaologia [della famiglia Savorgnan]', fol. 184, cited in note 56.

Though of rival branches of the same family, by the convention of the day Luigi and Lucina were distant cousins, and it is possible that they first met in Udine. On the evening of Wednesday, 26 February 1511, during the Carnival festivities, a dance was given by Maria Savorgnan in the family *palazzo* in Udine, when Lucina sang to the delight of the audience.[92] Perhaps Luigi was present, like Romeo in the *novella* uninvited because the hostility between the two branches of the Savorgnan family excluded him. The following day the faction fight in Udine occurred. If Luigi and Lucina had fallen in love by the time of the dance, the events of the *zobbia grassa* and its aftermath made their subsequent meeting very difficult. In the following June Luigi was seriously wounded. Three months later, in September, Luigi's uncle Antonio, having determined on treachery to Venice, fled to Austria with his only son, Niccolò, who was illegitimate.[93] He was also accompanied by two nephews, Francesco and Bernardino, sons of his recently deceased brother Giovanni; these nephews held property jointly with their uncle.[94] In response to the treachery the Venetian government put a price on Antonio's head and confiscated his property as well as that of his nephews.[95] Assassins were engaged to liquidate him and his son: he was struck down on leaving the cathedral of Villach on 27 May 1512, his

92 Amaseo, 'La zobbia grassa', in *Diarii udinesi*, p. 506, under Wednesday, 26 February 1511, after mentioning a reconciliation between Antonio Savorgnan and his adversaries remarked: 'Benché la sera medema, siando redutti in casa de madama Maria Savorgnana, dove se danzava, sonando dil continuo d'un clavizimbano, et in consonantia cantando degnamente madonna Lucina sua figliola, donzella pellegrina, et visto lì alquanti balli fin al tardi . . .'; cf. the brief mention in Sanuto, XII, 17. For Maria's *palazzo* in Udine, where these festivities took place, see Liliana Cargnelutti, 'I Savorgnan e la città di Udine: il patrimonio fondiario', in *I Savorgnan e la Patria del Friuli*, cited in note 32, pp. 61-2.

93 Antonio Savorgnan left Pinzano for the imperial camp on 19 September 1511, where on arrival Count Antonio Lodron negotiated on his behalf, see the letter of Girolamo Savorgnan from Osoppo, 19 September 1511, in ASV, 'Capi di Guerra, Lettere', busta 8, paraphrased in Sanuto, XII, 555, see also 237, and Amaseo, 'La zobbia grassa', in *Diarii udinesi*, p. 535. Antonio was granted his rights and property, as were his nephews, Francesco and Bernardino; see the decree of Maximilian, emperor-elect, dated 15 October 1511, printed in B. Vollo, *I Savorgnan* (Venice, 1856), pp. 132-4. Francesco was born at dawn on 10 February 1492, see the 'Memoriale', cited in note 89. Bernardino was perhaps born about 1493, since the two brothers and their uncle Antonio were granted Castelnuovo in 1509, following the death of their father, probably the previous year, see 'Genealogia [della famiglia Savorgnan]', fols. 216, 220, cited in note 56. Their mother was Maria Isabella, daughter of Count Vinciguerra Collalto, see A. Joppi, 'Studi e documenti della famiglia Savorgnan', vol. I, Biblioteca Comunale, Udine, MS 689, Ia. Antonio left Maria Isabella in control of Castelnuovo, which she surrendered to the Venetians on 13 November 1511, see Sanuto, XIII,231; she was still alive in 1537, though in poor health, see Amaseo, *Diarii udinesi*, p. 421.

94 For Giovanni and his two sons see note 93 above. Da Porto, *Lettere storiche*, p. 281, mentions Antonio's nephews, but does not name them or indicate they were two.

95 For the decision of 29 September 1511, taken secretly, to have Antonio assassinated, with 5000 ducats on his head (2000 granted by the Council, 3000 to be deducted from his property) see ASV, 'Consiglio dei Dieci, Criminale, reg. 1, fol. 168; Giacomo di Castello, Giovanni Gorgo di Zoppolla, and Girolamo di Colleredo, with others, were detailed for the task, see also Cargnelutti, 'Antonio Savorgnan e l'insurrezione', pp. 129-31.

son in the church of St Anne at Villach on 2 April 1518. In this manner Venice was wont to discourage treachery.[96]

Antonio's defection gave the rival Savorgnan branch of Girolamo its opportunity. In September Girolamo held Osoppo against imperial forces and remained loyal to Venice. Little by little thereafter he assumed the authority in the Friuli that had been Antonio's. In April 1514 Girolamo supplicated the Venetian government that he should be granted those lands and privileges of which Antonio and his two nephews had been deprived.[97] This petition was granted with the reservation that Girolamo should seek to persuade the two brothers, Francesco and Bernardino, who were living in exile in the duchy of Austria, to return to the Friuli, where on their taking an oath of loyalty to the Republic of Venice their inheritance would largely be restored. The Venetian government appreciated that if Antonio's two nephews were excluded permanently from their inheritances, the rivalry between the two branches of the family was likely to be perpetuated.[98]

In 1514, sometime after April, the Venetian lieutenant general in the Friuli decided that the problem could best be resolved by marriage; by 1515 he had in mind nuptials between one of the two nephews of Antonio in exile and one of Girolamo Savorgnan's many daughters.[99] Meanwhile Girolamo had made no serious attempt to contact the two brothers in exile, as he wished to retain their property; not surprisingly, he was adamantly opposed to the proposal regarding the marriage of one of his daughters.[100] Hence the Venetian authorities were forced to modify the scheme, and it is here that one returns to Lucina and the *novella* of 'Giulietta'. In 1517, probably in the summer, with general peace restored on the Italian peninsula, Francesco, Antonio's nephew, married Lucina, the niece of Girolamo, and by means of this matrimony the two rival branches of the Savorgnan

---

96 For Antonio's assassination on 27 May 1512 see Amaseo, 'La zobbia grassa', p. 541; for payment to the assassins in June see ibid., n.1; for the assassination of Niccolò, see ibid., p. 542 and n. 2. Cf. also Count de Mas Latrie, 'De l'empoisonnement politique dans la république de Venise', in *Mémoires de l'Académie des Inscriptions et Belles-lettres*, XXIV, part ii (1893), pp. 7- 67.

97 For the petition see under 20 April 1514 in Sanuto, XVIII, 144-5, and inserted under June in Amaseo, *Diarii Udinesi*, p. 241.

98 'Genealogia [della famiglia Savorgnan]', fol. 185, cited in note 56; Savorgnan, *Lettere storiche*, pp. 147-8; cf. G.P. Gri, 'Giurisdizione e vicinia nell' età moderna. Il caso di Buia', in *I Savorgnan e la Patria del Friuli*, cited in note 32, p. 186 notes 17, 18; see also note 99 below.

99 For the projected marriage of a daughter of Girolamo Savorgnan with Francesco urged by the Venetian authorities see Sanuto, LIII, 88. For the division devised in 1514, with half allocated to Girolamo and half to Giovanni's two sons on condition the latter deposited annually 500 ducats with the Treasury of Udine to compensate the *Castellani* for damage suffered in the February 1511 riots, see ibid., 87 and Cargnelutti, 'Antonio Savorgnan e l'insurrezione', p. 110; see also note 101 below for the return to Venetian territory of the two nephews, and note 102 for delays in making the required payments.

100 For Girolamo's refusal to marry one of his daughters to Francesco see Sanuto, LIII, 88. For his retention of the property allocated to the nephews see note 102 below.

family were united, and to some extent, at least, the Friuli was pacified in consequence. Francesco and his brother had returned to Venetian territory probably in the early summer of 1516, and taken the required oath of loyalty.[101] However, Girolamo refused to hand over the property of the two brothers, and this they recovered only on 19 May 1533, some four years after Girolamo's death.[102] Lucina, through her wedding, had become a pawn in Venetian endeavours to control more securely the Friuli.

One can reasonably assume that Luigi da Porto selected Lucina Savorgnan as dedicatee of his story because of the circumstances relating to her marriage to Francesco Savorgnan, which have their echo in the *novella*. After Luigi was wounded and until 1517 he resided most of the time in Venice, where daily he was wont to hobble to the Piazza di San Marco for news, so that he was likely to be well-informed as to the reasons of state behind the wedding.[103] In the story of 'Giulietta' the tribulations suffered by the lovers were a consequence of hatred, exacerbated by a vendetta, between their two rival families, which to a lesser degree paralleled that between the Del Monte and the Della Torre branches of the Savorgnan. The death of the two lovers, Giulietta and Romeo, resolved the rivalry and vendetta between the opposed families in the *novella*; the wedding of Lucina and Francesco was intended to reconcile the two branches of the Savorgnan. There is one fundamental difference: as far as is known Lucina was not in love with Francesco. In 1511 when he went into exile Francesco was aged nineteen, and Lucina was at least fifteen, already a woman by the

---

101 The precise date of the wedding remains unknown. The 'Libro d'oro matrimonio', ASV, reg. 2 ('Avogaria di Comun', 52 rosso), under 12 August 1542 registered very late two male children born of the marriage between Francesco and Lucina. Francesco then furnished the information that his son Giovanni was born on 4 June 1518 and his son Niccolò on 6 January 1523 M.V.; since Giovanni was legitimate the marriage of his parents was in 1517. The 'Cronaca matrimoni', compiled c. 1550 (ASV, 'Avogaria di Comun', 107 rosso), places the marriage under 1522, presumably from Niccolò's birthday, and added Lucina's name from the 'Libro d'oro matrimonio' indicated above. The earlier compilation by Pietro Barbaro, 'Cronaca matrimoni', for the period 1400-1538 (ASV, 'Avogaria di Comun', 106 rosso), does not mention Francesco, Lucina, or their children. Barbaro, 'Arbori patrizi veneti', cited in note 56, fol. 585 errs in dating Francesco's marriage to Lucina in 1522.

Francesco and Bernardino had returned to the Venetian state by the early summer of 1516, since on 19 July their property was assigned to them, though they were not permitted to go into the Friuli without permission of the Council of Ten, see Sanuto, LIII, 88.

102 Details of the dispute as it dragged on from 24 May 1519 to 20 July 1533 are in Sanuto, XXVII, 322; XXXIV, 362; XXXV, 134, 201, 234; XXXVI, 477, 625; XXXVII, 436-7; LII, 513, 529; LIII, 62, 85 (repeated in 87), 173; LIV, 528, 610, 611, 614; LVIII, 186, 187, 599. Documents concerning the complaints of the *Castellani*, who claimed they had not been compensated, and relating to payments from the estates of Francesco and Bernardino Savorgnan over the period from 30 April 1530 to 17 January 1547, are indicated by Cargnelutti, 'Antonio Savorgnan e l'insurrezione', pp. 109-11; see also 'Indice 140: Feudi', cited in note 67. Girolamo Savorgnan died in Venice on 30 March 1529.

103 See note 43 above.

convention of the time, since girls were deemed of marriageable age when they had attained their fourteenth birthday.[104]

The version of Luigi's 'Giulietta' dedicated to Lucina, hence supposedly presented to her, concluded with a tirade against the women of his day, as they lacked the fidelity and constancy until death exemplified by Giulietta. Witness his bitter remarks:[105]

> Oh, faithful love, that formerly reigned in the hearts of women, where art thou fled? In what breast dost thou dwell? Where is the woman that today would act as the faithful Giulietta did towards her dead lover? When will her fair name be celebrated by the most eloquent tongues? How many women are there now, who on seeing their lovers dead, would hasten to find others much sooner than die by their sides? And since I see that some women, even contrary to duty, reason, fidelity, and attachment, forget and abandon those lovers who were once very dear to them, not because they are dead, but only on account of their being somewhat buffeted by Fortune, what can we imagine they would do after their death? Wretched are the lovers of our day, who, neither by long and faithful services, nor by dying for their lovers, can ever hope that they will die for them; on the contrary, they can be certain of being dear to them only as long as they are able to provide effectually for their needs.

These are the final words of the *novella*. It appears that here, as in the dedication letter to Lucina, the author is referring to himself. Is it not he, with his wound and partial paralysis, who was somewhat buffeted by Fortune? Why should Lucina have been selected for this personal tirade on Luigi's part if in the latter's eyes it did not have a special relevance for her?

There is no entirely conclusive evidence that resolves the matter. However, my supposition is that by early 1511 Luigi and Lucina were lovers. The manuscript tradition of the 'Lettere storiche' gives Letter 49 as being sent from Cividale, dated merely '1510'; its addressee was Da Porto's Vicentine friend, Ghellino Ghellini, then in Venice. The skirmish described in the latter certainly is that in which Da Porto participated on 11 November 1510 (Bressan accordingly added the date '12 novembre' at the letter's head in his

---

104 For Lucina's probable age see note 89, and for the age at which a girl was deemed marriageable see note 91; for the date of Francesco's birth see note 93; for his supposed portrait see the Additional Note at the end of the essay.

105 *Hystoria novellamente ritrovata di due nobili amanti*, cited in note 24, fols. diii verso-div.
   At least from the early fifteenth century and Christine de Pisan the chivalric convention included knights who protested their love was true and that of their lovers was not; the manual of knighthood written in 1456 by Antoine de la Sale, 'Petit Jehan de Saintré', mocked women as deceived by their knights, see R.L. Kilgour, *The Decline of Chivalry as shown in the French Literature of the Late Middle Ages* (Cambridge, MA, 1937), pp. 310-11. Da Porto's tirade, however, seems to go far beyond the chivalric convention, and does not appear satire either.

edition). The letter concludes with the request to Ghellini to give Da Porto's greetings to 'cara mia Donna', the implication being that she was then in Venice. Letter 48 in the collection (following the manuscript tradition rather than Bressan's reordering) was likewise sent from Cividale, dated '. . . settembre 1510', the addressee being 'degnissima mia Nemica e Donna', in Venice. The core of this letter concerns a skirmish in which Da Porto displayed considerable valour, and which took place on 20 June 1510. While there is no certainty, both letters appear more genuine and less edited than most in the collection. In the letter to his 'Donna' Da Porto mentioned that he had taken prisoner Giorgino and his brother, defined as 'Germans', fighting as infantrymen. According to the letter, previously Giorgino had brought messages to Da Porto from the Donna, having been in her service, or that of her family. The letter specifically refers to the lovers as together having watched dawn break on several occasions, so presumably they had slept together. Who was this Donna? Given the dedication of the 'Giulietta', and apparent autobiographical details in the *novella* itself, the possibility is that the Donna was Lucina. Moreover, if one accepts that for some of the autumn and winter of 1510 she was residing in Venice, it seems that Da Porto had met her shortly after his posting to Cividale, and seduced her. The issue is complicated in that the Donna of the 'Lettere storiche' may have been invented to give a Petrarchan touch and love-interest. Luigi's poetry – certainly modelled on Petrarch – describes at least two different women whom he loved, one of whom died before him, so clearly cannot be identified as Lucina. By April 1528 one of his love-affairs had been renewed and prospered to the extent that Bembo warned his friend in a letter to act with moderation: it is possible this affair was with Lucina, whose husband was alive and unlikely to be complaisant.[106]

In the 'Giulietta' the two lovers were secretly married by a friar. Their passionate love was as man and wife. The analogy with Luigi's life is that he believed that he and Lucina were man and wife in God's sight, though this was unknown to their families. There is some confirmation of this supposition from another source: the *novella* of *Minetta e Polo*. The theme of this latter is akin to the 'Giulietta', and has the same moral sentiments, with the woman refusing sexual favours until after marriage. This *novella* appears to

---

[106] Letter 49 of the manuscript tradition corresponds to Da Porto, *Lettere storiche*, ed. Bressan, pp. 221-3 no. 54; Letter 48 corresponds to ibid., pp. 214-7 no. 52. For the skirmish of 11 November 1510 see Sanuto, XI, 642-4 and for that of 20 June 1510 see Amaseo, *Diarii udinesi*, p. 170, under that date, where reference is made to Da Porto's prominent part, and see also Sanuto, X, 618. The problem of Da Porto's poetry is considered in Clough, 'Lettere storiche', I, pp. cccxiii-xv, and see also the impressive notes to Da Porto's *Rime*, cited in note 86; for Bembo's letter of 20 April 1528 to Da Porto see Bembo, *Delle lettere*, III, p. 131: '. . . State sano, e godete moderatamente la vostra prospera amorosa ventura'.

have been dedicated to Lucina's younger brother, Giambattista Savorgnan of Udine. It was printed in Venice in 1551 as by an anonymous author, and this published text is the only early one known, the subsequent printings all deriving from it.[107] The text's grammatical constructions and language despite, one supposes, being partially masked in terms of the original, by the printer, still bear a close relationship to Da Porto's as evinced in his 'Giulietta' and his 'Lettere storiche'. Minetta's companion is called Peregrina, echoing Peregrino in 'Giulietta'. My suggestion is that *Minetta* is one of the *novelle* of Da Porto mentioned by Marzari as still extant in the late sixteenth century.[108] It probably passed to Bembo with Da Porto's literary papers. Bembo died in 1547 and certainly within a decade material that he owned, notably correspondence, had been made available by his son Torquato to the Venetian editor and publisher Francesco Sansovino; *Minetta* could have surfaced in this way.[109] It is possible that the printer's manuscript source did not indicate the author, as appears to have been the case with the manuscripts of 'Giulietta', merely providing the name of the dedicatee, which was published as 'Gianbattista da Udine', the name Savorgnan either not being given in the source or omitted by the printer. By a further twist the dedicatee has passed into history as the author of the *novella*.[110] In *Minetta* the two lovers were not married in a secret religious ceremony, as in 'Giulietta', but by the age-old token of Minetta allowing

---

107 Anon., *Lacrimosa novella di duo amanti genovesi [Minetta e Polo] novamente composta per il morigerato Giovan Batista da Udene* (Venice, 'Alessandro de Vian Venetian Ad instantia de Francesco librer [aio] da la Cucha', 1551), a copy in Venice, Marciana Library, Miscel. 2372, item 10 (formerly Apostolo Zeno, Miscel. Var. Tom. CLXVI, renumbered CXCIX.7). I am much indebted to Signorina Gigli for bringing this to my attention, and for associating it with Giambattista Savorgnan. For the reprints see the sources indicated in note 110. For Giambattista Savorgnan see note 113.

For the style, see my reconstructed text: 'Furono adunque (come io dico) in Verona sotto il già detta Signor le sopradette nobilissime famiglie di valorosi huomini et di richezza ugualmente dal Cielo, dalla Natura, et dalla Fortuna dotate . . . ,' cf. *Hystoria novellamente ritrovata di due nobili amanti . . .* , cited in note 24, fol. aiv verso; 'che per le sue bellezze, nobilitate, e richezze, meritamente tal nome le se puote attribuire, la quale tra tante sue gratie, da Iddio dalla Natura e d'Amore ricevute, di bellissime, gentili, & cortesi Donne più ch' altra città d'Italia era . . . ', see *Minetta e Polo*, fol. aii. The structure of the phrases in the two *novelle* are similar, with a long sentence that concludes with a verb; in both, too, the use of the participal is frequent. However the orthography of the two is far less close, and one can suppose the printer of the *novella* of *Minetta e Polo* revised that of the original manuscript, and even changed words, according to current usage; Da Porto, for instance, used *Deo* consistently, never *Iddio*.

108 For Marzari see the text above at note 81.
109 For instance, the editor Francesco Sansovino, in the 'Prefazione' to his *Delle lettere a Pietro Bembo scritte* (Venice, Francesco Sansovino, 1560), fol. aii, stated that the material published came into his hands by way of Bembo's son, Torquato.
110 The two early manuscripts of the 'Giulietta', see note 84 above. For the author as Gianbattista da Udine, see J.-C. Brunet, *Manuel du libraire* (5th ed., 9 vols., Paris, 1860–80), V (1864), cols. 999-1000, where the printings are indicated; G.B. Passano, *I novellieri italiani in prosa* (2nd ed., 2 parts, Turin, 1878), I, pp. 586-7, listing four reprints from the original of 1551, as well as a version in *terza rima* of 1832. Passano's note reads: 'Udine (Da) Giambattista fiorì nel secolo XVI, ma non si conosce né il suo casato, né l'epoca della sua nascita e della sua morte, né quelli studi facesse, e dove.'

Polo to take her hand and place a ring on her finger.[111] Thereafter they believed themselves to be man and wife, as did Romeo and Giulietta. It seems to me that the dedication of *Minetta* to Lucina's brother, in conjunction with that of 'Giulietta' to Lucina herself was not fortuitous.

My conclusion is that Giambattista knew of his sister's love for Luigi da Porto, and that she had plighted her troth to him.[112] Giambattista was born in 1498, just about the time of his father's death while fighting in Venetian service at Pisa. He himself was to serve as a military captain and was killed in the Garlasco campaign of 1524.[113] One can suppose that Luigi sent him a dedication copy of *Minetta*, or intended to do so. *Minetta* ends more positively than with a tirade. The two lovers were united in death in a tomb on which their star-crossed love was detailed – a tomb maintained by those women who honoured such sanctified and devoted love.[114]

It was the rivalry between factions and the hostility between two branches of the Savorgnan that had necessitated Lucina's love for Luigi being secret, though they had given their word to each other to be man and wife. Luigi believed that his wound and subsequent disability played its part in persuading Lucina to abandon him. Furthermore it must have been particularly embittering to Luigi that the very circumstances that had prevented his public marriage to Lucina – hostility between the two branches of the family – were those which for reasons of state motivated the wedding between Lucina and a cousin of the same faction as that represented by Luigi himself. Giulietta in the face of proposals to marry her to someone other than her lover Romeo had remained obdurate; Minetta was

---

111 *Minetta e Polo*, fol. aiv; cf. also the story of *Leonora e Ippolito*, where the couple swear mutual fidelity, and the woman accepts the man as husband thereafter, cited in Moore, *The Legend of Romeo and Juliet*, pp. 31-2. For an informal wedding with a religious ceremony that was kept secret in Florence in 1453 see G. Brucker, *Giovanni and Lusanna: Love and Marriage in Renaissance Florence* (London, 1986), pp. 19-21.

112 Giambattista presumably was a witness, and thereafter Luigi and Lucina had accepted each other as man and wife, which would explain the sexual implications of the dedication, as suggested in note 86 above. Presumably Giambattista, like Lucina, had chosen not to disclose that the wedding had taken place.

113 Lucina had a sister, Giulia, and her two brothers, Pagano and Giambattista were indicated as being babies in 1498 (see note 89). The latter's date of birth is given as 1498 in Barbaro, 'Arbori di patrizi veneti', fol. 581, cited in note 56; information regarding him is in 'Genealogia [della famiglia Savorgnan]', fol. 197, cited in note 56; by 1521 he was a captain in Venetian service, see Sanuto, XXXII, 422; XXXIV, 243; XXXV, 156. For his death see F. Sansovino, *Origine e fatti delle famiglie illustri d'Italia* (Venice, 1670), p. 509; in 1529 Pagano was granted his brother's property, see 'Indice 140: Feudi', cited in note 67, and this has resulted in some sources dating Giambattista's death to that year.

114 One can suppose that Luigi sent a copy of 'Minetta e Polo' to Giambattista because he knew of the wedding between Luigi and Lucina. The dedicatee's surname may not have been on the supposed dedication letter, which the printer in 1551 omitted, or alternatively the printer may merely have abbreviated the name. For the conclusion of *Minetta e Polo*, fol. civ: 'dove sin ad hoggi per specchio dell'altre Donne che dela santa honestate sono amiche, con grande riverentia la sacra tomba è conservata'.

weaker and did accept another as husband, but when Polo returned and committed suicide, she died too in testimony of her true love, because he really was in her sight and God's her husband. The evidence of Da Porto's love affair with Lucina is of necessity circumstantial, but what is revealed above in my view is the truth behind the story of Giulietta and Romeo. In many ways it is a real-life tragedy of the Veneto as touching as the *novella*.

Additional Note (see note 104)
The identification of a portrait of a Venetian nobleman by Titian, in the Bankes Collection, Kingston Lacy (The National Trust), as Francesco Savorgnan, dates to 1951. The recent discovery of the inscription CA ZORZI on the back of the canvas suggests rather that the sitter was a member of the Zorzi family, see *The Treasures of Britain*, ed. G. Jackson-Stops (exhibition catalogue) (New Haven, CT, 1985), pp. 560-61, item 498.

7

Benedetto Agnello, Mantuan Ambassador in Venice, 1530-56

David S. Chambers

Venice was closely observed for over a quarter of a century by the Mantuan Benedetto Agnello, who was serving as the resident ambassador of Mantua. His letters in the Gonzaga archives,[1] from his arrival in June 1530, overlap with the last three years of the *Diarii* of Marin Sanuto, whom he came to know personally, and thereafter almost provide a substitute, so rich are they are in all sorts of miscellaneous information. The annual total varies, though for some years there are well over a hundred from Agnello, with others from his secretaries and relatives; when he was absent, as happened for several quite long periods in the 1540s, the latter kept up the correspondence. In this essay I aim simply to give some idea of the writer and of the contents of his letters.

Benedetto Agnello was from one of Mantua's oldest families,[2] a branch of the Agnelli clan; born probably in the 1490s, he was one of the bright young chancery secretaries who flourished under the wing of the chancellor, castellan and littérateur, Gian Giacomo Calandra. Many of his letters are addressed to Gian Giacomo, until his death in 1543, or to his son Sabino Calandra; these complement the letters to Duke Federico Gonzaga and his successors.[3] He pointed out in 1547 that he had spent over thirty years in government service.[4] Before he came to Venice in 1530 he had been in Rome, the imperial court, Spain and Flanders, and had served for seven

---

1 Archivio di Stato, Mantua (ASMa), Archivio Gonzaga. References below refer to the relevant *busta* by number. In some *buste* each sheet (fol.) is numbered; in others, there is no numeration.
2 C. D'Arco, 'Delle famiglie mantovane', MS in ASMa, vol. I; on tav. V, p. 10, there are some details about Benedetto.
3 For instance, R. Quazza, *La diplomazia Gonzaghesca* (Milan, 1941), pp. 58-71; L. Mazzoldi, *Mantova: la storia*, II, pp. 397-401; Agnello had much in common with Annibale Litolfi, concerning whom see D.S. Chambers, 'A Mantuan in London in 1557: Further Research on Annibale Litolfi', in *England and the Continental Renaissance*, ed. E. Chaney and P. Mack (Woodbridge, 1991), pp. 73-107. On Litolfi's own visit to Venice in 1545 see below note 80.
4 Agnello to Sabino Calandra, 28 November 1547 (b. 1479), quoted in A. Luzio, *L'Archivio Gonzaga*, II (Verona, 1922), p. 83.

years in the wars. Part of this military experience had been with the army of the Holy League in 1527, commanded by the duke of Urbino, and his letters from that time also survive. Agnello recorded the army's slow progress towards Rome and on 21 May from Nepi he transmitted some of the details that he had heard about the sack of the city; this was a rather down-beat account, for while Agnello emphasised that terrible cruelties were committed, he stressed that the death toll was less high than had been feared and only selected a few salacious details, such as the landsknechts dressing up *a la cardinalescha*: he did not, he wrote, want to be tedious.[5] Not very much emerges about Benedetto's family; he had a younger brother, Giovanni, who distinguished himself as ambassador to Charles V in the 1530s but incurred heavy debts during the African campaign; he himself came to Venice in 1540.[6] Benedetto married in 1532,[7] but his wife Lucrezia is only occasionally mentioned in letters; she was once accused of smuggling salt[8] and was occasionally ill with dropsy, but she outlived her husband.[9]

What is best known about Benedetto – causing a number of his letters to be published or cited as long as a century ago – is that he moved in Venice's literary and artistic circles; above all, he knew Titian and Aretino and acted as their intermediary with the duke of Mantua.[10] His business dealings with Titian need not be repeated here, but that they were on rather close terms is suggested by evidence that they frequented each other's houses: for instance, on 14 February 1534, Titian visited Benedetto in his house about a portrait that was to be made of Ferrante Gonzaga,[11] and on 11 February 1536 Benedetto penned a letter to the duke in Titian's house.[12] On the other hand Agnello seldom offers any evaluative descriptions of the paintings which he saw in the artist's workshop, referring to opinions more expert than his own when praising the *St Mary Magdalene* early in 1531,[13] and venturing

---

5 Letters of 9 May from Deruta and of 15-26 May from Orvieto, Nepi and Isola (busta 874).

6 On Giovanni see *Dizionario biografico degli Italiani*; the letter of B. Agnello, 1 December 1535 (busta 1469, fol. 291); also his own letters from Venice in 1540 (busta 1474).

7 On 23 July 1532 he wrote that he was happy to have married the bride chosen for him by the duke (busta 1466, fol. 259).

8 B. Agnello to Cardinal Ercole Gonzaga excusing 'un errore comesso per ignorantia da mia moglie . . . per pura necessità et levita causata dal mal consiglio ', 18 November 1544 (busta 1476).

9 Lucrezia Agnello wrote of her bereavement on 21 January 1555(6) to Duchess Margherita Paleologo (busta 1489).

10 See W. Braghirolli, 'Tiziano alla corte dei Gonzaga a Mantova', *Atti e memorie della R. Accademia Virgiliana*, XIV (1881), pp. 59-124 and (more accessible but selective) the appendixes to J.A. Crowe and G.B. Cavalcaselle, *The Life and Times of Titian* (2 vols., London, 1881); also, A. Luzio, *Pietro Aretino nei primi suoi anni a Venezia e la corte dei Gonzaga*, (Turin, 1888); and A. Luzio, 'L'Aretino e il Franco', *Giornale storico della letteratura italiana*, XXIX (1897), pp. 229-83 (at 265-8).

11 B. Agnello to Duke Federico Gonzaga, 14 February 1534, 'M. Tician, qual è giunto qui in casa mia mi dice ha posto in ordine la tavola di far il quadro del Signor Ferrante . . . ' (busta 1468, fol. 74); see also, Crowe and Cavalcaselle, *Life and Times*, I, p. 457.

12 Busta 1470, fol. 20.

13 Agnello to Duke Federico Gonzaga, 11 March 1531 'quella che l'ha comincio, da quelli che hanno cognitione di pictura se è reputata cosa

only to judge that the first three of the Roman emperors, ready in September 1537, were *molto belli*.[14] Whatever the extent or limitations of his own interest in Venetian painting, Agnello was certainly eager, even in minor matters, to assist the progress of the arts in Mantua; he bought brushes in Venice for Giulio Romano,[15] tried to get work for Giulio's friend the saddle-maker Sebastianello da Bologna,[16] attempted to persuade Claudio da Correggio to go to Mantua as organist,[17] and even recommended a dyer, Giovan Maria Moretto, whose technique he thought would be appreciated there.[18] In 1551 he urged that the court architect Gianbattista Bertani should be allowed to come to Venice to submit a design for the new stone bridge at Rialto, offering to accommodate him in his house.[19]

Something about Agnello's character may explain the special appeal he held for writers and artists; not just for the *mecenatismo* he could exert indirectly, but perhaps for his geniality and wide interests. Benedetto Agnello and his brother Giovanni had first known Aretino in Mantua[20] and at first Benedetto was instructed to deliver to him gifts of money on the duke's behalf.[21] However, in September 1530 Agnello was warning Aretino that even if the duke had not said he wanted him beaten up on the Rialto for his malicious slanders, he might be in danger of this or worse,[22] and in subsequent letters he wrote indignantly about Aretino's insolence.[23] A violent assault on the Mantuan antique-dealer, Mainoldo, in February 1531 aggravated matters. Aretino was believed to have been the instigator, and Aretino suspected Agnello and Titian had passed on this report of his supposed involvement to Duke Federico Gonzaga.[24] In spite of these incidents, Agnello reverted to being on tolerably good terms with Aretino, reporting in 1533 that he was very anxious to be reconciled and had tried by many ways to get the ambassador to rehabilitate him;[25] by June 1534 it seems to have worked, for Aretino wrote that he had given a garment of

excellentissima' (busta 1465, fol. 82v; Crowe and Cavalcaselle, *Life and Times*, I, pp. 450-1).
14 Agnello to Duke Federico Gonzaga, 9 September 1537 (busta 1471; Crowe and Cavalcaselle, *Life and Times*, II, p. 497).
15 12 October 1535 (busta 1469, fol. 235).
16 Letters of 23 February, 4 March 1533 (busta 1469, fols. 47, 58).
17 Letter of 26 August 1553 (busta 1485).
18 15 January 1553 (busta 1485).
19 Agnello to S. Calandra, 21 January; 10, 20 February 1551 (busta 1483).
20 For instance, letters to G. Agnello, 11 November 1529, 26 November 1537 in P. Aretino, *Lettere: Il primo e il secondo Libro*, ed. F. Flora (Verona, 1960), pp. 24-5 no. 15, 318-19 no. 255.
21 For instance, 11, 15 July 1530 (busta 1464, fols. 48, 51v; Luzio, *Pietro Aretino*, p. 97).
22 Luzio, p. 100, n. 2.
23 For instance, on 4 October 1530 'poichè l'Aretino non può tacere certamente merita ch'el poltron sia castigato' (busta 1464, fol. 174) and called him on 7 October 'impudente . . . pazzo' (ibid; Luzio, *Pietro Aretino*, p. 101).
24 Agnello to Duke Federico, 5 February, and to Calandra 23 February 1531 (Luzio, 'Pietro Aretino', pp. 103-4).
25 Agnello to Duke Federico, 12 January 1533 (busta 1467, fol. 8; Luzio, *Pietro Aretino*, p. 105).

heavy black velvet and money, delivered to him in the house of Benedetto Agnello *mio honorato fratello*.[26] In 1541, when it was rumoured that Aretino was again going to lampoon the Gonzaga, Agnello denied this, acting once more as the appeaser.[27] Agnello remained at the same time the friend of Niccolò Franco, since 1538 one of the fiercest detractors of Aretino; in turn Aretino insinuated that Franco had even filled the mind of Agnello's housekeeper with vile ideas about him.[28] According to Franco's published letter-collection (1539), he and Agnello had been correspondents since the early 1530s, and when Franco came to Venice in August 1536 he lived for nearly a year in Agnello's house. In earlier letters Franco stressed the Mantuan ambassador's exceptional courtesy, and included a prefatory letter (dated 1531) extolling the nobility of the Agnelli family.[29]

Benedetto Agnello's letters do not betray much about his intellectual interests (they do not reveal, for example, whether he moved among the polymaths attendant on the bed-ridden Domenico Venier or knew Federico Badoer, projector of the ill-fated Academy), but other writers besides Aretino and Franco did cultivate him. They even cited him in their books on account of certain qualities or attitudes of mind, though whether these qualities were genuine or fictitious is sometimes hard to tell. For instance, Ortensio Lando included him in a short list of Erasmus's Italian admirers ('Benedictum Agnellum, virum spectata fide et virtute') — for which there is no supporting evidence — in his ambiguous dialogue about Erasmus's funeral (1540).[30] Lodovico Dolce dedicated to him his Italian translation of Philostratus's *Life of the Philosopher Apollonius*[31] explaining that this was on account of his literary merits as well as his prudence, modesty and other virtues, including hospitality.[32] Lando, like Franco, had also been a resident guest in Agnello's house; he seems to imply that Agnello's wife had been

---

26 Aretino, *Lettere*, p. 34, no. 24.
27 '... Aretino è persona che si acquieta facilmente con bone parole' he wrote to Calandra on 30 July 1541 (busta 1474).
28 Aretino, *Lettere*, p. 595, no. 124 (to Lodovico Dolce, 7 October 1539).
29 N. Franco, *Le pistole vulgari*, (Venice, A. Gardane, 1539). A letter of 6 August 1537 to Agnello (p. xlii) acknowledges 'la gentilezza che havete, la cortesia che possedette'. On Franco's staying with Agnello and his relations with Aretino see also P.F. Grendler, *Critics of the Italian World, 1530-1560: Anton Francesco Doni, Nicolò Franco and Ortensio Lando* (Madison, WI, 1969), pp. 38-42.
30 C. Fahy, 'Il dialogo "Desiderii Erasmi funus?" di Ortensio Lando', *Studi e problemi di critica testuale*, XIV (1977), pp. 42-60 at p. 54; S.S. Menchi, 'Ortensio Lando e altri eterodossi della metà del cinquecento', *Schweizerische Zeitschrift für Geschichte*, XXIV (1974), pp. 537-634 at p. 582 n. 152).
31 Philostratus, *La vita del gran philosopho Apolloni Tianeo*, trans. L. Dolce (Venice, G. Giolito, 1549 [1550]): noted by D'Arco, as above in note 2.
32 'Ho voluto nobilitare col publicarli sotto la luce del nome vostro, chiaro non meno per virtù che per generosità di sangue... per tacere gli ornamenti delle lettere che in voi risplendono a guisa di stelle: la prudenza, la bontà, la religione, la modestia, la pietà & la liberalità... s'aggiunge, che la casa vostra fu sempre, & è di continuo comune albergo a tutti i virtuosi' (fols. 2v-3).

accommodating about this, indeed that she never opposed her husband about anything,[33] and in another work, his voluminous 'Catalogues' of miscellaneous examples, he gives Agnello pride of place as an example of the generous host in modern times.[34] Agnello also features in Lando's *Dubbi*; he is cited in a sub-section of the book as proposer of some 'moral doubts', or extremely miscellaneous queries (for instance, 'Why did the ancients recommend temperance?'; 'Why did the Egyptians practise circumcision?'), but is also named as dedicatee of the last chapter, 'Dubbi religiosi', on grounds of his piety; prudently enough, none of the questions listed touch upon doctrinal issues of any importance.[35] Finally, in the same vein, Lando attributed to Benedetto a piece entitled: *Una lettera consolatoria alla Signora Susanna Valente che si doleva d'esser nata femmina*, in his collection of about forty such 'consolatory letters' supposedly written by prominent contemporaries. It has to be presumed that the link with Agnello was fictitious, unless maybe there was some concealed wit or irony intended, by using Benedetto's name in this instance as protagonist of the moral, intellectual and other attainments of women in antiquity and modern times.[36] Characteristically, seeing that he had so much to do with authors, it was Agnello who arranged for a Venetian printer to set up a press in Mantua in the winter of 1543-44;[37] this was evidently Venturino Ruffinelli, the first printer to work there since 1519,[38] who published there titles by Franco, among other writers.

Agnello's cultural interests and relationships must generally have enhanced his stature as ambassador and sometimes were of importance for the special duties assigned to him. For example, in 1534, he was expected to research the case for the duke of Mantua's claim to the duchy of Monferrato through his wife, Margherita Paleologo.[39] Agnello referred himself to most

33 Anonimo di Utopia [O. Lando], *Commentario delle piu notabili cose d'Italia* ([Venice], 1548), p. 38: 'il mio albergo fu nella casa del S. Benedetto Agnello, dove molto volentieri me n'andai, volentieri ci stetti, per essermi stato affermato da piu di dua, ch'egli era il padre de virtuosi & di perfetto cuore l'hospitalita esercitava, ne dal suo volere discorda punto la sua honoratissima consorte.'

34 O. Lando, *Sette libri de cathaloghi* (Venice, G. Giolito & fratelli, 1552) p. 534: 'Benedetto Agnello Mantovano, Re dell'hospitalità'.

35 [O. Lando], *Quattro libri de dubbi* (Venice, G. Giolito, 1552), especially pp. 106-7, 215-16: 'finalmente sonomi risoluto di consecrarli all'honorato vostro nome, et questo faccio non tanto per essermi voi sempre stato amorevole padrone, quanto per haverui conosciuto gentilhuomo religioso, amico di Iddio, et timoroso de suoi sancti giudici.'

36 [O. Lando], *Consolatorie de diversi autori novamente raccolte & da chi le raccolse* (Venice, 'al segno del pozzo', 1550), pp. 14-17. It is noted, as though by Agnello, in C. D'Arco, 'Mille Scrittori Mantovani', MS in ASMa, p. 61, but cf. Menchi, 'Ortensio Lando', cited in note 30, p. 582, n. 152; Grendler, p. 225 (appendix II) lists the few known copies; the printer, Andrea Arrivabene, was Mantuan by origin.

37 20 October 1543, 15 March 1544 to Sabino Calandra (b. 1475, 1476).

38 D. Rhodes, 'A Mantuan Bibliography', *La bibliofilia*, LVIII (1956), pp. 167-8.

39 Mazzoldi, cited in note 3, II, pp. 301-9; P. Marchisio, *L'arbitrato di Carlo V nella causa del Monferrato* (Turin, 1907), pp. 8-10.

of Venice's eminent historical writers, being tipped off by the family of Giacomo Giustinian that there was a valuable precedent in 1435. Finding that Andrea Navagero's heirs had destroyed all his papers after his death, Agnello then approached the ageing Marin Sanuto, of whom he had highest hopes, and planned also to consult Pietro Bembo.[40] In spite of illness,[41] Sanuto kept his promise: he searched in vain through his chronicles and also offered, health permitting, to do some research in the chancery.[42] Pietro Bembo was less helpful when the ambassador's emissary approached him in Padua,[43] and Giovan Antonio Egnazio found nothing;[44] but Benedetto did not give up. He even managed to penetrate government records, thanks to the doge's son, Lorenzo Gritti, who had a word with his father. Warning that such a request would not have been granted by the *Collegio*, the doge nevertheless sent a chancery secretary to make a search. Agnello also hoped to check the records of the Council of Ten.[45] In August Benedetto was still ploughing through Venetian chronicles, and in October he approached the Grand Chancellor for further access to records.[46]

If nothing came to light from all this historical research, the episode serves to illustrate Agnello's favoured access to high places in Venice. It also underlines the fact that Agnello's main function there was to promote the interest of the Gonzaga regime, and to gather political news. His letters are

---

40   19 May 1534: 'Ho parlato de questa cosa con li heredi del Navaggiero, ma loro me dicono non restar scrittura alcuna di quelle che lui haveva nel tempo di sua vita, perché alla morte sua ordinò ch'el tutto fosse abbrusato et che così fu fatto. Son anche stato con messer Marin Sannuto qual ha provision da la Signoria per scrivere le historie . . . lui m'ha promisso di cercare tra li suoi scritti . . . Penso che questo meggio di messer Marino sii il meglior in questa cosa che si possi usare, per essere persona molto diligente et che tien conto d'ogni minuta. Ho anche pensato di andare a Padua, quando mi venesse al manco il Justiniano et il Sannuto, per parlarne a messer Pietro Bembo, quale scrive li annali di Venetia, et questo perché si haverà grande difficultà ad ottenere gratia da la Signoria di potere far cercare nel'archivio publico . . . ' (busta 1468, fol. 205-v).

41   28 May 1534: 'messer Marin Sannuto s'è excusato meco non havere potuto cercare su le sue cronache per darne lume di quanto si desidera, per esser il povero gentilhomo molto indisposto. Pur mi ha promisso di fare ogni modo l'officio, et presto' (busta 1468, fol. 185v).

42   Agnello to Calandra, 29 May 1534: 'Messer Marin Sannuto ha cercato sule sue croniche ma non ha trovato cosa alcuna che faci al proposito nostro . . . Lui se offerte subito ch'el sia in termine di poter uscire di casa, per essere stà malato, di andar a cercare nelle scritture di cancelleria' (busta 1468, fol. 220).

43   'perchè la sua historia incommincia del 1484, né de le cose da quel tempo indrieto ha memoria alcuna' (8 June 1534: busta 1468, fol. 224).

44   27 June 1534: 'L'Egnatio mi disse non havere trovato cosa alcuna al proposito nostro ne li suoi scritti per le cose de Monferrato, ma vole cercare in certi altri loghi . . . Ho havuto da diversi gintilhomeni mei amici da vinti croniche antiche, le quale ho lette tutte diligentemente dal 143[0?] fin al 1440 . . . ' (busta 1468, fol. 245).

45   28 May 1534: 'mi è parso anche bene farne dire una parola al Serenissimo Principe, et ho usato in ciò del meggio di messer Lorenzo suo figliolo. Sua Sublimità m'ha fatto respondere che ricercandosi questa cosa al Collegio senza nissun dubio si haveria repulsa, ma che non havendosi molta presso ley vederà secretamente di fare cercare ad un secretario tra le scritture de la Cancelleria . . . ' (busta 1468, fol. 185v). In his letter of 8 June Agnello told Calandra 'resta solo da cercare in certi cassoni dove sono reposte le cose del Concilio di Dece' (busta 1468, fol. 224).

46   2 October 1534 (busta 1468, fol. 390).

full of specific matters in hand of rather ephemeral interest, though they also contain miscellaneous information from abroad, based on reports received in Venice, about anything from the Anabaptists of Münster to Ottoman plans to monopolise the eastern spice trade at Constantinople, or to the marital life of Henry VIII.[47] Agnello claimed, during his first year in Venice, to be too modest by nature for the status of ambassador, being content with the title of resident,[48] but it is clear that he was exceptionally suited to the post, perhaps the most important of any ambassadorship maintained by the duke of Mantua. Although Mantuan-Venetian relations had been habitually strained during the past half-century, reaching an all-time low-point when Federico's father had backed the League of Cambrai, had then been captured in August 1509, and held in Venice for nearly a year.[49] By the 1530s there were common interests to preserve, in the face of Spanish-dominated Lombardy and, from the Mantuan angle, many additional reasons to justify a resident embassy. Not that Mantuan ambassadors thought themselves maintained in a befitting style; indeed, Agnello complained often that he was kept short of funds, pointing with bitterness in 1535 to the very superior conditions enjoyed by Venetian diplomats abroad with their huge expense allowances; there was no ambassadorial residence in Venice so Agnello had to rent accommodation, at great cost.[50] He was even expected to accommodate special envoys such as those sent to congratulate a new doge, but – notwithstanding his reputation for hospitality – he refused to do this in 1553, on account of the inconvenience to his wife.[51] From the point of view of the Venetians the presence of such an able ambassador was very convenient; they did not condescend to appoint standing ambassadors to every Italian court, and could usually make use of the ambassadors sent to Venice for any relevant business of their own. Ambassadors of the Republic were only sent to Mantua for brief terms to mark special occasions, as in June 1537, when Francesco Giustinian arrived for a one-week visit to attend

---

47 On Münster, see for instance Agnello's letter of 10 December 1534 (busta 1469, fol. 42); on the Turks, 8 September 1530 (busta 1464, fol. 130r); on England, see Luzio, *L'Archivio Gonzaga*, II, pp. 121-2.

48 Agnello to Calandra, 23 February 1531: 'mi retrovo il più confuso homo del mondo, dubitando che non si creda ch'io vadi cercando questo fumo il che per il vero è in tutto alieno da la natura mia . . . me pare che questo titolo sii troppo honorevole alle conditioni che sono in me' (busta 1465, fol. 70).

49 See Luzio, *L'Archivio Gonzaga*, II, especially pp. 226-33.

50 For instance, Agnello wrote to Sabino Calandra, 5 January 1547: 'Io mi trovo in travaglio per causa dil padrone di la mia casa, quale mi ha fatto un protesto ch'io le debba vodar la casa o ch'io gli debbia pagare ogn'anno cento ducati . . . i fitti di le case e datii et altre angherie sono venuti a tale ch'è cosa diabolica, talche bisogna spendere un scudo ove si soleva spendere doi marcelli' (busta 1479).

51 16 June 1553: 'quando io non havea moglie allogiava in casa mia gli amb[assado]ri che venivano ad allegrarsi col nuovo Prencipe' (busta 1485).

the christening of the future Duke Guglielmo Gonzaga, accompanied by an enormous train of Venetian dignitaries, from Daniele Barbaro to the *piovan* of San Pantalon, not to mention Agnello himself.[52] Agnello was delighted to report that Francesco Giustinian made such a powerful *relazione* about Mantua on his return that Doge Gritti loudly praised him.[53] Another such occasion was the sending of Bernardo Navagero in 1540 to congratulate the acting regents upon the young Duke Francesco Gonzaga's accession; he was accompanied by Agnello and, in the latter's words, various *persone literatissime* including Vettor Fausto, Sperone Speroni and Paolo Manuzio.[54]

What do Agnello's letters tell us about Venice itself and the Venetians, his estimate of them and their regime? His impeccable credentials as a mainland nobleman, and his evident tact and prudence, must have been great advantages. In spite of the supposed restriction on social familiarity with ambassadors, Agnello built up a wide acquaintance during his first few years in Venice, which included members of the doge's family among his special friends,[55] and many other prominent patricians, not least the future doge, Francesco Venier.[56] Although at the beginning he was sometimes near despair because no one would tell him anything,[57] the impression is given that for an ambassador like himself, who knew how to play the game, there was little difficulty in penetrating Venetian society, or even Venetian secrecy; Agnello did not take on trust all that he was told, but he could usually find out something from his special friends. For instance, in 1532 he described Sebastiano Giustinian, who met him confidentially on his way home one evening, as a great friend of the duke's, and in 1539 he wrote that he believed Giovanni Dolfin more than the others (even if this does not imply much trust in the majority of Venetian nobles);[58] in 1541 he was recommending the procurator da Lezze as one of the *migliori amici* – also very rich – who wished to come to Mantua, and could stay with Giovanni Agnello.[59] There normally seem to have been no lack of those ready to leak information about what was going on, or provide details as to what foreign

---

52 Letters of 16-22 June 1537 (busta 1471).
53 17 July 1537: 'Il Serenissimo Principe disse ad alta voce ... "Signori, questo è un giovine d'una grandissima speranza ... " L'oration sua tutta è stata in narrare il sito, la fortezza et tutte l'altre qualità de la città di Mantua' (busta 1471).
54 Agnello to Cardinal Ercole Gonzaga and Duchess Margherita Paleologo, 23 August 1540 (busta 1474). For Navagero's *relazione* see A. Segarizzi, *Relazioni degli ambasciatori veneti al senato*, I (Bari, 1912), pp. 51-63.
55 On 11 April 1531 he reported a long talk with Zorzo Gritti, just returned from Constantinople (busta 1465, fol. 115); concerning Lorenzo Gritti, see also note 45 above.
56 See below, n. 87.
57 For instance, letter to Calandra, 23 September 1530: 'né mai posso intendere cosa alcuna di momento' (busta 1464, fol. 155).
58 Agnello wrote to Calandra, 11 June 1532, that Giustinian was 'uno di grandi amici che habbia il Signor nostro in questa città' (busta 1466, fol. 202); about Dolfin he wrote on 29 March 1539 (busta 1472).
59 Agnello to Calandra, 21 April 1541 (busta 1474).

reports had been delivered to the Senate.[60] Religious ceremonies provided a good opportunity for contact; at the consecration of the patriarch in December 1554 at which about 250 *gentilhomini principali* were present, he reported there was *gran commodità di parlare*[61] though he did not always believe all the indiscretions which came to his ears in church. One early December day in 1535, at SS. Giovanni e Paolo, a debtor, Paolo degli Agostini, in refuge there, told him that he had overheard about forty patricians discussing the emperor's resolve to confer the duchy of Milan on Federico Gonzaga.[62] Pleased as he was by the idea, Agnello did not have much faith in this informant.[63] Greater difficulties arose when there was a security alarm and clamp-down by the government, as in the autumn of 1542, when he complained the nobles would not talk to him, and that it was hard to find out anything;[64] or in 1547 after the Valier conspiracy. At that moment Agnello seems to have been greatly depressed, telling Sabino Calandra that he wanted to retire: it was a rotten and expensive life in Venice and no one spoke to him.[65]

Agnello did occasionally make incidental reports, or comments, about the domestic working of Venetian government. Sometimes he records elections to offices, but they are usually rather abnormal cases: for instance, the appointment as ducal councillor of the hundred-year-old nobleman, Francesco Michiel, who had never before sought office for himself,[66] or the election in 1543 of two exceptionally young men as *savi di Terraferma*, Bernardo Navagero and Marcantonio da Mula.[67] Holders of this post had some potential importance for Mantua, with its long Venetian frontier, just

60 For instance, letter of 23 May 1551 in which Agnello mentions he had found out from several *gentiluomini* the contents of letters concerning the Turks; or, 23 June 1551, those about France (busta 1483).

61 Agnello to S. Calandra, 11 December 1554 (busta 1486).

62 Agnello to Duke Federico Gonzaga, 4 December 1535: 'circa quaranta gentilhomini, tutti persone principali de'Pregadi et del Consiglio di X, fecero un circulo et incomminciorono a disputtare tra loro a chi l'impirator potrebbe dar il ducato de Milano . . . ' (busta 1469, fol. 295v).

63 'ne ho voluto dare aviso anchor ch'el author che m'è l'ha detto non sia persona molta authentica, benché credda quando non fosse vero, ch'egli non lo direbbe. Alcuni gentilhomini hanno ben anche parlato con me di questo, ma non han detto tanto' (ibid.).

64 6 November 1542: 'Questi gentilhuomini fugono pur anchor la conversatione de le persone publiche, et per questo con grandissima difficultà s'intende cosa alcuna di novo' (busta 1475).

65 Agnello to S. Calandra, 28 November 1547: 'la mala vita che ho in questa terra per la difficultà del negotiare et di penetrare le cose che sono neccessarie d'intendere per servitio delli patroni, per le gravissime spese . . . anche per essere privo d'ogni bona conversatione, perché non vi è alcuno di questa città che voglia conversare meco, per causa de gli ordini fatti quando fu impiccato il Valerio' (busta 1479).

66 2 September 1534: 'Uno gentilhomo di questa città chiamato messer Francesco Michele, quale alli 19 dil passato fornite cento anni, non havendo mai voluto alcun officio, né picolo né grande, fin a quest'hora, novamente ha dimandato l'officio dil consigliere, quale gli è stato concesso molto gratiosammente da tutto il gran consiglio' (busta 1468, fol. 341).

67 9 January 1543 (busta 1475).

as some Venetian patricians with particular mainland interests needed to cultivate special relations with Mantua: an example was Marco Garzoni, who liked to hunt every year in Mantovano.[68] Agnello followed with special interest the careers of Francesco Giustinian and Bernardo Navagero, who as mentioned already, had both been sent on official embassies to Mantua;[69] when Navagero was ordered to go to the imperial court in July 1543, and had urgent need of a horse, Agnello urged that he should be helped, since he was likely to become increasingly powerful in Venice and capable of doing many favours.[70] In 1547 Agnello mentioned another special friendship with a *savio di Terraferma* ('mio amico confidentissimo'), again mentioning a secret encounter in a church, this time the Frari.[71] Francesco Pisani, a former *avogador*, who was anxious to accompany him to Mantua on a private visit, he described in August 1551 as 'mio caro patrone'.[72] Likewise he mentioned the longstanding helpfulness of Girolamo Grimani, who became a *savio grande* in 1554.[73]

As befitted the servant of a prince, Agnello seems to have held the office of doge in some respect. He greatly admired Andrea Gritti, commenting at his death in 1538 that he had been a wise doge 'for these troubled times'.[74] Witnessing a vacancy in the dogeship for the first time Agnello sent to Mantua a printed description of the constitutional procedure,[75] and an account of some violent preliminaries in the Great Council expressive of rival factions.[76] Then he sent a complete list of the forty-one electors, the ultimate electoral committee.[77] In the light of all this, he was disappointingly uninformative about the outcome when reporting Pietro Lando's election a few days later.[78] Hearing a rumour that Doge Lando was dying in July 1545 he reported that the *pratiche* were quite unbelievable,[79] but he was not in Venice when the doge's death, and his successor's election, finally happened the following winter. It was his colleague Annibale Litolfi who accompanied the deputation to congratulate Doge Francesco Dona.[80]

68 11 December 1550 (busta 1482).
69 See above p. 136. Agnello mentions Navagero's high office in Padua and mission to France in a letter of 13 August 1548 (busta 1480), and on 29 May 1550 notes that he was going to Constantinople (busta 1482).
70 Agnello to Cardinal Ercole Gonzaga and Duchess Margherita Paleologo (26 July 1543): 'messer Bernardo, quel bono amico . . . et persona ch'ha da venire grande in questa città, et che per l'authorità sua potrà fare di piaceri asai' (busta 1475, fol. 47).
71 9 December 1547 (busta 1479).
72 25 August 1551 (busta 1483).
73 7 April 1554 (busta 1486).
74 29 December 1538: 'così savio signore in questi turbulenti tempi' (busta 1472).
75 6 January 1538 M.V. (busta 1472).
76 15 January 1539 (busta 1473); Luzio, *L'Archivio Gonzaga*, II, p. 230.
77 16 January 1539 (busta 1473).
78 19 January 1538 M.V. (busta 1472).
79 25 July 1545: 'E già s'erano fatte tante pratiche che è cosa da non credere, perché infiniti, et di quelli anchor che non sono degni di quel loco ambivano et procuravano di haverlo' (busta 1477).
80 Litolfi's letters of 22, 23 December 1545 record that he had an audience of the Doge, attended a session of the Great Council, and was taken to see the Arsenal also 'el thesoro, le sale, la libreria et qualche altra cosa' (busta 1477).

Agnello's general perception was that doges enjoyed, for all the legal limitations placed upon them, an unrivalled authority: this is shown in a letter some years later when he commented that Francesco Donà's ten-day absence, because of illness, had made it difficult to negotiate anything.[81] In 1553 he again sent a list of the forty-one electors and many speculations about rivalries;[82] and this time reported some details about the election of the compromise candidate, Marcantonio Trevisan, including the dinner given to his forty-one electors and all the ambassadors, with an oration in the slavic language (*lingua schiavona*) and a concert given by an orchestra of forty instruments.[83] According to Agnello the new doge was 'più presto huomo da paternostri che da governar stati' and the best thing about him was the reputation of his father.[84] Agnello noted his mortifications, which included the wearing of a hair shirt, and the measures he proposed to save nuns from prurient thoughts, which even related to cats and dogs.[85]

When Trevisan died of apoplexy, a year later, Agnello sounded quite relieved; he tipped as favourite the Procurator Marcantonio Venier,[86] but instead Marcantonio's brother, Francesco Venier, became doge. Agnello had reported each stage of this election in exceptional detail and was delighted by the outcome, contrasting favourably the new doge with his predecessor for being younger and rather more worldly-wise; more significantly, in a letter to Sabino Calandra, he revealed that Venier had always been one of his most helpful friends, and moreover had sworn to remain so; he would not even allow Agnello to kiss his hand by way of congratulation, but himself embraced the ambassador to everyone's astonishment.[87]

On the whole, Agnello does not seem to have had many illusions about the Venetian Republic or about its 'myth' of perfection. Even though in one of his letters he describes its intellectual champion, Gasparo Contarini, as

---

81 16 January 1550: 'Questo serenissimo principe già dece dì sta in letto indisposto di mal di gotta, et perché senza la presentia sua malamente si può far cosa buona' (busta 1482).

82 18, 25 May, 3, 5, 8 June 1553 (busta 1485).

83 27 June 1553, (busta 1485).

84 5 June 1553 (busta 1485).

85 Agnello to S. Calandra, 31 May 1554: 'Non hieri l'altro trovai dui gentilhuomini, quali fra loro raggionando della santa vita di questo lor Duge [sic], mi dissero che Sua Serenità era entrata in opinione che le monache di questa città non potessero tenere ne loro monasterii alcuna pittura che in alcuna parte del corpo fusse nuda, né anco galli tenendo galline, né gatti tenendo gatte, né cani tenendo cagne, acciò che venendo questi animali all'atto del coito, le monache domandando che cosa fusse, ne havessero da intrare in tentatione' (busta 1486). Other details about Doge Trevisan's austerities are in Agnello's letter to the Duke of Mantua, 7 June 1554 (ibid.).

86 He wrote of him on 18 May as 'gentilhuomo tanto raro quanto alcun altro hebbi questa città, et da ognuno è giudicato che serà duca', and repeated this prophecy on 31 May (busta 1486).

87 20 June 1554: 'sempre m'ha aiutato et consigliato in tutte le cose che mi è occorso negotiar con questo dominio ... de la nostra stretta e cordiale amicitia egli ne fece segno quando andai per baciarli la mano ... tre volte mi abbracciò stringendomi molto forte, et poi mi bacciò dicendomi "io vi sono quel vero et cordial amico che da qui indrieto son stato et serò sempre fin che vivo"' (busta 1486).

one of the duke of Mantua's greatest friends,[88] he seems rather to go out of his way to mention the defects rather than the supposed merits of the Republic. He reported attempts to clamp down on corruption and 'conventicles' in April 1531,[89] and the sequel in November 1531 concerning what had come to light about secret meetings to fix elections to offices for money.[90] He records that the *censori* had investigated the secret meeting spots, and found many nobles were involved, including those *di boni et di primi*; he himself believed it would have to be hushed up, otherwise there might be a conflagration so great that it could never be extinguished.[91] In April 1532 he mentions, as does Sanuto, the quantity of subversive *graffiti* appearing on all sides, and adds a comment of his own that never since Venice was founded had similar writings been discovered.[92] On the other hand he underlined the seriousness of the current scandal involving the imprisonment of Marco da Molin and other procurators of St Marks, under suspicion of misappropriating funds; this could lead to open warfare among the nobility and bring down the whole regime he declared; in any case he had heard that what was to blame really were the secret enmities between members of the nobility, which led to false accusations being made.[93] In 1540 he detected, rightly or wrongly, a crisis of confidence in the regime. Apparently it had been difficult to find anyone suitable to serve in the Council of Ten in 1540, and behind this was thought to lie a movement among the nobility – or even beyond – to end the cornering of power by the usual band of elderly *primi*.[94]

---

88 17 May 1535: 'Rmo. Girolamo Contarini: il più vero e caldo amico di vostra Signoria' (busta 1469, fol. 137). On 28 March 1532 Agnello mentioned an informal encounter *al matutino* with Contarini, who told him about proposals for an intergovernmental agreement against criminality (busta 1466, fol. 99).

89 14 April 1531: 'molte conventicule che havevano principio di factione' (busta 1465, fol. 122).

90 30 November 1531: 'in alcune bettole et barratarie si congregavano de molti gentilhomini quali facevano conventicule per meggio de le quali davano honori et dignità a chi non le meritava, et tutto se faceva per denari' (busta 1465, fol. 264v).

91 'molti dicono che la Illustrissima Signoria vorrà che la legge sii observata, et che non si haverà respetto a alcuno per grande che sia. Nondimeno io son d'altro parere, et tengo che . . . seria un apizare un foco troppo grande et forsi mai piu se amorzaria' (ibid.).

92 22 April 1532: 'per quanto intendo, mai pur dappoi che Venetia fu edificata non furono attacati scritti di simil sorte' (busta 1466, fol. 135); cf. Sanuto, LVI, 76, 78.

93 'debba nascere in questa cittade una guerra intestina tra questi nobili, il che Dio non voglia, perché senza niussun dubio seria la total ruina de questo stato. M'è detto che queste persecutioni si fanno per li odii et inimicitie occulte che sono fra questi nobili, non perché sii vero quel che se imputa alli procuratori, ma che li maligni sono quelli che stanno sempre de sopra, perché con li loro inganni et con testimonii falsi fanno credere alla maggior parte dei nobili che sono ignoranti quel che non è . . . ' (busta 1466, fol. 135).

94 3 August 1540: 'essendone stà proposti molti de li più vechii et di primi de la città, che sempre erano soliti versar in quel magistrato, non fu alcuno dessi che potesse remaner, havendo havuto contra quasi tutte le ballotte del Gran Consilio. La causa intendo esser perché la città vole levar in tutto et per tutto il governo di mano dei quelli che han retto fin hora, perché si arrogavano troppo . . . ' (busta 1474).

Agnello probably regarded the Venetian government's occasional drives against corruption as so much hypocrisy: he sounds astonished early in 1545 that many noblemen had been banned from office-holding for a year 'for no more than asking others to favour them for office'.[95] On the other hand in 1537 when some procuratorships were conferred for money, Agnello noted that many were voted down who had offered more money than those who were successfully elected.[96] Venetian cost-calculating irked him, 'the nature of republics is not to spend unnecessarily', he wrote scornfully in 1539.[97] He was also critical of the republican system of short-term elective offices: early in 1550 he complained explicitly about the difficulty of negotiating with republics where the office-holders were constantly changing.[98]

Agnello was not greatly impressed by Venice's elaborate public spectacles. At the first of such events which he witnessed, with dances and other effects sponsored by a *Calza* company, what struck him most vividly was simply the crowd itself.[99] A few months later he was rather sardonic about the mock naval battle staged for the duke of Milan.[100] Rather than describe contrived visual effects, he tended to stress things that went wrong. Thus he commented that the duke of Urbino's visit in 1532 was undignified because the duke was badly dressed;[101] and in 1534 another naval spectacle, produced on the occasion of Duchess Renée of Ferrara's visit, was reported as a disgrace.[102] Although Agnello was more approving of the ball given a few days later, he criticised the strictly limited access to it, and could not forbear mentioning that when a drunken Ferrarese boatman assaulted a member of the organising *Calza* company, the occasion nearly turned into a bloodbath.[103] At another festa in 1535 he reported that a spectators' stand collapsed in the piazza; many were injured and some killed.[104]

95 10 January 1545 (busta 1477).
96 6 June 1537 (busta 1471).
97 1 April 1539: 'per essere natura de le republiche di non entrare in spesa senza bisogno' (busta 1473).
98 16 January 1550: 'et questo aviene a chi negotia con republiche, che quando pensa d'haver tratto a fine li suoi negotii, li uffitiali si mutano et bisogna ch'egli retorni da capo' (busta 1482).
99 18 July 1530: 'molto più bella cosa era il numero infinito de li homini et donne che andavano a vedere la festa, però che per me non vidi mai maggior moltitudine di gente' (busta 1464, fols. 53-4).
100 Luzio, *Pietro Aretino*, cited in note 10, pp. 133-4.
101 8 May 1532: 'Il Signor Duca de Urbino quando fece l'intrata in questa terra era vestito molto miseramente' (busta 1466, fol. 158).
102 19 May 1534: 'Non heri l'altro fu fatta la battaglia navale per honorare la Illustrissima Signora Duchessa di Ferrara, la quale è reuscita tanto male et è vituperio a parlarne, che questi signori si doleno grandemente del Fausto . . . ' (busta 1468, fol. 205v).
103 23 May 1534: 'veramente questa festa seria stata de le più belle che mai fossero fatte in Venetia per un ballo, se vi fossi stato il libero adito ad ogniuno, et se non seguira un poco di disordine, che fu che un ferrarese barcharolo, qual se dice che era imbriaco, essendo venuto a parole con un gentilhomo di compagni de la calza, gli tirò di molte coltellate con una spada . . . in un tratto furon sfodrate più di cinquecento spade . . . ' (busta 1468, fol. 208).
104 6 February 1535: 'Non heri l'altro facendosi la festa su la piazza di San Marco che si sole fare ogni anno a simil giorno, si ruppe una baltrescha dove era sopra un gran numero di persone, de li quali molto restorono stroppiati et alcuni morti. Tra li morti fu Don Hieronymo Ghy-

He had an alert ear for public disasters, scandals and crimes, particularly if they involved the nobility. For example he reported the strange death of Benedetta Pisani in February 1544 – apparently suffocated in her bed or poisoned[105] – and the escape from gaol in 1547 of Marcantonio Erizzo, who was serving a life sentence for murdering his uncle.[106] Likewise he refers in 1553 to the case of Agostino Querini, who had murdered his daughter in order to avoid paying her dowry, then strangled himself in prison with his belt.[107] Reporting the discovery of 'a sect of sodomites' in January 1545, he remarked that the nobles among them had slipped away and would thus avoid prosecution.[108] In September 1554 he recounts the scandal of a gang of patrician youths who went on the rampage, a seventeen year old of the Donato family, a Zen and 'un populare richissimo'. They had injured whoever they encountered, apparently killing a fruitseller and a boy of twelve, whose head they slashed open. Agnello expected a severe sentence from the Council of Ten, and was surprised that the culprits seem to have got off relatively lightly – in fact none of the victims had died – on the grounds of being drunk.[109]

Agnello conveys an impression of Venice as a rather dangerous city, certainly no haven of security to the person. Serious assaults sometimes occurred on his very own doorstep. Once his secretary Ludovico Tridapoli was attacked outside the front door. This was the work of a gang thought to be in the pay of a patrician, Sebastiano Moro, of whom Tridapoli had spoken slightingly, or in consequence repeated remarks made about him by a *puttana* who knew them both. Tridapoli lost two fingers, though Agnello thought him lucky to have escaped alive.[110] However, when the Council of Ten came to make inquiries, Agnello's main concern was to hush the matter up.[111] He even interceded for Moro and suggested that another job should be found for Tridapoli in Mantua. Another incident on Benedetto's doorstep occurred in 1555 when a youth well known in the neighbourhood, infatuated with a woman apparently in the ambassador's household service ('inamorata d'una femina di mala vita che sta per mezzo la mia casa'), caused

mono tenorista de la capella di San Marco' (busta, 1469, fol. 41).
105 Agnello to Calandra, 5 February 1536 (busta 1470, fol. 14).
106 6 September 1547: ' . . . Marcantonio Erizo gentilhuomo venetiano, quale fu condenatto in vita alla prigione forte, per la morte del Bernardo suo barba, ha rotta la prigione et si n'è fuggito . . . ' (busta 1479).
107 12 August 1553 (busta 1485).
108 Agnello to S. Calandra, 29 January 1545: 'questi signori non attendano ad altro che far detener una setta di sodomitti che si ritrovava in questa città, et già se n'è preso una buona quantità, pur tutti populani, insieme con qualchi citadini, che gli gentilhomini che erano incolpati di tal delitto per esser delli buoni di questa città, essendo stati advertiti se ne sono fugiti' (busta 1477).
109 14, 27 September 1554 (busta 1486).
110 19 November 1542 (busta 1475).
111 25 November 1542 (busta 1475).

a rumpus and even threw stones at the windows when denied entrance; later he threatened one of Agnello's staff with violence. Benedetto was anxious that this outrage should be punished, and reported the matter to the Council of Ten. He disregarded the pleadings of his neighbours about the youth's character ('giovane da poco cervello'), but eventually wrote to the duke about the possibility of withdrawing the charge, which several noblemen were urging.[112] On one occasion the ambassador himself narrowly escaped injury; stones were thrown at his gondola when he was returning with his wife from a visit to Padua. The assailant may have been a minor government official, suspicious that there were smuggled goods aboard; the Council of Ten promised to make inquiries but nothing came of them. Agnello was most indignant that such an act should go unpunished.[113]

Finally, in addition to personalised cultural relations, political reporting and diplomatic business, the Mantuan ambassador devoted quite a lot of his time just to shopping for his patrons. Here again he had no illusions; to him, Venetian business practices were as suspect as their political practices; he commented, for instance, at a time of exceptional *acqua alta* in the winter of 1542-3, that merchants were trying to play down the damage to their flooded stores in order to keep up the price of spices.[114] During the 1530s he had much first-hand experience of commercial dealings; his letters are packed with references to exotic wares and artefacts, things he was seeking or bargaining for on behalf of Duke Federico Gonzaga, his wife Margherita Paleologo, his mother Isabella d'Este, his brother Ercole, or for Calandra and others. Many of the required goods were consumables, sweetmeats, spices and wine (almost every October there is a reference to the arrival or non-arrival of the new Malvasia wine).[115] Ginger and fruit-trees were bought through an agent known as the *prete spagnolo*[116] – there is no end to

---

112 16 April 1555: 'son stato necessitato farne querela alli Signori Capi del Conseglio di X . . . ma essendo poi stato ricercato con molta instanza da alcuni gentilhuomini mei amici a volergli perdonare, io ho lor risposto che quanto a me gli ho perdonato, ma che essendo principalmente offesa la Eccelenza Vostra, non mi pareva di poterlo fare senza sua commissione' (busta 1488).

113 Agnello to Sabino Calandra, 4 July 1547: 'il gastaldo o altri suoi che fossero dubitando che la mia gondola fusse barca venuta là per tuorgli il guadagno, comincioro a trarne de sassi, di maniera che se non se allargavamo presto, erano per farme qualche male' (busta 1479).

114 Agnello to Calandra, 18 January 1543: 'Il danno havuto da mercanti nelle loro mercantie, maxime nelle spetiarie, è iudicato grande, ma io le tengo molto maggior di quel che anche se dice, et la causa è perché li mercanti non voleno confessare che le loro robbe se siano bagnate, per poterli meglio dare exito anchor che siano deteriorate' (busta 1475).

115 For instance, in September 1530 he already sent a consignment 'de la migliore et de la più delectevole' (busta 1464, fol. 143); cf. letters 29 August 1532 (busta 1466, fols. 316-18); 13 September 1533 (busta 1467, fol. 177v); 2 September 1534 (busta 1468, fol. 359v); 3 September 1535 (busta 1469, fol. 200).

116 For instance, B. Agnello to Duchess Margherita Paleologo, 10 February 1535, and to Duke Federico Gonzaga, 8 December 1535, 13 May 1536 (busta 1469, fols. 50, 300; busta 1470, fol. 142).

the commodities he bought in Venice, down to seed for the Duchess's parrots.[117] Among the more costly items were intricately wrought clocks,[118] and glass objects. Agnello took trouble to look out for desirable pieces, and sometimes reported that it was difficult to find anything worth buying;[119] he interviewed glass-blowers and went in person to the workshops on Murano; on one occasion he and the English ambassador planned to go there together to specify what they wished to have made.[120] Agnello was not easily fooled by inferior quality, and once when seeking some so-called unicorn he noted that what was on offer was stag horn.[121] In Duke Federico's time, rare animals were frequently on the Gonzaga shopping list; during his first year in Venice Agnello's letters contain much detail about the creatures brought on the galleys from Beirut or Alexandria: there were, for instance, green parrots, monkeys, leopards and gazelles. Likewise, he tried over a long period to use his special acquaintance with Girolamo Cornaro to obtain sacred falcons from Cyprus.[122] In later years he was more occupied with obtaining costly fabrics for Margherita,[123] or miscellaneous items for Cardinal Ercole, which included tapestries, of which he sent a long list with prices of those available in January 1554.[124] Sometimes he met difficulties; he wrote in December 1548 that samples of gold cloth, which he had been asked to get, were no longer obtainable, in consequence of the Turkish occupation of Hungary.[125] Books were also among the items he purchased: he was in touch with the printer Giolito in January 1553, to keep him to a promise that when his edition of Vitruvius was ready the first copy would go to Cardinal Ercole Gonzaga.[126]

Agnello declared that the happiest day of his life, since he had come to Venice, was on 16 July 1553 when a congratulatory oration to Doge Trevisan was delivered by the special Mantuan emissary, Ippolito Recordati. What made Agnello so happy, presumably, was the combination of

117   11 July 1535 (busta 1469, fol. 174).
118   For instance, on 6 November 1535 Agnello wrote of a clock which struck every quarter of an hour (busta 1469, fol. 257).
119   For instance, his letters of 28 December 1532, 18 February 1534 (busta 1466, fol. 415; busta 1468, fol. 77).
120   [?] January 1535: 'non mando a Vostra Excellentia vasi da bevere perché a Murano non vi è cosa nova né che sii bella. L'ambassator d'Ingliterra et io havemo deliberato de andarlì uno de questi dì, et ambi doi studiaremo di far fare qualche bel bichero o tazza che le habbia da piacere' (busta 1469, fol. 34).
121   5 March 1537 (busta 1471).
122   Various letters in October 1535 (busta 1467, fols. 4, 229- 33, 245); of 25 November 1535 (busta 1469, fol. 134) 8 January 1538 (busta 1472).
123   For instance, about requests for damask and crimson silk. Agnello's letters of 17 January 1547 and 16 June 1553 (busta 1481, 1485).
124   Letters of 1 January to Carlo Maffei, 16 January to S. Calandra, 11 April to Duke Guglielmo Gonzaga concern these tapestries (busta 1486).
125   Agnello to Sabino Calandra, 23 December 1548 (busta 1480); also to Duchess Margherita Paleologo, 7 September 1554 (busta 1486).
126   Agnello to Sabino Calandra, 27 January 1553 (busta 1485). Apparently the edition was never printed by Giolito.

literary or rhetorical skill with prestige for Mantua. The speech was so much praised by the senators that many of them asked for a printed copy of the text, the ambassador proudly reported,[127] though much the same effect was produced by the oration of another Mantuan, Giulio Galvagno, a year later, after Francesco Venier's accession as doge.[128] Benedetto did not enjoy many more satisfactions. He had been ill quite often during his time in Venice; on various occasions he tried the waters of Abano, which sometimes worked for him.[129] In November 1555 his condition became much more serious. He took to his bed and became progressively weaker throughout the following month,[130] though just before Christmas his secretary, Ludovico Nello, reported that he was a bit better and, but for his dizziness, would have liked to converse with patrician friends when they called.[131] He lingered a while longer, but, after a crisis when he became violent, died on 16 January 1556.[132] His funeral ten days later took place at the parish church of S. Hyeronimo (Girolamo) with the vice-doge and about forty of the nobility present, the imperial, English and Urbinate ambassadors, and 'all the clergy of the city' (*tutte le chieresie di questa terra*). The wax candles and clergy's expenses were paid for by the government; about 400 mourners were present, and a crowd of 3000 gathered outside the church, in addition to those watching from the windows, Nello reported.[133] Agnello was buried at the church of the Servites; an oration was given which unfortunately was not up to the standards he would have expected; according to Nello it was written badly, and learnt, all in the space of two days.[134] Nevertheless, Nello was in no doubt about the extraordinarily high reputation which Agnello left behind in Venice ('egli ha lasciato tanto buon nome in questa città che si puol dire essere fatto immortale'). He died only a few months before Aretino: of the two it was not the good-natured Mantuan who was immortalised; he does not even have a niche in the *Dizionario biografico*.

---

127 Agnello to S. Calandra, 16 July 1553 (busta 1485).
128 30 July 1554 (busta 1486).
129 For instance, 6, 9, 15 June 1540 Agnello had complained in letters to Sabino Calandra he could not pass the water he drank at Abano and found the *gozza* most unpleasant (busta 1474).
130 Agnello to Sabino Calandra, 19 November 1555, complains of his 'indispositione del stomaco et flusso di corpo' (busta 1488).
131 23 December 1555 (busta 1488).
132 Letters of L. Nello 1 January 1555 M.V. (busta 1488); a subsequent letter mentions his *gran somnolentia* (busta 1489).
133 Nello to Sabino Calandra, 21 January 1556 (busta 1489); Giulio Agnello, on the same day, clarified that the Doge himself could not come because of illness (ibid.).
134 Nello to Sabino Calandra, 23 January 1556 (busta 1489).

8

Pietro Barbo – Paul II: *Zentihomo de Uenecia e Pontifico*

Ian Robertson

No less than three fifteenth-century popes were Venetian patricians – Gregory XII, Eugenius IV, and Paul II – linked, moreover, by family ties. Yet that century was no 'golden age' in relations between the papacy and the Venetian church and state. The Venetian popes confronted persistent conflict between the demands of loyalty to their *patria* and those of their wider responsibilities as Vicar of Christ. Inevitably, the latter generally triumphed – although, this essay will suggest, that victory may have been aided by the popes' very 'Venetian-ness'.

An unavoidable source of conflict between the papacy and the Republic of Venice lay in the area of jurisdictional theory and practice. The challenges to papal authority brought by the Great Schism and the fifteenth-century Councils had led to yet more highly-developed notions of omnicompetent papal monarchic sovereignty;[1] for its part Venice had by the time of the Schism long since come to see itself as a chosen city of God with divinely ordained institutions, heir to a Byzantine tradition which conceived the state as having an essentially confessional and sacral character.[2] Indeed, this tradition was still being elaborated in fifteenth-century humanist writing by such as Bernardo Giustiniani.[3]

By the fifteenth century, however, confrontation between the papal and Venetian jurisdictional traditions was complicated by anomalous and

---

1 Of the vast literature on this subject, I cite only the particularly helpful work of Anthony Black, *Monarchy and Community: Political Ideas in the Later Conciliar Controversy, 1430-1450* (Cambridge, 1970). For footnote references to archives, see list of abbreviations, above, p. xxix. I should like to thank my colleague Dr Ian Britain, for some helpful criticisms and comments. Dottoressa Silvia Fadda typed the text and Martin Sheppard retyped the notes.

2 Paolo Prodi, 'The Structure and Organization of the Church in Renaissance Venice: Suggestions for Research', in J.R. Hale ed., *Renaissance Venice* (London, 1973), pp. 409-30.

3 Patricia H. Labalme, *Bernardo Giustiniani: A Venetian of the Quattrocento* (Rome, 1969), pp. 295-6.

internally contradictory developments within both traditions, developments which were in certain respects similar and which seem to some extent to indicate an interpenetration of the two positions. The new papal theory of monarchical sovereignty, evolved during the clash between Eugenius IV and the Council of Basle, provided the basis for a policy of concordats which implied a certain equality between papal and secular monarchic authority. There was a 'Venetian' contribution here. Some of the members of Eugenius IV's 'team of clerical diplomats' who made the key contributions to the elaboration of the analogy between pope and emperor came from the 'imperialist environment of Venice' – most notably Piero dal Monte and Antonio Roselli, to say nothing of Eugenius himself.[4] Indeed, the interaction between papalist and Venetian concepts of sovereignty may also have operated through Venetian popes transposing to the papal context 'high' concepts of state sovereignty absorbed in the patrician society of their native Venice. Moreover, the way in which the pope-council conflict was eventually resolved gave new importance – diplomatic, military and financial – to the task of rendering the exercise of papal sovereignty over the papacy's temporal dominions in Italy more effective and direct.[5] A parallel Venetian development was to open up a new front of persistent and often bitter conflict.

Although the Venetian tradition of integration of lay and religious society was still alive as part of the 'myth' of Venice, ecclesiastical and secular authorities were starting to distinguish their spheres of influence. Prodi suggests that the key to these changes must be sought in the Venetian conquest of the *Terraferma* from the early fifteeth century. The absorption under Venetian dominion of the ecclesiastical structures of these 'western' areas entailed a radical change in relations with the papacy, above all by virtue of 'the government's need to put trusted men in charge'.[6] But the conquest of the *Terraferma* also had another impact on relations between Venice and a papacy which was itself now more interested in effective control of its own territories on the mainland. Confrontation over issues of ecclesiastical jurisdiction per se began to be eclipsed by confrontation over political, diplomatic and military issues raised by Venetian territorial expansion. These issues also involved other major territorial powers of the Italian peninsula, and the popes were able when in need to exploit rich reserves of anti-Venetian feeling.[7]

4 Black, *Monarchy and Community*, pp. 86-8, 99-100.
5 Ibid.; Paolo Prodi, *Il sovrano pontefice: un corpo e due animi: la monarchia papale nella prima età moderna* (Bologna, 1982); Peter Partner, 'The Budget of the Roman Church in the Renaissance Period', in E.F. Jacob ed., *Italian Renaissance Studies* (London, 1960), pp. 256-78.
6 Prodi, 'Structure and Organization', especially pp. 411-12.
7 Nicolai Rubinstein, 'Italian Reaction to *Terraferma* Expansion in the Fifteenth Century', in Hale ed., *Renaissance Venice'*, pp. 197-217.

The pontificate of Paul II (1464-71) offers the best opportunity to illustrate these themes. His policies and actions as pope indicate he was an enthusiastic heir to the highly-developed notion of papal monarchical sovereignty elaborated by his uncle Eugenius IV's 'team of clerical diplomats'. Some of this group, such as the Castilian Rodrigo Sánchez de Arévalo, became Pietro Barbo's closest collaborators after his election as pope, flanked by others including Domenico de' Domenichi and Teodoro de' Lelli, bishops in the Veneto. It is arguable that Paul II's 'high' concept of papal sovereignty was reinforced by the transposition to the papal context of native Venetian 'high' concepts of state sovereignty. But most significant perhaps was Paul II's logical extension of the post-conciliar concept of papal sovereignty to papal temporal government. Although the analogy between the church and the secular state had been fundamental to the arguments of Eugenius IV's ideologues, they had rarely addressed explicitly the problem of the Papal States: the temporalities had not on the whole been a controversial issue in the pope-council dispute. However, the ideologues' arguments had certainly had implications of which Paul II seems to have been almost obsessively conscious. A fundamental premise of his temporal government – which distinguishes him from other fifteenth-century popes – seems to have been a conviction that every opportunity should be exploited to bring back all the territories of the Papal States under the direct government of the church. In embracing this conviction, Paul II extended to the full range offered by fifteenth-century developments the occasions for confrontation between his papacy and his native Venice.

Pietro Barbo was born in February 1417 or 1418 in the parish of San Giovanni in Bragora in the vast *sestiere* of Castello,[8] in a relatively modest house of originally Byzantine form fronting on to the Rio della Pietà which still survives (N. 3709-14) (*Fig. 15*). His mother Polissena was niece to Angelo Correr (Pope Gregory XII) and sister to Cardinal Gabrielle Condulmer, later Pope Eugenius IV. Pietro's father (d. 1434) was Nicolò di Paolo Barbo.[9] The patrician status of the Barbo had

---

8 Michele Canensi, in his 'De vita et pontificatu Pauli Secundi P.M. opus', in *Le vite di Paolo II di Gaspare da Verona e Michele Canensi*, ed. Giuseppe Zippel, *RIS* (1904-11), III, xvi, p. 76, gives 1417; but the details on Paul II's tomb inscription seem to indicate 1418: Iiro Kajanto, *Papal Epigraphy in Renaissance Rome* (Helsinki, 1982), p. 70. It may be a case of *more veneto*.

9 For family background and early biographical details, see the biographies of Gaspare da Verona and Michele Canensi in *Le vite di Paolo II*; and *Platynae historici Liber de vita Christi ac omnium pontificum (AA. 1-1474)*, ed. Giacinto Gaida, *RIS* (1913-32), III, i, pp. 363-98.

been established by the 1290s, and they had accumulated sufficient wealth by 1379 to rank quite highly in the *Estimo* of that year. Although linked to *case grandi* like the Contarini, the Michiel and the Bragadin, the Barbo remained a smallish clan. Nonetheless, largely due to the rich ecclesiastical benefices which some of their members and connections came to possess, the Barbo enjoyed a degree of political influence amongst the *Primi* disproportionate to their size.[10] In particular, Pietro's elder brother Paolo, born in 1416 and admitted to the *Consiglio Maggiore* in December 1434, was to become a front-ranking figure in Venetian government. When he returned to Venice in 1447 after a period at the papal court, he regularly occupied key offices in both the city and its *Terraferma* territories, and he served on a number of vital diplomatic missions, for example as Venetian representative in the negotiation of the Peace of Lodi in 1454.[11] The Barbo family connections – Barozzi, Bragadin, Contarini, Michiel, Soranzo, Zane, Zeno – seem to have been primarily amongst the so-called *case vecchie* or *longhi* clans, the twenty-four houses credited with having founded Venice before the ninth century, who around 1450 were reportedly the victims of a conspiracy amongst the *case nuove* or *curti* clans to exclude them from the dogeship – although there was a connection between the Barbo and the Moro, one of the sixteen conspiratorial *case nuove*.[12]

Pietro was initially destined for commerce;[13] but it would appear that the election of his uncle as pope in 1431, together possibly with the death of his father in 1434, induced a change of plan. He decided to devote himself to a clerical career – 'etiam contra volunta de li parenti soy, et potentissimum de la Matre vedoua', he recalled years later[14] – and, probably in 1435 or earlier 1436, he left Venice for the court of his uncle the pope, since June 1434 in exile from Rome in Florence. As pope, Barbo was concerned to stress that his decision had been dictated by vocation, and not simply careerist opportunism:

---

10 Robert Finlay, *Politics in Renaissance Venice* (London, 1980), pp. 82-4; Stanley Chojnacki, 'In Search of the Venetian Patriciate: Families and Factions in the Fourteenth Century', in Hale ed., *Renaissance Venice*, pp. 67, 72-5.

11 On Paolo Barbo, see S. Borsari in *Dizionario biografico degli Italiani*, VI (Rome, 1964), pp. 254-5; G. Degli Agostini, *Notizie istorico-critiche intorno la vita, e le opere degli scrittori viniziani* (Venice, 1752), I, pp. 333-45. For his role in connection with the Peace of Lodi, see Marin Sanudo, 'Vite de' duchi di Venezia', in *RIS*, XXII (Milan, 1733), col. 1152c.

12 Finlay, *Politics*, pp. 92-4, 145-6; Chojnacki, 'Venetian Patriciate', pp. 49-50. For the connection with the Moro, see G. Spiazzi, 'Barozzi, Giovanni', in *Dizionario biografico degli Italiani*, VI, pp. 500-1.

13 Platina, op. cit. note 9, p. 364; Canensi does not mention this particular.

14 ASMi, 'Roma', 60, 19 July 1466 (Agostino de' Rossi and Giangiacomo Ricci).

... Relictis omnibus se ne vene ala corte, et Immediato pigliò lhabito, et se misse in sacris senza hauere vno minimo beneficio al mondo, per non hauere poy casone de potere mutare sententia, perche era omnino deliberato àquella via ... '[14]

Nonetheless, the accumulation of ecclesiastical benefices soon began. In succeeding years he was the beneficiary of a steady stream of grants *in commendam* of abbacies, priories, canonries and prebends, some far afield, but probably mostly in Venice and its territory, including Friuli and Dalmatia. His brother Paolo was to administer the temporalities of the latter after his return to Venice in 1447.[15] The Venetian government seems to have surrendered tolerantly its jurisdictional claims in the matter of ecclesiastical appointments so as to allow this lucrative 'portfolio' to be assembled — a point of interest in the light of later conflicts. Some time around 7 November 1438, Pietro Barbo was also granted the bishopric of Cervia *in commendam*;[16] and his curial career was significantly advanced in July 1440 when he was made cardinal deacon of Santa Maria Nuova.[17] Nicholas V improved on this in June 1451, translating Barbo to be cardinal priest of San Marco, with its appropriately Venetian resonances.[18] At the same time, he was provided with the bishopric of Vicenza — which the Venetian Senate again meekly accepted, despite having previously elected Giacomo Zeno, then bishop of Belluno and Feltre.[19]

After 1435 or 1436 Pietro Barbo's only return to Venice seems to have been in October-November 1451, on his way to and from taking formal possession of his see of Vicenza[20], although there were some discussions about possible further visits in 1454[21] and (as pope) in 1466, 1467 and 1468.[22] However, he did not lose affection for his native city and its people, nor his sense of his responsibilities as a Venetian 'gentleman'. For most of his career as cardinal, the potential tensions between such patriotic feelings and his curial responsibilities were contained. Together with other Venetian cardinals such as Francesco Condulmer

---

15 A book of accounts kept by Paolo Barbo is in Vatican Library, MS Vat. lat. 7285 (14 August 1447-28 March 1460).
16 ASegVat, reg. Vat. 375, fols. xxxv verso, lxviv-v.
17 ASegVat, arm. XXXI, t. 52, fols. 48v, 49.
18 C. Eubel, *Hierarchia catholica medii aevi* (Münster, 1914), II, p. 30 (Appendix I, p. 142).
19 C. Cenci, 'Senato veneto: "probae" ai benefizi ecclesiastici', in C. Piana and C. Cenci, *Promozioni agli ordini sacri a Bologna e alle dignità ecclesiastiche nel Veneto nei secoli XIV-XV* (Florence, 1968), pp. 387-88, n. 96; Tommaso Riccardi, *Storia dei vescovi vicentini* (Vicenza, 1786), pp. 169-71.
20 ASV, 'Senato', 19, fols. 92-93, 94v.
21 ASV, 'Senato', 20, fol. 30v.
22 ASMa, 843, 6 November 1466, 5 March 1467; ASMi, 61, 14 Feb. 1467; 62, 9 April 1467; 65, 13 June 1468, 14 Oct. 1468; ASMo, busta 1, fol. 9 (i), no. 19 (27 Sept. 1467); ASV, 'Senato', 23, fol. 71, 3 Sept. 1467.

and Lodovico Trevisan, Cardinal Barbo functioned in effect as a permanent ambassador at the papal court, fulfilling expectations that he would advocate the Venetian case on all issues involving the Republic's interests.[23] When he came to Venice in 1451, he came in part as a papal ambassador, but the Senate in speaking with him decided 'tanquam cum uero ciue nostro aperte loqui, et aperire omnem mentem nostram'. And he remained content with the replies to the questions he raised, even about the Venetian occupation of Ravenna, which was to concern him as pope.

However, signs of the fragility of the Venetian cardinal's position, both vis-à-vis his *patria* and vis-à-vis the pope, were never far away. In December 1451, for instance, the Senate instructed its ambassador in Rome to reinforce a request for loans from the Venetian cardinals by pointing out

> quod eorum beneficia, siue loca in quibus sita sunt, aquisiuimus maxima cum expensa et periculo ac nostrorum sanguinis effusione, et similiter maxima cum expensa illa tenemus, et animaduertendum est, quod nisi ea loca habuissemus, non est credendum quod ea beneficia tenerent . . .

At the same time the ambassador was instructed to meet objections by reminding the pope:

> quod beneficia huius nostre Ciuitatis, ab ipso principio urbis nostre, et per continua tempora pro domibus possessionibus, et bonis eorum tulerunt onera, quemadmodum ciues nostri . . . .[24]

A concession to Pietro Barbo in response to his pleas of impecuniosity was accompanied by the remark that: 'non dubitamus, Quod considerabit, quod ipse nobilis noster est, et nolet in hoc contendere, sed dabit modum repperiendi pecunias predictas . . . '.[25] No further mention of the matter suggests that he took the hint.

The delicacy of Pietro Barbo's position is also suggested by a case which is of particular interest in the light of later conflicts. In 1454-55 there was a dispute between Pope Nicholas V and the Republic over the right of nomination to the bishopric of Stagno and Curzola in Dalmatia.[26] Cardinal Barbo eventually resolved the conflict by negotiating an

---

23 ASV, 'Senato', 19-20, passim.
24 ASV, 'Senato', 19, fol. 107.
25 Ibid., fol. 114.
26 Cenci, 'Probae', p. 389n.; ASV, 'Consiglio dei Dieci', 15, fols. 1v, 7-9, 36v-37.

agreement between the respective nominees which allowed the papal nominee to take possession with Venetian approval. The acrobatic finesse of this achievement is underlined by the terms in which Barbo was reminded of his duties to his native city. An emissary sent by the Council of Ten was instructed to point out to the cardinal that:

> ipse qui nobilis ciuis noster est, et cui honor nostri dominij commendatus esse debet, Ita subiacet in eo quod ad se spectare potest legibus et ordinibus nostris, sicut laici . . . ;

and he was also to make known to the cardinal that

> in nostris consilijs esse statutum, Quod si dominium cum consilijs terre scripserit Romano pontifici, et aliquis ciuis, seu sacer, seu non sacer audebit contrarium tentare, aut dicere aut scribere, ipso facto ab omni nostro dominio alienus efficitur, et priuatur bonis etc . . .[27]

The delicacy of the cardinal's position vis-à-vis the papacy, on the other hand, is dramatically illustrated in Pius II's account of his request, around the fatal year 1459, that 'litteras omnes arrestari, que de rebus sub ditione Venetorum consistentibus se inconsulto decernerentur', a request accompanied with the assertion that this had been 'a Calisto concessum'. Pius' reaction represents the other end of the cardinalatial tightrope:

> Ergo . . . non me Veneti, sed cardinalem Sancti Marci summum pontificem adorabunt? si potuit Calistus superiorem ferre, non potest Pius mortalem hominem; deo tantum et sacris litteris subiecta est auctoritas nostra.[28]

Ironically, as pope, Barbo was to react similarly to cardinals' deference to other powers.[29]

Pietro Barbo's balancing-act came to an end in February 1459, through his nomination by Pius II to the bishopric of Padua.[30] Fantino Dandolo having

---

27 ASV, 'Consiglio dei Dieci', 15, fol. 8.
28 Pius II, *Pii II Commentarii rerum memorabiliumque temporibus suis contiguerunt*, ed. Adriano van Heck (2 vols., Vatican City, 1984), I, p. 124.
29 ASMa, 842, fasc. XXXI, no. 532 (Giovanni Pietro Arrivabene, 29 Jan. 1465).
30 On the affair of the bishopric of Padua in 1459-60, see Pius II, *Commentarii*, ed. Van Heck, I, pp. 138-9, 204, 245, 258; Cenci, 'Probae', pp. 391-3, n. 99; Sanuto, *Vite dei duchi*, cols. 1166E-1167E; Domenico Malipiero, 'Annali veneti dall' anno 1457 al 1500', *Archivio storico italiano*, series i, VII (1843-4), pp. 652-3; Gasparo Zonta, 'Un conflitto tra la repubblica veneta e la curia romana per l'episcopato di Padova (1459-60), *Atti e memorie della R. Accademia di Scienze, Lettere ed Arti in Padova*, n.s. XL (1924), pp. 221-38.

died on 17 February, the Senate on the following day instituted its normal procedure of a *proba*. The names of interested candidates were gathered, and most votes went to Gregorio Correr, protonotary apostolic and abbot of San Zeno in Verona, with Giacomo Zeno, Bishop of Belluno and Feltre, as runner-up. The Senate immediately wrote to Pius II recommending Correr's appointment. However, on 22 February, before receiving this recommendation, Pius II – then nearing Siena on his journey to his congress in Mantua – had appointed Cardinal Barbo. The Senate refused to accept his nomination and a year-long battle ensued.

Such battles between pope and republic had long been quite regular occurrences, but this one was to be fought tenaciously. In a deliberation of 5 March, the Senate described Cardinal Barbo, *ciuis noster*, as 'immemor obligationis naturalis quam habere debet ad patriam suam'. He had, they claimed, insistently solicited the appointment 'non habito respectu ad honorem nostri dominij, nec ad voluntatem et intentionem nostram, et huius consilij'. They declared:

> vt Libertatem nostram, iam ultra annos mille conseruatam et de bono in melius auctam, per hos indirectos modos et vias, suppeditari et uiolari non permittamus . . . .

They ordered that the cardinal's brother Paolo should come before them and be given twenty days to persuade Pietro to renounce the bishopric, so that Correr could have it. The cardinal's revenues from benefices in Venetian jurisdiction were sequestrated, and Paolo Barbo himself was threatened both with banishment and confiscation of all his goods should he fail to persuade the cardinal.[31] There is some indication that Pietro Barbo may have been prepared to renounce. Indeed, a letter of 27 March from the Senate to the pope somewhat bafflingly asserts that he had done so, and expresses great joy.[32] However, the Senate may have been the victim of false information or wishful thinking, the cardinal may subsequently have changed his mind, or – most likely, as we shall see – such a renunciation may not have been allowed by the pope. Certainly, the situation long remained unresolved, and Paolo Barbo disappears from the Venetian political record between February 1459 and mid 1460.[33] Only in March 1460 did Pietro finally renounce the Paduan see *sponte et libere*, and Pius II – apparently determined not to concede the Venetians a total victory – nominated to the

---

31 ASV, 'Senato', 20, fols. 179v-180 (published by Zonta, 'Conflitto', pp. 230-1).
32 Ibid., 180v (Zonta, 'Conflitto', pp. 232-4).
33 He still figures as an *avogador di comun* on 21 Feb. 1459 in ASV, 'Consiglio dei Dieci', 15, fol. 171v. He reappears as a *savio di terraferma* on 7 June 1460, ASV, 'Senato', 21, fol. 9v.

see not Gregorio Correr, but the runner-up, Giacomo Zeno.[34] The Senate, probably so as not to obstruct cooperation with the pope in an expedition against the Turks, accepted this. Shortly before, Paolo Barbo successfully challenged the validity of the measures taken against him and, on 5 March 1460, three *capita* of the Council of Ten annulled the senatorial decree of exactly a year earlier.[35]

This episode had great impact on Pietro Barbo personally, and ended his career as a Venetian agent at the papal curia; hereafter his name rarely appears in the Senate registers. The Venetian ambassadors sent to Pius II's Congress of Mantua in September 1459 were specifically prohibited by the Senate from visiting Cardinal Barbo there, and on their return to Venice in January 1460 were disciplined by the Council of Ten for having had dealings with him.[36] Indeed, Cardinal Barbo came to be credited with systematic obstruction of Venetian requests at the curia. A Venetian envoy sent to Rome in March 1462 about the contentious matter of reform at the Madonna dell'Orto was instructed, if he visited or saw Cardinal Barbo, to say to him:

> quod si ei non scripsimus, non miretur, quoniam sicut informati sumus in omnibus que obtinere quesiuimus apud Summum pontificem et presertim in facto monasterij Sancte Marie ab orto, Ipse semper fuit contrarius uotis nostris . . . .[37]

By December 1463, when arrangements for a fleet against the Turk were under way and Cardinal Barbo was one of the cardinals assigned to arm a galley[38], it was contemplated that he should be one of the curial cardinals on whom Lodovico Foscarini (one of the ambassadors to Mantua in 1459) should call as ambassador to the pope.[39] Nonetheless, mutual confidence was not restored, and the Paduan episode was to be repeatedly invoked.

This conflict has to be seen in a wider context than that of a personal clash between Cardinal Pietro Barbo and the Venetian government. On the Venetian side, it is clear that the case reflected intensified preoccupation with defence of the Republic's jurisdiction in ecclesiastical affairs. For one thing the Senate saw Barbo's appointment as one *in commendam*, being understandably convinced that he had no intention of residing in Padua.[40] This they

---

34 ASegVat, reg. lat. 559, fols. 120-122 (26 March 1460).
35 ASV, 'Senato', 20, fol. 179v.
36 ASV, 'Senato', 20, fols. 191v-192v, for the instructions; ASV, 'Consigio dei Dieci', 15, fol. 196v, for the proceedings against the ambassadors. See also Sanuto, *Vite de' duchi*, col. 1167CE.

For another example of Barbo being singled out in a hostile manner, see ASC, 'Consiglio dei Dieci', 15, fol. 195v (2 Jan. 1460).
37 ASV, 'Consigio dei Dieci', 16, fol. 93v.
38 Sanuto, *Vite de' duchi*, col. 1178A.
39 ASV, 'Senato', 21, fol. 211v.
40 ASV, 'Senato', 20, fols. 179v-180.

took as a slur on the honour of Padua, 'inter alias italie vrbes, famosa et preclara satis': in human memory the see had never been conceded *in commendam*, but always to a resident bishop agreeable to them.[41] But the Senate also related the case to a broader campaign against such appointments which, they intoned ritually, led to many evils:

> diuinus non celebratur cultus; dissipantur ecclesiarum ornamenta; patrimonium hiesu christi, sancteque religionis nostre, his modis Labefactari, et in exitium dari . . .

They connected the matter with demands presented to Pius II by the embassy sent to swear obedience to him in 1458 (demands also made by a similar embassy to Calixtus III in 1455), and they reminded Pius of his promise no longer to make appointments *in commendam* in Venetian territory. For another thing, the Senate also argued on grounds of general diplomatic practice. They pointed out that it was normal for popes in such matters to accommodate the wishes of secular authorities, as indeed past popes had done for Venice herself.[42]

On the same day as it promulgated the decree about the Paduan appointment, 5 March 1459, the Senate also decreed that no papal nominations to ecclesiastical benefices in Venetian territory with revenues of over 100 ducats could be accepted, except by a favourable vote in the Senate of two-thirds of at least 120 voters.[43] This seems to have disconcerted Pius II rather more than Paduan affair itself, and probably led him to block quick resolution of the Paduan question through an early renunciation by Barbo. Papal protests were met by the Senate with bland assertions that the decree was no new assault on papal prerogatives or ecclesiastical liberties because the Senate had always invested appointees to benefices with their temporalities. This argument enabled the Senate eventually, in January 1460, to content the pope with the revocation of the decree, 'ita quod res ista remaneat, sicut prius erat'.[44] Another sign of growing tension in Venetian-papal relations came in November 1459 when the Council of Ten, concerned at ambassadorial reports from Mantua that the pope knew everything that went on in Venice's governmental councils, renewed a decree of 1411 (in the time of the Venetian Pope Gregory XII) requiring that *papalisti* –

---

41 Ibid., fol. 180.
42 Ibid., fol. 180v (Zonta, 'Conflitto', pp. 232-34). For the instructions to the ambassadors to Calixtus III and Pius II, ASV, 'Senato', 20, fols. 62-63v, 164-165v. For the diplomatic argument, ibid., 205-v.
43 Zonta, 'Conflitto', p. 225 (citing, ASV, 'Senato, Terra', 4, fol. 100-v; Cenci, 'Probae', p. 321.
44 Pius II, *Commentarii*, ed. van Heck, I, pp. 245, 258; Cenci, 'Probae', p. 321; ASV, 'Senato', 20, fol. 205-v.

anyone who held a benefice from the pope, or whose father, son, brother, son's son or brother's son held any such benefice – should be excluded from discussions relating to the pope or curial affairs.[45] Behind everything, by November 1459, was also the complex relationship between Venice and Pius II over the projected crusade.[46] Hesitancy prompted by Venice's delicate 'front-line' position vis-à-vis the Turks and suspicion of Pius's broader agenda provoked papal resentment, while fear of papal claims to the yields of tenths, preachings and indulgences in Venetian territories was also awakened.[47] There seems, in fact, little doubt that the eventual resolution of the Paduan problem owed most to its being submerged in the diplomatic give-and-take necessitated by the projected crusade.

On the papal side, the Paduan affair has to be seen in a broader context of increasing papal assertiveness of plenitude of power. Pius II's conciliarist and imperialist pasts were now long forgotten, and he had become an uncompromising proponent of the 'high' papalism forged in the debates of the conciliar period. Pius's attitude emerges, for instance, in his reaction to Pietro Barbo's claim to intervene in all curial decisions regarding Venice. The crusade was also an attempt to reclaim for the papacy in a concrete way the leadership of Christendom. The congress of Mantua also promulgated in January 1460 the bull *Execrabilis* anathematising conciliar appeals. In more direct relation to the Paduan case, Pius II was also very assertive of his overriding powers to provide to episcopal sees vacant *apud sedem apostolicam*, having made a general reservation to that effect at the beginning of his pontificate – as he recalled in the bull nominating Giacomo Zeno.[48]

There was, then, on both the papal and the Venetian sides, a convergence of developments which promised that the 'Venetian' pontificate to begin in 1464 would be one of stormy confrontation.

Pietro Barbo was elected pope in Rome on 30 August 1464 (*Fig. 15*). The Venetians determined to put on a brave face. Sanuto reports that news of the election was celebrated with 'grandi dimostrazioni d'allegrezza, di suoni, e di luminarie assai';[49] and the Senate gave formal expression to its joy in letters to pope and cardinals on 8 October, on receipt of the bull solemnly communicating the pope's assumption of office.[50] On 5 September, the

---

45 ASV, 'Consiglio dei Dieci', 15, fols. 192v, 193v; E. Friedberg and F. Ruffini, *Trattato di diritto ecclesiastico cattolico ed evangelico* (Turin, 1893), p. 101.
46 ASV, 'Consiglio dei Dieci', 15, fols. 192v, 193v, 195.
47 ASV, 'Senato', 21, fol. 2.
48 ASegVat, reg. lat. 559, fol. 120 (Zonta, 'Conflitto', pp. 223-4).
49 Sanuto, *Vite de' duchi*, col. 1181BC.
50 ASV, 'Senato', 22, fols. 45v-46.

Senate had also decided to honour the new pope by sending an unusually large embassy of ten to swear obedience.[51]

For his part, Pietro Barbo certainly did not lose all his patriotic loyalties. On the day of his election, he even proposed to take the very Venetian name of Mark II – until Pius II's confidant Cardinal Jacopo Ammannati, to be one of the new pope's most persistent critics, pointed out that such a choice would have the unacceptable consequence of making acclamation of the pope – 'Marco! Marco!' – simultaneously acclamation of Venice. Barbo therefore chose the name of Paul II.[52] But throughout his pontificate, he continued to identify himself as a Venetian patrician,[53] and ambassadorial observers continued to note – often with apprehension – his affection 'ala patria et in genere ala cita'.[54] Late in his pontificate, Paul II still expressed affectionate memories in particular of his native neighbourhood in Venice. In December 1470, in a bull establishing a *Studium Generale* in Venice, he recalled that he had been born in the parish of San Giovanni in Bragora and that 'in ipsa Ecclesia Sacri Baptismatis unda renati exstitimus'; and 'pro ipsius Ecclesiae decore et nostri reminiscentia', he nominated the then rector of S. Giovanni and his successors chancellors of the new university.[55]

Now he was pope, the tightrope which he had been walking as cardinal demanded even more dextrous balancing. On one occasion, he gave an indication of his own sense of this when he described himself as torn between his identity as a 'zentilhomo de uenecia uolendo il bene de la sua terra' and his role as 'pontifico' desiring 'la salute de lanime'.[56] The problem had earlier provided a theme for the elegant oration which the Venetian humanist Bernardo Giustiniani delivered before Paul II on his arrival as ambassador in January 1466. He urged the pope to maintain a balance between his attachments to Venice and to the church:

> Licet enim ecclesia te puerum a nobis abduxerit, adolescentem Cardinalem fecerit; nunc denique creaverit summum ponteficem. Natale tamen solum et illa prima cunabula ubi natus, altus, educatusque es negare non potes . . . . Sit Roma tibi cara ut esse debet; sit romana ecclesia sponsa tua, filia tua. Istis illa nominibus contenta sit, dum patriae nomen Venetiis tuis relinquat. Neque tu dedignabere . . .[57]

51 Ibid., fol. 37; ASV, 'Maggior Consiglio', 23 (Regina), fol. 58.
52 ASMa, 'Roma', 56, 30 August 1464 (Stefano Nardini, archbishop of Milan).
53 E.g., ASMa, 843, 2 March 1466 (Bartolomeo Marasca).
54 ASMi, 'Roma', 65, 14 Oct. 1468; see also ibid., 56, 11 Sept. 1464.
55 The text of the bull is given in Sanuto, *Vite de' duchi*, col. 1192A-1193D.
56 ASMa, 843, 2 March 1466 (Bartolomeo Marasca).
57 Bernardi Iustiniani, *Orationes* (Venice, per B. Beralio, n.d [?1492]), fol. gi.

But the claims of spouse or daughter and fatherland were not easily reconcilable. On the one hand, there was the problem of relations with other powers suspicious of Venice. It was necessary that any cooperation should be seen to proceed from consideration of the good of the church, rather than from 'laffectione de la patria', which Paul felt constrained to insist on occasion, 'per essersi uestito de questo ecclesiastica, haueua deposta'.[58] On the other hand, there was the problem of incompatible jurisdictional claims. More than once Paul II said that, if he were to ally himself with Venice, he would have to give himself to them *in commendam* and content himself with being treated as their chaplain – and he cited warnings from his uncle Eugenius IV to this effect.[59] The issue was, of course, yet further complicated by his own past relations with Venice.

In the first days of his pontificate, Paul II had a long conversation with the Milanese ambassador Ottone del Carretto, in which he spoke *molto male* of the Signoria of Venice. Apart from mentioning that he intended to ask them to return the Romagnol centres of Cervia and perhaps Ravenna to the church, and saying that he did not want too many Venetians in his household, Paul II claimed to

> hauere legitima cagione de essere Inimico a quella Signoria, laquale li ha fatta tanta Iniuria a luy et a tuti li suoy parenti et amici, et sono stati cagione con le persecutione loro fare morire Inanci tempo il fratello suo . . . .

He did speak well of Doge Cristoforo Moro, and affirmed his benevolence 'aluy et ala Citta in genere'; but, he said, 'ali altri che gouernano non potria may essere amico'.[60] A few days later, when he heard of the election of the ten Venetian ambassadors to swear obedience to him, he told a close collaborator that they were really coming simply to spy on his intentions, and to ensure that promised papal funds for the enterprise against the Turk did not slip from their grasp. Moreover, he claimed, four of them were 'soy mortali Inimici' who had never tired of working against himself and his brother.[61]

Paul II's personal resentments against the Venetian government – stemming primarily from the Paduan episode – are evoked repeatedly through his pontificate, both in his own reported remarks and by ambassadorial and curial analysts.[62] These resentments constitute an important determinant of

---

58 ASMa, 843, 11 June 1467 (G.P. Arrivabene).
59 ASMi, 'Roma', 57, 22 June 1465 (Agostino de' Rossi); see also ibid., 65, 11 Oct. 1468.
60 ASMi, 'Roma', 56, 11 Sept. 1464.
61 Ibid., 16 Sept. 1464 (S. Nardini).
62 ASMi, 'Roma', 57, 22 June 1465; 63, 28 Dec. 1467; 65, 14 Oct. 1468.

his relations with Venice as pope. Particular emphasis is placed consistently on the treatment accorded his brother. Paolo Barbo had died not long after the affair, probably on 19 November 1462, at the age of only forty-six.[63] It may be that his death was hastened by his treatment, as Paul II dramatically insisted; but at the same time it should be noted that he had been able to resume his distinguished political career from mid-1460, holding various significant offices including membership of the Council of Ten,[64] and serving with Bernardo Giustiniani as ambassador to the new King of France, Louis XI, in 1461-62.[65]

The way in which Paul II's resentments are expressed also suggests another possible dimension of the Paduan affair. There are tantalising hints at its connection with factional divisions inside the Venetian patriciate. Mention has already been made of the reported splintering of the patriciate around 1450 through a conspiracy of sixteen *case nuove* or *curti* to exclude the *case vecchie* or *longhi* clans from the dogeship, and of the fact that most of the connections of the Barbo seem to have lain amongst the latter group. Does Paul II's reiterated distinction between the city in general and 'alcuni de quilli che gouernano' reflect a factional alignment?[66] It is interesting that Pius II in his *Commentaries* says of Venetian reaction to Barbo's appointment to Padua that:

. . . illis nihil molestius uisum est, rabida invidia et, que presulem latebant, ciuili simultate agitatis . . . .[67]

Certainly, precisely whilst the affair was dragging on, the Venetian Council of Ten had occasion to express concern at the spreading of 'aliqua seditiosa, et periculosa uerba' by 'aliquem seu aliquos seditiosos et maledictos', which was disrupting the traditional unity of the patriciate.[68] Who were Paul II's four 'mortal enemies' amongst the ten Venetian ambassadors of September

---

63 The date 19 November 1462 is implied in a quittance granted by Paul II to his sister Elisabetta Barbo in 1470: ASegVat, arm. XXXIX, t. 12, fols. 45-46v.

64 ASV, 'Senato', 21, fols. 9v-58 (references to him as a *savio di Terraferma* between 7 June 1460 and 28 Sept. 1461); 'Consiglio dei Dieci', 16, fols. 51-61 (member of Council of Ten from 1 Oct. 1460; references to 26 March 1461); 'Maggior Consiglio', 23 (Regina), fol. 39v (20 Dec. 1461: extension of term as Podestà of Verona); ASV, 'Consiglio dei Dieci, 16, fols. 100-115 (*avogador*: references from June 1462 to 15 Oct. 1462).

65 ASV, 'Senato', 21, fols. 61v-63 (12 Oct. 1461: *Commissio*). For Paolo Barbo's *Oratio* of 8 Dec. 1461 to Louis XI at Tours, see Augustini Valerii, *De cautione adhibenda in edendi libris* (Padua, 1729), pp. 183-92.

66 ASMi, 'Roma', 65, 14 Oct. 1468 (Agostino de' Rossi).

67 Pius II, *Commentarii*, ed. Van Heck, I, pp. 138-9; note also report on p. 176 of how Barbo's rival Trevisan went to Padua and Venice, 'quibus in locis aduersus cardinalem Sancti Marci multa molitus ne patauinam consequeretur ecclesiam'.

68 ASV, 'Consiglio dei Dieci', 15, fol. 187, 4 Sept. 1459.

1464?[69] Five of the ten belonged to the conspiratorial *curti* clans (Barbarigo, Gritti, Mocenigo, Trevisan, Tron); at least two of them had personally taken part in the vote on the senatorial provision of 5 March 1459 relating to the Paduan affair (Triadano Gritti and Niccolò Tron); and two others belonged to houses with members known to have participated in the vote (Barbarigo, Trevisan) (although we do not know which way any particular individual voted).[70] Were these the four? It unfortunately seems impossible to answer these questions. Moreover, the matter is somewhat complicated by Paul II's singling out of Doge Cristoforo Moro for praise, the Moro having been one of the conspiratorial *case nuove* – perhaps this had something to do with the family connection between Barbo and the Moro.[71] However, the possibility seems to exist that another factor determining Paul II's relations with Venice was family involvement in patrician factionalism. There are hints that behind Paul II's repeated contemplation of a visit to Venice *per farsi vedere*,[72] was the notion that thereby he might upset the current factional balance, neutralising his enemies in the government by using personal magnetism to promote a wider consensus – as Cardinal Francesco Gonzaga put it, 'parendoli che quando el fosse li, piu facilmente se acordaria piu presto à le uoglie suoe'.[73]

Paul II had sought to calm the concern of the Milanese ambassador that he would 'fill his house with Venetians';[74] and certainly his court and household were not to be totally dominated by them. Nonetheless, amongst his principal collaborators there was a strong presence from Venice itself, or from the Venetian territories. This does not, however, seem to have done much to render papal policy more accommodating to Venetian demands – as the Milanese ambassador feared it might. Indeed, some of the key 'Venetians' in Paul II's entourage seem rather to have been enemies of Venice. The principal place was quickly assumed by the pope's distant relative Marco Barbo, described by a Ferrarese ambassador as 'lo ochio destro del papa'.[75] Paul II himself noted that Marco, who had been master of

---

69 The ten ambassadors were (ASV, 'Senato', 22, fol. 37): Girolamo di Francesco Barbarigo, Vittore Capello, Lodovico Foscarini, Triadano Gritti, Andrea di Niccolò Lion, Pietro di Leonardo Mocenigo, Ettore Pasqualigo, Niccolo Soranzo, Zaccaria Trevisan, Niccolò Tron. After the departure of the other eight in late December 1464 or early January 1465, Barbarigo and Gritti remained on in Rome until the end of March 1465.
70 ASV, 'Senato', 20, fols. 178-179v. Of the voters, the names of only eighteen (doge, *consiliarii*, etc.) are given. The 135 votes were distributed as follows: *De parte*, 84; *Non*, 13; *Non sinceri*, 38.
71 See above, note 12. Another family connection, Pietro Barozzi, later bishop of Padua (1487-1507), during Cristoforo Moro's term as doge (1462-71), produced a poem in praise of him: *Cristoforo Moro Doge* (Venice, P. Naratovich, November 1866).
72 ASMi, 'Roma', 65, 14 Oct. 1468 (Agostino de' Rossi).
73 ASMa, 843, 6 Nov. 1466.
74 ASMi, 'Roma', 56, 1 and 11 Sept. 1464.
75 ASMo, 'Ambasciatori, Roma', busta 1, fol. 9 (i), n. 15, 19 Sept. 1467 (Giacomo Trotti).

his household as cardinal, had 'insieme con luy' been 'maltractato da venecianj'[76] – although he seems to have come to play a mediatory role in papal-Venetian relations. Another distant relative, Lorenzo Zane, treasurer-general and soldier-governor in the temporalities, had had many troubles with the Council of Ten, which ended in 1463 with banishment from his see of Spalato for ten years.[77] And a Mantuan observer commented on the death of another close collaborator, Teodoro de' Lelli, bishop of Treviso, that 'molto era odiato presertim da uenecianj magnati'.[78]

In the sphere of ecclesiastical jurisdiction, Paul II came into conflict with Venice primarily over provision to benefices in Venetian territory and over clerical taxation. About the former, the Venetians were initially quite indulgent of the pope's wishes, just as he had gratified them after Andrea Bondemiro's death in August 1464 by confirming as patriarch of Venice the candidate successful in the senatorial *proba*, Gregorio Correr. Misfortune, however, did not desert Correr, for he died in November 1464 before taking up the office.[79] Thereby the patriarchate became a divisive issue. In the *proba* of late November 1464, the successful candidate was Marco Barbo; but, presumably in deference to other papal plans, he refused the office.[80] In January 1465, Paul II made his own appointment – Giovanni Barozzi, then bishop of Bergamo, his own cousin once removed.[81] The pope's intention was discerned by the Milanese ambassador: 'lo manda la per stare, et tractare tutte le facende che accaderano tra la sua Beatitudine et quella Signoria'.[82] The Venetian government accepted the appointment, but it was a source of tension. Barozzi in turn died in April 1466. The Senate elected Maffeo Gherardi, the Camaldolensian abbot of San Michele di Murano, whom Paul II refused, making clear to the Venetian Ambassador 'quod volebat habere patriarcham qui suae beatitudini obediret'. The Venetians continued to insist on Gherardi, invoking familiar arguments about long-established custom and practice elsewhere. Only in December 1468 did Paul II finally agreed to confirm him.[83]

An even more delicate political situation – involving imperial interest as well as Venetian concern for its recently consolidated control of Friuli – led

76 ASMi, 'Roma', 56, 11 Nov. 1464 (Ottone del Carretto).
77 ASV, 'Consiglio dei Dieci', 16, references spread between fols. 49 (27 Aug. 1460) and 150 (9 Feb. 1464). See also ASMi, 'Roma', 61, 19 Feb. 1467.
78 ASMa, 843, 31 March 1466 (Bartolomeo Marasca).
79 See Cenci, 'Probae', pp. 395-6, n. 101; Sanuto, *Vite de' duchi*, col. 1174A; Malipiero, *Annali*, p. 654; AMi, 'Roma', 56, 17/18 Sept. 1464 (S. Nardini); ASV, 'Senato', 22, fols. 44v-45, 8 Oct. 1464.
80 Cenci, 'Probae', pp. 397-8, n. 102; Sanuto, *Vite de' duchi*, col. 1182BC.
81 ASMa, 842, fasc. XXXV, n. 583, 7 Jan. 1465 (Baldassarre Suardo).
82 ASMi, 'Roma', 57, 27 Jan. 1465.
83 Cenci, 'Probae', pp. 398-400, n. 103; Sanuto, *Vite de' duchi*, col. 1183B; ASV, 'Senato', 22, fols. 158, 163-v; 23, fols. 71, 112v, 117v, 130, 145v, 154v.

to a six-year vacancy in the once-powerful patriarchate of Aquileia, after the death of Cardinal Lodovico Trevisan in March 1465.[84] Marco Barbo was eventually appointed in 1470, but only in the midst of a yet more remarkable brawl involving also the pope's appointments of his two young cardinal nephews, Battista Zeno and Giovanni Michiel, to the bishoprics of Vicenza and Verona respectively.[85] Marco Barbo's appointment was eventually accepted by the Senate in September 1471,[86] early in the next pontificate; but the other appointments remained blocked, not just because of long-standing Venetian objections to the principal bishoprics of their *dominio* being alienated *in commendam*, but also because of a storm which broke around the head of Battista Zeno. In May 1471, the Council of Ten found that he had been obtaining Venetian state secrets in correspondence with members of his family, and using them against Venetian interests. Besides barring him from all benefices in Venetian jurisdiction, they imprisoned his mother, Elisabetta Barbo, Paul II's sister, and various other relatives and connections.[87] The two cardinals were not to obtain possession of their bishoprics until 1476/7.[88]

Governmental taxation of the clergy provoked strife above all in the levying of *decime* or tenths to sustain Venice's war effort against the Turks.[89] After the failure of Pius II's efforts to launch a crusade, Venice was left to face the Turkish problem virtually alone, at an annual cost estimated at over 700,000 ducats.[90] For most of his pontificate, Paul II's commitment to the crusade remained merely formal: he gave priority to immediate local political problems. He would not countenance Venetian arguments for agreement with the Turks,[91] but was generally inattentive to Venetian appeals for financial support.[92] However, when the Venetian government unilaterally continued to levy from the clergy the *decime* originally approved by Pius II,[93], he protested vigorously at infringement of clerical prerogative. The Mantuan observer, Bartolomeo Marasca, reports a speech to

---

84 ASV, 'Senato', 22, fols. 88v, 108, 110v; AMi, 'Roma', 58, 24 Jan. 1466 (Agostino de' Rossi).

85 On the whole affair, see Cenci, 'Probae', p. 401n.; Giovanni Soranzo, 'Contrastata nomina del card. Michiel al vescovato di Verona', *Zenonis cathedra*, special number, *Nova historia*, VII, fasc. iii-iv (1955), pp. 73-83. See also ASMi, 'Roma', 67, 10 June 1471 (Pietro da Modegnano, protonotary apostolic).

86 ASV, 'Senato', 25, fol. 68, 16 Sept. 1471 (cited in Cenci, 'Probae', p. 401n.).

87 ASV, 'Consiglio dei Dieci', 17, fols. 167-v, 177, 182v-183, 184v-185, 187v, 188-v, 189v-191v, 193v. See Malipiero, *Annali*, pp. 661-2.

88 ASV, 'Consiglio dei Dieci', 18, fol. 207, 30 April 1476 (cited in Cenci, 'Probae', p. 401n.); R. Predelli, *I libri commemoriali della Repubblica de Venezia: regesti*, V (Venice 1901); Deputazione veneta di storia patria, *Monumenti Storici*, series i, X, pp. 222-3 (*Libro* XVI, nos. 102-4, 18-19 Feb. 1477).

89 The issue is recurrent throughout ASV, 'Senato', 22-24.

90 ASV, 'Senato', 22, fols. 120v-121.

91 Ibid., fols. 51v-52, 68-v.

92 Ibid., fols. 56-57, 65-66.

93 For a senatorial survey of the history of the *decime*, see ASV, 'Senato', 22, fol. 110.

Venetian prelates in 1466, in which the pope identified such perversity as a product of Venetian expansion into the *Terraferma*:

> prima che hauesseno in terra erano bonj hominj. Modo per la Signoria de terra sonno fatti diauoli senza conscientia in mettere taglie e colte ale chiesie contra dio e la sede apostolica . . . .

And he went on to elaborate the consequent evils in terms which echoed Venetian complaints about *commende*:

> sonno sequiti tanti malj che molte poure chiesie priuate de calice e libri; per la impotencia de preti pouerj, sonno abandonate, et consequenter gli parochianj de quelli sonno senza ministratorj de sacramenti . . . .

Justifying thereby his bulls prohibiting the *Signoria* from taxing clerics, it was in this context that Paul II described the conflict within himself between *zentilhomo de uenecia* and *pontifico*. He said he wished *decime* to be imposed by diocesan bishops and then consigned to the Patriarch of Venice, who in turn should concede them to the *Signoria* when needed.[94]

The Venetian government, apart from stressing the need for funds for an effort in the general interest of Christendom, responded with characteristic appeals to custom established *ab urbe condita*, to practice *cepta iam mille et amplius annos*. The Senate claimed that:

> consueta est ciuitas haec . . . in omnibus bellis et difficultatibus occurris, non secus a bonis praelatorum, et presbyterorum exigere portionem eorum grauedinum, quam a ciuibus laicis . . . .

Moreover, they asserted, previous popes had not objected.[95] Through the efforts of the Patriarch Barozzi, and later of Paul II's legate Cardinal Juan Carvajal, accommodations were reached which enabled the levying of two *decime* annually with papal approval[96]; but the pope was anxious to reduce this concession when the Turkish threat receded,[97] while the Venetians were ever ready to go it alone should papal permission be denied.[98] The prickly issue was aggravated by Venetian orders to provincial rectors to sequestrate ecclesiastical property and income in cases of failure to pay.[99] Perhaps

---

94 ASMa, 843, 2 March 1466 (Bartolomeo Marasca).
95 ASV, 'Senato', 22, fol. 76-v; see also fols. 90-91.
96 Ibid., fols. 105-106, 146-v, 161-v; 23, fols. 3, 4v-5, 8v-9.
97 Ibid., fols. 135v, 139.
98 ASV, 'Senato', 22, fol. 170v.
99 Ibid., fols. 161-v, 170; 23, fol. 129-v.

Bartolomeo Marasca best defined the problem when he reported from Rome in July 1466 that:

> tuta questa corte crida contra uenecianj, *dicendoli essere douentati papi* per che propria auctoritate poneno decime a chierici et sequestrano loro benj . . . .[100]

Paul II's presentation of Venetian policy as a result of *Terraferma* expansion highlights the signs of transmutation of age-old clashes between church and state over clerical immunity into broader jurisdictional clashes between two rival 'states'. Venice's new involvement in Italian peninsula politics was paralleled by a new papal determination to render the papacy's control of its Italian temporal dominions more effective and profitable. Pressures in this direction appear to have been mounting for some time before Paul II's pontificate.[101] Even though as cardinal he had little direct involvement in the government of the Papal States, Paul II seems to have responded to these pressures enthusiastically, and to have incorporated their logic into his conception of papal sovereignty. It seems likely that his response derived at least in part from adherence to concepts of state sovereignty inculcated in him as a *zentilhomo de uenecia*, which gives an extra poignancy to his consequent conflicts with Venice. He repeatedly gave evidence of the seriousness with which he took the clause in the electoral capitulation of the 1464 Conclave forbidding the alienation of church territories;[102] and he quickly earned a reputation as a pope whose consistent aim was 'de subiugarsi tutte le terre de la chiesa, che immediate non gli sono sottoposte'.[103] As he declared:

> . . . cordi nobis est iura Camere Apostolice non modo conservare sed, ubi cum honestate et iustitia possit, ubilibet ampliare . . . .[104]

By mid 1465, Paul II had had an early success in imposing direct rule on the lands of the Anguillara in the Patrimony, when news of the impending

---

100 ASMa, 843, 9 July 1466 (Bartolomeo Marasca) (my italics). In the last year of the pontificate, the problem of clerical taxation came to the fore in another guise through papal excommunication of the Venetian officials who levied gabelles and other such taxes from clerics: ASV, 'Senato', 24, fol. 118-v; 25, fol. 12-v; 'Consiglio dei Dieci', 17, fols. 162v, 164.

101 Giovanni Soranzo, 'Sigismondo Pandolfo Malatesta in Morea e le vicende del suo dominio', *Atti e memorie della deputazione di storia patria per le provincie di Romagna*, series iv, VIII (1917-18), p. 240.

102 He took refuge behind it, for example, in dealings over Sora and Mondavio in October 1468; and in April 1470 he used it to justify rejection of a proposal to give Rimini as a dowry for the suggested marriage between one of his nieces and Costanzo Sforza. For the latter, see ASMo, busta 1, fol. 9 (iv), no. 10, 27 April 1470 (Giacomo Trotti).

103 ASMi, 'Roma', 64, 27 Jan 1478 (Giovanni Bianchi).

104 ASegVat, reg. vat. 525, fols. 47v-48.

death of the ailing Malatesta Novello of Cesena turned his attention to the northern province of Romagna. By the terms of the peace of 1463 which ended the long struggle between Pius II and the Malatesta brothers of Cesena and Rimini, what remained to them of their former territories were to return under the direct dominion of the Holy See on their deaths. Paul II was determined to enforce the observance of this agreement; and in the case of Cesena, soon after Malatesta Novello's death in late November 1465, he was successful.[105] It was beginning to seem – as the young Cardinal Francesco Gonzaga was later seductively to suggest in one of his many intimate conversations with the pope, comparing Paul II's situation with that of Nicholas V – that:

> hora La Beatitudine Vostra e lo stato de chiesia è in altra reputatione e potentia, e de magiore terrore, che non soleua . . . .[106]

The success over Cesena prompted the formulation of plans to bring other areas of the Romagna under direct papal rule – what another Mantuan observer baptised as Paul II's 'desegno de romagna'.[107] It was inevitable that Paul II should become preoccupied with the Romagna. There, the effective exercise of papal sovereignty had long been nullified by the independence of long-established local *signorie*. Nominally they ruled as papal vicars, but generally the papacy did not even receive payment of the required *census*. As Cardinal Gonzaga reported in July 1466:

> . . . La Sanctitate de nostro signore hauendo fatto examinare le Inuestiture che pretendeno hauere questi Signori de Romagna, troua che in uero niuno de lor gli ha ragione alcuna; e per questo da qui inanti ha deliberado de non acceptare da Lor censo, ne uideatur approbare, e col tempo ha animo de tirarse ugni cosa sotto . . . .[108]

Many of the *signorie* were notoriously unstable, their ruling families rent by internecine feud; their inability to guarantee good government had led to the formation of factions anxious for an alternative regime, such as that of the church – all of which provided the pope with further pretexts, opportunities, and indeed responsibilities. Finally, the Romagna was the strategic frontier area in which emergent papal territorial power confronted most

---

105 Ian Robertson, 'The Return of Cesena to the Direct Dominion of the Church after the Death of Malatesta Novello', *Studi romagnoli*, XVI (1965), pp. 123-61.

106 ASMa, 843, 9 Sept. 1467.
107 Ibid., 3 June 1466 (Gian Pietro Arrivabene).
108 Ibid., 31 July 1466.

directly the already consolidated power of the other large territorial states which had emerged to dominance in the north of the peninsula – Milan, Florence and Venice. Control of the Romagna was vital to the consolidation of the Papal States.

The very fragmentation and disorganisation of the Romagna had led it to serve as a buffer zone, in which the surrounding greater powers could indulge their hegemonic aspirations without wholesale confrontation. The emergence of these larger territorial powers had also revealed the nonviability of the petty Romagnol *signorie*. They were forced to prop themselves up precariously through ties of political clientage which took precedence over obligations to their papal sovereign. Such a situation obviously provided another motive for papal intervention, but at the same time it imposed crippling disabilities on a papacy seeking to assert its sovereign rights. The papacy's military and diplomatic resources were inadequate to ensure the success of uncompromising unilateral action. The fate of Paul II's *desegno de romagna* provides graphic illustration of this. It soon became clear that his success with Cesena had depended very largely on the indifference of the outside greater powers. Alarmed at the grandiosity of Paul II's wider strategy, these powers felt their interests in other Romagnol centres to be more vital. In various combinations and ways they intervened – or failed to intervene – so as to frustrate the pope's aims.

Venice's involvement in the affairs of the neighbouring Romagna was particularly close, and this became perhaps the major determinant of the relations between Paul II and the Republic. Since 1441 Venice had controlled Ravenna, and in 1463 purchased the important salt-manufacturing centre of Cervia from Malatesta Novello of Cesena. At the opening of his pontificate, Paul II expressed the intention to ask for the return of Cervia, and perhaps of Ravenna as well.[109] In the case of Cervia, he persisted in attempts to enforce a sentence of the Auditors of the Rota regarding the nullity of the sale, provoking the Venetians' disbelief that he would move against them 'in re minima sicut est locus cervie'.[110] After Venice had obligingly stood aside to allow the resumption of Cesena in December 1465,[111] the principal objectives of the *desegno de romagna* were to be Faenza, Forlì and Rimini. In each case, interests which Venice was not prepared to waive stood in the pope's way.

---

109 ASMi, 'Roma', 56, 11 Sept. 1464.
110 ASV, 'Senato', 22, fols. 163-164; see ASMi, 'Roma', 58, 8 and 24 Jan. 1466; 59, 22 April 1466. The sentence of the Auditors of the Rota is in ASegVat, AA., arm. I-XVIII, no. 1443, fols. 40-44; see also Vittorio Franchini, 'L'annulabilità della concessione di Cervia e delle sue saline del 1463', *La Romagna*, VIII (1911), pp. 205-40.
111 ASV, 'Senato', 22, fols. 126v-127, 128.

For Paul II, the vicariates of the Manfredi of Faenza and the Ordelaffi of Forlì had lapsed through failure to pay the *census*, and he refused to accept Astorgio Manfredi's proffered payment of past *census* in November 1465, 'che vna fiada e descazuto da omne rasone'.[112] In the case of Forlì, the alleged crimes through which Pino Ordelaffi acceded to sole rule in January 1466 constituted another basis for removal, and Paul II instituted formal legal proceedings.[113] The recovery of Sigismondo Malatesta's Rimini was the balance of the task of enforcing Pius II's settlement of 1463, begun successfully with Cesena.

Although in each case Paul II had to confront the interest of the other major powers, the three centres had long since gravitated principally towards Venice's sphere of influence, being received 'in protectionem et commendationem nostram'.[114] Their rulers were given Venetian military contracts and other subsidies, on occasion military aid,[115] and they were guided by resident Venetian commissioners, or ambassadors, and sometimes direct consultations in Venice.[116] The Senate coolly analysed their situations in terms of what was good *pro statu nostro*.[117] Their interest in Rimini, for instance, was particularly lively: 'ob situm Ciuitatis Ariminj diuidentem, et discriminantem territorie Sanctissimi pontificis a territorio nostro . . .';[118] and moreover:

> pro vetustissimo amore, et paterna affectione nostra in Magnificam domum de malatestis per quamplura centenaria annorum ostensa desiderium nostrum semper fuit et est, quod status ille in domo ipsa manteneatur, et conseruetur. . . .[119]

Indeed, they had the 'salutem, et conseruationem Ciuitatis ipsius non minus caram, ac si nostra esset'.[120] There was justification for the suspicion that the Venetians would take over these Romagnol centres totally, should the local regimes cease to serve their interests.[121]

Paul II protested repeatedly. He objected to the infidelity of his subjects, who placed themselves under the protection of outside powers, departing

---

112 ASMi, 'Romagna', 165, 13 Nov. 1465 (Ludovico de' Ludovisi, from Bologna).
113 Ibid., 30 Jan. 1466, 1 and 3 Feb. 1966; ASMi, 'Roma', 58, 19 Feb. 1466, 4 March 1466; ASMa, 843, 5 July 1466.
114 E.g., ASV, 'Senato', 20, fol. 84-v; 22, fol. 10.
115 *Condotte*: Predelli, *Commemoriali*, V, pp. 152-3, 158, 162, 167; ASV, 'Senato', 23, fols. 101, 107; ASMi, 'Romagna', 166, 30 April 1467. Military aid: ASV, 'Senato', 22, fols. 15v, 61-v, 165v.
116 Emissaries: ASV, 'Senato', 22, fols. 61-v, 168v; 23, fols. 43-v, 48, 139v-140, 163v; 24, fol. 23; ASMi, 'Romagna', 166, 30 April 1467; 167, 31 May 1467. Direct consultations: ASV, 'Consiglio dei Dieci', 17, 103; 'Senato', 23, fols. 152, 158; ASMa, 843, 19 Jan. 1469 (Carlo Manfredi).
117 E.g., ASV, 'Senato', 23, fol. 168v.
118 ASV, 'Senato', 23, fol. 163.
119 Ibid., fol. 144.
120 Predelli, *Commemoriali*, V, pp. 158-9.
121 ASMa, 843, 27 June 1466 (Niccolò Secco, from Forlì); ASMi, 'Roma', 60, 1 July 1466 (Agostino de' Rossi).

thereby 'da la deuotione et protectione de sancta gexa'.[122] His frustration at being robbed of initiative is vividly illustrated in an outburst against Pino Ordelaffi in summer 1467. Borso d'Este's envoy Giacomo Trotti reports the pope saying:

> Il non delibera per alcun modo mai lassare forli come il sta al presente, sotto la protectione de venetianj; et che piu tosto el douentaria zudio, et turcho per modo parlare, che mai mai deuiare da questa voglia, et patire tanta infamia, tanto charicho, et tanta vergogna, che vn suo vicario fratricida, et matricida, tristo et cussi gran ribaldo, se gli ribelli et faccia beffe de soa Sanctita, et non lo stimi vn ficco per ombra chel habia de essere Jn protection de venetiani . . . .[122]

Paul II objected to the *poca cortesia* of outside powers who sought to 'condurre suoi hominj e suoi feudatarij senza sua licentia'.[123] In the renewals of the general Italic League which he sponsored in 1468 and in 1470, he was indignant that Venice and the other major powers determinedly nominated papal subjects like the Manfredi, the Ordelaffi and the Malatesta amongst their confederates and adherents. He declared:

> non esse Justum neque conueniens, quod aliquis potentatuum in pace predicta comprehensorum nominet alterius potentatus similiter in dicta pace comprehensi subditos . . . .

As he pointed out to the Venetians, he could as well nominate Padua, Vicenza, Verona, and so on – to say nothing of possessions of the church under Venetian control like Ravenna and Cervia.[124] To such complaints, the Senate calmly replied:

> Alijs itaque obijcenda est rabies ista dominandi, et augendi principatus, non nobis . . . Non rem inusitatam, non inauditam facimus. Sed potius quod florentini, et alij potentatus sepenumero, consulentibus rebus suis fecerunt . . . [125]

This specious Venetian excuse contained much truth, as the pope was to become increasingly aware. His natural inclination would have been to accomplish his *desegno de romagna* independently, not through force, but rather through judicial proceedings, persuasion with the lure of alternative

---

122 ASMo, 'Ambasciatori, Roma', busta 1, fol. 9 (i), no. 10, 24 Aug. 1467 (Giacomo Trotti).
123 ASMi, 'Roma', 61, 20 Dec. 1466 (Lorenzo da Pesaro).
124 Predelli, *Commemoriali*, V, pp. 169-76.
125 ASV, 'Senato', 23, fol. 55; see also fol. 71.

territories, or conspiratorial exploitation of internal divisions.[126] But he soon realised that there was no alternative to proceeding militarily, in alliance with one or more of the outside powers with interests in the region. When Venice dealt into the game of Romagnol politics the wild card of Bartolomeo Colleone in summer 1467, the pope saw new opportunities to realise his *desegno*, but he had to face the dilemma of choosing between alliance with the League of Milan, Florence and Naples, or alliance with Venice.[127] He chose alliance with the League; but the League soon deserted him, leaving him obliged to shelve his plans for Faenza and Forlì,[128] and even eventually to concede new vicariates there to the Manfredi and the Ordelaffi, in December 1468 and February 1470 respectively.[129]

Paul II turned instead to Venice for assistance. Ironically, despite conflicts, negotiations towards an *intelligentia* had been going on sporadically for a long time.[130] They finally bore fruit in 1469, in an alliance formalised in May of that year.[131] By now, the focus of the papal *desegno* had shifted to Rimini. Sigismondo Malatesta, who had resisted all Paul II's efforts to beguile him into surrendering Rimini for other territories,[132] had died in October 1468.[133] His son Roberto, having broken a promise that he would take Rimini on the pope's behalf,[134] had joined with Isotta degli Atti and her son Sallustio Malatesta to perpetuate the Malatesta regime. Venice had firmly intervened in support,[135] but seems to have been alienated by signs of division between Roberto and the others,[136] and by Roberto's inclination to seek support from the rival league.[137] Venetian interests now seemed to demand a combination with the pope to block the League from gaining a

---

126 On wishing to proceed independently, without interference, see ASMi, 'Roma', 59, 11 June 1466 (Agostino de' Rossi). On exploitation of internal divisions, see Agostino de' Rossi's reports on the activities of Lorenzo Zane from his base in Cesena: ibid., 16 May 1466. In the case of Rimini, Paul II also tried a three-year tax exemption, granted in June 1466 and renewed in June 1468: ibid., 25 June 1466 (copies of briefs).

127 See the report of his long exposition of his dilemma at the consistory of 10 June 1467: ASMa, 843, 11 June 1467 (Gian Pietro Arrivabene).

128 On papal reaction to the truce between the League and Colleone, see ASMi, 'Roma', 63, 16 Aug. and 10 Sept. 1467 (Agostino de' Rossi).

129 Manfredi: ASMi, 'Roma', 65, 9 Dec. 1468 (Protonotary de Rocha); Sixtus IV's confirmation of the vicariate on 31 August 1471 makes no reference to any grant by Paul II (see ASeg-Vat, arm, XXXV, t. 37, fols. 98-100). Orde-

laffi: ibid., fols. 297-302v, 9 Feb. 1470.

130 ASMa, 843, 6 Aug. 1466 (Bartolomeo Marasca); ASV, 'Consiglio dei Dieci', 17, fols. 44v, 49v, 51, 68, 76v; 'Senato', 23, fols. 159v, 161v-162, 163-v, 166; 24, fols. 10, 12v-13v, 18-v, 20v- 21v.

131 Predelli, *Commemoriali*, V, p. 178.

132 ASMi, 'Roma', 58, 8 Jan. 1466; 60, 20 Aug. 1466 (Agostino de' Rossi).

133 ASMi, 'Roma', 65, 17 Oct. 1468; 66, 7 Oct. 1468 (Agostino de' Rossi; filed with Sept. 1470); ASV, 'Senato', 23, fols. 139v- 140.

134 ASMi, 'Roma', 65, 21 Oct. 1468 (Agostino de' Rossi), 23 Oct. 1468 (Sagramoro, from Montefiascone); ASMi, 'Romagna', 169, 29 Oct. 1468 (Roberto Malatesta, from Rimini).

135 ASV, 'Senato', 23, fol. 144.

136 ASMi, 'Romagna', 169, 16 March 1469 (Roberto Malatesta).

137 ASV, 'Senato', 23, fols. 139v-140, 163-v; 24, fol. 10; ASMi, 'Romagna', 169, 24 Dec. 1468 (duke of Milan).

foothold in Rimini. A desperate pope may also have dangled before the Republic baits which betrayed his proclaimed principles of action: some Venetian reports refer to a Venetian-approved plan to give Rimini to a papal nephew, Paolo Barbo's son Agostino.[138] However this may be, by June 1469 the Senate was declaring to the pope: 'De negotio autem vrbis arimini, percupidi certe sumus, vt res pro desyderio, et cogitatione sanctitatis vestre succedat . . . '.[139]

Cooperation did not last long, however, papal troops launched the enterprise against Rimini with some initial success early in June 1469, but Venetian reinforcements failed to cross the Po – because they were needed to contain Turkish assaults in Istria and Friuli, or so the Senate explained later.[140] The enterprise thereby lost the impetus which might have brought success. Although papal efforts to secure Rimini by one means or another long continued, the pope became increasingly embittered and hopeless before the realisation that 'niuna potenza d'Italia non uuole che egli habbia Rimini'.[141] Eventually, the escalation of the Turkish menace (Negroponte fell in July 1470) made Rimini seem peripheral, and the enterprise was abandoned.[142] Paul II's only significant victory was the denial to Roberto Malatesta of an apostolic vicariate[143] – but Paul II's more pliable successor, Sixtus IV, granted Roberto that too, in 1473.[144]

When Paul II suddenly died in July 1471, he had become a rather tragic figure. He had said that as pope 'de rasone doueria essere el piu libero Signore del mondo'.[145] Perspicaciously, informed opinion in Rome – *etiam de capelli rossi* – had discerned: 'che ogni studio opera et diligentia del papa miri et tendi ad farsi et mantenersi Judice dele appellatione in Italia, et per consequens fuori de Italia . . . '. Paul II had been seen as wanting to leave the memory: 'che lhabij possuto disponere et fare et dire ad suo modo, la quale non hano possuto lassare li suoy precessori . . . '. His supreme aim was identified as being 'chel voglia essere dominus dominantium'.[146] Such grand aspirations had certainly not been realised: he left a memory of impotence rather than omnipotence thanks to a complex of forces, but undoubtedly the policies and actions of his native Venice loomed large

---

138 Malipiero, *Annali*, p. 237; ASV, 'Senato', 24, fol. 34.
139 Ibid., fol. 34.
140 Ibid., fol. 40v.
141 ASMo, busta 1, fol. 9 (viii), no. 1, 7 Aug. 1469 (Giacomo Trotti).
142 ASMa, 844, no. 42, 24 Sept. 1470 (Cardinal Francesco Gonzaga).
143 Ibid., no. 45, 6 Oct. 1470 (Cardinal Francesco Gonzaga).
144 ASegVat, reg. vat 558, fols. 204-219v; see also arm. XXXV, t. 37, fol. 119.
145 ASMi, 'Roma', 59, 17 June 1466 (Agostino de' Rossi').
146 ASMi, 'Roma', 64, 27 Jan. 1468 (Giovanni Bianchi).

amongst them. His last months were haunted by the failure of the enterprise against Rimini, attributable to the self-interested perfidy of the Venetian *Signoria*; and by Venetian denial of possession of their sees to his cardinal nephews, and imprisonment of various relatives. No pope with the high post-conciliar concept of his office could have had an easy relationship with the mighty Republic of Venice, but in his case the relationship seems to have been particularly fraught, precisely because he was Venetian. The *zentilhomo de uenecia* who had become *pontifico* was confronted with the problem that the *ueneciani* were *douentati papi*.

9

Architectural Taste and Style in Early Quattrocento Venice: The Façade of the Ca' d'Oro and its Legacy

Richard J. Goy

For centuries the Grand Canal façade of the Ca' d'Oro has been regarded as a paradigm of Venetian gothic architecture in its mature, 'florid' stage (*Fig. 16*). Here I intend to summarise the origin of the palace, to outline the approach to its design by the young nobleman who built it, Marin Contarini, and to suggest ways in which the completed work relates to Quattrocento style as a whole.

The construction of the palace was the result of one broad, general influence, together with two catalysts that were highly specific in character. The first was the political and economic climate in the *Dominante* in the first two decades of the new century, an era of unparalleled expansion on the *Terraferma*; a period in which peace generally predominated over war, and of consolidating prosperity, following the crisis of 1380.

The two specific contributory factors were first the still shadowy career of Marin's father Antonio and secondly Marin's own marriage to Soradamor Zeno in 1406. Antonio seems to have been an ambitious man, who had accumulated much of his own wealth in these first years of the Quattrocento[1] and whose later career was probably linked to the rise and reign of Doge Tommaso Mocenigo. Soon after the latter's election, Antonio became a procurator of San Marco, one of the pair *de ultra*;[2] patronage, perhaps, but also an indication of his prominence in the Palazzo Ducale.[3]

---

1 For an analysis of the 1379 *estimo*, see S. Chojnacki, 'In Search of the Venetian Patriciate' in *Renaissance Venice*, ed. J.R. Hale (London, 1974), pp. 47-90; see also D. Queller, 'The Venetian Family and the *Estimo* of 1379' in the forthcoming Festschrift for Bryce D. Lyon. Antonio Contarini was then living at San Moisè; his declared wealth was 2000 *lire di grossi*, by no means a very large sum, but he was still a young man.

2 F. Sansovino and G. Martinioni, *Venetia città nobilissima* (Venice, S. Curti, 1663) part ii, F. Sansovino, 'Cronico particolare', p. 44; and R.J. Goy, *The House of Gold: Building a Palace in Medieval Venice* (Cambridge, 1992), chapter 6.

3 For a summary of the procurators' duties, see M. Sanuto, *De origine, situ et magistratibus urbis Venetae ovvero La città di Venetia*, ed. A.C. Aricò (Milan, 1980), pp. 104-5; Venice, Biblioteca del Museo Civico Correr, MS Cicogna 969, fols. 50-51. The procurators were elected by universal ballot of the *Consiglio Maggiore*.

A decade later, amid the bitter in-fighting that preceded his successor's election, Doge Mocenigo exhorted the *Consiglio Maggiore* to elect either Antonio Contarini, or one of a handful of like-minded senior politicians, whom he considered suitable candidates to follow him and continue his policies.[4] The decade of Mocenigo's reign is the period in which the metaphorical foundations for the new palace were laid; it thus seems possible that one underlying motive was Antonio's hope that the house might become the home of the next Serene Prince.

Marin, Contarini's first son, had been born in 1386 and at twenty was betrothed to the second daughter of Bachalario Zeno, from another prominent *lungho* family.[5] Her elder sister Caterina had already married into the Dandolo *casada*, while Caterina's husband and his brother (Fantin and Piero) then held the controlling interest in the large Byzantine palace at S. Sofia.

In 1407 Marin began renting the Zeno house from his parents-in-law for 75 ducats a year;[6] in June 1412, just before the expiry of the statutory five-year lease, he bought the house outright.[7] The price was 320 *lire di grossi*, although the contemporaneous renegotiation of his wife's dowry recouped 240 *lire* from the Zeno-Dandolo.[8] By then it is likely that Marin, under Antonio's direction, had decided to rebuild it.[9]

The first site-records date from 1421,[10] by which time the old Zeno house had been carefully dismantled. Contarini began by buying a considerable quantity of stone from the Milanese master, Matteo Raverti,[11] and at the same time appointed his master builder, Marco d'Amadio, and his carpenter, Zane Rosso.[12] Little progress was made, however, until 1423, the year of the ducal election although, with the site cleared, Marin was committed to a new palace. His first contract with his other mason, Zane Bon, pre-dates the election by some months,[13] although as soon as Francesco Foscari was presented as doge to his people on 13 April 1423 it was clear that the new house was not to be the home of a doge's family after all.[14]

4 'Renga de messer Thomado Mocenigo doxe alla Signoria', in *Bilanci Generali*, series ii, I, 1, part i (3 vols., Venice, 1912); see also M. Kretschmayr, *Geschichte von Venedig* (Stuttgart, 1934), II, p. 618.
5 For Marin's marriage contract, see ASV, 'Proc. di S. Marco de Citra', B. 269 bis, unmarked bundle, doc. 2.
6 For the lease, see ibid., doc. 5.
7 For the purchase of the house, ibid., doc. 3.
8 For Soradamor's dowry, ibid., doc. 7.
9 See note 7 above. The key phrase in the contract is the slightly ambiguous one referring to the 'usum veterem vendite quam postea vendidistis ad usum novum'.
10 All of the very earliest building accounts are in ASV, 'Proc. di S. Marco de Citra', 269 bis, Marin Contarini, *libretti di spese*, III, esp. fols. 2-v, 4-v, 5. Subsequent references to these four account books are to 'Contarini, *Spese*', I-IV.
11 Ibid., III, fols. 2v, 3.
12 Ibid., fols. 4-v, 5 for Marco; fol. 2v for Zane Rosso.
13 ASV, 'Proc. di S. Marco de Citra', 269 bis, miscellaneous papers, no. 10, dated 18 Jan. 1422 M.V. (=1423). See also Goy, *House of Gold*, appendix 4.
14 Sansovino and Martinioni, *Venetia 'Vite de' Principi'*, lib. xiii, p. 576.

It is thus tempting, and perhaps inescapable, to regard the Ca' d'Oro as it came to be built as something of an act of defiance on the part of the Contarini *casada*, at having Antonio's ambitions thwarted by a 'new man' from a 'short' family;[15] it can equally be regarded as a rather self-conscious proclamation of Contarini wealth, of the power of 'old money', and of the undoubtedly considerable continuing influence of the clan.

Nevertheless, Foscari's election apparently provoked something of a crisis in the Contarini household, still based at S. Felice.[16] The hiatus on site lasted for some months,[17] but when work began in earnest it is clear that although Antonio underwrote the project financially (and perhaps iconographically, too), thereafter he played no part in its construction, which now came under Marin's sole control.[18]

So Marin built his *Domus Aurea*, and the manner of its building was more than a little erratic and eclectic. From the beginning, he had no clear idea of the final result that he wished to see; he drafted no overall contract with a master builder for the fabric; he employed no *proto* to coordinate the trades on the site.[19] He must have harboured only the most general vision of what the completed palace would look like, and had little idea as to how to achieve this goal. As the accounts so clearly attest, Marin intended to take the role of the *proto* (or superintending master architect) for himself, and this simple statement explains the almost organic fashion in which the house was both designed and built.[20]

Marin's first prudent act was to salvage many Byzantine bas-reliefs from the Zeno house, to be worked into his new façade, with great ingenuity, by

15 For some observations on the 'long' and 'short' families and their relative wealth and influence, see the studies cited in note 1 above.

16 Antonio is recorded as resident at S. Felice by 1400 on the evidence of his will, dated 13 April 1400: ASV, 'Proc. di S. Marco de Citra', 269. He moved there some time after the 1379 *estimo*. See also Queller, 'The Venetian Family'.

17 The hiatus on site lasted until spring 1424, when Contarini signed with Bon a new contract, by which he lent Bon 40 ducats to complete the purchase of his house at S. Marzilian: ASV, 'Proc. di S. Marco', 269 bis., Misti, papers, no. 2. Very soon afterwards Bon began carving stone for him.

18 The last of the few records of Antonio's involvement in the building process date from *c*. 1425: 'Contarini, *Spese*', IV, fols. 4v, 5.

19 For full discussions of the building trades, see G. Caniato and M. Dal Borgo, *Le arti edili a Venezia* (Venice, 1990); see also R.J. Goy, *Venetian Vernacular Architecture: Traditional Housing in the Venetian Lagoon* (Cambridge, 1989), chapters 4-7. For stonemasons in particular, see S. Connell, *The Employment of Sculptors and Stonemasons in Venice in the Fifteenth Century* (London and New York, 1988). It is significant that Marin's first agreement with his master builder related solely to the well refurbishment and the building of the ground floor walls, and not to the whole fabric of the house: 'Contarini, *Spese*', III, fol. 4; IV, fol. 7v.

20 Most of the major elements of the house were let by quite separate contracts; for example, the agreements with Bon for the ground floor screen and the crenellation; that with Zuan da Franza for the decoration of the façade; that with Antonio di Martini for completing many items of general builders' work; see below, pp. 180-1.

the Bon workshop.[21] He also took the literally fundamental decision to retain most of the original foundations (except those to the façade)[22] and the well-tank of the earlier house. This had a profound effect on the new plan, which in consequence had perforce to be designed around the existing location of the *cortile* and its large subterranean tank.[23]

The decision saved time and money and in itself was not unusual; but it led directly to the asymmetrical plan and façade, with its two unequal wings. Pragmatism and prudence thus left Marin no choice but to come to terms with an asymmetrical palace. Individual asymmetrical elements are often found in later Trecento palaces, usually the result of successive modernisations,[24] but, as we will see, many new Quattrocento houses were purely symmetrical, evidence – among other factors – of a stronger desire for order, but probably also indicative of greater wealth and the consequent ability to rebuild from a cleared site.[25] However, it should be noted that, despite its bipartite form, Marin's façade is almost purely symmetrical within each element.

Contarini's involvement in the long building process was very close, at times almost obsessively so. His attention to the details of the façade in particular led directly to the piecemeal nature of this rich screen, in which the relationships between several elements are not precisely coordinated. Not only did Marin pay the men on site every week, he also took on something of the design role of a *proto*, as is evinced by his direct involvement in drafting specifications for such elements as the crenellation, and his several additions to the façade as work progressed.[26]

His overall approach remained fragmented, a fragmentation exacerbated by his appointment of two stone-carving *capo-maestri*, Raverti and Bon, with their respective workshops. Although their roles were different and even complementary, the decision still meant that work from one *bottega* was assembled adjacent to that from the other. Raverti's contribution to the façade was in fact limited to the design and execution of the two great *logge*

---

21 Bon later had to carve some pieces of stone to match these existing fragments: ASV, 'Proc di S. Marco de Citra', 269 bis, miscellaneous unnumbered fragments. See also, Goy, *House of Gold*, appendix 6.

22 For the façade, see 'Contarini, *Spese*', IV, fols. 18v, 19, 22v (for the supply of *tolpi* for the piles), 31v, 32 (for their installation).

23 For Marco's refurbishment of the well, see 'Contarini, *Spese*', III. fol. 4; Goy, *House of Gold*, chapter 18.

24 Palazzo Sagredo Morosini is perhaps the mostapposite example here, but see also the Palazzo Badoer and Palazzo Zaguri.

25 Accurate dating remains difficult for many of these mid Quattrocento houses, but for a detailed stylistic analysis, and attempts at chronology, see E. Arslan, *Venezia gotica* (Milan, 1970), pp. 317-24.

26 Notably Bon's crenellation, the decoration of the façade and Nicolò Romanello's balconies; see below, pp. 180-1.

on the *piani nobili*,[27] while Bon was employed more as a traditional all-round *capo-maestro*,[28] responsible for all remaining stonework on the façade. Yet even this responsibility stopped short of being the *proto* for the entire project. Bon was indeed initially employed on the basis of an annual salary, but after this short period, he, too (like Raverti) undertook specific elements of work for an agreed fee, as did Romanello and Rosso, both former members of Raverti's *bottega*.[29]

Marin's elemental approach means that analysis of the façade as a whole is neither feasible nor really desirable. Its antecedents belong neither to a specific place nor a specific time, and it remains a collage of details from a variety of sources. Before discussing its influence, it is useful to summarise the chief elements and their own origins.

The ground floor colonnade (one of the first elements to be carved) was designed by Bon, although largely executed by others.[30] The design appears archaic, recalling such Byzantine precedents as Ca' da Mosto; but it is likely that Marin's own pragmatism played a part here, and we know that the four capitals are Byzantine, adapted by Bon to suit their new location.[31] The broader central arch may well have been introduced simply to provide a more spacious access from the Grand Canal.[32]

Directly above Bon's *riva* is the lower of Raverti's two splendid traceried screens, carved in 1425-26 (*Fig. 17*).[33] Both screens express on the façade the broad transverse *loggia* behind them, and here again there are echoes of Byzantine forms (Ca' Barzizza, Ca' Loredan), where a wide *loggia* terminates the axis of the *pòrtego*. Such plans, though, were archaic long before the early Quattrocento.[34]

Raverti's tracery to the lower *loggia* has itself become something of a paradigm of late Venetian gothic, and it has an important ancestry since its

27 The original contracts with Raverti (of which there seem to have been two) have not survived, but see ASV, 'Proc. di. S. Marco de Citra', 269 bis, miscellaneous papers, no. 20, which refers to these *pati*. See also Goy, *House of Gold*, chapter 26. Raverti's men included Iacomo da Como, Nicolò Romanello, Gasparin Rosso, Antonio and Paolo Bregno (very briefly) and various members of the Frison clan from Milan and Como.

28 For Marin's first contract with Bon, ASV, 'Proc. di S. Marco de Citra', 269 bis, miscellaneous papers, no. 10; see also, Goy, *House of Gold*, chapter 19 and appendix 4.

29 For Rosso, see 'Contarini, *Spese*', IV, fols. 41, 57v, 58 (item 3); for Romanello, ibid., fols. 56v, 57, 60-v. See also, Goy, *House of Gold*, chapter 36.

30 'Contarini, *Spese*', IV, fols, 16v, 17; Arslan, *Venezia gotica*, p. 228; Goy, *House of Gold*, chapter 24.

31 'Contarini, *Spese*', IV, fol 34. Bon was paid eleven ducats on 9 Feb. 1425 M.V. (=1426).

32 For more detailed discussion, see Arslan, *Venezia gotica*, p. 228.

33 For purchases of stone, 'Contarini, *Spese*', III, fol. 4v; IV, fols. 17v, 18. For the execution of the work, ibid., III, fol. 10v; IV, fols. 10v, 44v. For Romanello's capitals: IV, fols. 13v, 14.

34 For examples, see P. Maretto, *La casa veneziana nella storia della città* (2nd ed., Venice, 1987), pp. 57-107; P. Maretto, *L'edilizia gotica veneziana* (2nd ed., Venice, 1978), particularly p. 59; S. Muratori, *Studi per una operante storia urbana di Venezia* (Rome, 1959) provides examples of the urban context in which these houses were built.

basic form (and indeed its geometrical setting-out) derives directly from the first floor *loggia* of the Palazzo Ducale.[35] The symbolic significance of 'borrowing' from such an august parent was probably not lost on Marin's contemporaries, and the more perceptive among them would have been aware that Raverti's tracery is even more refined (and consistent in its geometry) than that of the palace of the *Serenissima* itself. Raverti was indeed a master of rare sensitivity and technical skill.[36] Contarini may have referred him initially to the recent modernisation at the Morosini house almost next door (the present Palazzo Sagredo),[37] where a row of quatrefoils had been inserted above an earlier *quadrifora*, but Raverti took little note of such an awkward compromise and instead took his own inspiration directly from the Palazzo Ducale. His design here was taken up, with variants, on a number of important later Quattrocento houses.[38]

The *loggia* is flanked by two large lights with complex pendant-traceried heads. They are the work of the Bon workshop,[39] as is the second pair of similar windows lighting the *albergo grando* on the right side of the façade. The lights have only the most tenuous relationship with Raverti's screen; the tracery is much smaller and their whole aesthetic different, the direct result of apportioning the work to two masters, apparently working in isolation in two different *botteghe*.[40]

Although the Bon are closely associated with the difficult form of the pendant-light, their similar windows at the Misericordia are almost certainly later, from the 1440s,[41] and the only local precedents for the Ca' d'Oro windows seem to be the small-scale examples at the Frari and the Addolorata Chapel at SS. Giovanni e Paolo; no lay examples seem to have survived. However, Bon may have been encouraged to develop the form by Raverti's *compagni*, several of whom came from Como and may have worked on the new cathedral façade there (after c. 1396), where two large

---

35 See my own forthcoming paper on 'Matteo Raverti at the Ca' d'Oro', to be published shortly in *Renaissance Studies*; see also Arslan, *Venezia gotica*, p. 231.
36 Goy, *House of Gold*, chapter 26, n. 7.
37 ASV, 'Proc. di S. Marco de Citra', B. 269 bis, miscellaneous papers, no. 20, where the Morosini house is cited by name. See also Arslan, *Venezia gotica*, p. 230; P. Paoletti, *L'architettura e la scultura del rinascimento in Venezia* (2 vols., Venice, 1893), I, p. 22; Goy, *House of Gold*, chapter 26.
38 Goy *House of Gold*, chapter 42; see especially Arslan, *Venezia gotica*, pp. 244-50, and figs. 204-

23. The chronology of the carving of both *logge* is a little odd, and the capitals were carved in reverse order, those to the second *piano nobile* before those to the first. In both cases, Raverti carved the first one as a model for Romanello to carve the remainder. See 'Contarini, *Spese*', L.IV, fols. 13v and 14.
39 'Contarini, *spese*', L.IV, fols. 7, 20v, 21; Goy, *House of Gold*, chapter 25.
40 Bon carved the *fiori* to the pendant-lights himself; 'Contarini, *Spese*', L.IV, fol. 24v: [i fiori] che va soto i quatro strafori de pergolij [che] va in el soler de soto . . . '
41 Goy, *House of Gold*, chapter 25.

pendant-lights can be seen.[42] This was not the only ecclesiastical motif that Contarini was to employ.

Not only do Bon's windows bear no direct relationship with Raverti's screen, they are not consistent beween themselves. One of the four is smaller, and has simpler tracery, while of the larger three, only two are nearly identical, the second and fourth from the left. A detail in a state of transition, therefore, although Marin apparently accepted such anomalies of detailing. There were others. In a note written to Raverti in the autumn of 1426, Marin summarised the work still outstanding;[43] of the half-dozen clauses, none was eventually executed in precisely the way that Contarini described them. At the time, he intended to decorate the façade with two high-level *scudi*; later, he changed his mind and instead settled on a single larger one, in the schematic centre of the façade.[44]

Another clause leads again to the matter of the widespread reuse of materials from other sources. Raverti was instructed to 'compir 5 cholone lavorade e fregade de piera de ruigno a longeza e grossezza de quele se in la mia balchonada granda del primo soler'.[45] In fact, Marin then acquired three columns of pink Verona *broccatello*, the dimensions of which now determined the size of the other two, of white marble. All are shorter and narrower than those of the lower *loggia*. Romanello had already carved their capitals,[46] but Raverti now had to lower all of his tracery, which resulted not only in the curious blank band on the façade above the architrave, but in a slight misalignment between Romanello's capitals and Bon's flanking ones.[47] This upper tracery is both lighter and more complex in its geometry than the lower tracery, and appears to be without precedent in the city. The

42 See note 27 above.
43 ASV, 'Proc. di S. Marco de Citra', 269 bis, miscellaneous papers, no. 20.
44 Ibid.: 'e me resta a dar 2 arme . . . le qual dovea andar sora le dite fenestre', i.e. those to the *balchonada* of the *soler de erto*. Comparisons in the display of *scudi* on façades in this period are instructive. There appear to have been no original *scudi* on the façades of Palazzo Loredan degli Ambasciatori, Palazzo Contarini degli Scrigni, Palazzo Giovanelli or Palazzo Pisani Moretta. That on Palazzo Bernardo at S. Polo is a model of discretion, facing a narrow *rio*, while that on Palazzo Bembo at the Rialto is similarly modest. Both *scudi* here form part of an heraldic ensemble.
45 Ibid.
46 'Contarini, *Spese*', L.IV, fol. 13v; Arslan, *Venezia gotica*, p. 229; Paoletti, *L'architettura*, I, p. 23; Goy, *House of Gold*, chapter 26.
47 Difficulties also arose over the matter of floor levels between the two *logge* and the *pòrtego* behind; there is a single step to the lower *loggia*, but three steps to the upper one.

The traditional practice of the reuse of building materials (particularly those of high value such as marble columns) was widespread in this period, and indeed for some time afterwards. Some other examples relating to Venice are: 1) In 1458 the nuns of S. Zaccaria bought ten columns from the bishop of Torcello, which had been salvaged from an (unnamed) former monastery at Lio Maggiore: ASV, 'S. Zaccaria', 31, *Fabbriche*, I (1458-89), p. 26. 2) A long time later, in 1528, a large column was bought from the *piovan* of S. Maria Formosa from which four smaller columns were to be carved to build one of the altars in the Miani chapel at S. Michele in Isola: ASV, 'Proc. di S. Marco de Citra', B. 67, 19, *quaderno* no. 1, p. 10. 3) Two further columns were acquired from the monastery of S. Elena in the same year; ibid.

very few other examples (comprising interlocking four-centred arches with quatrefoils in the interstices) are certainly later; one may be seen at Ca' Foscari, from the 1450s.[48]

Yet further evidence of Marin's accumulation of motifs from a variety of sources can be seen at the top of the façade, capped by a strongly moulded row of blind trefoil arches, above which is the unique crenellation. Both are the work of the Bon *bottega*, and were the subject of a comprehensive specification dated 20 April 1430.[49]

The blind arcade successfully unifies the complex, heterogeneous façade below it, but the detail was again taken from ecclesiastical rather than patrician sources. Several early examples survive, chiefly on *campanili*, and by the later Trecento most church façades (and some flank walls) were terminated in this manner, including San Stefano, the Frari and the Madonna dell' Orto. They are usually of brick, with stone corbels,[50] and as far as is known only Contarini seems to have applied the feature to a private house, and with such success.[51] The crenellation, though, is quite different in character, and there are no ecclesiastical precedents here. The only important surviving original example is the more refined crenellation on the Palazzo Ducale, and ultimately both derive from similar motifs in such Muslim cities as Cairo and Beirut, with which Venice had strong trading links.[52]

Brief mention should be made of one or two secondary elements on the façade. The strongly-moulded corners, designed by the Bon workshop, also appear unique, although they are again related to the rather less robust colonnettes on the Palazzo Ducale.[53] Their upper termination offers a further example of Marin's unsure path in design matters; Bon carved the original cappings for these columns in 1429,[54] but the present ones are apparently replacements, again carved by Bon only two years later.[55] They terminate the columns satisfactorily enough, but have no direct relationship with the arcading above them, and the resolution of these elements appears arbitrary.

---

48 Arslan, *Venezia gotica*, pp. 246, 248; figs. 209-11.
49 ASV, Proc. di S. Marco de Citra', 269 bis, unnumbered fragment. The agreed price was 210 gold ducats. See also Goy, *House of Gold*, app. 6.
50 The Frari example is typical: it is all of brick, apart from the stone corbels. That applied to SS. Giovanni e Paolo is far more elaborate and all in stone.
51 The De' Barbari prospective map of Venice shows a number of apparently rather similar examples, now lost. The crenellation of the palace of the duke of Ferrara (Fòndaco dei Turchi) was rebuilt in the nineteenth century; its fidelity appears questionable.
52 Goy, *House of Gold*, chapter 33 and n. 22.
53 'Contarini, *Spese*', IV, fol. 17v. See also Arslan, *Venezia gotica*, p. 229.
54 'Contarini, *Spese*', IV, n. 34.
55 These formed part of several minor works that Bon was to carve as part of the contract for the crenellation: ASV, 'Proc. di S. Marco de Citra', B. 269 bis., unnumbered fragments.

Several of the other minor details, which add yet further richness to the façade, do in fact derive closely from more indigenous sources. The square stone outer frames to the windows, with their *tondi* of porphyry, take their place in the florid style; earlier examples may be seen at Palazzo Soranzo (San Polo) and elsewhere. The *tondi* have a long history, originating in Byzantine *paterae* such as those on the Ca' da Mosto.[56] The *fiori* at the window-heads, too, were a widespread detail by now, surviving into the 1470s. Marin thus incorporated several more typical motifs intermingled with the more inventive and esoteric ones.

While the crenellation was being fixed in 1431[57] Marin drafted his specification for decorating the façade. This, of course, resulted in the palace's famous soubriquet, itself the result of Zuan da Franza's painstaking application of 22,075 sheets of gold leaf to many prominent details of the façade. It was already destined to become memorable as a result of the plethora of rich stonework, but with the decoration,[58] and Marin's contemporaneous instruction to his builder to clad the rest of the palace with marble,[59] the place of the house in history was assured. Although evidence is very limited, we know of no other palace decorated in such a manner[60], and only a decade later, when the Bon had nearly completed the Porta della Carta, do we have considerable gilding applied to a lay structure.[61] Even after Zuan's decoration (which also incorporated expensive ultramarine pigments)[62] Marin continued to add to his façade; in 1433 Romanello was commissioned to carve three elaborate balconies for the first *piano nobile*,[63] immediately followed by three more for the second.[64]

---

56 Marin's *tondij* were carved by Gasparin Rosso: 'Contarini, *Spese*', IV, fols. 57v, 58.

57 See the specification for the many and varied works undertaken by Marin's last master builder, 'Antonio di Martini, in ASV, 'Proc. di S. Marco de Citra', 269 bis, miscellaneous papers, no. 3. See also Goy, *House of Gold*, especially appendix 7, where the text is provided in translation.

58 ASV, 'Proc. di S. Marco de Citra', 269 bis, unmarked bundle; see also 'Contarini, *Spese*', L.IV, fols. 58v, 59, 59v, 60; and Goy, *House of Gold*, chapter 35 and appendix 8.

59 See note 57 above.

60 By about 1484 it seems already to have been referred to as the 'House of Gold'; see G. Tassini, *Curiosità Veneziane* (9th edition, Venice, 1988), p. 104, under *Ca' d'Oro*, ' . . . questo Pietro [Marcello, who in 1484 married a daughter of Pietro Contarini] era detto dalla Ca' d'Oro perché acquistò, per la moglie, la casa dorata al di fuori di cà Contarini a S. Sofia . . . ', citing the genealogist Priuli, writing *c*. 1630.

61 For the decoration of the Porta della Carta see S. Romano, *The Restoration of the Porta della Carta* (Venice, 1980), trans. Ashley Clarke and Philip Rylands and in particular there, K. and G. Hempel, 'A Technical Report on the Condition of the Porta della Carta and its Restoration by the Venice in Peril Fund', pp. 37-9, with illustrations.

62 'Contarini, *Spese*', L.IV, fols. 58v-60. Zuan was not able to begin for some months because Contarini only then had decided to install two fireplaces in the two *alberghi grandi*, together with the necessary flues and chimneys.

63 Ibid., fols. 56v, 57.

64 ASV, Proc. di S. Marco de Citra', 269 bis, miscellaneous unnumbered fragments; see also 'Contarini, *Spese*', IV, fols. 59v, 60, 60v; and Goy, *House of Gold*, chapter 36.

Elsewhere, I have described Marin's approach as magpie-like in his accumulation of motifs from many sources.[65] There is evidence of this propensity in his own hand: in 1426 Raverti was instructed to carve modillions 'e qual dovea andar ai laj (de) la sua balchonada lavorado per tuto chome sie quele dela chasa de ser Nicholo moresinij fo de miss. Gasparin del suo soler de erto'.[66] This was the present Sagredo house on the nearby *campo*. Five years later, Romanello's first three balconies were to be 'a modo de quelo e de la chasa fo di ser Chostatin de priolij e suso el chanton in versso sam zacharia'.[67] Further, as we see, many other elements can be traced in more general architectonic terms, if not by written references such as these.

Nevertheless, Marin was no more alone in 'borrowing' from other sources of design than he was in recycling Verona marble, although he was certainly less well coordinated than some other Quattrocento patrons, as will be discussed below. Indeed, the overt emulation of details from elsewhere was widespread. A decade or so after Nicolò's balconies, Bartolomeo Bon was employed by the monks of the Carità to carve most of the stone for their new church. On 1 June 1443 he was paid 20 ducats 'per parte de lochio de la giexia davanti el quale de eser facto como è quelo de santa maria da lorto', this latter being another church with which Bon himself is closely associated.[68] Many other such elements had been similarly developed from one church to another since the mid Trecento, as a short survey of several of their façades will reveal.

Rather more than a decade later, in 1458, we find the nuns of S. Zaccaria instructing their own master mason, Bertuzi de Iacomo, in a very similar vein regarding six new windows to be inserted in their rebuilt church: 'quatro fanestre de la grandeza e largeza e condition de quele de la giexia de la carita messe suxo la frixa e do ala condition de quele sono dal zadi (lato?) del trageto de la dicta ghiexia'.[69] Further evidence, therefore, of the handing down of details from one church to another.

To a large extent, of course, such actions are an intrinsic part of the evolutionary nature of any long-lived architectural style, and in many cases (*vide* Raverti) the emulator refines the detail in question a little beyond its model. Very few examples of stone tracery in early Quattrocento Venice are truly *sui generis*, and most fit within the developing florid style. Nevertheless, there is a significant, indeed a fundamental difference of approach between, on one hand, the incorporation of an individual feature, such as

---

65 Goy, *House of Gold*, especially chapter 41.
66 ASV, 'Proc. di S. Marco de Citra', 269 bis, miscellaneous papers, no 20.
67 'Contarini, *Spese*', L.IV, fol. 56v.
68 ASV, 'S. Maria della Carità', parte terza (doc. cartacei), 3, fol. 47.
69 ASV, 'S. Zaccaria', B. 31, *Fabbriche*, I (1458-89), p. 24.

these windows at the Carità and San Zaccaria – which were chosen individually and inserted into the structural shell – and, on the other hand, Marin's complex accumulation of details from a variety of sources, both lay and ecclesiastical.

Contarini finally completed his *capolavoro* in 1436;[70] he died there only four years later, aged fifty-four. What was the legacy and influence of his eclectic masterpiece, and how typical was his approach to its design? Other than in certain specific details, it must be said that its influence was neither long-lasting nor widespread. Indeed, in two key aspects, its elaborate decoration and its asymmetry, it appears to have provoked a noticeable reaction in quite the other direction.

Of the individual details of note, Bon's pendant-tracery was developed further by his own *bottega*, first at the Misericordia, and then – above all – at the Porta della Carta. Others, too, took up the motif, but on a smaller scale, as seen at Ca' Giustinian and Ca' Bernardo.[71] Raverti's *logge* were the most influential individual features, and they seem to have acted as a spur to the development of several similar geometrical forms, although none follows his own proportions precisely. However, these great multi-light windows in houses such as Palazzo Giovanelli and Ca' Foscari are undoubtedly the most mature, refined and prominent features of such mid-century houses.

Ca' Foscari deserves singular mention. Its place in the last generation of truly gothic palaces is arguably of the greatest importance of all, not simply for its noble dignity, but above all for its order and symmetry. Its significance is thus pivotal, both in urbanistic and architectural terms. Foscari's views on design could hardly have been more different from those of Contarini; his house and its successors derive in a highly disciplined manner from the long, steadily developing palace tradition in their detailing, in their materials and in the hierarchy of their component parts. Istrian stone is similarly restricted to the traditionally detailed elements such as windows, quoins and cornices (*Fig. 18*).[72]

Although Ca' Foscari was almost certainly unfinished at the time of the doge's fall from power and subsequent death, the image that he left behind acted as a powerful counter-force to Contarini's legacy. Order and discipline are the hallmarks of Foscari's own legacy, and one may thus identify a widespread, conscious effort to eschew the perceived excesses of Contarini

---

70 The last building account of all is dated 25 February 1440 M.V. (=1441), and summarises Marin's final payments to Romanello. His handwriting is very shaky and he most likely died shortly thereafter.

71 For a fuller analysis of *gotico fiorito* after the *Ca' d'Oro* see Arslan, *Venezia gotica*, pp. 317-24. For some further notes on the later works of the Bon, see Goy, *House of Gold*, chapter 43.

72 Arslan, *Venezia gotica*, pp. 320, 324.

in favour of propriety, although there does not appear to be any evidence that the Palazzo Ducale itself directly influenced this process. Even the striking asymmetry of Marin's façade seems again – to an indefinable extent – to have provoked this last generation of gothic palace builders to react against it, to insist more rigorously on balance, continuity and dignity, attributes which, after all, epitomised the patriciate's perception of the *Serenissima* herself.

The most significant single aspect of the many houses built after about 1450 is thus their harmony and symmetry. The matter of the perceived importance of the latter quality to the patriciate is difficult to evaluate, particularly since it is so intimately bound up with more mundane considerations such as the shape and size of the site, the available funds, and the concomitant feasibility – or otherwise – of starting afresh with a cleared site. Foscari was indeed fortunate in being able to do so,[73] and had the further advantage of a superb site from which to dominate the Canalazzo. Nevertheless, the increased discipline of many such façades is notable, contrasting sharply with the minor irregularities that are so frequently found in slightly earlier houses.

In itself, this does suggest that a cleared site was a more frequent starting-point than it had been earlier. Such rebuildings from the ground (often, in the Quattrocento, to increase density and accommodation) must themselves have either been built from entirely new, symmetrical foundations (an expensive course of action), or they were built anew from earlier footings that were also – fortunately – symmetrical. That is, these earlier, perhaps originally Byzantine, palaces had also been built to a regular, tripartite form, consisting in principle of four parallel, equidistant rows of foundations. If necessary, such foundations would then have been brought forward towards the new façade, thus obliterating any remnant of a surviving Byzantine transverse loggia. Some Byzantine houses certainly had such a regular basic plan (Ca' Loredan and Palazzo Donà, for example), which could thus in theory have been modernised with a new florid gothic façade.[74] At the Ca' d'Oro, too, the only completely new foundations necessary were those to the canalside *riva*.

Putting aside the ultimately almost insoluble matter of the extent to which constraints imposed by earlier foundations influenced rebuilding works, great desire for rationality and harmony is manifested in several

---

73 For a summary of the history of the site, see Tassini, *Curiosità*, under 'Foscari', pp. 255-7.
74 For Byzantine examples, see Maretto, *La casa*, pp. 76-95; for gothic examples, ibid., pp. 108-

57. See also Maretto, *L'edilizia gotica*, especially the floor-plans facing pp. 62, 86, 124; and on pp. 63 (Ca' Loredan, Ca' Farsetti), p. 66 (Ca' da Mosto), p. 90-91 (Palazzo Soranzo at S. Polo).

16 Ca' d'Oro, Venice: façade to the Grand Canal (*Photo: Richard Goy*)

17 Ca' d'Oro: detail of *loggia*, by Matteo Raverti, *c.* 1425–26 (*Photo: Richard Goy*)

18 Ca' Foscari, Venice: the eight-light window of the *piano nobile* and the windows to the top storey, derived from Raverti (*Photo: Richard Goy*)

19 Palazzo Giovanelli, Venice: principal façade towards the Rio di Noale (*Photo: Richard Goy*)

20 Palazzo Cavalli (later Franchetti), Venice: façade to the Grand Canal (*Photo: Richard Goy*)

21 Palazzo Venier Contarini, Venice: façade to the Grand Canal (detail) (*Photo: Richard Goy*)

22 Porta della Carta, Palazzo Ducale, Venice: central window by the Bon workshop (detail) (*Photo: Richard Goy*)

23 Giorgione, *Rustic Idyll* (*Museo Civico, Padua*)

24 Giorgione, *The Judgement of Solomon* (detail) (*Uffizi, Florence*)

25 Giulio Campagnola, St Jerome (engraving) (*Department of Prints and Drawings, British Museum, London*)

26 (*Above*) Unidentified fifteenth-century German artist, *John the Baptist* (woodcut) (*Kupferstichkabinett, Berlin*)

27 (*Right*) Konrad von Megenberg, *Buch der Natur (Augsburg, 1482)* (woodcut) (*Germanisches National Museum, Nuremberg*)

28 Giorgione, *The Preaching of John the Baptist* (Pearl Collection, Washington DC)

29 Unidentified fifteenth-century artist, woodcut in the anon. *Plenarium* (Augsburg, 1489)

30 Lucas Cranach, *The Preaching of John the Baptist* (woodcut) (*Albertina, Vienna*)

31 Albrecht Dürer, woodcut in Sebastian Brant, *Das Narrenschiff* (Basle, 1494), fol. 22 (*Germanisches National Museum, Nuremberg*)

32 Giorgione, *The Epiphany* (*National Gallery, London*)

33 Giorgione, *The Preaching of John the Baptist* (detail) (*Pearl Collection, Washington DC*)

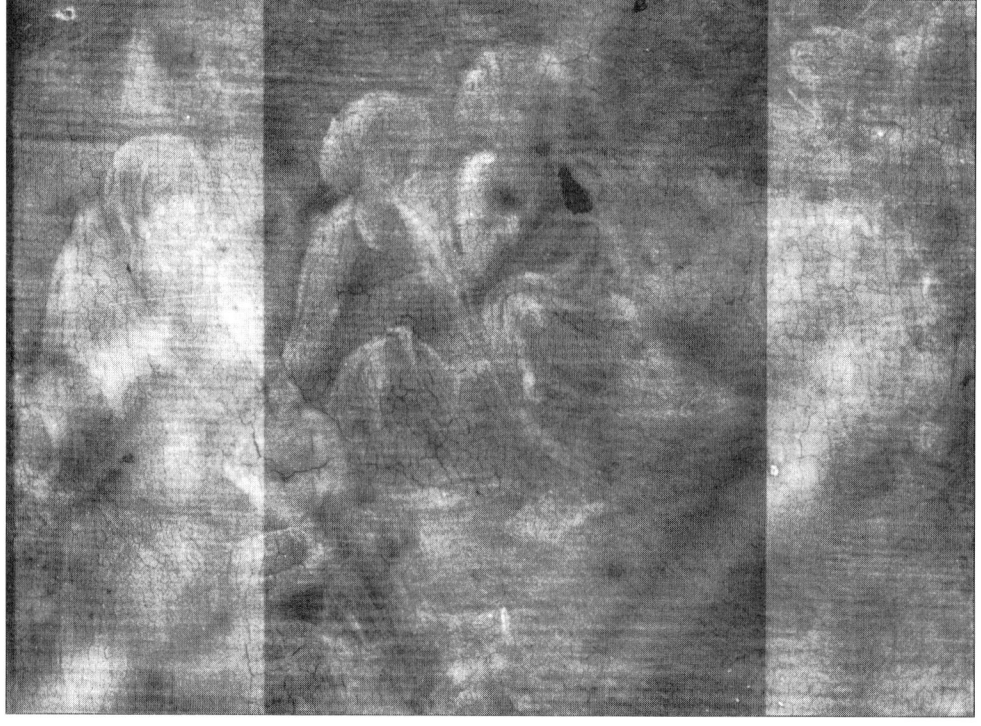

34 Giorgione, *The Preaching of John the Baptist* (X-ray photograph) (*Pearl Collection, Washington DC*)

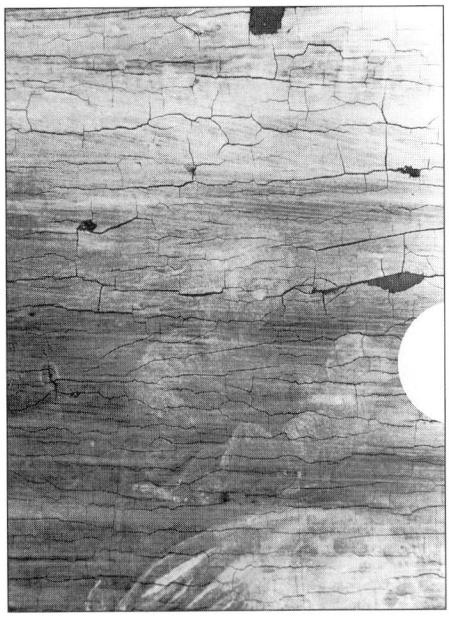 

35 Giorgione, *Rustic Idyll* (detail of X-ray photograph) (*Museo Civico, Padua*)

36 Giorgione, *Rustic Idyll* (detail of X-ray photograph) (*Museo Civico, Padua*)

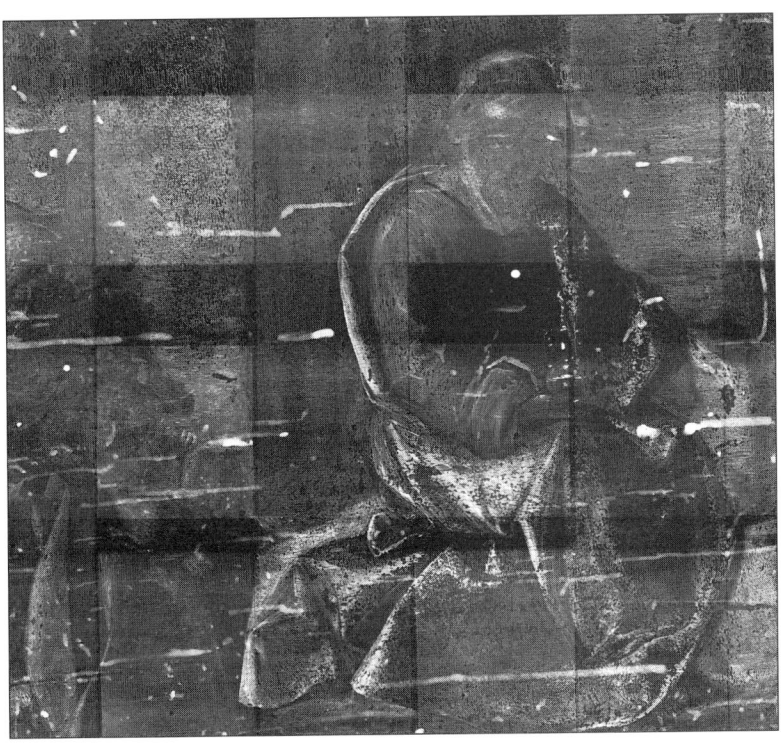

37 *The Epiphany* (detail of X-ray photograph) (*National Gallery, London*)

38 Horatio Brown (*Bristol University Library*)

ways: in the careful modulation of spaces between flanking windows; in the attention lavished on the great central light; in the elimination of asymmetrical quirks; and in the 'weight' given to each storey. To a large extent, these considerations were simply the more disciplined imposition of rhythms and patterns that had long been part of the palace tradition; even as far back as Palazzo Donà (early Duecento), one finds the essential fenestration rhythm established.

Among this last generation of examples, one thinks particularly of Palazzo Giovanelli, dominating even its own very restricted urban context with stately order and careful modulation, the only more daring features being the unusual corner windows (themselves derived from Palazzo Priuli of the early 1420s) and the notable *pòrtego* window (*Fig. 19*).[75] Palazzo Priuli itself offers a good example of the slightly earlier, less disciplined, more organic approach, incorporating several idiosyncratic details.[76]

Palazzo Cavalli is perhaps an even finer example than Palazzo Giovanelli (*Fig. 20*). Perfect in its symmetry (even before Franchetti's interventions), it incorporates two fine *pentafore* to the superimposed *piani nobili*: on the lower a row of interlocking semicircular arches – a rare form – and on the upper a form derived from Raverti's second floor loggia at the Ca' d'Oro. Although the debt to Raverti is clear enough, the façade as a whole is balanced and dignified, a derivation but also, in a sense, a reproach to Contarini's 'excesses'. Some of these very last houses were built nearly half a century later than the Ca' d'Oro, but remain imbued with the essential *palazzo* tradition, now often subject to a most rigorous aesthetic discipline. Marin's *Domus Aurea*, too, still fits broadly into this tradition, certainly functionally, but aesthetically rather uncomfortably since its character, like that of its creator, is so particular.

The vertical rationalisation of some of these last houses is almost as prominent as their lateral discipline. At Palazzo Giovanelli, for example, the lowermost two storeys form a substantial plinth on which the *piano nobile* stands; above it there is a clearly-defined attic. Here we see a conscious attempt to rationalise the façade into these three almost classical elements of base, *piano nobile* and attic; there is a similar arrangement at Palazzo Cavalli, although here we have two superimposed *piani nobili*. Nevertheless, the tall two-storey plinth is a prominent feature at both houses, and despite heavy

---

75 For the Palazzo Priuli, see Arslan, *Venezia gotica*, pp. 247-8, with a measured drawing of the corner window.

76 Ibid., pp. 92-3. Arslan believes that the Palazzo Priuli dates, at least in part, from the later Trecento, or even earlier.

restorations, in both cases seems to be original.[77] Elsewhere, though, more complex vertical gradations are apparent, as for example at Ca' Bernardo, where a fairly tall ground storey is surmounted first by a 'minor' *piano nobile*, secondly by the *piano nobile* itself, then by a generous attic.

Building to higher densities, and the more frequent use of such superimposed *piani nobili*, gave rise to certain hierarchical difficulties, which were resolved with varying degrees of success. The requirement itself usually made a simple vertical tripartite arrangement impossible, and there is often a duality between the two principal storeys. Chiefly the result of the necessity to house two branches of a *casada* under a single roof, these dualities are not always entirely happily resolved; indeed, they are often exacerbated by the use of different tracery in the *pòrtego* windows at the two levels, as we noted above at Palazzo Cavalli. One is tempted here to identify something of the strong Venetian tradition of eclecticism surfacing once again, a trait that is perhaps most pronounced at Ca' Bernardo. Here there are two *piani nobili*, the lower with fairly simple florid gothic lights, and the upper more complex tracery of the Palazzo Ducale/Raverti type, but flanked by the elaborate little pendant-lights derived from Bon at the Ca' d'Oro. The dual role of the house is clearly evinced on the façade, too, by the well-known pair of separate water-gates.[78]

Frequently, though, this strongly reemerging desire for greater order and symmetry could not be achieved for a variety of reasons. Sometimes the shape of the site (compounded by demands of accommodation) made it quite impossible; Palazzo Soranzo van Axel, for example, makes up in its ingenious planning what it perforce lacks in symmetry in every plane.[79] But the strength of the desire for order is also evinced – a little surprisingly perhaps – in a number of 'secondary' *palazzi*: houses in which in earlier periods we might have expected less discipline than in the greatest palaces. The façade of the recently restored Palazzo Venier Contarini has a purity and balance from which all extraneous, unharmonious elements have been carefully excised (*Fig. 21*). It also incidentally incorporates a pair of Marin's square lights, although here used with discretion and perfectly balanced.

The development of the role of the *proto*, that is, as already defined, the superintending master architect, may have had a significant effect on this new spirit of rationality. Although one is hampered by an acute shortage of

---

77 The Osvaldo Böhm Collection contains a photograph of the Palazzo Cavalli before its restoration; see G. Perocco and A. Salvadori, in *Civiltà di Venezia*, III (Venice, 1976), p. 1228, fig. 1501. The Palazzo Giovanelli was altered by Meduna, but it is not clear to what extent he modified the façade: Arslan, *Venezia gotica*, p. 248.

78 For plans, see Maretto, *La casa*, p. 147. Arslan, *Venezia gotica*, p. 248 dates the Palazzo Pisani Moretta to c. 1470.

79 For plans, see Maretto, *La casa*, p. 148.

data on private palace-building, the picture in the public or institutional realm is a little clearer, and may offer some useful guidance. The original title of *proto* or *protomaestro*, of course, was bestowed by the *Signoria* on certain chief masters in the service of the Republic, and in particular of the procurators of San Marco *de Supra*, and the *provveditori al Sal*, as the funding agency for public works at San Marco, Rialto and elsewhere. Whilst it remains difficult to plot the spread of the use of the title itself elsewhere, the function of the *proto*, as a salaried master responsible for the design and supervision of the whole project, can be seen to be well-established outside government circles in the period immediately after Marin's house was built. The essence of such posts was indeed that they were salaried, thus providing vital continuity, and the terms of their appointment were almost certainly derived from those used by the *Signoria*. As Professor Goldthwaite has observed, this was an era still notable for fluidity of roles,[80] and his remarks regarding the Florentine context certainly apply equally to Venice; nevertheless, a prestigious work such as the rebuilding of S. Zaccaria after 1458 was undertaken by first appointing Antonio Gambello, a *proto* in every practical respect, including the use of the title. Gambello was salaried, was provided with a house on site, and given all the powers generally recognised as those of an architect.[81] Codussi's appointment in 1483 was accompanied by similar terms.[82]

Not surprisingly, the evidence suggests that the appointment of a *proto* bore a close correlation with the size, complexity and prestige or status of a project; a full-time salaried *proto* simply could not be justified on buildings below a certain size or importance. At the Carità church, for example, which was rebuilt from 1441 to 1456, there was no *proto*, and the fabric as a whole was probably designed by the church's first master builders, Stefanino and his son Piero; Bartolomeo Bon's role was to provide almost all of the carved stonework, but he was not a salaried *proto*, being paid on an 'elemental' basis for each of the works that he carved. The church was not a difficult or unusual building to design or construct and closely followed several recently built examples elsewhere in the city.[83] On an even more humble level, when in 1438-45 the procurators of San Marco built the charitable almshouses known as the Corte Nova, attached to the Misericordia, there was no question of a *proto* being employed, although a prodigious

80 R. Goldthwaite, *The Building of Renaissance Florence* (2nd edition, London and Baltimore, 1982), p. 237.
81 ASV, 'S. Zaccaria', B. 31, *Fabbriche*, vol. 1 (*1458-89*), p. 8: 'Mo. Anthonio de marco protomaistro super la fabrica con salario de duc. C°.

al 'ano e la casa de bando . . . '
82 For Codussi at S. Zaccaria, see ibid., pp. 169, 180, 187.
83 For the Carità, see ASV, 'S. Maria della Carità', parte terza (doc. cartacei), B.3, fols. 43, 45v, 46r-v.

number of different craftsmen were occupied on the project at one time or another, including the Bon workshop once again.[84]

In the case of private palaces, the physical evidence strongly suggests that powers similar to those given to a salaried *proto* were delegated with increasing frequency after about mid century by these patrician patrons. Such general powers of overall design and coordination resulted directly in façades such as those of Ca' Foscari and Palazzo Giovanelli, disciplined and structured. That this pattern was still by no means universal at this time is again illustrated by more 'organic' examples such as the grandiose, rambling Palazzo Pesaro at S. Beneto, where idiosyncracies and asymmetry remain extensive.[85] But it must have become apparent to these patrons that balance, order and symmetry could only be achieved by giving design control to a single master; ideally, he would be salaried and permanent but, even if he were not, control had to be vested in one man, whether he was a *murer* or *taiapiera* by his original training.

In the end, it was the influence of houses such as Ca' Foscari that had a critical and profound effect on mid century façades, and we must therefore reluctantly consign the Ca' d'Oro to what can now be seen to be effectively an architectural cul-de-sac. It is true that we find occasional small-scale flourishes of something resembling the Contarini *brio* in such delightful (and unique) examples as Palazzo Contarini Fasan, a miniature *tour de force*, but ultimately the only true inheritor of Marin's aesthetic mantle is the Porta della Carta. Rather than siring numerous, richly apparelled progeny, the influence of the Ca' d'Oro was the reverse; even the illustrious Doge Foscari, confronted by Marin's glittering façade, did not emulate it but reverted to, and refined further, the traditional discipline. Contarini's gauntlet, thrown at Foscari's feet in 1430, was not taken up twenty years later *in volta dil Canal*, or indeed anywhere else.

The picture is not quite as simple as this. Although Marin was alone in completing an elaborate all-stone façade, he was not the sole patron who desired to have one built. The other outstanding exception to this Foscari-led return to traditional brick façades with stone detailing was the fragmentary and ill-fated Ca' del Duca. But this grandiose project, too, was a special case, and one has to wait until the work of Lombardo and Codussi for a genuine *rinascimento* of this particular desire.

---

84 For the Corte Nova development, see ASV, Proc. di S. Marco de Citra', B. 54: *Commessaria Baseggio, Zorzi, quaderno* no. 2.

85 Arslan, *Venezia gotica*, p. 319: 'Siamo lontani dal "rigore" architettonica che caratterizza Cà Foscari: continua qui lo spirito prettamente veneziano cromatico, di tanti edifici trecenteschi . . .'.

The Ca' del Duca is indeed unique, but by no means unconnected with Contarini's *capolavoro*. Connell has identified as Bon the 'maystro Bartolomeo' who is recorded in letters sent by Benedetto Ferrini and Antonio Guidobono (respectively the Florentine architect and the Milanese ambassador to Venice) to their patron, Francesco Sforza, in Milan.[86]

The palace had been begun by Marco Corner in *c*. 1457 with Bon as his *proto*, and although only a small fragment of the façade had been completed by 1460 – that which is to be seen today – it seems highly likely that Bon, by no means a young man by then, had begun a façade that was to be most unusual by Venetian standards.[87] As Corner wrote: 'la dicta fazada a do torre da lado, como la Caxa del Marchixo da Farara le qual torre sono de marmoro a diamante, e la riva fra le do torre con colone grossisime de marmoro . . .'[88] Reading these words, it is perhaps not surprising that Bon was apparently so reluctant to let either Ferrini or Guidobono see his drawings for the façade, which Sforza had expressly asked them to do; it seems to have been regarded by Bon as – potentially – his own late *capolavoro*. Although by no means fully Milanese in style (Sforza later said that he might retain Bon's façade 'al modo venetiano') it certainly incorporated some 'revolutionary' and unVenetian elements.[89]

On Sforza's orders, Ferrini had two models made (*disegni de relevo*), almost certainly so that he could decide whether to proceed with the palace *ala venetiana* or *ala milanese*.[90] In the event, of course, the whole grandiose project came to nothing, but one of the lessons from this still elusive and

86 Connell, *The Employment* pp. 19-21. See also L. Beltrami, *La Ca' del Duca' sul Canal Grande ed altre reminiscenze sforzesche a Venezia* (Milan, 1900) and J.R. Spencer, 'The Ca' del Duca in Venice and Benedetto Ferrini', in *Journal of the Society of Architectural Historians*, XX (1971), pp. 3-8.

87 Many of the detailed circumstances surrounding the early works (that is those executed before Ferrini's letter to Sforza in 1461) are still rather obscure, although the documents cited by Connell make it clear that Bon had been engaged by Corner for the period to August 1460: Connell, *The Employment*, p. 20.

88 As Connell, *The Employment*, p. 20, has observed, this brief description does indeed suggest a house closely modelled on the overall massing of that of the marquis of Ferrara; that is, it would be Veneto-Byzantine in its basic form, but clearly not so in its rustication, and in the grandiose scale of its waterfront colonnade or *riva*.

89 According to Ferrini, Bon 'non me vole dare el desegnio perche dice vorebe luy havere lhonore et lutile'. Bon clearly felt that he had created something unusual; according to Guidobono, the drawing was 'in vero . . . bellissimo'; cited by Connell, *The Employment*, p. 20.

90 Spencer has concluded, with convincing evidence, that Ferrini was in fact Sforza's only appointed architect, and that the often-cited involvement of Filarete had little direct practical bearing on the matter, as Beltrami had suggested. However, the works executed prior to 1461 (when Ferrini was working up his models of the two alternative designs) were certainly the work of another master, that is, Bon. For Ferrini's letter to Sforza see Spencer, 'The Ca' del Duca', p. 5, citing, ASMi, 'Sezione Storico, Autografi Ingegneri', 82/5. He does not emphasise the point but the phrase at the beginning of this letter ('Mandarvi per el presente portatore el disegno secondo è fondata la casa del nostro Illustrissimo signore [Sforza]) indicates that either he had prised the drawing from Bon's reluctant hands, or that he had made a record drawing of the completed fragment.

complex episode seems to be that even such a quintessentially Venetian master as Bon could rise to Corner's original challenge, to begin a work that was to be not only more monumental in scale than any (gothic) palace yet seen in Venice, but which incorporated such motifs as bold rustication and *diamante* ashlar, foretastes of the classical Renaissance. When we recall that fifteen years earlier Bon was being urged by the *Signoria* to complete the Porta della Carta in its own essentially Venetian florid gothic style,[91] it is clear that Bon (by then at least fifty years old) must still have kept a creative, imaginative mind, and one which was by no means a closed book (*Fig. 22*).

The Ca' del Duca cannot be located happily within the Venetian palace style in any sense, partly because so little remains, partly because in Sforza there would have been strong foreign stylistic influences at work, had building been continued. Nevertheless, the matter indicates the degree of artistic freedom that was becoming feasible in the later 1450s. Much more powerful, though, for at least a couple more decades, was Foscari's native palace tradition, surviving into the almost inevitable transitional period that itself resulted in such curious hybrids as Palazzo Moro Lin, with its wilful conjunction of gothic and Renaissance motifs. It also resulted in the unlikely but extraordinary success of San Zaccaria.

By the 1480s, the stylistic vocabulary had finally changed and half a century later, when one surveys the city for Marin's legacy, one finds it only at the Porta della Carta. The Bon *bottega* once again provides the practical link, although there are naturally few other close connections in functional or iconographic terms. The great central window is the clearest expression of the most refined later work of Bon, although we might hazard some contribution from the technically skillful Raverti.[92] To some degree, the Porta della Carta, as the expression of the collective will of the *Signoria* and the Republic, finally put Contarini back in his place as simply one patrician among many, even though Marin died before the Porta was completed and so triumphantly decorated. Here, then, appropriate tribute was made to Caesar (or rather his Senate) in the lapis lazuli and gilding with which the Porta was illumined. Ultimately, the Ca' d'Oro can only be understood as the direct expression of the character of its patron. Although its refined arches have one foundation in the long, powerful tradition of the indigenous style, the other footing rests firmly on the personality of its creator, Marin Contarini.

---

91 For the record of the *Signoria*, exerting pressure on Bon to complete the work in 1442, see ASV, 'Collegio dei Provveditori al Sal', III (1411-1520), fol. 84.

92 For Bon's original contract for the Porta della Carta, ibid., fol. 8.

10

Giorgione's Pre-Venetian Beginnings: A New Proposal

Terisio Pignatti

While the literature about Giorgione proceeds on its troubled path, one period still remains very ill-defined: that of his early years. Not even the conference at Castelfranco in 1978, despite bringing together almost all the experts on the subject, seems to have resolved two of the most difficult questions: when did he begin to paint, and who were his masters?[1] Recently, however, a trend in criticism has emerged which has tended to push back his artistic beginnings to the years before 1500.[2] A number of scholars – including the present writer – have linked these beginnings to figurative sources from north of the Alps: in particular to Dürer, on account of his first Italian journey of 1494-5, to the diffusion of prints and book illustrations, and also to the part played directly by German artists, some of whom are documented as having had workshops in Venice and the Veneto.[3]

As a consequence, a whole group of paintings can be linked with Giorgione; in the preceding literature they were slowly sinking into the limbo of minor works of art and adding to the so-called 'school of Giorgionism' – a category historically vague and difficult to define in critical terms because of its great variety. I refer in particular to the group of 'small landscapes' (*paesetti*), some of them so exiguous in size and cursory in

---

1 The *Atti del convegno internazionale di studi giorgioneschi*, conference held at Castelfranco, 29-31 May 1978, have been published in the volume *Comune di Castelfranco Veneto, Giorgione* (Castelfranco Veneto, 1979), referred to below as *Giorgione* (Castelfranco, 1979).

2 K. Oberhuber, 'Giulio Campagnola', in *Early Italian Engravings* (Washington, DC, 1970), pp. 390-413; A. Chastel, 'Titien', in *Tiziano nel quarto centenario della sua morte; lezioni all' Ateneo Veneto* (Venice, 1977), pp. 11-26; Jaynie Anderson, *I tempi di Giorgione* (Castelfranco Veneto, 1979), pp. 153-8, n. 2; A. Ballarin, 'Una nuova prospettiva su Giorgione . . . ', *Giorgione* (Castelfranco, 1979), pp. 227-52; K. Oberhuber,

'Giorgione: The Graphic Arts of his Time', ibid., pp. 313-20; R. Rearick, 'Chi fu il maestro di Giorgione?' ibid., pp. 187-94; A. Ballarin, 'Tiziano prima del Fondaco dei Tedeschi', *Tiziano e Venezia* (Vicenza, 1980), pp. 493-9, n. 3; A. Chastel, 'Dürer et Venise', in *Giorgione e l'umanesimo* (Florence, 1981), pp. 459-63; S. Freedberg, *Painting in Italy, 1500-1600* (Harmondsworth, 1983), p. 679, n. 27; C. Hornig, *Giorgiones Spätwerk* (Munich, 1987), pp. 167-76; T. Pignatti, *Venezia: mille anni d'arte* (Venice, 1989), p. 157.

3 L. Testi, *Storia della pittura veneziana*, 2 vols, (Bergamo, 1915), II pp. 301-8 (with bibliography). See also below n. 7.

execution that they have tended to be classed with furniture painting, *cassone* panels etc., without being considered at all as the *opera prima* of a young artist.

After much hesitation and many changes of mind, it now seems to me that the time has come to reclaim for the catalogue of Giorgione's autograph work a number of paintings, modest only in appearance, such as the three small panels already linked under the names of 'The Master of the Phillips *Astrologer*' (Phillips Museum, Washington, DC), the *Leda and the Swan*, and the *Rustic Idyll* (both in the Museo Civico, Padua) (*Fig. 23*), together with the others already linked under the name of 'The Master of the *Venus and Cupid*' (National Gallery, Washington, DC), and the *Homage to a Poet* (National Gallery, London). These 'small landscapes' constitute a sufficiently homogeneous group to be listed as early works of Giorgione.[4] Indeed, they become difficult to understand at all if they are placed in the later period, when Giorgione's style reached maturity in such a work as the *Tempesta*. The subsequent stage of development can be discerned in the *Moses* and the *Solomon* both in the Uffizi (*Fig. 24*).[5] The 'small landscapes' can therefore be dated earlier than the hitherto prevailing opinion: around, if not before, 1500.

Significant in this respect are some of the very similar works of Giulio Campagnola, and his acclaimed *Giorgionismo*. In the case of this Paduan engraver, too, the trend has inclined towards an earlier dating, so as to include his prints containing northern motifs in landscape executed before his arrival in Venice, where he is documented only after 1507.[6] In this way some of his engravings were typical of the cultural milieu in which Giorgione developed, for instance the *Saturn*, signed at Padua (Kristeller, no. 5) – dateable perhaps to the end of the Quattrocento – or the *St Jerome* (Kristeller, no. 15) – probably a little later – which could lend themselves to indicate what might be the echoes of lost paintings by Giorgione (*Fig. 25*). Closely resembling the 'small landscapes', they are thus with better reason believed to constitute the origins of Giorgione's mature style. In the *St Jerome*, for example, the landscape with towers, water-mills and rustic houses of northern appearance (like those in the Giorgionesque paintings in Padua) belongs to this iconography. Identical, too, is the rendering of leaves,

---

4 T. Pignatti, *Giorgione* (Venice, 1969), cat. nos. A 66, A 40, A 41, A 65, A 22, A 34. Cf., however, the same author's *Giorgione* (Milan, 1955), where most of the paintings listed above were already attributed, significantly, to Giorgione.

5 Pignatti, *Giorgione* (1969), cat. nos. 7, 8. For the *Solomon* there remains some doubt as to whether an assistant may not have done some of the figures.

6 Oberhuber, 'Giulio Campagnola', p. 401; D. Landau, 'Giulio and Domenico Campagnola', *The Genius of Venice*, exhibition catalogue, ed. C. Hope and J. Martineau (London, 1983), pp. 310-11; M.A. Chiari Moretto Wiel, 'Per una nuova cronologia di Giulio Campagnola incisore', *Arte veneta*, XLII (1988), pp. 41-57; P. Kristeller, *Giulio Campagnola* (Berlin, 1907).

similar to the manner of the Uffizi paintings, with delicate touches and high-lighting, which enlivens the separate leaves in characteristically fan-shaped clusters. Such elements of painterly language characterise the few drawings by Giulio's hand: the delicacy of touch is noteworthy in his *Landscape with Two Figures* (Louvre, no. 1959, Kristeller, pl. xxiii). Also to be noted in this example is the fan-shaped foliage, outlined distinctly upon the somewhat rigid and vertical oak branches. Likewise suggestive of Giorgione is the undergrowth of flowering bushes, with their wide leaves, either spiky or round-shaped: the latter a motif which seems to be derived from numerous prints of the late Quattrocento, (*Fig. 26*) like the anonymous *St John the Baptist* (Illustrated Bartsch, 23, New York, 1985), p. 60), or in the *Buch der Natur* of Conrad von Megenberg printed and published at Augsburg in 1482 (*Fig. 27*). Thus the circle closes upon the German connections of the young Giorgione and fellow artists in the Veneto.[7]

There is no doubt that *The Preaching of the Baptist*, which recently reappeared in the collection of Piero Corsini and is now in Frank Pearl's collection in Washington, DC, belongs to this period and to the area of the Veneto influenced by masters from beyond the Alps (*Plate I*; *Fig. 28*). Notwithstanding northern motifs, such as the rustic theme and realistic iconography, it is clearly beyond dispute that the glazed oil-painting technique and tonality hark back to features characteristic of the 'small landscapes' of Giorgione's earliest period.[8] As in many of these, the setting is a wood of leafy oak trees and the figures are rendered with a lightness of touch and with particularly sparkling colours, against a soft green meadow, where the play of shadow heightens the atmospheric value. Typical here – as with Campagnola – is the rendering of the foliage on leafy boughs receding in depth, with a fan-like design which the light brightens in minute detail. The development is similar in many of the subsequent works which are unanimously attributed to Giorgione in his first Venetian period, from the *Benson Madonna* to the *Allendale Adoration*, and from the London *Epiphany* to the small panels in the Uffizi. Nor should it be overlooked at this point, that Treviso and the surrounding region, where Giorgione spent the formative

---

7 On the theme in general, see T. Pignatti, 'The Relationship between German and Venetian Painting in the Late *Quattrocento* and Early *Cinquecento*', *Renaissance Venice*, ed. J.R. Hale (London, 1973), pp. 244-73 (with bibliography); C. von Megenberg, *Buch der Natur* (Augsburg, 1482), part IV, p. 839.

8 Painted on poplar panel (34.3 x 27.9 cm.). Acquired by Piero Corsini from Christie's, New York, 11 December 1986, Lot 149, as 'Circle of Lucas Gassel'. After my attribution, it was shown in the exhibition *Places of Delight* (National Gallery of Art, Washington, DC, 1988), no. 4. See R. Cafritz, L. Gowing, D. Rosand, *Places of Delight* (Washington, DC, 1988), p. 48, fig 13 (attributed to Giorgione).

period of his life before he settled in Venice, was an area of German culture.[9] Indeed the Germanic component is always present in the first works of Giorgione, as long ago Suida pointed out, when he insisted on linking the *Benson Madonna* and other works with the prints of Schongauer and Dürer.[10]

It also seems to me beyond doubt that the iconographical features of *The Preaching of the Baptist*, generally so unusual for Venice, are in keeping with those of German origin. There is nothing strange about the costumes of peasants and soldiers, for which the German sources are only too evident in the vernacular manner of innumerable book illustrations of the late Quattrocento: for instance, in the *Plenarium* printed at Augsburg in 1489 (fol. 10r) (*Fig. 29*). We seem to be confronted by a series leading to the *Preaching of the Baptist* by Cranach (1516), in which the identical rustic types are seen, roughly clad in their shapeless garments, with the same straw hats and even the identical saint, with his curious balustraded podium constructed out of branches laced together with cross-bars (*Fig. 30*).[11] Nor can there be any doubt that these clothes are taken from Dürer's series of book illustrations for *Der Ritter vom Turn* (Basle, Michael Furter, 1493) or perhaps Sebastian Brant's *Das Narrenschiff* (Basle, Johannes Bergmann von Olpe, 1494) (cap. 22), (*Fig. 31*), works which could easily have come to the attention of the twenty-year-old Giorgione, seeking inspiration for his first small paintings, even before 1500.

Other persuasive comparisons confirm that there is continuity here with the themes and compositional devices of more mature works of Giorgione, such as the Uffizi *Moses* and *Solomon* or the London *Epiphany* (*Fig. 32*). There are many typological similarities among the figures placed

9 There are also numerous documentary sources proving the active presence of a German artistic colony between Treviso and Venice, where the Fondaco was the pole of attraction; see G. Nepi Scirè, 'Pier Maria Pennacchi', *Bollettino d'arte*, 6th ser. LXV (1980), pp. 37-48; M. Lucco, 'Riflessi lombardi nel Veneto', *Lorenzo Lotto a Treviso* (Treviso, 1980), pp. 33-66; D. Dematte', 'Giovanni Maria Teutonico pittore in Treviso', *Arte veneta*, XXXVI (1982), pp. 45-54 (with bibliography).

10 W. Suida, 'Spigolature giorgionesche: Giorgione e Schongauer', *Arte veneta*, VIII (1954), pp. 153-55. See also Pignatti, 'The Relationship', pp. 259-61.

11 As Henk van Os of the University of Groningen has confirmed, the theme of the Baptist preaching in the solitude of the woods of Judeaea is of mediaeval origin. A not too remote source for the Veneto might have been for example the fresco of Lorenzo and Jacopo Salimbeni in the church of San Giovan Battista, Urbino, in which the motif appears of peasants sitting in a semi-circle around the prophet, see P. Zampetti, *Gli affreschi di Lorenzo e Jacopo Salimbeni . . .* (Urbino, 1956), Pl. XXII. The saint preaching in the woods also appears – as has been noted already – in numerous book illustrations, and in the prints of Cranach of 1516 (F.W.H. Hollstein, *German Engravings*, VI, no. 62) with striking points of identity with our picture and with Crabbe (Hollstein, *Dutch Engravings*, V, no. 95). Flemish painters also take up the motif of the prophet leaning against a balustrade of branches, as in the background of Patinir's paintings of the *Baptism of Christ* now in the Metropolitan Museum, New York, and in the Kunsthistorisches Museum, Vienna; it also occurs in two other paintings of the *Baptist Preaching* in the Royal Museum, Brussels, and in the Philadelphia Museum. All this is evidence that the theme enjoyed widespread popularity and it is not too hazardous to suppose that it was diffused by means of vernacular prints, probably now lost.

in a semi-circle, as in *The Preaching of the Baptist* (*Fig. 33*). To take the soldiers, one is leaning against a tree in the *Preaching* in a pose identical with that of the groom on the right hand side of the *Epiphany*; the feathers in the cap of the seated soldier in the *Preaching* also recall those worn by one of the soldiers in the Uffizi *Moses*, while the red woollen cap of the last auditor on the left in the *Preaching* is painted with little dabs of carmine just like those of the groom whose head appears above the horse in the *Epiphany*.

The style of *The Preaching of the Baptist* also relates, without too many differences, to the Giorgionesque works already cited. In particular the figures should be noted; rather summary in execution, the drapery is lightly rendered with a brush dipped in a mere touch of colour in a manner similar to the 'small landscapes' of Padua and Washington and others up until the London *Epiphany*. There is no doubt that this could be a manner typical of Giorgione only at the beginning of his career, and that it becomes attenuated after his encounter with Bellini in Venice, toned down, shaded, with more body to it, fluid in the brushwork yet more accurate in the drawing.

It is important to add that the stylistic analogy between *The Preaching of the Baptist* and the earliest works of Giorgione is also supported by the X-ray evidence (*Figs. 34-7*). I have in fact examined the X-ray plates of the *Preaching* and found them wholly in keeping with what Mucchi read from the X-ray plates of the Uffizi *Moses*: 'The picture is elaborated with a small, thinnish brush, with little colour mixture and slight contrast. The folds in the drapery are done with dry and narrow brush strokes, rich in white, often angular. The faces appear to be painted carefully but with softness; a thin brush-stroke of white is employed to highlight the profiles of the noses. For the hands, a thin brush-stroke should be noted, outlining the backs of the fingers . . . for the bodies, a colour mixture is sufficiently rich in white to make them stand out sharply against the background, which is already clear from the brush strokes mentioned above. The foliage, the tree-tops, are painted with small touches in the various parts, the branches and leaves . . .'[12]

Just as many similarities link the X-ray vision of the *The Preaching of the Baptist* to the Padua *Rustic Idyll* and the London *Epiphany*: the same sketchy brushwork, rendered with little colour but with evident dabs and streaks of white lead: the same summary technique in sketching the faces with softness, with light touches of the brush and indicating the landscape features in minute detail.[13] At this point the decisive question has to be asked: what degree of

---

12 L. Mucchi, *Caratteri radiografici della pittura di Giorgione* (Florence, 1978), p. 25 (preface by T. Pignatti).

13 Radiography and its reading by Paolo Spezzani of the Soprintendenza of Venice (by kind communication, 1987).

relevance do all these Giorgionesque elements have in *The Preaching of the Baptist* to lead us to the conclusion that it is an autograph work? And, if it is, to what stylistic period of Giorgione does such a painting belong?

First of all, the high quality of the painting is beyond doubt. It strikes the beholder with its suggestion of warm afternoon sunlight, filtering down through the woodland trees, their shadows lengthening behind the tiny sparkling figures, each of whom is strongly characterised in both pose and physiognomy. They appear linked indissolubly to their setting, through the artist's individual medium: a palette which builds up atmosphere precisely by means of colour, shading down the tonal values, grading the half-tints, yet retaining an emotionally climatic liveliness. As Vasari wrote, it was Giorgione, and only Giorgione at Venice, who knew how 'to paint in both harsh and sweet tints, without a preliminary drawing'.[14] And that characteristic was not only in his late works, to which perhaps the Florentine art critic was more accustomed, but ever since his youth, when the Germanic sources still showed through strongly.

Indeed, all of Giorgione's paintings which I have compared to *The Preaching of the Baptist* – from the small landscapes at Padua and in the Uffizi to the London *Epiphany* – are dateable to the end of the Quattrocento or the very earliest years of the Cinquecento, and could not be much later than the beginning of its first decade. In the case of the *Preaching of the Baptist* it seems to me that one can therefore postulate a wholly youthful creation, in short: perhaps one of the very first works of Giorgione.

The painting seems to represent the slightly ingenuous, almost rustic, poetic inspiration of the twenty-year-old painter at the very moment – perhaps a traumatic one – of Venice's first impact upon him, which we date to the last years of the Quattrocento. This is the same date offered for the Giorgionesque *Christ* in Boston, if it is true that this was one of his first works, copied from a painting by Bellini dateable to 1500 (now at Toledo, Ohio). Likewise the date 1500 is confirmed for the *Benson Madonna*, because of its Bellini-like characteristics of style, its colours sweetened by tonal shading, the drapery still retaining the outlines of a print by Schongauer. All this reinforces the argument that the *Preaching of the Baptist* belongs emphatically to Giorgione's earliest period. The iconography and the figurative language, astonishing by Venetian standards, can be best explained as the expression of northern influence. Thus an image takes shape of a youthful Giorgione still linked to motifs

---

14 'macchiare con tinte crude e dolci, senza far disegno', G. Vasari, *Le Vite* (Florence, 1568), ed. G. Milanesi (Florence, 1878-85), VII, p. 427.

and iconography derived from German art, just at the time when colour was about to overwhelm the Venetian scene. Prevailing there already were the tonal values and exquisite sensitivity which Giorgione would derive from Giovanni Bellini, in whose workshop, as Vasari wrote, he was apprenticed to 'make his earliest beginnings' (*suoi primi principi*).[15]

The Preaching of the Baptist seems therefore to reveal an unexpected side to the painter from Castelfranco: slightly raising that curtain of mystery behind which his early work has hitherto been concealed. The magic suggestion of a moment of repose in the deep silence of the woods, after it has just been shattered by the voice of the prophet, transports us into that typical atmosphere of profound lyrical resonance, into one of those dream-like memory landscapes that Giorgione would continue to evoke. It is almost in the mode of a passage written by his friend the poet Pietro Bembo, taking a philosophical stroll and discussing the subject of love, along the grassy slopes, the brooks and shady olive-groves of the beloved valleys near Asolo.[16]

---

15 Ibid., III, p. 172.
16 P. Bembo, *Gli Asolani* (Venice, A. Manuzio, 1505), fol. e 1, at the end of Bk. C: 'per ombre et per rive et per piagge dilettevoli s'andarono diportando'.

11

The Language of Sanudo's *Diarii*

Anna Laura Lepschy

In what language are Sanudo's *Diarii* written? This is a question historians must often ask themselves as they try to determine the exact value of a given expression of this frequently consulted work. But for students of literature and linguistics too, who tackle the problem more directly, not only in order to interpret the text, the answer is by no means obvious. In this essay I shall try to illustrate and clarify the problem, using as my corpus a portion of the *Diarii*, leading to 17 September 1523, in homage to the dedicatee of this Festschrift, born exactly 400 years later. The corpus I have chosen consists of about twenty-five columns of vol. XXXIV (cols 390-422) which contain over 12,000 words. In describing various phenomena I shall not attempt to give a complete concordance, but the examples will be plentiful; as the lexical usage of the *Diarii* is rather uniform, my illustrations may give a fair idea of Sanudo's vocabulary as a whole.

The first question to ask is whether the text is written in Venetian or in Italian. It will soon become clear that neither alternative is a satisfactory answer, and in any case even the terms of the question need clarification.

In the past, in fact until our own age with its widespread use of tape-recordings and its creation of archives of the spoken word, it was very difficult to reconstruct speech on the basis of written documentation. Not only has the written word its own rules, thus transforming the spoken word which it reports, but there are linguistic realities belonging to speech that are unlikely to find their way into a written text. If we try to imagine the tongues which could be heard in Venice in the Renaissance, we are faced with an enormous diversity – from the various Italian dialects to the European languages spoken by the pilgrims on their way to the Holy Land and by the merchants (for instance the Germans at their Fontego), the Yiddish and Ladino of the Jews, Slav, Turkish, Arabic, and the *lingua franca* that flourished in the Levant and in the Mediterranean ports. A pale literary reflection of this variety of languages can be found within the tradition of polyglot comedies.

Venetian was undoubtedly the everyday language of the resident population of Venice, from the origins of the city, and it still is, to a large extent, even today. It is documented from the thirteenth century[1], and subsequently in later centuries in a rich literary production, with playwrights, like Goldoni in the eighteenth century, and Gallina in the nineteenth, providing valuable linguistic evidence.

It is hard to try and define what Italian was in the early Cinquecento. These are the years in which the Bembian norm was being elaborated – the *Prose* were published in 1525 – a mixed blessing which Venice bestowed on the Italian peninsula as on the rest of Europe, a norm which for centuries to come was to provide the model for literary Italian. It was a written language, codified on the basis of Petrarch's *Canzoniere* and Boccaccio's *Decameron*, rejecting (at least in theory, and up to a point in practice too) both the innovations introduced into Quattrocento Tuscan usage and the moderate eclecticism of the *lingua cortegiana* – the other two principal positions debated in the *questione della lingua*. Bembo's proposals prevailed, not least because in the context of the opposition between the various Italian powers of the period, it was the only solution which avoided identification with the prestige of one state at the expense of another. But it was a language for scholars, acquired through a demanding literary apprenticeship and the practice of imitation, and as such was unsuited for the spoken language, or for everyday written usage which covered the practical areas of administration, law and bureaucracy. In northern Italy the Trecento and the Quattrocento had seen the formation of literary languages, or *koinaí*, based on Tuscan, partly because of the outstanding prestige of the Tuscan literature of the Trecento, but with strong northern colouring in spelling, morpho-syntax and lexis. An obvious example of this contrast between a Northern *koiné* and the Bembian norm is provided by a comparison between Boiardo's *Orlando innamorato* and Ariosto's *Orlando furioso*. The latter, in its three editions, came progressively nearer to an ideal Tuscan literary model, and in its third edition (1532) it tried to adopt the rules given in his *Prose* by Bembo, who is quoted in Canto XLVI amongst other famous characters:

> . . . là veggo Pietro
> Bembo, che 'l puro e dolce idioma nostro,
> levato fuor del volgare uso tetro,
> qual esser dee, ci ha col suo esempio mostro.

---

1 See A. Stussi, *Testi veneziani del Duecento e dei primi del Trecento* (Pisa, 1965).

The *volgare uso tetro* is precisely the northern *koiné* of the *Innamorato*, a poem which was soon to undergo recasting into the new literary language, while the original disappeared from publishers' lists, to re-emerge only in the mid nineteenth century in London, edited by Panizzi, who initiated its modern *fortuna*.

Exactly how these *koinaí* spread (and even how outside Tuscany people learnt to read authors like Dante, Petrarch and Boccaccio) is a question which still requires an answer. The term *koiné* is taken from *koinè diálektos*, that is the 'common dialect', based on Attic, which during the Hellenistic period came to replace classical Greek dialects. It is worth noting that the term 'dialect' was in fact borrowed from the Greek *diálektos*, and introduced into European culture by Italian humanists between the Quattrocento and Cinquecento to express the variety of vernacular languages (whilst in the Latin tradition it was an almost non-existent concept, as it was unitary norm rather than variety which prevailed). But in the passage from Greek to vernacular the term 'dialect' acquired a value which it did not have in its Greek context, with reference to varieties which were subordinate to the standard language, to the language of greater prestige, which is the role that literary Tuscan had assumed in Italy.[2]

In this context it is difficult to imagine that in Renaissance Venice the term 'dialect' would have been used, as it is today, for the Venetian of daily conversation, or for the *koiné* with Venetian colouring of Sanudo's *Diarii*.

Why did Sanudo choose to write in this *koiné*? He had a humanistic training as a pupil of Giorgio Merula, and he belonged to Manuzio's circle;[3] his letters are evidence of his command of Latin.[4] He also had the ability to write in Tuscanising Italian, as bear witness his dedicatory letters, for instance the one accompanying *La spedizione di Carlo VIII in Italia*.[5] But he chose another medium, and it is worth noting the remarks he himself makes about the language of his works. We find that he makes a distinction between the vernacular of his texts and the Venetian expressions he inserts: for example in the *Itinerario per la Terraferma veneziana* (1483) he uses without comment the Northern *mio barba*, whereas he elaborates '*chiodi*,

---

2 For these ideas on 'dialect' see M. Alinei, *Lingua e dialetti, struttura, storia e geografia* (Bologna, 1984), pp. 169-99 (the article 'Dialetto: un concetto rinascimentale fiorentino' originally appeared in *Quaderni di semantica*, II (1981), pp. 147-73); P. Trovato, "Dialetto" e sinonimi ("idioma", "proprietà", "lingua") nella terminologia linguistica quattro- e cinquecentesca', *Rivista di letteratura italiana*, II (1984), pp. 205-36.

3 R. Finlay, 'Politics and History in the Diary of Marino Sanuto', *Renaissance Quarterly*, XXXIII (1980), pp. 585-98 (p. 586).

4 [Rawdon Brown], *Ragguagli sulla vita e sulle opere di Marin Sanuto* (Venice, 1837), p. 12.

5 M. Sanudo, *La spedizione di Carlo VIII in Italia*, ed. R. Fulin (Venice, 1883), p. 17.

vel, ut sermone nostro veneto utamur, agudi'.⁶ The letter to Doge Agostino Barbarigo dedicating the *Spedizione* (1495) to him explains that, unlike Sabellico who wrote in Latin, he has chosen to write *vulgari sermone*, to be accessible to both *dotti e indotti*.⁷ It is in order to reach this wide readership that, as he comments in another dedicatory letter to Barbarigo, he wrote the *Cronachetta* (1493) 'nel sermone materno', imagining that in this work it would be 'non lo stile ma la fatica' which would be appreciated.⁸

On two occasions in 1521 he was persuaded to continue with his diaries after having expressed the desire to terminate them, so that they could be polished and used for a more orderly history, as a sequel to his *Spedizione*. In March he notes:

> ho deliberato sequitare il mio cotidiano scrivere in forma de diaria; et cussì in questo libro sarà descripto, giorno per giorno, quello se intenderà di novo et cosse mi parerano degne di farne mentione, lassando l'ornato et più limato stile a scrivere in altro tempo et quando si seguirà la historia principiata.⁹

Again in July he notes:

> ho deliberato seguitar il rozzo, inornato et basso stile mio, e per giornata descriver il successo di tempi . . . Per tanto seguirà per jornata qui driedo ne farò mentione giorno per giorno, perchè poi si meterà ne la ordita et ben tessuta mia historia a honor di questo Excelentissimo Stato, et memoria a li *posteri mei* venitiani.¹⁰

When writing to the *Capi del Consiglio dei Dieci*, Sanudo puts his work in the context of other histories: 'L'ho voluta scriver vulgar considerando che . . . Lunardo Aretin scrisse vulgar la historia di Fiorenza, trasse da un Zuan Vilani, qual scrisse in lingua rozza toschana. Bernardin Corio ha scritto la historia di Milano in volgar.'¹¹

Gaetano Cozzi, in his illuminating article on Sanudo's approach to history, has pointed out how the language of the *Diarii* corresponded to a

---

6 M. Sanudo, *Itinerario . . . per la Terraferma veneziana nell'anno 1483*, ed. Rawdon Brown (Padua, 1847), pp. 134 and 41.
7 M. Sanudo, *La spedizione*, p. 17.
8 M. Sanudo, *Cronachetta*, ed. R. Fulin (Venice, 1880), pp. 2 and 3.
9 M. Sanudo, *I diarii di Marino Sanuto*, eds. N. Barozzi, G. Berchet, R. Fulin and F. Stefani (58 vols., Venice, 1879-1903) [hereafter Sanuto], XXX, p. 5.
10 Sanuto, XXXI, 7.
11 M. Sanudo, *De origine, situ et magistratibus urbis Venetae ovvero la città di Venezia*, ed. A. Caracciolo Aricò (Milan, 1980), pp. xv-xvi. On the official use of the vernacular in Venice being later than in Florence and Milan, see P. Frasson, 'Tra volgare e latino: aspetti della ricerca di una propria identità da parte di magistrature e cancelleria a Venezia (sec. XV-XVI)', *Stato, società e giustizia nella repubblica veneta (sec. XV- XVIII)*, ed. by G. Cozzi (Rome, 1980), I, pp. 588ff.

particular view of historiography. Unlike Sabellico's Venice 'tutta fatta di grandezza politica, di elevatezza religiosa, di saggezza civile', Sanudo's world was more comprehensive, it presented 'non solo i lati più appariscenti, ma tutti quei nessi minuti esistenti tra fatto e fatto e dovuti spesso all'operato di personaggi minori'.[12]

Sanudo had hoped to succeed Sabellico as the official historian, but Andrea Navagero was chosen instead, and on the latter's death, in 1529, Sanudo was once more passed over when in September 1530 Pietro Bembo was given the post. To add to Sanudo's bitterness his diaries were to be officially consulted by Bembo for his own history in Latin, with the small consolation that he was to be recompensed by the Venetian government with an annual sum of 150 ducats. In spite of his mortification at being made to hand over his diaries, Sanudo managed to write positively to Bembo, referring to 'la longa benevolentia ch'è stata sempre tra li nostri padri e progenitori et la servitù mia a Verona essendo Camerlengo quando el clarissimo vostro padre era podestà de lì'.[13] He claimed he was pleased on two counts: 'l'uno perchè è sta conosuto la mia faticha esser grata a questo excellentissimo Dominio, l'altra per il ben dila Patria, che sarà mediante la latina eloquentia et stil di Vostra Signoria, che ben si pol dir siate l'onor di questa terra *item* di tutta Italia.'[14]

Sanudo's 'rozzo, inornato et basso stile' was the subject of discussion among his nineteenth-century editors, who were evidently not unanimous in wanting to retain the original language. Cesare Cantù gives us the options:

> Si aveva a conservare il dialetto veneziano, o darvi la terminazione letteraria? In quel dialetto, quale parlavasi nel Consiglio e sotto le Procuratie di S. Marco, occorrono voci che ora non son più intese, nemmeno fra le lagune; si avevano ad eliminar e surrogarsi delle conosciute?[15]

Fortunately respect for the original prevailed.

I shall now try to characterise some of the linguistic features of the *Diarii*, isolating elements which belong to the speech of the Veneto (or more specifically of Venice), in contrast to the Tuscan literary tradition (in some

---

12 G. Cozzi, 'Marin Sanudo il Giovane dalla cronaca alla storia', *Storiografia veneziana fino al secolo XVI. Aspetti e problemi*, ed. by A. Pertusi (Florence, 1970), p. 347. I am grateful to Gaetano Cozzi for a helpful conversation on the subject of my article.

13 G. Berchet in the introduction to the *Diarii*, I (Venice, 1903), p. 98; see D.S. Chambers, 'Marin Sanudo, Camerlengo of Verona (1501-1502)', *Archivio veneto*, CIX (1977), pp. 37-66.

14 Cited by G. Berchet in Sanuto, I, p. 98.

15 C. Cantù, 'Diarj di Marin Sanudo', *Archivio veneto*, XXXV (1888), p. 426.

cases the Venetian form, for example: *fusse*, may coincide with that used in contemporary Tuscan, but still differ from the literary one, *fosse*).

(a) In the field of SPELLING AND PHONOLOGY we find the following phenomena:

(i) The use of **single consonants** instead of double, e.g. *aviso, cavali, fato* ('fatto'), *leto* ('letto'), *loto* ('lotto'), *schiopetieri* ('schioppettieri'), *sguizari* ('svizzeri'), *vene* ('venne'), *zuchari* ('zuccheri'), and, correspondingly, the use of abnormal double consonants, indicating uncertainty in spelling, which was not guided by a pronunciation in which all consonants were single, e.g. *falitto* ('fallito'), *qualli* ('quali'), *rippe* ('ripe' or 'rive').

(ii) **Voiced** instead of voiceless consonants, e.g. *anotada, avogador, cargo, caxa, Cazude, deputadi, dispensade, Domenega, donadi, eceptuadi/exceptuadi, fuogo, fradello, Governador, intrada, invidar, papado, pagador, partido, portado, Pregadi, prestadi, Provedador, refudava, savemo* ('sappiamo') *scuoda* ('riscuota'), *stado, sussitadi, vachado, veludo, vendede* ('vendite'), *zudegando*.

To these one can add the instances where the sonorisation of *p*, and late Latin *v*, is followed by its **disappearance**, as in *Cai, sora*, and the truncated participles like *acostà, balotà, butà, computà, confortà, conzà, mandà, stà*. There are numerous alternations, like *havea/haveva* (as well as *avia, havia*), *haveano/havevano, volea/voleva*.

(iii) **Fall of final vowels** (which is not characteristic of the whole of the Veneto): *e* after *l, n, r*, and *o* after *n*, and sometimes *l*, e.g. *ambassador, baston, ben, boletin, castelan, cavalier, caxaruol, citadin, comun, condition, condutier, creation, cremexin, criminal, cuor, damaschin, deliberation, dotor, eletion/elezion, explorator, faction, favor, fin, Governador, Imperator, iuridition, mal, man* (sing. and plur.), *Milan, motion, Muran, opinion, oration, orator, patron, pension, procurator, provedador/proveditor, provision, qual* (sing. and plur.), *quartiron, raxon, requisition, restitution, retention, sanser, Texin/Tisin* (but also *Tisino*), *ubligation, untion, Urbin, val, vien, vol*.

Following this rule, all infinitives end in -*r*. We find: *abandonar, aceptar, alozar, andar, butar, cavalchar, compiacer, concieder, condur, confirmar, convegnir, conzonzer, dar, decider, defender, dir, disnar, donar, dubitar, elezer, esser, exborsar, expedir, far, ferir, gionger, guazar* ('guadare'), *habitar, haver, incontrar, indusiar, intrar, invidar, lassar, lezer, manchar, mandar, manzar, meter/metter, morir, murmurar, numerar, obedir, obviar, pagar, partir, passar, pensar, penzer* ('spingere'), *piover, prestar, proveder, referir, restar, retenir, saper, scampar, scriver, scuoder, sigilar, solicitar, sparger, sperar, spinger, star, supplir, tardar, temer, tornar, trovar, tuor, ubligar, unir, vardar, veder, vender, venir, voler, zonzer*. I have noted only a few cases of the infinitive with a final *-e*; two are used as nouns: *il parlare* (402.24),[16] meaning faculty of speech, and *a suo piacere* (406.18).

(iv) Use of **alveolar affricates**, normally rendered with a *z*, where the equivalent words in Tuscan have palatals, rendered with *c* and *g*. These sounds were at that time still affricates in Venetian, as their reduction to sibilants (which is without exception today) seems to have taken place in the eighteenth century. Here are some examples: *abrazado, alozamento, alozar, alozato, arzento, aziò* ('acciò'), *Chioza, comenzando, cominzava, conzonzersi, elezer, fazi* ('faccia', subjunctive of 'fare'), *Franza, fuzito, hozi/ozi, lanze, leze* ('le leggi'), *lezer* ('leggere', infinitive), *lizieri* ('leggeri'), *manzar, mazor, penzer* ('spingere'), *pezo* ('peggio'), *pezorando, precio, precii* ('prezzo, prezzi'), *rezimento, stacii* (plur. of 'stazio'), *Verzeli/Verzei/Verzelli, zà, zeneral/zenaral, Zenoa, zenovese, zente/gente* (sing. and plur.), *zentilhomeni/zentilhomini, zercha* ('circa'), *zivanza* ('civanza'), *zoè, zonzer/gionger, Zonta* ('Aggiunta'), *zornata, zorno, Zorzi, Zudei, Zugno, Zuliano*. In certain cases we have a spelling which seems a hypercorrection, like *scocesi* ('scozzesi'). Other spellings may indicate a pronunciation with a sibilant instead of an affricate, as in *brusor* and *grisoni* (where the etymology does not require an affricate), *contradiseva, Croxe, Tisin/Texin*.

(v) **Absence of the palatal element**, with *s* and *i* corresponding to forms which in Tuscan present *sc* and *gl*, as in *lassar, foraussiti, ussito/usito*, and with hypercorrect spelling *prescidii*; *Consejio, consier, gaiarda, medaie, mia* ('miglia'), *mioramenti, moier, Oio* (but also *Oglio*), *Alexandria di la paia, taia, taiato a pezzi/pezi* (also *tagliati a pezi*). In the context of the rendering of palatals, we also find the spelling *artellerie/artellarie, seraggio* ('serraglio'), and *Cologna*.

(vi) Various **vocalic outcomes**, which are different from the equivalent literary Tuscan forms, as in words without anaphonesis: *adoncha, fameglio, gionta, longo*; in those without a diphthong, like *eri/heri* ('ieri') *homini* ('uomini'), *novo* ('nuovo'), and in others like *do* ('due'), *soa* ('sua'), *ditto*

---

16 The two numbers separated by a dot refer to column and line in Sanuto, XXXIV.

('detto'), *cussì* ('così'); in those where unstressed vowels have fallen: *disnar* ('desinare'), *fodrà* ('foderato'), or where they have been preserved: *anderà, haverà, parerà, vederà, vegnirà*, or where they have opened in front of *r*: *passarà*.

(vii) **Consonantal outcomes**, like *v* as opposed to *gu, g*: *Avosto, vadagnava, vardar, varito*.

(b) In the field of MORPHOSYNTAX:

(i) **Verbal morphology**:

In the **Present Indicative**, the first person plural, exemplified in our corpus only in *-ere* verbs, is in *-emo*: *havemo, savemo, volemo*, apart from a single *habiamo* (403.10). The third person plural of verbs in *-ere* and *-ire* is in *-eno* and not in *-ono*: *accadeno, dieno* ('devono'), *giongeno, reduseno, scriveno, tieneno* (also *tengono* (398.13)), *vieneno, voleno*.

In the **Imperfect Indicative** there are Venetian forms for certain verbs: *feva* ('faceva'), *fevano* ('facevano').

In the **Past Historic**, a tense which has since disappeared from Venetian morphology, in the third person singular we find *disse*, but *contradise* instead, always with one *s* (used as an official term in public discussions); in the third person plural we find forms in *-ono* (and in some cases *-orono*) for verbs in *-are*, *-eno* for verbs in *-ere*, and *-ino/-iteno* for verbs in *-ire*:

-*are*: *acceptorno, andono, introno, mandono, mostrono, negorono, restorono, serono* ('chiusero'), *tagliono, trovono*;
-*ere*: *disseno, messeno, preseno, risposeno, scorseno, scrisseno, tolseno, volseno* ('vollero'), and from the irregular *star*: *steteno*;
-*ire*: *fuziteno* ('fuggirono'), *riferiteno, servìno, ussiteno, veneno*, and in one instance *venono* (402.41);
for *essere* in the third person singular we find *fu, fo*, and in the plural *fono, furono, furon*; for *avere*: *ave, have, avi*.

In the **Present Subjunctive** the forms with *i* as the thematic vowel prevail in all three conjugations, so we do not only find third person singular *cavalchi*, third plural *balotino, butino, pagino* ('paghino'), but also *dagi* ('dia'), as well as an instance of the Italian *dia* (407.42), *fazzi* and *fazi, habbi, possi, si provedi, respondi, si scuodi* ('si riscuota'), *vadi, vagli* ('valga'), *vendi*, voglii; and *si parti, si servi, vengi*; and for the third plural *habino, possino, vadino, voglino*. But there are also forms like *contano* (396.4) and *passano* (405.13) which in the context seem to be subjunctives, and other forms in *a* like *debbasi, se intenda, si veda*, with plurals *debbano, debano, vengano* (and also a form in *e: dieno* (392.13)).

In the **Imperfect Subjuntive** the third person plural is consistently in *-no: calaseno, fosseno, havesseno, restaseno, zonzesseno*.

In the **Conditional**, the forms are always etymologically based on the imperfect (hence in *-ia*) and not on the past historic (Tuscan *-ei*, Venetian *-ave*). In the third person singular we find: *aldiria* ('udirebbe'), *cavalcheria, daria, haveria, mancheria, moriria, partiria, potria, risponderia, saria*; and in the third plural: *fariano, passeriano, potriano, responderiano, sariano, trariano*. However there is an isolated *parerebe* (406.12), and a first person plural corresponding to the present-day dialect form: *governeressimo* (404.18) ('governeremmo').

In the **Gerund** the form in *-ando* is found not only for *-are* verbs: *comenzando, stagando* ('stando'), but also for *-ere: vendando*.

(ii) **Singular verb with plural subject**. Modern Venetian has no verbal forms in the third person plural. Plural subjects in the third person agree with a third person singular verb. This phenomenon is frequent, but not prevalent, in our corpus. Here are some examples: *questi do morite su la corda* (390.31); *dovea passar dicte zente* (390.41); *le galie vien di Fiandra* (393.14); *et merchadanti di le galie è venuti in terra* (394.39); *si ben è uterini* (396.1); *4000 lanzinech vien in aiuto* (396.25); *li Procuratori serve la Signoria di danari* (397.27); *le quali decime . . . butava ducati* (400.23); *fu remessi* (401.30); *Fo mandati segretarii* (401.47); *è avisati* (402.29); *che anglesi . . . havea dato una rota* (403.12); *i qual sia* (404.11); *che le zente nostre cavalchava* (404.16); *e le zente soe passarà* (405.30); *dove è le medaie* (407.45); *e fo electi do* (407.48); *è quelli bronzi* (408.4); *vene do man di letere* (409.37); *ch'è gran cose* (410.24); *e li do coletori li scuoda* (411.22); *zonse letere* (412.29); *si andava le povere persone* (421.21). The formula *fo letere* is the customary one.

(iii) **Auxiliaries**. When the verb is accompanied by a *si* form (be it a reflexive or an impersonal), the auxiliary in Venetian is prevalently *avere*, while in modern Italian it is always *essere*, although in earlier periods *avere* is also frequently found. In our corpus I have noted nine *si* constructions where an auxiliary is used: in only one case is it *essere: s'è dito* (394.28), in all the others we find *avere*: *si havea reso* (393.13), *non si ha acostà* (393.26), *si havia voluto tuor taia* (393.43), *si haveva messo* (394.20), *per aversi mal portado* (395.44), *si à auta* (399.26), *si havia messo* (409.13), *si ha reso a francesi* (421.28).

(iv) **Absence of *che***. A noteworthy feature in this text is the frequent absence of the form *che*. The **conjunction** *che* is omitted in a few cases – in about ten compared to the hundred or so where it appears. They are instances of constructions with the subjunctive or the conditional, which would not be abnormal even in literary Italian, as in: *la causa che la Signoria vol [che] resti per Baylo* (391.36); *fo scrito a sier Lunardo Emo . . . [che] si lievi et vadi* (397.31); *pregava li officiali . . . [che] restaseno* (401.45); *disseno [che] cavalcheria* (402.47). Sometimes the *che* is omitted even with the indicative: *era fama [che] todeschi di l'Archiducha haveano* (396.17); *dicendo [che] il signor Prospero volea* (398.11).

But what is more striking is a feature which is common to many vernacular Renaissance texts (including Tuscan ones), that is the absence of the **relative pronoun** *che*, whether object, or, more frequently, subject. It is present in about twenty cases, and absent in about a hundred (not counting the numerous cases in which the relative *quale, il quale* is found). Here are some examples in which the relative pronoun does not appear, as object: *per saper di quello [che] fece quel Visconte* (390.28); *portò alcuni avisi [che] manda il suo signor* (391.2); and as subject: *quelli [che] stà qui e in terra ferma* (392.11); *le galie [che] vien di Fiandra* (393.14); *sier Piero Marzello [che] fo podestà a Padoa* (395.43): this is perhaps the most frequent type of example, indicating a function exercised by a certain person, as in *sier Polo Malipiero [che] è di Pregadi* (395.46); *4000 lanzinech [che] vien* (396.25); *300 fanti spagnoli [che] vi erano a custodia* (398.30); *el suo ambasador [che] è qui* (403.11), etc. The relative pronoun which I have inserted in square brackets is of course not intended as a 'correction', but merely indicates the position where the pronoun might appear, clarifying the syntactic structure of the sentence, which on its own might appear as a main clause, while instead the contexts demand that it be interpreted as a relative: 'le galee che vengono dalla Fiandra', and not 'le galee vengono dalla Fiandra'.

(v) **Pronouns and their combinations**. Here we note the use of *li* for the dative, masculine and feminine, singular and plural: *li fazi intender la causa* (391.36) (a lui); *li rispose* (393.7) (a lui); *li contò li ducati* (393.45) (a loro); *li è molto contrario* (397.3) (ad essa), etc.

In clusters one comes across *se li*, equivalent to modern Italian 'gli si': *se li daria ducati 3000* (403.46); *se li prepara* (405.32), *se li darà* (405.33); *no se li pol obviar* (406.17) ('non gli si può impedire').

We also find the presence of *ge* (presumably with velar prounciation as in modern Venetian *ghe*), as in *ge responderiano* (421.30) (a lui), and in the clusters *ge lo volesse concieder* (410.2) (glielo); *dargelo* (410.3) (glielo); in *fo terminà ge li sia dato* (407.47) the juxtaposition of the two dative pronouns, which would be odd, turns out to be a misreading for *ge le* of the manuscript,[17] with *le* referring to *medaie*.

In many cases there are a tonic dative and a clitic paired together: *li rispose al Doxe* (393.32); *a' quali la Signoria li darà soldo* (397.41); *Al qual il Doxe li disse* (398.32). The unstressed pronoun is sometimes also picked up in the accusative: *la qual nova la portò* (393.16).

Sometimes we have the tonic subjects *lui* and *lei*: *et lui sarà subito* (397.38); *habbi lei* (408.11), or the atonic subjects, Venetian style: *come el mandava* (394.31); *come l'era contento* (394.47); *come l'havea voluto metter in Novara 2000 fanti . . . e lui star . . .* (394.23); *che'l vengi* (395.4); *come el stava* (402.19); *che i siano ritornati* (396.37); *quello [che] i vorano far* (421.43); in *et che i non haveano voluti tuor* (393.45) the negative particle has a different position from modern Venetian.

The use of *quale* and *il quale* is noteworthy, as both forms serve as relatives (*li lanzinech . . . quali doveano* (394.22); *Veneno in Collegio li oratori di la comunità di Treviso, li quali fono . . .* (397.51)), and as resumptive adjectival expressions (*Li qual spagnoli sono . . .* (393.49); *Quali ducati 8000 expedirà* (397.16)).

(vi) **Da and per introducing an agentive**. The form *per* seems to prevail over *da*, in expressions where there is an agentive with an impersonal passive, as in formulas like *fu posto: Fu posto, per li Savii* (391.41 and passim); *fu posto, per li Consieri* (396.3); *fo messo, per il Serenissimo* (393.28); *fo scritto per Collegio* (391.32); and in constructs with *si*: *che si teniva per foraussiti* (391.21); *per uno . . . s'è dito* (394.27); *per li cardinali si atendeva a far pratiche* (402.26).

With personal passives the preposition is usually *da*: *occupati da foraussiti* (390.12); *fo expediti da . . . contestabili* (391.31); *fusse stà expedito dal Signor* (391.35); *alcune parole non ben intese da lui* (410.10); and even with the passive *si* construction: *la qual vittoria si à auta da solum zercha 5000 hongari* (399.26).

(vii) **Accusative and infinitive**. There are frequent latinising constructions, like the accusative and infinitive, which are unexpected in the spoken vernacular, but which do not appear out of place in an official account like

---

17 Venice, Biblioteca Marciana, MS Ital., Cl.VII, cod. 262 (2249), fol. 222v.

that of the *Diarii*. These constructions normally follow verbs of saying, knowing, etc.: *Fo dito esser aviso* (393.11); *afirmò . . . esso ducha non esser francese* (395.2); *era nova il re di Franza haver fato trieva* (398.22); *scrive esser zonto il reverendissimo cardinal* (399.21); *significhando haver lettere* (401.31); *avisano el signor Prospero aver abandonato* (402.36); *se intese esser zonte lettere* (403.5). In these expressions the main verb *avere* is often used in the sense of 'aver notizie, informazioni': *hanno esser stà morto Nicolò Varola* (390.31); *Di le galie di Fiandra si hanno, quelle esser a Liesna* (394.38); *aver da Milan, el signor Prospero quel zorno esser intrato* (405.10).

(c) LEXIS. Many terms fit into both categories, of Venetian and of a Northern *koiné* based on Tuscan. Naturally there are official Venetian terms, like *Cai dil Consejo di X, Pregadi, Avogador*, etc., and other words with a Venetian form, like *Domenega* (404.13) and *Zuobia* (413.37), for 'domenica' and 'giovedì' (modern dialect *zioba*), *fuogo impiato* (421.28) for 'fuoco acceso' (modern dialect *impissà*), *mancho* (400.26) for 'meno', *moier* (404.37) for 'moglie', *nova* (393.16) for 'notizia', *si negorono* (399.19) for 'si annegarono', *serate* (405.16) for 'chiuse', *piovesto* (421.20) for 'piovuto', *safil* (408.5) for 'zaffiro', *zoso* (399.4) for 'giù', etc. But it is not on the basis of the presence of dialectal words such as these that one can characterise the language of the *Diarii*.

As mentioned above, one can ask whether this text is written in a language with its own grammatical system (belonging to the sphere of Saussurean *langue*, or of Chomskian 'competence'), or whether we are in fact dealing with a mixture, on the level of expression (in the sphere of Saussurean *parole*, or of Chomskian 'performance') – a mixture of two different linguistic systems, one being Venetian and the other that of the Tuscan-based literary tradition. It is difficult to give a clear-cut answer, and this may be because a distinction which is relevant for an analysis of the spoken language in its spontaneous use, is less so for the literary language which commonly embodies different traditions. But even in the case of the spoken language, for instance in the so-called popular Italian of today, it is difficult to decide whether this is analysable in terms of its own grammar, or whether it is a mixture of two different grammars – of the dialect and of written literary Italian. This latter solution, which might seem the most reasonable, turns out to be problematic if one considers that speakers of popular Italian often do not have complete command of either the dialect or the literary language.

In the case of Sanudo, it is clear that the language of his *Diarii* is not the spoken language of conversation (i.e. Venetian), which, being the vehicle for informal communication would have been unsuited to the permanent and official account of public events, of the discussions and decisions taken by the various organs of the Venetian government. In the fourth section of this essay I listed some features which may strike a reader of Sanudo. They are mostly Venetian. But this ought not to lead us to think that we are dealing with a Venetian text. I feel that the more familiar one is with the dialect, the more Sanudo's text appears different from it. Behind the idea of isolating dialect features lies in fact the assumption that such features characterise a work which, in its basic texture, is not written in dialect. Neither is it written in the *volgare* based on an imitation of Petrarch and Boccaccio, which Bembo advocated, and which also would have been unsuitable, being too distant from the language used by the Venetian government for its affairs. What we have in the *Diarii* is a written language with strong local colouring, based on the literary *koiné* which had been created over the preceding two centuries on a Tuscan foundation. Gamba describes it as 'quel rozzo italiano che più veramente s'accosta al veneziano vernacolo'.[18] It is a language rich in Latin elements which are clearly visible in spelling (etymological *h* as in *hanno*, *t* as in *licentia*, non-assimilated clusters as in *aceptar*, *exceptuadi*) and in technical formulas (*ad consulendum, maxime, videlicet, item, de praesenti, immediate, ut in parte, cum sit, quod inquiratur* etc.). It is the vernacular of chancery usage, the 'volgare cancelleresco veneziano', or 'veneziano cancelleresco', as Cozzi calls it,[19] which still deserves to be studied in greater detail in its different contexts.[20]

I hope these considerations will be confirmed by a comparison of the following three brief passages which give an idea of the three idioms which I have mentioned. The first is a dialogue in Venetian, taken from *La Veniexiana*, the second, a passage in the literary Tuscan of Bembo, and the third in the Venetian-type *koiné* of Sanudo's *Diarii*.

---

18 B. Gamba, *Serie degli scritti impressi in dialetto veneziano* (Venice, 1832), p. 57; (2nd edition, Venice and Rome, 1959), ed. N. Vianello, p. 60.
19 G. Cozzi, 'Marin Sanudo', pp. 344 and 353.
20 In general, see the relevant section in M. Tavoni, *Il Quattrocento*, (Bologna, 1992). Tavoni points out the connection between chancery usage and the formation of the *koinè*. For a detailed study of the Milanese variety, see M. Vitale, *La lingua volgare della cancelleria visconteosforzesca nel Quattrocento* (Milan and Varese, 1953); idem 'La lingua volgare della cancelleria sforzesca nell'età di Ludovico il Moro', *Milano nell' età di Ludovico il Moro* (Milan, 1983), pp. 353-86; see also Anna Laura Momigliano Lepschy, 'Santo Brasca: The Language of his *Viaggio*', *Italian Studies*, XXI (1966), pp. 31-41; P. Bongrani, *Lingua e letteratura a Milano nell'età sforzesca* (Parma, 1986)

I

Oria: Madona Valiera, che voleu pagar? ché ve dirò de gnovo. *Valeria*: Che? bestia! de la çizeta! che xè vegnua? *Oria*: Digo altro che çizeta! che xè meio. *Valeria*: Che cosa? *Oria*: Nol voio dir, perché m'avé ditto 'bestia'. *Valeria*: No ti scorozar, cara fia. Dilo voluntiera. *Oria*: Non sciò chi 'l gera, che in la calle m'ha parlao, non so che, de vu. *Valeria*: Che distu? de mi? che zànzestu? *Oria*: Vàrdame Dio! no l'ho volesto scoltar una parolla. *Valeria*: Chi xèlo costù? Chi te ha parlao? *Oria*: Un forrestier vestio da sbisao, cun la spa', col penachio in la bereta, col vestio a la corta, de veluo. *Valeria*: Xèlo un zovene forrestier co i cavei negri? *Oria*: Madona sì: negri, trezolai.[21]

II

Egli si potrebbe dire in questa sentenza, messer Ercole, molte cose; perciò che primieramente si veggono le toscane voci miglior suono avere, che non hanno le viniziane, più dolce, più vago, più ispedito, più vivo; né elle tronche si vede che sieno e mancanti, come si può di buona parte delle nostre vedere, le quali niuna lettera raddoppiano giamai. Oltre a questo, hanno il loro cominciamento più proprio, hanno il mezzo più ordinato, hanno più soave e più dilicato il fine, né sono così sciolte, così languide; alle regole hanno più risguardo, a' tempi, a' numeri, agli articoli, alle persone.[22]

III

A dì 17. La matina comenzò a piover, ch'è molti zorni non ha piovesto, *adeo* gran sicità de aqua in la terra, che si andava le povere persone a porta a porta chiedendo aqua, nè si vedea altro che aqua mo' andar vendando per la terra.

Vene in Collegio il signor Thodaro Triulzi, et disse come havia pensado zercha il star qui e haver ducati 3000 a l'anno, et che li pareva non aceptar il partido, et dimanda licentia. Il Doxe lo persuase a voler indusiar fin si veda la fin di questo fuogo impiato, et quello farà francesi a Milano. A la fin, instando lui aver licentia, li fo ditto fin tre zorni ge responderiano con il Senato.[23]

---

21 *La veniexiana*, ed. G. Padoan (Padua, 1974), p. 77.
22 P. Bembo, *Prose e rime*, ed. C. Dionisotti (Turin, 1966), pp. 111-12.
23 Sanuto, XXXIV, 421, lines 19-31.

12

Horatio Brown, John Addington Symonds and the History of Venice

Brian Pullan

On a day between 27 March and 9 April 1888, John Addington Symonds, aesthete, biographer of the Italian and English Renaissance, called by some the English Burckhardt, translator of Benvenuto Cellini and failed (or unappreciated) poet, moved with his wife and daughters on to the *mezzanine* of an ample Venetian house, no. 560 the Zattere. This palazzo was newly named the Ca' Torresella, after the canal that flanked it, and the canal itself commemorated an ancient towered palace of the noble families of the Venier and the Donà, demolished many years before.[1] Henry James had been another potential tenant, and the matter of the five-year lease on the apartment had been the subject of much debate in the Symonds household. Would it exile them irrevocably from England, where they had sold the family house in Bristol to take refuge in the mountain retreat of Davos, for the sake of lungs assailed by tuberculosis? Would it hinder wider exploration in Italy? Would it curtail the education of their daughter Margaret?[2] Those doubts dispelled, however, the distinguished lodger surrendered freely to the pleasures of the palace and the joys of Venetian society – to the superbly placed apartment, to the prospect of the Giudecca Canal, brilliant with painted sails or ghostly and arctic in the winter weather, to the intimate view of the crowds flowing over the bridge beneath the window, to the sad cypresses seen in the garden of a close neighbour, widow of the murdered Tsar Alexander II. As he wrote to Edmund Gosse on 12 May 1890:

---

1 See Giulio Tassini, *Curiosità veneziane: ovvero, origini delle denominazioni stradali*, new edition, ed. Lino Moretti (Venice, 1964), pp. 689-90.

An earlier version of this essay was delivered in 1988 as the first in a series of lectures at the University of Edinburgh, founded by Horatio Brown's great-niece, the late Bud Brown. I am most grateful to all concerned for giving me the incentive to reexamine Horatio Brown's work.

2 H.M. Schueller and R.L. Peters, ed., *The Letters of John Addington Symonds* (3 vols., Detroit, 1967-9 [hereafter LS]), III, pp. 202, 210, 273-4, 301-5.

> I cannot describe the curious mosaic of this Venetian existence . . . It is a jumble of palaces and pothouses, princesses and countesses, gondoliers and facchini, hours and hours by day upon the lagoons, hours and hours by night in strange places of the most varied description . . . It is good for me, meanwhile, to be able to string all these things upon the thread of my dear old friend H.F. Brown, who is both sympathetic and wise, and upon the sense of duty to my wife and three daughters who are with me.[3]

'H.F. Brown', formally designated by initials and surname like the public schoolboy he was when their acquaintance formed at Clifton College in the 1860s, was the owner of the Ca' Torresella, and had been for about three years.[4] He came of an enterprising, literary, Scottish landowning family whose seat was Newhall, on the borders of Midlothian near the village of Carlop,[5] and was a cultivated amateur scholar who moved easily between the 'sumptuous country-houses of the West of England'[6] and the town house on the Zattere, which was scarcely less imposing. His Venetian property was not in itself a display of opulence. As Brown himself testified in his first book of essays, 'House rent is cheap in the city of fallen palaces', and as Mrs Prest has it in *The Aspern Papers* (of 1888), 'a big house here, and especially in this *quartier perdu*, proves nothing at all: it is perfectly compatible with a state of penury. Dilapidated old palazzi, if you will go out of the way for them, are to be had for five shillings a year'.[7] But the Ca' Torresella was not as remote as the residence of the reclusive Misses Bordereau, extensive repairs and alterations were made, and it became a place where generous hospitality was extended to English-speaking visitors who aspired to culture or knowledge or both.

It took time for Brown to become the principal British host. In the days of Symonds, it fell to Brown's senior, Sir Henry Layard of Ca' Capello, despite his execrable cuisine, to entertain Queen Victoria's daughter, the Empress Frederick, and her entourage. It was under Layard's roof that she and Symonds talked of Michelangelo on her visit in October 1892.[8] But Brown's Monday evenings became a more lasting institution, and on one of them he earned a dubious immortality by introducing the illustrious Lord Rosebery, 'firm, grave, sleek, plump as a church cat', to the incubus of the British colony, Frederick Rolfe, Baron Corvo. With other pillars of the

---

3 Ibid., III, pp. 515-6, 522. See *Fig. 38* for a photograph of Brown.
4 Ibid., II, pp. 677-8, 691; III, pp. 77, 79.
5 See Brown's own article, 'Newhall on the North Esk, with its Artistic and Literary Associations', *Scottish Historical Review*, XVI (1919), pp. 177-90.
6 LS, III, pp. 509-11.
7 Horatio F. Brown, *Life on the Lagoons* (4th edition, London, 1904), p. 219; Henry James, *The Aspern Papers and Other Stories*, ed. S. Gorley Putt, Penguin Modern Classics (Harmondsworth, 1976), p. 16.
8 LS, III, pp. 762-3.

Edwardian community he attracted the ornate scurrilities of *The Desire and Pursuit of the Whole*. Travestied as Nelson McTavish, 'merry magenta McTavish', he parades as the bumbling host of the Palazzo degli Incurabili – a sly allusion to the old pox hospital of the sixteenth century which rises above the Zattere between the Ca' Torresella and the customs point. Corvo's malice depicts the *salonnier*, equipped with laborious small talk, as a collector displaying his latest acquisitions – 'a long flaxen pair of scissors who handled little books, a German prince with onyx studs who talked of little red houses in excellent English, a white and scarlet rolling-footed crumpled-skirted Academician, a shy reader of archives with a cockney twang, a dyspathetic featureless old-youngster . . . .' Even Corvo, however, could not quite suppress the cordiality of his host, or ignore his genuine if inadequate response to the news that his guest was sleeping in his boat at nights because poverty had brought him close to starvation, and not because he was imposing an endurance test upon himself.[9]

More gracefully, Horatio Brown makes unobtrusive appearances in the biographies and papers of literary men more respectable than Corvo. It is he who sends Robert Louis Stevenson 'translations from old Venetian boat-songs', and brightens Stevenson's sick room in Davos with his own 'spirited and happy book', *Life on the Lagoons*.[10] It is he who waits with a gondola at the station when Havelock Ellis, fresh from a medical convention in Rome in 1894, takes a trip to Venice.[11] It is he who sends A.E. Housman, a regular guest at the Europa Hotel, a kind invitation to Sunday lunch in September 1901. To Brown the Ducal Palace was a sublime example of 'a nation's self-portraiture through painting and through sculpture'; Housman had privately described it as 'like a clothes-horse with a blanket on it'.[12] But seemingly they got on well, for it is Brown whom Grant Richards, the publisher they shared, arriving breathless and late at the Café Royal, finds dining with Housman and just reaching the *canard à la presse*, perhaps in July 1904.[13] Years later, he joins a select body of literary men who receive complimentary copies of Housman's *Last Poems*,

---

9 Frederick Rolfe, Baron Corvo, *The Desire and Pursuit of the Whole: A Romance of Modern Venice* (New York, 1953; reprint, Westport, 1977), pp. 163-4, 226, 231-4, 236-7, 250-1, 261. Cf. A.J.A. Symons, *The Quest for Corvo* (Harmondsworth, 1940), and Donald Weeks, *Corvo* (London, 1971).

10 Sir Sidney Colvin, ed., *The Letters of Robert Louis Stevenson* Tusitala edition (5 vols., London 1924), II, pp. 145-7; Robert Louis Stevenson, 'Underwoods', in *Poems*, Tusitala edition (2 vols., London 1923), I, pp. 76-7.

11 Vincent Brome, *Havelock Ellis, Philosopher of Sex: A Biography* (London, 1979), p. 84.

12 H.F. Brown, *Venice: An Historical Sketch of the Republic* (London, 1893), p. ix; Henry Maas, ed., *The Letters of A.E. Housman* (London, 1971), pp. 57, 59.

13 Grant Richards, *Housman, 1897-1936* (London, 1941), p. 39; George L. Watson, *A.E. Housman: A Divided Life* (London, 1957), pp. 181-2, 184.

a distinction which puts him in the company of Gosse, Masefield, Bridges, Hardy and Drinkwater.[14]

Was Horatio Brown, like J. Alfred Prufrock, not Prince Hamlet but an attendant lord – merely an adjunct to John Addington Symonds, an entertainer, introducer and landlord of the great and eccentric, an object, therefore, of the poor writer's scorn and a subject for the casual allusions of other men's biographers? Predictably, he figures in a judgement by the editors of Symonds' bulky correspondence as one of a string of 'minor writers' whom Symonds influenced. Gremlins, however, will invade the footnotes of the most scholarly compilations, and, as if to atone for their patronising verdict, the professors have credited him with becoming Master of the Rolls.[15] Venetian historians will know that he was never that, but rather one who worked for the Master as an agent of the London Public Record Office in the Venetian State Archives. They may see him as a historian of sounder judgement than his friend and mentor Symonds, of narrower range but deeper attachment to a particular Italian city. To Corvo, one of Brown's offences lay in being a man of means who could afford to take little for his writing and so spoil the market for the needy professionals.[16] Be this as it may, the long years in Venice financed by his fortune gave him an unrivalled sense of the place and its people, of the harmony and concord between the Venetians, their city, and the lagoons, of their perfect accommodation to each other. It is said that he was not a trained academic historian, and came to history through literature.[17] Both statements are true, but not surprising; in his Oxford days, the School of Modern History had only recently detached itself from the School of Jurisprudence,[18] and in the provincial university colleges Chairs of History and English Literature were often held by the same professor, as they were by Rowley in Bristol and Ward in Manchester. Autodidacts may well, in the '80s and '90s, have outnumbered the professionally trained, especially among those who wrote history rather than taught it.

Most remarkable was the discipline which Horatio Brown developed within himself, despite the seductions of a sociable existence and the freedom from any need to compete for an academic post. Venice was notorious for discouraging hard work; as Henry James observed, 'The

---

14 Norman Page, *A.E. Housman: A Critical Biography* (London, 1983), p. 132.
15 LS, I, p. 36, III, pp. 87-8.
16 *The Desire and Pursuit*, p. 250.
17 Cf. T.W. Allen, in *Dictionary of National Biography, 1922-1930* (London, 1937), pp. 120-3.
18 John Kenyon, *The History Men* (London, 1983), p. 145; cf. Peter Slee, *Learning and a Liberal Education: The Study of Modern History in the Universities of Oxford, Cambridge and Manchester, 1880-1914* (Manchester, 1986).

effort required for sitting down to a writing table is heroic, and the brightest page of MS. looks dull beside the brilliancy of your *milieu*.'[19] Will-power and good organisation enabled the gentleman scholar to deal systematically and incisively with a mass of record evidence preserved in the archives of the vanished Venetian Republic. On his death in 1926 the obituary notice in the local historical journal listed thirty-one substantial and varied publications.[20] These included a volume of verse entitled *Drift*, conventional in language if not always in sentiment, but capable of sudden forays into adventurous metaphor, as

> Love's Bank is large, fear not an overdraft,
> While youth is Cashier and the Banker daft.[21]

At the other extremity of achievement lay five portly volumes of the *Calendar of State Papers Venetian*, which were, incidentally, counted as only one item among the thirty-one. So, for that matter, were two chapters in *The Cambridge Modern History*, bracketed together for this purpose as Item 13. Amateur or not, Brown had produced five articles for that most professional of journals, the *English Historical Review*, and one for its Scottish equivalent. Modestly signing himself 'L. Smith', the author of the obituary (perhaps Logan Pearsall Smith) depicted Horatio Brown as a writer of broad human sympathies who, being far more than a historian in any narrowly academic sense, had revolutionised the British perception of Venetian history, and freed it both from Ruskin's puritanical judgements and from the fantasies of Ruskin's romantic rivals, who were no less divorced from reality.

Horatio Brown's friendship with John Addington Symonds does something to account for his rare combination of sensibility and application, of scholarly rigour and literary elegance. Symonds' letters reveal the younger Horatio as a more complex and emotional man than either the breezy undergraduate or the affable host who figure in the *Dictionary of National Biography*. The friendship with Symonds, and the duties it imposed, came to cloud Brown's reputation, not among students of Venice, but among those of Victorian literature and sexual behaviour. As literary executor, he was faced after Symonds' death in Rome in 1893 with the problem of dealing with an extraordinary essay in morbid psychology, entrusted to his

---

19 Henry James, 'Venice' (1882), in *Italian Hours*, New York, n.d.), p. 13.
20 In *Archivio veneto-tridentino*, X (1926), pp. 223-7.
21 From 'Awake! Awake!' in Horatio F. Brown, *Drift* (London, 1900), p. 46.

care. This was the manuscript autobiography which disclosed the intolerable tension between Symonds' homosexual nature and his public persona as an affectionate father and a respected if provoking critic and man of letters; which proclaimed his sense of injustice at the legal system which dubbed him a criminal; and which at the same time conveyed his tortured perception of himself as a profoundly abnormal, even monstrous, being.[22] 'It is doubtful', he had written to Brown from Davos, 'when or whether anyone who has shown as much to the world in ordinary ways as I have done, will be found to speak so frankly about his inner self. I want to save it from destruction after my death, and yet to reserve its publication for a period when it will not be injurious to my family'.[23]

Faced with censorship from the Symonds family and from Professor Henry Sidgwick of Trinity College, Cambridge, Brown resorted to compromise. Superficially his solution savoured of the historical method – publication of the documents and banishment of the historian himself from the book – which he was then practising in the Venetian archives as the Record Office's agent. He published parts of the Autobiography, whilst describing it irreproachably as the product of a particular period in Symonds' life, organised, as it were, around a particular emotional crisis.[24] Where possible, he preferred to rely on materials contemporaneous with the events and inner experiences they described, and drawn from the huge collection of letters, diaries, and other materials which Symonds had bequeathed to him. Severe biographers and editors, who now have access to the full text of the Autobiography which Brown deposited in the London Library in 1925, have accused him of distorting the truth, of mutilating letters and running them together without explanation, of funking any public mention of homosexual behaviour, and even of laying a false trail by implying in nebulous language that Symonds was tortured by religious doubt. Why did he publish at all if he could not tell the truth,[25] and disclose – amid the decade which consigned Wilde to Reading Gaol – what Symonds called his second 'incurable malady', 'that more deeply rooted perversion of the sexual instinct (uncontrollable, ineradicable, amounting to monomania) to expose which in relation to my whole nature has been the principal object of these memoirs'?[26]

---

22   See Phyllis Grosskurth, ed., J.A. Symonds, *The Memoirs* (London, 1984).
23   Ibid., p. 289; LS, III, pp. 642-3.
24   H.F. Brown, *John Addington Symonds: A Biography* (2nd edition, London, 1903), pp. x-xii.
25   Phyllis Grosskurth, *John Addington Symonds: A Biography* (London, 1964), pp. 319-22; LS, II, pp. 717-20.
26   Symonds, *Memoirs*, p. 281.

Brown, too, is unkindly remembered as the censor who tried to conceal the evidence of Symonds' collaboration with Havelock Ellis on his volume dealing with 'Sexual Inversion', even to the extent of attempting to buy up and suppress the entire English first edition.[27] 'The long conspiracy against the revelation of truth has gradually given way', optimistically wrote in 1902 the editors of *The Cambridge Modern History*.[28] Was the editor of the *State Papers Venetian* himself just such a conspirator, a Trojan horse in the first volume of that solemn collaborative enterprise, to which he contributed a piece on Venice? His recent critics may not have measured the force of the conflict between his desire to honour a very dear friend by writing his life, and his fear of wounding that friend's family and exposing them to ridicule or opprobrium. Despite the fashionable talk in England of making history a science, even *The Cambridge Modern History* made no pretence of total objectivity — whatever the justice of John Kenyon's description of it as 'a solid, reliable compendium of stodge'.[29] 'The point of view of any individual writer', observed Bishop Mandell Creighton, 'influences not only his judgement of what he presents, but his principle of selection; and such is the wealth of matter with which the writer of modern history has to deal, that selection is imperative'.[30] Brown could say, after all, that, though selective in his evidence, he used very few words that Symonds himself did not use: had not the documents spoken for themselves, in so far as they could properly do so?

Symonds and Brown shared an admiration for the Venetian friar Paolo Sarpi, and his best known maxim, uttered in conversation with a minor German prince in 1608, had been 'I never tell a lie; but I do not tell the whole truth to everyone'.[31] Symonds saw Sarpi as the Christian Stoic who worships the providence of God and sees God as spirit, not God in a human manifestation or God as presented by any organised and embattled Christian Church.[32] Superficially at least this bore some resemblance to Brown's portrayal of Symonds himself in the introduction to the *Biography*, as a man tortured by the contrast between all the available man-made representations of God and the 'universal, all-embracing *theos* of which he was in search'.[33] In so far as Symonds recognised Sarpi as a kindred spirit, and was writing in

27 Brome, *Havelock Ellis*, pp. 92-5.
28 A.W. Ward, G.W. Prothero and Stanley Leathes ed., *The Cambridge Modern History*, I (Cambridge, 1902), 'Preface', p. v.
29 Kenyon, *The History Men*, p. 143.
30 *Cambridge Modern History*, I, 'Introductory Note', p. 5.
31 Paolo Sarpi, *Lettere ai protestanti*, ed. M.D. Busnelli (2 vols., Bari, 1931), II, pp. 121-32.
32 J.A. Symonds, *Renaissance in Italy: The Catholic Reaction*, part II (London, 1886), especially pp. 257-8.
33 Brown, *John Addington Symonds*; pp. xiii-xiv.

part about himself, Brown may have come closer to the truth about his master and subject than is generally now acknowledged.

Be this speculation as it may, when a discreet account of the late Baron Corvo appeared in the *London Mercury* in 1923, Horatio Brown commented with fellow feeling: 'If it was necessary to modify concerning Rolfe – a freelance with no ties – imagine what I was forced to do in my John Addington Symonds books, with his daughters and their husbands insisting on seeing the MS before it was printed!'[34] It is worth recalling that an edition of Housman's letters, published as recently as 1971, had to exclude all Housman's correspondence with his close friend Moses Jackson.[35]

In the quest for Horatio Brown as a person in his own right, it is possible to turn the tables and use Symonds as the biographer of Brown's early years, especially by drawing (as Brown himself did) upon Symonds' letters. Horatio was a pupil at Clifton College when Symonds, fourteen years his senior, offered the headmaster some lectures on Greek literature, to be delivered to the Sixth Form and to 'the ladies of Clifton'. The lecturer later described his proposal as a stratagem designed to give access to the object of a great passion, Norman Moore; it was by yielding to that urge, he said, that he released and developed the creative powers that made him a prolific and famous writer. His connexions with the school then led him into a wider circle of friendships, more conventionally restrained by the relationship of teacher and pupil, and lasting for years beyond the departure from Clifton.

> Though I dearly loved them, and felt the physical charm of one or another, I entered into no relations like that I had begun with Norman. The duties of a teacher prevented this; and besides, I felt that it would be a mistake to repeat what I gradually came to recognise as more or less a failure. Consequently, these friendships grew up without jealousies, sentimentalities, and etherealized sensualities.

One of the boys named was Horatio Brown.[36]

Brown's first fleeting appearance in the bulky correspondence occurs in November 1867, when he was thirteen, and he takes on sharper outlines in July 1868: 'Brown was like an Olympian – perhaps a parvenu among

---

34 Quoted in Weeks, *Corvo*, pp. 395-6.
35 See, for example, Michael Holroyd's review of Henry Maas's edition of Housman's *Letters* (above, n. 12), reprinted in his *Unreceived Opinions* (Harmondsworth, 1976), pp. 201-5.
36 Symonds, *Memoirs*, pp. 193-5, 204-5.

divinities with a trace of his low breeding left'.[37] He did not lack ancestry – on his mother's side, from the Chiefs of Glengarry; but there was room for improvement, and the charm increased quite rapidly with the years. At first he emerges as an amiable but soft-centred youth, mysteriously in trouble in the winter of 1871 and incurring the headmaster's disfavour: 'he has a natural tendency to Aesthetical Sybaritism', wrote Symonds.[38] But during the young man's student days in Oxford, from 1873 to 1877, he came to recognise in the sybarite the presence of a 'good Scots will',[39] which made for hard reading and a valiant attempt to carry off a distinguished degree; he was to speak later of Brown's 'blent Calvinism and Aestheticism',[40] which may well have procured the blend of scholarship and elegance which he achieved in later life.

The numerous letters both to and about Brown pursued at least four different themes, each representing a different level of emotional and intellectual engagement. For much of the time they were friends swapping experiences of delightful things, and exchanging essays and poems, for the relationship was not based solely on an older man's pedagogic advice to a protégé, and Symonds valued Brown's judgement on his verses. With the decay of Symonds' health, Brown became in a sense his observer of the world, clambering up to vantage points beyond the reach of invalids, and sending him rich descriptions of what he saw: so, perhaps, he developed his talent for sketching in words, for writing of sea and sky and mountains and people, that showed in his first published work.

In another mood, Symonds was very much the brisk and business-like tutor, analysing degree results – the Second in the Oxford School of Literae Humaniores – and planning to discover from his brother-in-law, the philosopher T.H. Green, just how strong an element of First Class had shone through Brown's papers: 'a second, if nothing to be proud of, is nothing to be ashamed of. You have done your duty to yourself and the College; and you have done, even so, far more than I believe when you left Clifton, Percival [the headmaster] expected of you'.[41] He was more charitable than R.H. Tawney's father, who, in similar circumstances, asked him what he proposed to do to live down the disgrace.[42] About Brown, Symonds tended to write to other people in the tones of one worried about a late developer, talented but slow to find his metier, desultory, inaccurate, prone to disintegrate into morbidity and introspection.

37 LS, I, pp. 778, 830.
38 Ibid., II, pp. 132.
39 Ibid., II, pp. 424-5.
40 Ibid., II, pp. 560-2.
41 Ibid., II, pp. 481.
42 Asa Briggs in *Dictionary of National Biography, 1961-1970* (Oxford, 1981), p. 994.

> I am not very happy about him. He is 26, and he does not seem to get a grip on any vocation, though he has abundant good gifts, mental moral emotional and social. I wonder whether he will get into public life and make anything of it. Tom [T.H. Green] told him, it appears, that 'literature is only justified by success'. That is true of everything a man attempts – equally true and false, I mean, for all possible careers. What I doubt is, whether Brown has the quality of success. He cannot spell: he wrote 'sucess'. Will he make a secretary?[43]

This last was a glasshouse remark, for Symonds himself had occasional trouble with such words as 'tobogganing' and 'Robert Louis Stevenson'[44] – but perhaps these terms, though useful to a resident in Davos, were not as crucial as the word 'success' to a young man in need of it. Even six years afterwards, when Brown had scored his first modest successes, become an 'Inglese Venezianato' and applied himself to work in the Venetian archives,[45] Symonds was still worrying away retrospectively at Clifton's failure to perform an act of intellectual obstetrics and deliver Brown of his real self:

> The development from his aesthetical and inaccurate boyhood is somewhat singular. Men of his kind make me often wonder what is wrong in public school education. Perhaps it is in the nature of some people to find their real selves very slowly. But education ought to be maieutic of the real self, which in a case like Brown's it certainly was not.[46]

Beside the tutor walked the literary counsellor, steering Brown through his early disappointments. Determination and stoicism, Scottish or Calvinistic or from any other available source, were undoubtedly needed, for the first collection of essays on Venetian history was decisively, even brutally, rejected by Symonds' own publisher, George Smith of Smith Elder and Co.;[47] and the original manuscript of *Life on the Lagoons* was consumed in a fire at the publishing house of Kegan Paul in 1883 before it could be either accepted or rejected.[48] But in November 1881 there was a modest triumph to share, when three pieces, 'Burano', 'Malamocco' and 'A Venetian Ghost Story' were published by John Morley in the *Pall Mall Gazette*, and Symonds was quick to realise that Brown's special gift lay in expressing through these vignettes his sympathy and love for Venice and its people. About thirty were needed to make a book, he calculated; and when the book

---

43 LS, II, pp. 633-5.
44 Ibid., II, pp. 581, 664.
45 Ibid., II, pp. 824; III, pp. 46-8.
46 Ibid., III, pp. 124-7.
47 Ibid., II, pp. 686-8.
48 Ibid., II, pp. 824-5, 842-3.

in question went up in flames, he welcomed the calamity for the chance it gave to rewrite and build the essays into a more coherent whole.[49] There was a proposal, urged by Jowett, the Master of Balliol, that Symonds and Brown should collaborate on the vast *History of Italy* to which Symonds considered devoting himself after completing his many volumes on the Renaissance. But Symonds would have none of it: 'I see great difficulties in the scheme. Two men cannot (at least you and I cannot) write, arrange material, give form in common'.[50] Prepared to acknowledge Brown as a disciple as well as a friend,[51] Symonds insisted admirably on his preserving independence, and positively refused to give him specific advice or encouragement concerning an early essay on Caterina Cornaro, Queen of Cyprus.[52] 'Take heed now to be *yourself*', he wrote in November 1881. 'Do not get known as *scuola di* [school of] anybody'.[53]

Lastly, the friends exchanged much deeper confidences, sharing melancholy and self-doubt. Symonds recognised in Brown something of his own nature, and urged him on to adopt his own remedy, 'self-effectuation',[54] discovery and development of the real, inner self through ceaseless, unremitting labour, turning it outwards towards the world and never allowing it to turn destructively inwards upon itself. He preached the parable of the talents in diluted religious language. At the age of twenty-three or twenty-four, Brown suffered a traumatic experience when his friend Giuseppe Erba, 'the sheet-anchor of his heart', died tragically of typhoid fever. 'He is very sad', wrote Symonds, 'with the *maladi de la jeunesse*, that undefinable sickening of life, before life has been tried or grasped'.[55] Though writing at intervals as though they were two of a kind, Symonds still reproved Brown for self-indulgent melancholy and urged upon him as remedy an ethic of service to the world. As late as 1883 he wrote,

> I do not feel that you yet are living resolutely 'Im Ganzen Guten Schonen [in the Whole, the Good and the Beautiful]', that is, not in yourself and in the dark atmosphere which your own trouble has thrown around you, but in the world and in its luminous exhilarating ether. It seems to me blasphemy for anyone, with health and good means, to take pleasure in coming to 'realise that life after all is not so very long'. I have not a very defined religion; but that attitude of mind strikes me as distinctly irreligious. Suppose you were to die and find yourself out there alone, with what is called eternity before you, where would

---

49 Ibid., II, pp. 701-5.
50 Ibid., II, p. 763.
51 Ibid., II, pp. 865-6.
52 Ibid., II, p. 668.
53 Ibid., II, p. 707.
54 Ibid., II, pp. 665-6; III, p. 588.
55 Ibid., II, pp. 560-2, 571, 574-7, 580-2.

you then be if your life on earth had provided you with courage and unselfish sympathies, but had taught you only to expect the end – the end then of something which, *ex hypothesi*, could never end? The fact is, we ought to learn to live outside our own lives in something.[56]

He struck a chord, no doubt, in the puritanical leanings of the Venetian historian, who reconciled at last the grind of the tenacious scholar with the graces of the genial *salonnier*, the austere archival morning with the agreeable messing about in boats after the closing hour. In this sense, and not through being a pallid imitator, Brown was perhaps '*scuola di* Symonds'.

Himself at ease with the great, Brown sensed with his mentor the power of Venice itself, and the power of love or friendship between men, to dissolve the barriers of rank and degree. Venice was a medieval city still, without the social antagonisms and residential segregations of an industrial society, and Symonds captured in a letter of 1892 the ease of his own movement from one social circle to another, from the Empress Frederick to Angelo Fusato, the gondolier, and Augusto Zanon, the porter, from the Ca' Capello to the boatmen's wineshop.[57] Prominent in Brown's book of verse, *Drift*, are people of low degree, splendid physique, enormous strength: soldiers bathing, a Swiss waggoner, the stoker of a broadgauge engine on the Great Western Railway, who becomes a muscular extension of the mechanical power latent in the great locomotive itself.[58] One of his light pieces bears the title 'Bored: At a London Music':

> Two rows of foolish faces blent
> In two blurred lines: the compliment,
> The formal smile, the cultured air,
> The sense of falseness everywhere;
> Her ladyship superbly dressed –
>   I liked their footman, John, the best.
>
> 'The tired musicians' ruffled mien,
> Their whispered talk behind the screen,
> The frigid plaudits, quite confined
> By fear of being unrefined.
> His lordship's grave and courtly jest –
>   I liked their footman, John, the best.

---

56 Ibid., II, pp. 854-5.
57 Ibid., III, p. 767; cf. p. 808.

58 Brown, *Drift*, pp. 3-11, 107-8.

> 'Remote I sat, with shaded eyes,
> Supreme attention in my guise,
> And heard the whole laborious din,
> Piano, 'cello, violin;
> And so, perhaps, they hardly guessed
>   I liked their footman, John, the best.[59]

In Venice, as he relates, an invitation from Antonio Salin, his gondolier ('Will you sup with me, Signorino?') would release him, at least briefly, from the tedium of *table d'hôte* and waiters with white ties.[60] It was in the traditions of the gondoliers and the organisations of the ferry stations, which he came to know and describe in exact detail (for his readers must be made to understand precisely how they worked), that he found the ancient spirit of the Republic most perfectly preserved. For the people held to the past, even when the aristocracy had deserted the city and rented out most of their palaces, returning briefly and unwillingly from their country estates only in order to pacify their wives.[61] *Life on the Lagoons* and *In and Around Venice* made no pretence of being serious history, but may prove to be the work of Brown's that most interests historians today, when their discipline flirts with social anthropology and looks eagerly for ethnographers of past times to provide the material. Serious or not, Brown's vignettes record the passions that could be aroused by archival discoveries, as when he revealed in a gondoliers' cafe his conclusion that the faction of the *Castellani* had won more games at the *Forze d'Ercole* (the making of human pyramids) than the faction of the *Nicolotti*.[62]

Behind these pieces lies the desire to record the traditions and the rituals – rigorously determined by the forces of *costume* – of a society beginning to be threatened by the intrusions of an uglier if more efficient industrial world from beyond the shore. Gone were the days when an American consul could proclaim, 'There never was a pile-driving machine known in Venice; nor a steam-tug in all the channels of the lagoons'.[63] Ruskin lived to complain that 'the development of civilization now only brings black steam-tugs to bear the people of Venice to the bathing-machines of Lido', where, as Henry James remarked, a 'little cockney village' and a 'third-rate boulevard' had recently sprung up.[64] Some optimists reflected, as did

---

59 Ibid., pp. 104–5.
60 *Life on the Lagoons*, pp. 291-2.
61 See 'A Country Gentleman', in *In and Around Venice* (London, 1905), pp. 200-14.
62 *Life on the Lagoons*, p. 280. On the *Castellani* and the *Nicolotti*, see now R.C. Davis, *Shipbuilders of the Venetian Arsenal: Workers and Workplace in the Preindustrial City* (Baltimore and London, 1991), pp. 135-49.
63 W.D. Howells, *Venetian Life* (New York, 1866), p. 299.
64 John Ruskin, *St Mark's Rest* (Orpington, 1884), p. 5; James, *Italian Hours*, p. 28.

Augustus Hare, that Venice had suffered less than other Italian cities, that the steamers, so much abused, were 'really no disfigurement and a great convenience', that the houses were too strong to pull down, that there was no room to build any more, and that the only grave cause for concern was the disappearance of well-heads on a large scale into the hands of antique dealers.[65] But the desecration of Sant' Elena by an iron-foundry was generally deplored; the wash and competition of the steamboats threatened to ruin the gondoliers, and Brown won their hearts by bringing a successful action against the steamboat company; and by 1904 the first steam-hammers were poised in readiness to drive piles into the clay bed of the lagoon.[66] Brown hastened to record and translate the shanties, with their echoes of the fifteenth and sixteenth centuries, of the workmen who would soon be displaced by the new technology – the songs they sang as they hoisted huge weights with a pulley and dropped them on to the piles:

> Up with it well,
> Up to the top,
> Up with it well,
> Up to the summit.
> Saint Joseph, he
> Was an old fellow,
> With his adze he,
> Plane and hammer he,
> Went for to make
> A great ship,
> All for to fight
> The great Sultano,
> Him of the Turks,
> Those fools of Turks,
> All for to get
> Hold of his treasure,
> All for to seize
> All he had pride in,
> Naples the fair,
> And Rome the holy.
> Inside Rome
> They sing the Masses,
> Inside Rome

---

65 A.J.C. Hare, *Venice* (5th edition, London, 1900), pp. 2, 13.
66 Brown, *Life on the Lagoons*, pp. 130-3; *In and Around Venice*, pp. 123, 129; obituary of Horatio Brown, *The Times*, 21 August 1926, p. 7.

> There is the Master.
> Also the friars
> Of San Bruson,
> And eke the nuns,
> Nuns of Malamocco,
> Nuns with fine skin,
> Over the artichoke.[67]

However, he was no besotted romantic, and was never blind to the darker side of Venetian life, for he drew attention to the high mortality of infants and to the strutting masculine conceit which folk-songs betrayed.[68] His purpose was to make a sober attempt to preserve what was best in the people's memory of the city's past.

What made him unique was his capacity both for presenting the place and the people of his own time in terms that were neither sentimental nor patronising, and for piecing together a very hard-headed account of the Republic's past. The combination of the two was peculiarly his. As a systematic observer of nineteenth-century Venice he certainly had at least one formidable rival, in William Dean Howells: this American consul had published a far more comprehensive account of Venetian social life at all levels, but it was ruled by a half-contemptuous, half-affectionate vision of the Venetians as cafe-loafers or as *lazzagnoni*, of the *poverini* of Venice as an idle and corrupt if good-natured breed devoted either to the plucking of geese (which seemed to be the principal industry of Venice in the 1860s) or to the fleecing of foreigners.[69] Like most visitors or foreign residents the consul had written of gondoliers, but concluded that they 'trouble themselves as little with the past as with the future', and did nothing but repeat apocryphal tales supposedly culled from the Republic's history, like the gruesome story of 'Biagio *luganegher*', the sausage-maker who (like Sweeney Todd's accomplice in the pieshop) introduced his Venetian customers to unwitting cannibalism.[70] Howells realised that there must be something badly wrong with Pierre Daru's vision of a 'merciless' or tyrannical Venice, for if that was a true portrait then why should so many Venetians chafe under Austrian rule and look back with nostalgia to their own Republic?[71] Seeing the future salvation of Venice in the new men, in the lawyers, the physicians, and the Jews released from the Ghetto, he also knew that 'the last great name in Venetian literature is that of the historian

---

67 *In and Around Venice*, p. 131.
68 *Life on the Lagoons*, pp. 225-6, 255-8.
69 Howells, *Venetian Life*, pp. 34-5, 83, 117, 159, 181, 300, 301.
70 Ibid., pp. 288-91.
71 Ibid., p. 3.

Romanin, a Jew'.[72] None the less, he concluded that 'One learns in these old lands to hate and execrate the past', and it was left to Horatio Brown to interpret Romanin, whom he and other British historians recognised as their principal guide, for English readers of Venetian history.[73]

Admittedly there was a divorce between Brown's two approaches to Venice, since in his general statements about Venetian history he obeyed convention by writing almost entirely about the achievements of the patriciate rather than the people. He may have regarded social history in general as the proper business of the art historian Molmenti, whose volumes on the 'private life' of the Venetians (much of it lived in public) he eventually translated into English.[74] Hence, in his own most comprehensive book, there is an all-pervading tension or contradiction. He was avowedly determined to write a collective biography of the Venetian state and people as a living organism capable of 'vitality' and 'maturity', to identify and define the 'spiritual complexion of a whole people' and its 'mental attitude'. At the same time he was unable or unwilling to describe in detail anything much other than a 'young oligarchy' or 'nascent aristocracy', whose greatest achievement was to 'extrude' 'the people' from their ancient rights.[75] He argued with conviction that Venice never suffered from a 'feudal system' of caste-like social divisions imposed from without by a landed aristocracy, but had to admit that an equally strong hierarchy, justified chiefly by the extraordinary stability of its government, was created from within by a corpus of successful merchants.[76] However, he liked to dwell on the benevolent paternalism of the ruling order, and to suggest that the city had functioned like a joint-stock company in which everyone was a shareholder.[77] He described with relish those moments in Venetian history when popular sovereignty seemed to mean something again – as in the war of Chioggia when the Genoese blockaded the lagoon, and the sheer strength of the Venetian people's patriotic ardour forced the reluctant government to reinstate the disgraced admiral Vettor Pisani, that he might lead them to victory.[78]

If weak on social history (as distinct from social observation), Horatio Brown was strong on economic motives. He may not have cut Venetian

72 Ibid., p. 197; see also pp. 334–6, and Samuele Romanin, *Storia documentata di Venezia* (10 vols., Venice, 1853-61).
73 Howells, *Venetian Life*, p. 207. Compare the tribute to Romanin in Thomas Okey, *Venice and its Story* (London, 1903), p. v.
74 P.G. Molmenti, *Venice: Its Individual Growth from the Earliest Beginnings to the Fall of the Republic*, trans. H.F. Brown (6 vols., London, 1906-8).
75 Brown, *Venice*, pp. ix, 105, 141, 163-4, 167, 181, 233, 237, 262.
76 Ibid., pp. 80, 97, 112-3, 163-4.
77 In his chapter, 'Venice', *Cambridge Modern History*, I, p. 283.
78 Brown, *Venice*, p. 229.

history loose from Ruskin at one blow, or indeed have wholly discarded Ruskin himself, but he did concentrate on the more provable side of Ruskin's thesis – on the primacy of commercial interest in determining Venice's public actions, rather than on 'the vitality of religion in private life'. Brown strove to define a collective character for the Venetians, whom he presented as a 'race' divorced from other Italians, the product of their peculiar environment, and destined to quite separate development. In so doing he called them 'able, self-reliant, astute, single-minded, selfish, practical'. Thus Doge Enrico Dandolo, conspirator against Constantinople in the early thirteenth century, was 'the personification of the community which he ruled'.[79] In explaining the 'marring of Venice' which occurred between about 1405 and 1540 after the 'making' was completed,[80] he did not simply fall back on his own metaphor of the live organism which must, sooner or later, wither into senility. For the process was a logical consequence of Venice's pursuit of self-interest – of the 'crime' committed when the shaking of the Byzantine Empire weakened the barrier which stood between the Mediterranean and the Turks, and created (in nineteenth-century language) an Eastern Question.[81] It was also, and more immediately, the consequence of Venice's entanglement in mainland politics at the start of the fifteenth century, which was crucial in drawing the Venetians away from their proper element, the sea, into an environment in which they could not survive, the *Terraferma*. But this fatal move did not, in Brown's eyes, spring merely from corrupt ambition, but from a highly rational self-interest which originated in Venice's need to survive as a metropolis and a commercial power: in the need to secure supplies of grain, and above all in the need to secure direct access to the passes over the Alps into Germany.[82] Venice's over-extension and consequent financial exhaustion accounted for her decline into the status of a third-rate power, especially when the invasions of Italy brought the Republic into alliance or collision with the great monarchical states of Europe.

Like Ruskin, Brown believed that after 1530 or 1540 the vital, expansive power of Venice had failed and she was living on as a magnificent pageant, in which lavish expenditure concealed an unsound economy and an impoverished exchequer.[83] But his verdict was more indulgent than Ruskin's, for he depicted 'the Venetians' (the term referred increasingly to a frivolous aristocracy) as 'enjoying, in a way which attracted and dazzled Europe, that lovely home which they had constructed for themselves . . . The osseous

---

79 Ibid., p. 116. Compare John Ruskin, *The Stones of Venice* (3 vols, London, 1906), I, p. 6.
80 Brown, *Venice*, especially pp. 260-1.
81 Ibid., pp. 129-30, 131-2.
82 Ibid., pp. 190-1, 263.
83 Ibid., pp. 349-51.

structure, the rib-work of the constitution, remained long after the spirit had departed.'[84] Fortunately, too, he did not in practice follow Ruskin's precept that 'after 1600 the record of Venice is only the diary of expiring delirium, and by those who love her will be traced no further'.[85] Indeed, much of his writing dealt with the early seventeenth century, and drew upon the fruits of Venetian diplomacy. This, as he saw it, was a by-product of Venetian decline: a calculating science based on acquiring and summarising information about the strengths and weaknesses of other states, that served as a substitute for actual military force.[86] Between 1884 and 1891 it was on the cards that he would take up appointment as editor of the *Calendar of State Papers Venetian*.[87] First launched in the days of Lord Palmerston, this was an ambitious project designed to track down, and to summarise or even translate in full, all documents in the Venetian archives, and especially those compiled by ambassadors and other diplomatic agents, that had some bearing upon English affairs. Eventually, perhaps after completing work on his own big book on Venetian printing,[88] he began to devote himself to this labour for the benefit of British scholars, and brought out five volumes of carefully presented documents which spanned the years from 1581 to 1613.[89]

By this route he came to approach one of the most significant periods in British-Venetian relations. Half way through these years the rigid frontier between Catholic and Protestant Europe began to dissolve. Diplomatic relations between England and Venice were officially resumed after the death of the excommunicate Queen; her Scottish successor James I had, as he told a Venetian envoy, been taught by his tutor, the irascible George Buchanan, to admire the Venetian Republic.[90] An especially powerful rapport began to develop with the Interdict of 1606, when the Venetian Republic defied a direct order of Pope Paul V to rescind its laws controlling bequests and gifts of property to religious institutions, and refused his demands that clerks guilty of atrocious crimes be handed over for trial to the clerical authorities.[91] As Brown's documents showed, the English government of Lord Salisbury approved the actions of the Venetian Republic

---

84 Ibid., pp. 417-19.
85 Ruskin, *St Mark's Rest*, p. 61.
86 Brown, *Venice*, pp. 347-8.
87 LS, II, p. 912; III, pp. 87-8, 564-6, 649-50.
88 Horatio F. Brown, *The Venetian Printing Press* (London, 1891; reprint, Amsterdam, 1969).
89 *Calendar of State Papers and Manuscripts, relating to English Affairs, existing in the Archives and Collections of Venice, and in Other Libraries of Northern Italy*, VIII-XII (London, 1894-1905).
90 *Calendar*, X, doc. 78, pp. 52-3; cf. D.H. Willson, *King James VI and I* (London, 1963), pp. 19-27.
91 The Venetian version of events is given in Paolo Sarpi, *Istoria dell' interdetto*, ed. M.D. Busnelli and Giulio Gambarin (Bari, 1940). For a modern account, see W.J. Bouwsma, *Venice and the Defense of Republican Liberty* (Berkeley-Los Angeles, 1968), pp. 339ff.

because of their propaganda value in persuading the Catholic minority in England of the propriety of obeying a lay prince rather than the pope.[92] There were others, in the English embassy in Venice, who would go much further than that. Sir Henry Wotton, the English ambassador, seeing the strategic value of Venice in a grand design for overturning Habsburg and papal domination of Europe, exploited diplomatic privilege and excited the suspicion of the papal nuncio by launching a campaign for the spread of Protestantism in Venice, in which King James' own published attack on Catholicism was to play a crucial part.[93]

It may well have been absorption in the task of reconstructing these episodes that drew Horatio Brown back to Paolo Sarpi, the Republic's consultant-in-law at the time of the Interdict. Symonds had suggested in 1881 that Brown should write the life of Sarpi, in the moment of disappointment when his Venetian studies were rejected by George Smith.[94] Symonds had written on Sarpi himself, eloquently and forthrightly and in the ringing tones of one who knows exactly what to praise or blame, in one of his volumes on 'The Catholic Reaction'. He had hung his portrait against a stylised background, presenting Sarpi as the last heroic spirit defying the sinister advance of the Jesuits and momentarily postponing the decline of Venice. 'This friar incarnated the Venetian spirit at a moment when, upon the verge of decadence, it had attained self-consciousness'.[95] Brown made Sarpi the subject of his Taylorian lecture at Oxford in 1900, and this was to lead him to other high academic honours, including an honorary doctorate of the University of Edinburgh. 'The University rejoices to show her appreciation of the high scientific value and the literary grace of his writings', declared the Dean of the Faculty of Law, under whose auspices the degree was bestowed.[96] Some evidence of these qualities lies in the contrast between the exuberance of Symonds and the judiciousness of Brown, for the pupil resists the temptation to which the master succumbs. Symonds makes Sarpi an honorary Victorian Briton, 'a staunch Whig', 'a Macaulay of finer edge', 'a Dean Stanley of more vigorous build'.[97] Brown places Sarpi in a much longer Italian tradition, reaching back to and beyond Marsilio of Padua, of resistance to the expansion of papal authority beyond its proper and purely spiritual sphere, and into the conquest of secular

---

92 *Calendar*, X, doc. 532, pp. 359-62.
93 See *Calendar*, X-XI, passim, and L.P. Smith, *The Life and Letters of Sir Henry Wotton* (2 vols., Oxford, 1907), I, pp. 87ff.
94 LS, II, p. 686.
95 Symonds, *Catholic Reaction*, part II, chapter X, 'Fra Paolo Sarpi'.
96 Edinburgh University Library, Special Collections: *Laureation Addresses by Professor Sir Ludovic J. Grant, Bart., Dean of the Faculty of Law, 1894-1910*, I, pp. 91-2.
97 Symonds, *Catholic Reaction*, part II, pp. 208-9.

power. Both writers knew that Sarpi was not the crypto-Protestant that Macaulay and Hallam had assumed him to be, and they ventured on a subtler interpretation of his religious outlook. Brown fully appreciated that 'it is precisely because the defence of secular princes came from a Catholic living in a Catholic State that it made so deep an impression upon Europe'.[98] They did not consider Lord Acton's opinion that Sarpi was not a Christian at all, which one recent historian, David Wootton, has hailed as a remarkable insight;[99] but unlike Acton they knew the difference between Sarpi and the Pseudo-Sarpi, the gulf between the real Sarpi and the Machiavellian writings which were put out under his name.[100]

As *Venice: an Historical Sketch of the Republic* reaches its centenary (it was published in 1893, with a second 'revised' edition two years later), it is worth asking how well Brown's work has survived the years of investigation, debate and changes of fashion that have passed, especially since his death in 1926. Most of the *Sketch* administers a strictly chronological, doge-by-doge treatment to Venetian history, moving between external affairs and inner constitutional developments. True to Ruskin's outlook, there is much stress on deeds of heroism and feats of leadership, especially overseas. There is much talk of evolution, of natural selection, of the adaptation of the distinctive Venetian species to its environment and its inability to survive away from the sea. These things may sound unattractively dated, but the fashions of popular history have changed very little. Lord Norwich's acclaimed *History of Venice* still gives pride of place to doges, wars and conquests rather than social analysis;[101] the title of Christopher Hibbert's lavishly illustrated *Venice: The Biography of a City* echoes, perhaps unconsciously, the stated intention of Horatio's Brown's preface: 'In this volume I proposed to write a biography of Venice, and if it had seemed advisable I should have prefixed that title to my book'.[102] And a respected professional historian, Frederic C. Lane, began his own work of synthesis by stating with as much conviction as Brown that 'From the sixth century A.D. to the end of the eighteenth, the Venetians were a separate people.'[103]

---

98 H.F. Brown, 'Paolo Sarpi, the Man', in his *Studies in Venetian History* (2 vols., London, 1907), II, pp. 233-4. Cf. Symonds, *Catholic Reaction*, Part II, pp. 208-9, 218, 234, 244-5.

99 Lord Acton, 'Fra Paolo Sarpi', in his *Essays on Church and State*, ed. Douglas Woodruff (London, 1952), pp. 251-60; David Wootton, *Paolo Sarpi: Between Renaissance and Enlightenment* (Cambridge, 1983), pp. 42-3.

100 LS, II, pp. 971-2.

101 John Julius Norwich, *A History of Venice* (one-volume edition, London, 1982).

102 Christopher Hibbert, *Venice: The Biography of a City* (London, 1988); Brown, *Venice*, p. ix.

103 F.C. Lane, *Venice: A Maritime Republic* (Baltimore and London, 1973), p. 1.

Venetian historians are more serene and less contentious than those of Florence, but they tend to divide into the factions of myth-makers, who stress Venice's virtues, its stability and its love of justice, and of iconoclasts, who dwell upon its vice and corruption. One of the least reverent, Professor Donald Queller, has written with gusto a kind of encyclopaedia of the crimes and peculations of the Venetian aristocracy in the late middle ages, and he identifies Horatio Brown as one who fostered the legend of the unique selflessness of Venetian nobles and their submergence of personal interest in the greater whole of the Venetian state. Brown would have enjoyed the suggestion that 'his words appear almost fit to be set to music',[104] and he could happily have swapped quotation for quotation from his own works.

> There was, of course, another aspect of the patrician class. The vicious nobles became poor, the poor corrupt, and political and social life both suffered in consequence. The Council of Ten was frequently called upon to punish the betrayal of State secrets and the unbridled license of the nobility.[105]

Brown was disinclined to catalogue the details of patrician peccadilloes, but he did argue that when, by the time of Doge Foscari, the oligarchy had accomplished its task of bridling the doge and 'extruding' the people, its integrity was lost, it sank into corruption through turning inward upon itself, and there arose a 'pauper nobility open to bribes'.[106]

No doubt one should quarrel with Brown's assumption that the Venetian constitution was somehow fixed and fully developed by 1310, so that the only significant subsequent development lay in the strengthening of executive authority, personified by the Council of Ten. He certainly trivialised the later struggles to contain the powers of that Council and underplayed the genuine shifts which occurred after 1582 between the 'narrow' government of the Ten and the 'broad' government of the Senate,[107] to say nothing of the enormous extension during the sixteenth century of government machinery for the regulation of economic life and the control of disease and famine.[108] If he described the formation of the ruling orders of patricians

---

104 D.E. Queller, *The Venetian Patriciate: Reality versus Myth* (Urbana-Chicago, 1986), pp. 21-2.
105 *Cambridge Modern History*, I, p. 284.
106 Brown, *Venice*, p. 282.
107 See, for example, Gaetano Cozzi, *Il Doge Nicolò Contarini: ricerche sul patriziato veneziano agli inizi del seicento* (Venice-Rome, 1958); Robert Finlay, *Politics in Renaissance Venice* (London, 1980); Felix Gilbert, *The Pope, his Banker, and Venice* (London, 1980).
108 E.g. Maurice Aymard, *Venise, Raguse et le commerce du blé pendant la seconde moitié du XVIe siècle* (Paris, 1966); Brian Pullan, *Rich and Poor in Renaissance Venice* (Oxford, 1971); Richard Palmer, *The Control of Plague in Venice and Northern Italy, 1348-1600* (University of Kent Ph.D. thesis, 1978).

about 1300, he said little of the creation in the fifteenth and sixteenth centuries of a second estate of citizens, both merchants and civil servants, who came to exercise an informal influence over Venetian government that is still very difficult to gauge.[109] His allusions to citizen secretaries tend to portray them as mere go-betweens or even as traitors and spies, like the Muscorno who helped to bring down Antonio Foscarini, ambassador to England in the early seventeenth century; with less than his usual felicity he wrote of 'a secretary of the Council, Giovanni de Imperiis, a man with a long pale face, but a trusty servant'.[110]

In the sphere of economic history, within a few years of Brown's death, the researches of a young American scholar, Frederic Chapin Lane, had cast serious doubt on one of the assumptions that Brown and others took for granted: the belief that the Venetian spice trade was irrevocably and finally destroyed by the Portuguese discoveries of the Cape Route to the Indian Ocean.[111] Indeed, one of the strongest tendencies of Venetian historical writing in recent years has been to distinguish more clearly between relative and absolute decline, and to portray what looks like absolute decline as structural change, in which the decay of traditional areas of activity is counterbalanced by the rise of new ones.[112] Nevertheless, Brown's own researches, published in the *State Papers Venetian*, themselves provided ample evidence that there was much Venetian prosperity left in the 1600s for the English and Dutch to destroy when they not only by-passed but invaded the Mediterranean, took away the trade between Venice and her own colonies, and exposed the woollen industry of the city to direct competition from London and Leyden.[113] One only wishes that he had traced more sharply the line of descent between the Venetian patricians who turned to the mainland in the sixteenth century and the entrepreneurial capitalistic landlord of the late nineteenth whom he sketched so vividly from the life in his essay 'A Country Gentleman'.[114] Even so, he showed a remarkable talent for opening up subjects that have since proved to be of the most enduring interest for scholars – the organisation of crafts, the censorship of

---

109 Cf. Giuseppe Trebbi, 'La cancelleria veneta nei secoli XVI e XVII', *Annali della Fondazione Luigi Einaudi*, XIV (1980), pp. 65-125; Mary Neff, *Chancellery Secretaries in Venetian Politics and Society, 1480-1533* (Ann Arbor, 1985).
110 Brown, *Venice*, p. 293.
111 F.C. Lane, 'Venetian Shipping during the Commercial Revolution', *American Historical Review*, XXXVIII (1933), pp. 219-39. See Brown, *Venice*, pp. 324-6.
112 See especially R.T. Rapp, *Industry and Economic Decline in Seventeenth-Century Venice* (London, 1976), and Jean Georgelin, *Venise au siècle des lumières* (Paris and The Hague, 1978).
113 Cf. his own essay, 'The Commercial and Fiscal Policy of the Venetian Government', *Studies in Venetian History*, I, pp. 335-66; and Domenico Sella, 'Crisis and Transformation in Venetian Trade', in Brian Pullan ed., *Crisis and Change in the Venetian Economy in the Sixteenth and Seventeenth Centuries* (London, 1968), pp. 88-105.
114 See above, n. 61.

the press, the impact on printing and bookselling of the papal indexes of prohibited books, the activities of the Holy Office, on which he was already doing a little research at Symonds' request in the 1880s.[115]

It is all too easy to tell other scholars, especially dead ones, what they should have done. Like all of us, Horatio Brown had ambitious plans which he never brought to completion, and wrote essays where he dreamed of writing books. His full biography of Sarpi and his monumental history of the Venetian economy never saw the light. Perhaps of all creatures he most envied Nini, the white tomcat who lived at the café opposite the archive, as witness the epitaph he wrote on his death in 1894:

> Had I, the poor day-working wight,
> Had half your chance, O archive cat!
> What tomes with *lumen siccum* bright,
> Had proved, beyond all cavil, that
> Yours was indeed a happy plight,
> For down the Frari corridors
> The ghosts of ancient senators
> Conversed with you by night.
>
> Now three o'clock, the closing hour,
> Sends me to home, and each sad ghost
> Will pace the passages, and scour
> In search of furry friend they've lost.
> What will and learning died with you!
> What wisdom in your mournful mew!
> Take these poor verses, archive cat,
> Indited by an archive rat.[116]

---

115 LS, III, p. 103. See especially P.F. Grendler, *The Roman Inquisition and the Venetian Press, 1540-1605* (Princeton, NJ, 1977).

116 Brown, *Drift*, pp. 112-3. See also James Morris, *Venice* (London, 1960), pp. 74-5.

Index

Abano, 145
Acrocorinth, 39
Acton, J.E.E. Dalberg-, 1st baron, 232
Adige, river, 10, 11, 12, 22, 26, 63, 65
Adria, bishop of, *see* Novello, Tito
Adriatic Sea, 55, 58, 63, 66, 85, 86
Agnadello, battle of, 24
Agnello, Benedetto, Mantuan ambassador in Venice: as ambassador, 134-6; cultural relationships, 130-4; family and early career, 129-30; letters of, 129, 132, 134-5; Venice and Venetians portrayed in, 137-44
—, Giovanni, brother of Benedetto, 130, 131, 136
—, Lucrezia, wife of Benedetto, 130, 132-3, 135, 143
Agostini, family, 81
—, Paolo degli, 137
Albania, 43, 45, 84
Alexander VI, pope, 75, 93
Alexandria, 144
Alviano, Bartolomeo d', 102 n. 10
Amadio, Marco d', master builder, 174, 176 n. 23
Amboise, Charles II d', seigneur of Chaumont, 109
Ammannati, Jacopo, cardinal, 158
Anabaptists, 135
Andrews, Kevin, 30, 36, 38, 39
Angiolello, Agostino, 114
Anguillara (Papal States), 165
Apulia, 44, 46, 63, 66, 67

Aquileia, patriarchate of, 163
Aragona, Alfonso d', duke of Calabria, 58, 64, 66, 68 n. 46
—, Eleanora d', duchess of Ferrara, 59
—, Ferrante d', king of Naples, 58, 75
architecture, military, *see* fortifications
—, Venetian palazzi: 'borrowing' of design features, 182-3; Byzantine, 184; love of symmetry, 176, 184-6; post-1450, 184-90; role of *proto*, 175, 176, 177, 186-8; Trecento, 176; *see also* Ca' d'Oro
Aretino, Pietro, 130, 131-2, 145
Ariosto, Lodovico, *Orlando furioso*, 200
Arquà Petrarca, 67
Atti, Isotta degli, 170
Austria, 120, 121

Badoer, Antonio, 111 n. 61
—, Federico, 132
Bagnolo, peace of, 69, 83, 86
Balastro, Andrea, *camerlengo* of Modon, 34, 51, 52, 53, 54, 55
Barbarigo, family, 161
—, Agostino, doge, 79, 87, 88, 90, 91, 92 202
—, Girolamo di Franceso, Venetian ambassador to papal curia, 161
Barbaro, Daniele, 136
—, Francesco, governor of Brescia, 7
Barbeta, pirate, 43
Barbo, family, 149-50
—, Agostino, son of Paolo, 171

—, Elisabetta, sister of Pietro, 160 n. 63, 163
—, Marco, cardinal, 161-2, 163
—, Nicolò di Paolo, father of Pietro, 149, 150
—, Paolo, brother of Pietro, 150, 151, 154, 155, 160
—, Pietro, *see* Paul II, pope
Barozzi, family, 150
—, Giovanni, bishop of Bergamo, patriarch of Venice, 162, 164
—, Pietro, bishop of Padua, 161 n. 71
Basle, council of, 148
Bayezid II, sultan, 43, 44, 46, 47, 52, 53
Beirut, 144, 180
Bellini, Giovanni, 195, 196, 197
Bembo, Antonio, of Modon, 35 n. 17
—, Bernardo, 203
—, Bernardo di Niccolò, *visdomino* of Ferrara, 97
—, Pietro, 36, 119, 134, 197, 211; letters, 114, 115, 116, 124; and Luigi da Porto, 102 n. 11, 113, 114-6, 124, 125
—, —, *Historia Viniziana*, 114, 203; *Prose e Rime*, 200, 212
—, Torquato, 125
Bendoni, Benedetto, printer, 113-4, 115, 116, 117
Bentivoglio, Giovanni, *signore* of Bologna, 81
Bertani, Gianbattista, architect, 131
Bhogana, river, 42
Biancardo, Ugoletto, *condottiere*, 13, 14, 22
Black Sea, 40

Boccaccio, Giovanni, 113, 200, 201, 211
Boiardo, Matteo Maria, *Orlando innamorato*, 200-1
Bologna, 84, 85
Bologna, Sebastianello da, saddle-maker, 131
Bon, Bartolomeo, Zane and workshop, 174, 175 n. 20, 176, 177, 178, 179, 180, 181, 182, 183, 186, 187, 188, 189, 190
Bondemiro, Andrea, patriarch of Venice, 162
Borgia, family, 93
—, Cesare, 77, 79, 81
—, Lucrezia, 77
Borgo, Teodoro dal, *condottiere*, 107
Bosphorus, 40, 46
Bragadin, family, 150
—, Andrea, 63
Brant, Sebastian, *Das Narrenschiff*, 194, *Fig. 31*
Bregno, Antonio and Paolo, masons, 177 n. 27
Brescia, 5, 6, 7; Broletto, 5
Brescia, Fra Antonio da, engraver, 118
Bressan, Bartolomeo, historian, 123-4
Brienne, Walter of, duke of Athens, 4
Brindisi, 44
Bristol, 213; Clifton College, 214, 220, 221, 222
Brown, Horatio F.: as historian, 216-7, 234-5; literary acquaintances of, 215-6; relationship with John Addington Symonds, 217-24; *Fig. 38*
—, 'A Country Gentleman', 225 n. 61, 234; *Calendar of State Papers Venetian*, 217, 230-1, 234; *Cambridge Modern History*, 217; *Drift*, 217, 224-5, 235; *English Historical Review*, 217; *In and Around Venice*, 225, 226-7; *Life on the Lagoons*, 214 n. 7, 215, 222-3, 225, 226 n. 66, 227 n. 68; 'Paolo Sarpi, the Man', 231-2; *Scottish Historical Review*, 217; translation of P.G. Molmenti, *Venice . . .*, 228; *The Venetian Printing Press*, 230; *Venice . . .*, 228-30, 232-4
Bruni, Leonardo (Aretino), *History of Florence*, 202
Bruno, Cola, secretary of Pietro Bembo, 115, 116
Buchanan, George, 230
Bursa, 46

Ca' d'Oro, Venice: chief features of and their sources, 177-82; design and building of, 175-7; legacy of, 183-4, 185, 188, 190; origins of, 173-5; *Figs. 16, 17*
Cairo, 180
Calandra, Gian Giacomo, 129
—, Sabino, son of Gian Giacomo, 129, 131 n. 19, 132 n. 27, 133 n. 37, 134 nn. 42, 45; 135 nn. 48, 50; 136 nn 57, 58, 59; 137, 139, 142 nn. 105, 108; 143, 144 n. 124, 145 nn. 127, 129, 130, 133, 134
Caleffini, Ugo, 'Cronica di Ferrara', 73 n. 2, 77, 78, 88, 90, 93
Calixtus III, pope, 153, 156
Cambrai, league of and war of, 10, 24-5, 99, 102-7, 135
Cambridge Modern History, 217, 219
Camisano (territory of Vicenza), 99
Campagnola, Giulio, engraver, 192; *St Jerome*, 192-3, *Fig. 25*; *Saturn*, 192; *Landscape with two figures*, 193
Campomorto, battle of, 64
Canal, Giovanni di Girolamo da, *visdomino* of Ferrara, 81, 94
Canale, Niccolò da, captain general of Venetian fleet, 41
Candia, 44
Capello, family, 88
—, Domenico, 88 n. 98
—, Giovanni, 60
—, Vittore, Venetian ambassador to papal curia, 161 n. 69
Caraman mountains (Anatolia), 47
Caravello, Marino, of Coron, 35 n. 17
Carrara, family, 14, 15, 58

—, Francesco 'il Vecchio', 11
Carretto, Ottone del, Milanese ambassador to papal curia, 159
Cartari, Bartolomeo, Venetian ambassador to Ferrara, 82-3
Carvajal, Juan, cardinal, 164
Castelguglielmo (Polesine), 92
Castellana, Fra Jacopo della, 41 n. 39
Castelnuovo, fief (duchy of Milan), 62
Castiglione, Baldassare, *Book of the Courtier*, 109
Castracani, Castruccio, 3-4, 6, 9
Cattaro, 47
Cavalli, Nicolao, *condottiere*, 20 n. 54
Cavarzere, 60
Cellini, Benvenuto, 213
Cephalonia, island, 50
Cergnocco, Gianbattista, of Udine, 110-11
Cerigo, 43, 48
Cervia, 88, 151, 159, 167, 169
Cesena, 166, 167, 168
Charles IV, emperor, 6
Charles V, emperor, 1, 130
Charles VIII, king of France, 75, 76
Chaumont, *see* Amboise
Chioggia, war of, 228
Chipsala (near Gallipoli), 47
chivalry, 108-9
Cippico, Coriolano, galley captain, 42 n. 43
Cividale, 104, 107, 110, 123, 124
Codussi, Mauro, 187, 188
Colleoni, Bartolomeo, *condottiere*, 58, 61, 62, 170
Cologna (near Berra), 80
Coltrin, Jacomo, military engineer, 45 n. 54
Comacchio, 59, 78, 89
Como, cathedral of, 178-9
Como, Iacomo da, mason, 177 n. 27
Condulmer, Francesco, cardinal, 151-2
—, Gabrielle, *see* Eugenius IV, pope
—, Polissena, mother of Paul II, 149
Connell, S., 189
Constantine the Great, emperor, 39

Index

Constantinople, 29, 30, 39, 40, 41, 42, 44, 46, 47, 135, 229; Castello del Mar Mazor, 53; Peace of, 62
Contarini, family, 60, 150
—, Antonio, father of Marin, 173-4, 175
—, Francesco di Paolo, *visdomino* of Ferrara, 94
—, Gasparo, 139-40
—, Gianvettore, *visdomino* of Ferrara, 59-60, 67, 87, 88, 94
—, Girolamo, commander of Venetian fleet, 50, 51, 53
—, Marin: builds Ca' d'Oro, 174-83, 188
—, Pietro, *provveditore* in Verona, 16
Corfu, 35, 44, 46, 47, 50, 55, 62
Corinth, Gulf of, 42, 48, 49, 50
Corio, Bernardino, historian of Milan, 202
Cormons, 107
Corna da Soncino, Francesco, chronicler, 24
Cornaro, Caterina, queen of Cyprus, 223
—, Federico, 79
—, Giacomo, lieutenant-general of Friuli, 121
—, Girolamo, 144
—, Marco, 189, 190
Coron, 29, 46, 48, 49, 50; fortifications of, 38-9, 40, 54, *Fig. 12*
Correggio, family, 77
—, Claudio da, organist, 131
Correr, Angelo, *see* Gregory XII, pope
—, Gregorio, patriarch of Venice, 154, 155, 162
Corsini, Piero, 193
Cortese, Alberto, Ferrarese ambassador to Venice, 60, 61, 68, 81-2
Cozzi, Gaetano, 202, 211
Cranach, Lucas, 194, *Fig. 30*
Creighton, Mandell, bishop of London, 219
Cremona, 90, 93
Crete, 35, 41, 46, 51, 53, 55
Curzola, war of, 40
Cyprus, 55, 144
Czernovic, Giorgio, 43

Dalla Corte, Girolamo, *Storia di Verona*, 13
Dalmatia, 44, 151, 152
Dandolo, Enrico, doge, 229
—, Fantin, 174
—, Fantino, bishop of Padua, 153-4
—, Piero, 174
—, Vinciguerra di Marco, *visdomino* of Ferrara, 95
Dante Alighieri, 113, 118, 201
Da Porto, family, 99, 100
—, Bernardino, brother of Luigi, 113, 114, 115
—, Girolamo, 102 n. 10
—, Luigi (Alvise), 99, 100; *condotta* in Venetian army, 101-2; and faction fight in Udine, 109, 110-11; literary papers of, 115, 116, 125; and Lucina Savorgnan, 120, 123-4, 126; military service, 103-9, 124; *novelle* of, 116; poetry of, 115, 117 n. 86, 124; *see also* Bembo, Pietro
—, 'Lettere Storiche', 114-5, 116, 123, 125; *Lettere Storiche*, 101, 102-3, 104, 105, 106, 108, 109, 112; *Minetta e Polo, novella*, 124-7 'Giulietta e Romeo', 104-5, 112; Bendoni edition (1st), 113-4, 115, 116, 117; Bendoni edition (1st rev.), 114, 116; literary sources of, 113, 118; and Lucina Savorgnan (dedicatee), 113, 116, 117-8, 121-4, 126-7; MSS of, 113, 114, 115, 116, 117, 125; Marcolini edition, 113, 115, 116
—, Simone, cavaliere, uncle of Luigi, 100, 101
Dardanelles, 40, 47, 48, 50
Daru, Pierre, historian, 227
Davos (Switzerland), 213, 215, 218
Della Rovere, Bartolomeo, bishop of Ferrara, 59, 89
—, Francesco Maria I, duke of Urbino, 130, 141
Della Scala, family, 2, 11, 12, 14, 16
—, Antonio, *signore* of Verona, 11
—, Brunoro, son of Guglielmo, Bavaria branch, 16

—, Cangrande I, *signore* of Verona, 12
—, Cangrande II, *signore* of Verona, 10
—, Fregnano, illegitimate son of Mastino II, 10
Djem, prince, 43
Dolce, Lodovico, 132
Dolfin, Dolfino, 68
—, Giovanni, 136
Dolgoronki, princess, widow of Tsar Alexander II, 213
Domenichi, Domenico de', bishop, 149
Donà, family, 213
—, Francesco, doge, 138, 139
—, Girolamo di Antonio, *visdomino* of Ferrara, 79, 97
—, Pietro di Lorenzo, *visdomino* of Ferrara, 95
Donato family, 142
Duodo, Pietro di Luca, *visdomino* of Ferrara, 96
Dürer, Albrecht, 191; illustrations for *Der Ritter vom Turn*, 194, *Das Narrenschiff*, 194, *Fig. 31*

Egnazio, Giovan Battista (G.B. Cipelli), historian, 134
Ellis, Havelock, 215, 219
Enrichi, pirate, 43
Epirus, 50
Erasmus, Desiderio, 132
Erba, Giuseppe, 223
Erizzo, Antonio di Marco, *visdomino* of Ferrara, 82-3, 95-6
—, Marcantonio, 142
Este, family, 2, 3, 6, 59, 90, 93
—, Alfonso I d', duke of Ferrara, 75, 76, 77, 79
—, Azzo VIII d', *signore* of Ferrara, 3, 4, 6
—, Beatrice d', duchess of Milan, 75
—, Borso d', duke of Ferrara, 169
—, Ercole I d', duke of Ferrara: alliances, 75-6, 77; financial difficulties, 74; neutrality, 76, 77
—, relations with Venice, 77, 78, 79, 90, 92-3; formal diplomatic exchanges, 80-1;

friends and informers in, 81-2; hostile politicians in, 60; various disputes with, 58-9, 87-8, 91; and *visdomini*, 59-60, 76, 79, 80, 81, 82-3, 87, 88, 91
—, Ferrante d', son of Ercole I, 76, 77
—, Isabella d', marchioness of Mantua, 143
—, Niccolò III d', marquis of Ferrara, 58-9
—, Renée d' of France, duchess of Ferrara, 141
Eugenius IV, pope, 147, 148, 149, 150, 159

Fabri, Antonio da, *condottiere*, 49-50
Faenza, 167, 168, 170
Fausto, Vettor, scholar, 136
Ferrara, 2; Castel Vecchio, 93; San Marco, 78; San Silvestro, 89; woodcut panorama, 75 (fig.); *Diario ferrarese . . .*, 74 n. 13, 76, 77, 78; First Venetian War (1313), 84; peace of (1428), 21
—, and Venice: disputes over citizenship, 90-1; disputes over contraband, 88-89; disputes over borders, 92-3; tax immunity, 83-6, 89-92; *visdomini*, 58, 76, 78, 79, 82-3, 85, 86, 87, 88, 90, 91, 93, 94-8
—, war of (1482-4): background to and causes of, 57-61, 73, 83; campaign, 63-6; costs and consequences of, 73-5, 77-9; financing of, 62-3, 70; map of, 56; military preparations for, 61-2, 63; peace negotiations, 70-1; peace treaty, 71, 75, 83, 92; role of Senate and Council of Ten, 68-9; Venetian attitudes to, 59-60, 61, 66-9
Ferreti, Ferreto de', *Historia rerum in Italia gestarum*, 2 n. 15, 4
Ferrini, Benedetto, architect, 189
Ficarolo, 64, 67, 84
Florence, 4, 7, 10, 74, 76, 150, 167, 187; Captain of the People, palace of, 4; Executor of the Ordinances of Justice,

palace of, 4; Fortezza da Basso, 1, 7; Loggia dei Lanzi, 7; Palazzo Vecchio, 4, 7; Piazza della Signoria, 7; Porta a Faenza, 1; Signoria, palace of the, 4
Florentine exiles, 1, 7-8; Pazzi war, 57-8
Forlì, 167, 168, 170
fortifications: in Greek colonies, 40, 44-5; artillery fortifications, 38-9; coastal fortifications, 40; river forts, 65-6; *see also* Coron; Hexamilion; Lepanto; Napoli di Romania; Negropont
—, in Italian cities, 2-8, 9-10, 11 nn. 7, 26; *see* Verona, Cittadella
Foscari, Francesco, doge, 6, 174-5, 183-4, 188, 190, 233
—, Niccolò, 83
Foscarini, Antonio, Venetian ambassador to England, 234
—, Lodovico, Venetian ambassador to Mantua, 155; to papal curia 161 n. 69
France, 43, 55 n. 100, 65, 77, 78, 79; French men-at-arms, 108-9
Franchetti, baron, 185
Francis I, king of France, 25
Franco, Niccolò, writer, 132, 133
Franza, Zuan da, craftsman, 175 n. 20, 181
Frederick, empress, 214, 224
Fregnano da Sesso, captain of Cittadella, 17, 20
Friuli, 39, 61, 66, 106, 109, 112, 121, 122, 151, 162, 171; Adunanza of, 106, 110, 111 n. 61; factions in, 103, 110, 111, 112, 126
Furter, Michael, printer, 194
Fusato, Angelo, gondolier, 224

Gabriel, Marco, rector, Modon, 49 n. 74, 50, nn. 77, 80, 82; 51, 52, 53, 54
Gallina, Giacinto, playwright, 200
Gallipoli, 44, 46, 47
Galvagno, Giulio, Mantuan envoy, 145

Gamba, Bartolomeo, 211
Gambello, Antonio, *proto*, 187
Garlasco campaign (in duchy of Milan), 126
Garzoni, Marco, 138
Genoa, 1, 3; *Castelletto*, 76; Doria, 3
Ghellini, Ghellino, 123-4
Gherardi, Maffeo, abbot of San Michele di Murano, 162
Giacomazzo of Bologna, soldier, 23
Giolito de' Ferrari, Gabriel, printer, 144
Giorgione: German influences on, 191, 193, 194, 196-7; influence of Campagnola on, 192-3
—, *Allendale Adoration*, 193; *Benson Madonna*, 193, 194, 196; *Christ*, 196; *Epiphany*, 193, 194, 195, 196, *Figs. 32, 37*; *Homage to a Poet*, 192; *Leda and the Swan*, 192, 195, 196; 'Master of the Phillips Astrologer', 192, 195; 'Master of the *Venus and Cupid*', 192, 195; *Moses*, 192, 193, 194, 195, 196; *Preaching of the Baptist*, 193-7, Plate I, *Figs. 28, 33, 34*; *Rustic Idyll*, 192, 195, 196, *Figs. 23, 35, 36*; *Solomon*, 192, 193, 194, 196, *Fig. 24*; *Tempesta*, 192
Giovanni of Cremona, master builder, 18
Giuliano, Andrea, *provveditore*, Verona, 20
Giustinian, Antonio, 111 n. 61
—, Benedetto di Pangrazio, *visdomino* of Ferrara, 94
—, Bernardo, humanist, 60, 147, 158, 160
—, Francesco, Venetian ambassador to Mantua, 135-6, 138
—, Giacomo, 134
—, Sebastiano, 136
Goldoni, Carlo, 200
Goldthwaite, R., professor, 187
Gonzaga, family, 129, 132, 134
—, Carlo, 109
—, Ercole, cardinal, 136 n. 54, 138 n. 70, 143, 144
—, Federico II, duke of Mantua,

129, 130, 131, 133, 136, 137, 140, 143, 144
—, Ferrante, 130
—, Francesco III, duke of Mantua, 136
—, Francesco, cardinal, 161, 166
—, Gianfrancesco, marquis of Mantua, 22, 23 n. 70, 135
—, Guglielmo, duke of Mantua, 136, 139 n. 85, 144 n. 124
—, Ludovico III, marquis of Mantua, 108-9
Goro (near Ferrara), 85
Gosse, Edmund, 213
Gradani, Martin, light cavalryman, 104
Gradenigo, Luigi, lieutenant general of Friuli, 108
Gradisca, 107
Grassi, Francesco, *condottiere*, 24
Green, Louis, 4
—, T.H., philosopher, 221, 222
Gregory XII, pope, 147, 149, 156
Griffoni, Matteo, *condottiere*, 119
Grimani, Antonio, naval commander, later doge, 44, 48, 49, 50, 92
—, Francesco, soldier and magistrate, 30 n. 6
—, Girolamo, *savio grande*, 138
Gritti, family, 136, 161
—, Andrea, doge, 43 n. 47, 46, 47, 99, 100 n. 2, 101, 102 n. 10, 103, 104, 134, 136, 138
—, Lorenzo, son of Andrea, 134, 136 n. 55
—, Triadano, naval commander, 42, 161
—, Zorzo, 136 n. 55
Guarda, 92
Guardati, Tomaso (Masuccio of Salerno), *Giannozza e Mariotto*, 113
Guardazola, 92
Guicciardini, Francesco, 1-2
—, Jacopo, 68 n. 46
Guidobono, Antonio, Milanese ambassador to Venice, 189
Guidoni, Aldrovandino, Ferrarese ambassador to Venice, 80, 82, 83, 87, 89

Hainault-Bernberg, Rudolf of, prince, 101
Hale, Sir John, ix-xi, 1, 9, 26; bibliography of, xvii-xxvii
Hallam, Henry, historian, 232
Hare, Augustus, 226
Henry VIII, king of England, 135
Hexamilion (*Semili*), 39, 40
Hibbert, Christopher, *Venice: The Biography of a City*, 232
Housman, A.E., 215-6, 220
Howells, William Dean, *Venetian Life*, 225, 227-8
Hungary, 47, 144

Iacomo, Bertuzi de, master mason, 182
Imperiis, Giovanni de, a secretary of Council of Ten, 234
Istria, 171

Jackson, Moses, 220
James I, king of England, 230, 231
James, Henry, 213, 216-7, 225; *The Aspern Papers*, 214
Jowett, Benjamin, master of Balliol, 223
Justinian, emperor, 39

Kenyon, John, 219
Knights of St John, 44, 46

Landi, Marc'Antonio, count, 115-6
Lando, Ortensio, 132-3; 'Catalogues', 133; *Dubbi*, 133
—, Pietro, doge, 138
Lane, Frederic C., historian, 48, 232, 234
Lanfredini, Giovanni, 69 n. 52
language, 199; Italian, 200; *koinaí*, 200, 201; Tuscan, 200, 201; Venetian, 200, 201; *see also* Sanudo, M.
Layard, Sir Henry, 214
Lazara, Marco, medical doctor, 107-8
leagues: Holy (Italian, 1495), 76; Holy (1527), 130; Italic (1468, 1470), 169; of Milan, Florence and Naples (1467), 170; Triple Alliance (1480), 58, 59, 61, 64, 65, 66, 67, 69, 71

Legena, castle, 49
Legnagno, Fra Francesco da, 47
Lelli, Teodoro de', bishop of Treviso, 149, 162
Lepanto, 29, 40, 46, 47, 48, 49, 50; fortifications of, 38, 39, 42
Levant, 35, 44, 91
Lezze, Donado da, *Historia Turchesca*, 30, 34
Lezze, da, procurator, 136
Lion, Andrea di Niccolò, Venetian ambassador to papal curia, 161 n. 69
Lionora e Ippolito, anon. *novella*, 113
Litolfi, Annibale, 138
Lodi, Peace of, 57, 150
Lodron, Antonio, count, 120 n. 93
Lombardo (Pietro di Martino Solari), 188
Lombardy, 12, 21, 61, 64, 65, 67, 70, 85, 92, 135
Lonigo, 103, 104
Loredan, family, 88
—, Antonio, naval commander, *provveditore generale*, Ferrara, 42, 63, 67
—, Leonardo, doge, 69, 80-1, 110 n. 59
—, Tommaso, 88 n. 98
Loreo, 60
Lorraine, René II, duke of, 65, 71
Loschi, Antonio, secretary to Giangaleazzo Visconti, 8 n. 56
Louis XI, king of France, 71, 160
Louis XII, king of France, 77, 90, 93
Lucca, 1, 6; *Augusta*, 3-4, 6, 9; Dal Portico palace, 4

Macaulay, Thomas Babington, 1st baron, 232
Machiavelli, Niccolò, 10, 11, 12, 22, 25; *Discourses on the First Decade of Livy*, 1, 2, 8; *History of Florence*, 10; *Prince*, 112
Maffei, Carlo, 144 n. 124
Mainoldo, antique-dealer of Mantua, 131
Malatesta, Domenico (Malatesta Novello), 166, 167
—, Sallustio, 170

—, Sigismondo Pandolfo, 9, 166, 168, 170
—, Roberto, 62, 63, 64, 170, 171
Malipiero, Domenico, 44; *Annali veneti . . .*, 42 n. 41, 61, 67, 70, 71, 78
Manfredi, family, 168, 169, 170
—, Astorgio, 168
Mantovani, family, 88 n. 98
Mantovano, the, 138
Mantua, 65, 84, 85, 131, 133; Congress of, 154, 155, 156, 157; relations with Venice, 135-6, 137-8, 145
Manuel II Palaeologus, emperor, 39
Manuzio, Aldo, printer, 201
—, Paolo, printer, 136
Marasca, Bartolomeo, 163-4, 165
Marcello, Giacomo, 67
—, Giacomo Antonio, 22, 23
—, Pietro, *provveditore generale*, 104
—, Valerio, galley commander, 51-2, 53 n. 93
Marche, 85
Marmora, Sea of, 40
Marsilio of Padua, 231
Martini, Antonio di, master builder, 175 n. 20, 181 n. 57
Marzari, Giacomo, notary of Vicenza, 116, 125
Mason, 104
Massa Fiscaglia (Ferrara), 87
Masuccio of Salerno, *see* Guardati, Tomaso
Maximilian, emperor elect, 25, 101
Medici, Alessandro de', duke of Florence, 1, 7
—, Lorenzo de' (*il Magnifico*), 7, 58, 69
Megenberg, Conrad von, printer, *Buch der Natur*, 193, *Fig. 27*
Merona, castle, 49
Merula, Giorgio, humanist, 201
Messenia, 49
Mezzo, Giacomo da, commissary, 63, 67
Michael VIII Palaeologus, emperor, 40
Michiel, family, 150
—, Francesco, *provveditore*, 60, 61 n. 12, 63, 67, 70

—, Francesco, 137
—, Giovanni, cardinal, 163, 172
Milan, 5, 11, 43, 57, 58, 59, 62, 65, 71, 77, 78, 85, 87, 90, 137, 167
Minio, Giovan Antonio, member of *Collegio*, 60
Mocenigo, family, 161
—, Andrea, 17
—, Francesco, brother of Giovanni di Pietro, 81
—, Giovanni, doge, 59, 60
—, Giovanni di Pietro, *visdomino* of Ferrara, 79, 81, 96-7
—, Piero, naval commander, 42
—, Pietro di Leonardo, Venetian ambassador to papal curia, 161
—, Tommaso, doge, 20, 173, 174
Modena, 3-4, 6, 74
Modon, 29, 40, 46, 47, 48, *Fig. 6*
—, fortifications of, 30, 32 (fig.), 33 (fig.), 34, 35-8, 54, 55, *Figs. 7, 8, 9*; Bembo bastion, 36; Torre Maestra, 37, 55
—, siege and fall of, 45, 49-54, 55, 77
Mohammed II, sultan, 40
Molin, Marco da, procurator of St Marks, 140
Moline, castle, 49
Molmenti, P.G., historian, 228
Monemvasia, 29, 40
Monferrato, duchy of, 133-4
Monte, Piero dal, clerical diplomat, 148
Montefeltro, Federico da, duke of Urbino, 4, 58, 61, 64
Morea, 29, 30, 35, 39, 46, 50, 54, 66
Moretto, Giovan Maria, dyer, 131
Morley, John, editor of *Pall Mall Gazette*, 222
Moro, family, 150, 161
—, Cristoforo, doge, 159, 161
—, Cristoforo di Lorenzo, *visdomino* of Ferrara, 79, 97-8
—, Damiano, patron of the arsenal, 63, 66, 67
—, Sebastiano, 142
Morosini, Francesco, 30, 54
Mucchi, L., 195
Mula, Alvise da, *visdomino* of Ferrara, 98

—, Marcantonio da, *savio di Terraferma*, 137
Münster, 135
Murad II, sultan, 39
Murano, 144
Muscorno, Giulio, 234

Naples, 1, 24, 43, 44, 58, 61, 77
Napoli di Romania (Nauplia), 29, 40, 43, 46; fortifications of, 37, 38, 45, 54, *Figs. 10, 11*
Navagero, Andrea, historian of Venice, 134, 203
Navagero, Bernardo, *savio di Terraferma*, 136, 137, 138
Navarino Bay, 50
Nepi, 130
Negropont, 29, 41, 53, 171; fortifications of, 30
Nello, Ludovico, secretary to B. Agnello, 145
Newhall (near Carlop), 214
Nicholas V, pope, 151, 152, 166
Nicodemia, 46
Nobili, Armanno, envoy, 87 n. 93
Norwich, John Julius, *History of Venice*, 232
Novello, Carlino di, infantry captain, 61
—, Tito, bishop of Adria, 73-4

Olpe, Johannes Bergmann von, printer, 194
Ordelaffi, family, 168, 169, 170
—, Pino, 168, 169
Orsini, Niccolò, Count Pitigliano, captain general, 99, 103
Osmo, Pietro d', light cavalryman, 105
Osoppo, 121
Otranto, 66
Ovid (Publius Ovidius Naso), *Art of Love*, 113, 117 n. 86; *Metamorphoses*, 113

Padua, 11, 99, 100, 101, 116, 134, 143, 169, 192; bishopric of, 153, 155, 156, 157, 160
Paleologo, Margherita, duchess of Ferrara, 133, 136 n. 54, 138 n. 70, 143, 144
Palmier, Piero, 34

Pandolfini, Pier Filippo, 71 n. 62
Panizzi, Sir Anthony, 201
papacy: relations with Venice, 147-8, 154, 155-7, 165; *see also* Paul II, pope
Papal States, 77, 149, 165, 166, 167
Papas, cape, 49
Parma, Communal palace, 5, 7; Communal piazza, 5, 7; palace of the podestà, 5; palace of the captain of the people, 5
Pasqualigo, Ettore, Venetian ambassador to papal curia, 161 n. 69
—, Gianfrancesco di Alvise, *visdomino* of Ferrara, 96
Patinir, Joachim, painter, *Baptism of Christ*, 194 n. 11
Patras, 39, 50
Patrizi, Francesco, humanist, *De institutione rei publicae*, 2
Paul II, pope, 147, 156; as cardinal, 151-3; ecclesiastical benefices of, 151, elected pope, 157; family of, 149-50; and papal sovereignty, 149, 165; and Romagna ('desegno de romagna'), 166-71; *Figs. 14, 15*
—, relations with Venice, 149, 152-3, 155, 158-64, 167-71, 172; Paduan affair, 153-5, 156, 157, 159, 160, 161
Paul V, pope, 230
Pazzi War, 57-8, 60
Pearl, Frank, 193
Pera, 46
Peregrino of Verona, supposed light cavalryman, 104
Pesaro, Marco da, 60, 82
—, Niccolò, 69 n. 52
Petrarch, Francesco, 124, 201, 211; *Canzoniere*, 117 n. 86, 118, 200
Piccinino, Niccolò, *condottiere*, 10, 22, 23, 24
Picino, master engineer, 18, 19
Pico, family, 77
Pio, family, 77
'Piramus et Tisbé', 113, 118
Pisa, 4, 6, 8, 43, 44, 119, 126; Pisan War, 76
Pisani, Benedetta, 142
—, Francesco, *avogador*, 138

—, Girolamo, *provveditore* of fleet, 51-2
—, Vettor, admiral, 228
Pitigliano, count, *see* Orsini, Niccolò
Pius II, pope, 153, 154-5, 156, 157, 163, 166; *Commentaries*, 160
Plenarium (Augsburg, 1489), 194, *Fig. 29*
Po, river, 62, 73, 89, 92, 103, 171; river fleets in, 63, 65, 66, 70
Pocapoina, Arcolini di, son of Alboino, of Verona, 13
Pola, 44
Polani, (Battista?), galley commander, 51
Polesella, 92
Polesine di Rovigo, 59, 63, 64, 71, 77, 81, 92, 93
Pomposa, abbey of (near Ferrara), 74
Pontecchio, 92
Pontelagoscuro (Lagoscuro), 66, 67, 78
Prevesa, 50
Pellegrino, Prisciani, historian, diplomat, 83 n. 75, 90, 91
Prodi, Paolo, 148
Pseudo-Asconius, 2
Puglia, *see* Apulia

Queller, Donald E., professor, 233
Querini, Agostino, 142
—, Giovanni, 78

Rangoni, Baldassare, military commander of Verona, 26 n. 88
Rapallo, Giovan'Antonio da, engineer, 45 n. 54
Ravenna, 152, 159, 167, 169
Raverti, Matteo, stone mason, 174, 176-7, 177-8, 179, 182, 183, 185, 186, 190
Recordati, Ippolito, Mantuan emissary, 144-5
Refugio de' miseri, anon. *novella*, 113
Remer, Antonio, galley officer, 52
Rhodes, 44, 46, 47
Riario, Girolamo, *signore* of Forlì and Imola, 59, 63, 69
Richards, Grant, publisher, 215
Rimini, 62, 165 n. 102, 166, 167, 168, 170, 171, 172; Castel Sismondo, 9
Roberti, Antonio de', *condottiere*, 20
—, Niccolò, envoy, 87 n. 93
Rolfe, Frederick, Baron Corvo, 214-5, 216, 220
Romagna, 63, 67, 76, 166-70
Romanello, Nicolò, mason, 176 n. 26, 177, 181, 182, 183 n. 70
Romanin, Samuele, historian, 227-8
Romano, Ezzelino da, 2
—, Giulio, 131
Rome, 64, 129, 130; Santa Maria Nova, 151
Rosatto, abbey of, 105
Rosebery, Archibald Philip Primrose, 5th earl of, 214
Roselli, Antonio, clerical diplomat, 148
Rossi, family, 63, 64, 71
—, Pier Maria, 62
Rosso, Gasparin, mason, 177, 182, 181 n. 56
—, Zane, carpenter, 174
Rovigo, 93
Ruffinelli, Venturino, printer, 133
Ruskin, John, 217, 225, 229, 230, 232

Sabellico, Marc'Antonio, historian, 202, 203
Sacchi, Bartolomeo (Platina), *Historia . . .*, 23 n. 70
Salimbeni, Lorenzo and Jacopo, fresco of, 194 n. 11
Salin, Antonio, gondolier, 225
Salisbury, Robert Cecil, 1st earl of, 230
Sańchez de Arévalo, Rodrigo, clerical diplomat, 149
Sanmicheli, Michele, architect, 25, 26
Sanseverino, Roberto da, count of Caiazzo, 61, 62, 63, 64, 65, 68, 71
Sansovino, Francesco, 42 n. 43, 125
Santa Maura, island, 50
Sanudo, *see* Sanuto

Sanuto, Francesco, 66 n. 33, 67
—, Marin, 134, 201-3; *Chronachetta*, 202; *Itinerario . . .*, 24, 73, 201; *La Spedizione . . .*, 201, 202; *Vite de' duchi*, 157
—, *Diarii*, 25, 30, 47, 48, 80, 129, 140; language of, 199, 201, 202-3, 210-12; lexis, 210; morphosyntax, 206-10; spelling and phonology, 204-6
Sapienza, island, 48, 50
Sarpi, Paolo, friar, 219-20, 231, 232, 235
Sathas, C.N., 30
Savonarola, Girolamo, 2
Savorgnan, family, 109-10, 121; Del Monte branch, 110, 112, 119, 122; Della Torre branch, 110, 122, 126
—, Antonio, uncle of Luigi da Porto, 106, 109, 110, 111, 112, 120-1
—, Bernardino, nephew of Antonio, 120, 121, 122
—, Francesco, nephew of Antonio, 120, 121, 122, 124, 126
—, Giacomo, father of Lucina, 118-9, 126
—, Giambattista, brother of Lucina, 125, 126
—, Giovanni, brother of Antonio, 120
—, Girolamo, son of Pagano, collateral-general, 99, 110, 112, 119, 121, 122
—, Lucina, 119, 121; medallion of, 118, *Fig. 13*; see also Da Porto, Luigi
—, Maria, mother of Lucina, 119, 120
—, Niccolò, father of Antonio, 110
—, —, son of Antonio, 120, 121
—, Pagano, son of Tristano, 110
—, Tristano, 109, 110
—, Urbano, grandfather of Antonio, 110
Savoy, Bona of, duchess of Milan, 59
Sbrojavacca, Bernardino, of Udine, 119 n. 89
Schongauer, Martin, engraver, 194, 196
Scipione, Baldassare, captain,

light horse, 106, 107 n. 38, 108 n. 44
Scutari, 42-3, 63
Sforza, Francesco I, duke of Milan, 10, 22, 23, 189-90
—, Francesco II, duke of Milan, 141
—, Ludovico, duke of Milan, 62, 63, 64, 69, 75, 76, 77, 78, 82
Sidgwick, Henry, professor, 218
Siena, 1, 3, 7, 154
Sigismund, emperor, 16
Sixtus IV, pope, 58, 61, 63, 64, 70, 171
Smith, George, publisher, 222, 231
—, Logan Pearsall, 217
Soave, 104
Sommariva, Giorgio, poet, military engineer, *Relazione*, 23
Soranzo, family, 150
—, Benedetto, archbishop of Cyprus, 69 n. 52
—, Niccolò, Venetian ambassador to papal curia, 161 n. 69
—, Vettore, captain general of sea, 63
Spain, 55 n. 100
Speroni, Sperone, 136
Stagno and Curzola, Dalmatia, bishopric of, 152
Stefanino, master builder, 187; son Piero, 187
Stefano of Cremona, master builder, 18
Steno, Michele, doge, 14, 15
Stevenson, Robert Louis, 215
Suida, W., art historian, 194
Suligo, Bartolomeo, engineer, 30
Symonds, John Addington, 213-4, 216, 235; Autobiography, 217-8; 'The Catholic Reaction', 219 n. 32, 231; and Horatio Brown, 217-24; letters, 213-4, 216, 217, 218, 220-4, 235; and Paolo Sarpi, 219, 231-2
—, Margaret, 213
Syracuse, 2
Syria, 46

Tarsus, 47
Tartaro, river, 63
Terraferma, 15, 18, 71, 93, 112, 148, 150, 164, 165, 173, 229
Timoleon, Greek statesman and general, 2
Titian (Tiziano Vecelli), 130-1; *St Mary Magdalene*, 130
Torri di Quartesolo (near Vicenza), 99
Trecenta, 92
Trevisan, family, 60, 161
—, Benedetto, *visdomino* of Ferrara, 59
—, Lodovico, cardinal, 152, 160 n. 67, 163
—, Marcantonio, doge, 139, 144
—, Melchior, commander of Venetian fleet, 49, 50
—, Niccolò, *visdomino* of Ferrara, 90 n. 112
—, Zaccaria, Venetian ambassador to papal curia, 161
Treviso, 24, 193-4
Tridapoli, Ludovico, secretary to B. Agnello, 142
Trissino family, 100
Tron, Niccolò, Venetian ambassador to papal curia, 161
Trotti, Giacomo, envoy of Borso d'Este, 169
Turks, 29, 30, 35, 39, 135, 157, 159, 164, 229; artillery, 29, 40-1, 50, 51, 52, 54; navy, 40-1, 44, 46, 47, 48-9
—, First Turkish War (1463-79), 29, 30, 59, 61, 62, 155, 163, 171; warfare in, 39, 41, 42-3
—, Second Turkish War (1499-1503), 29; battle of Zonchio, 48-9; causes of, 43-4; military preparations for, 44-7; siege of Modon, 37, 49-54, 55
—, Third Turkish War, 29
Tuscany, 61, 85

Udine, 106, 108, 109, 110, 111, 118, 120; San Francesco, 118
Urbino, 4

Valier conspiracy (1547), 137
Vasari, Giorgio, 196, 197
Vendramin, Alvise, 82
—, Andrea, doge, 82
Venice: Ca' Barzizza, 177; Ca'

Index

Bernardo, 183, 186; Ca' Capello, 214, 224; Ca' da Mosto, 177, 181; Ca' del Duca, 188-90; Ca' Foscari, 180, 183, 188, *Fig. 18*; Ca' Giustinian, 183; Ca' Loredan, 177, 184; Ca' Torresella, 213, 214, 215; Canalazzo, 184; Carità, church, 182, 183, 187; Corte Nova, almshouses, 187; Fondaco dei Turchi, 180 n. 15, 189; Frari, 138, 178, 180; *Generale Studium*, 158; Giudecca canal, 213; Madonna dell' Orto, monastery, 155, 180, 182; Misericordia, 178, 183, 187; Palazzo Badoer, 176 n. 24; Palazzo Cavalli, 185-6 *Fig. 20*; Palazzo Contarini Fasan, 188; Palazzo Donà, 184, 185; Palazzo Ducale, 178, 180, 184, 186, 215; Palazzo Giovanelli, 183, 185-6, *Fig. 19*; Palazzo Moro Lin, 190; Palazzo Pesaro, 188; Palazzo Priuli, 182, 185; Palazzo Sagredo Morosini, 176 n. 24, 178, 182; Palazzo Soranzo (S. Polo), 181; Palazzo Soranzo van Axel, 186; Palazzo Venier Contarini, 186, *Fig. 21*; Palazzo Zaguri, 176 n. 24; Porta della Carta, 181, 183, 188, 190, *Fig. 22*; Rialto, 131, 187; San Felice, 175; San Giovanni in Bragora, 149, 158; San Marco, 151, 173, 187; San Pantalon, 136; San Stefano, 180; San Zaccaria, 179 n. 47, 182, 183, 187, 190; Sant' Elena, 226; Sant' Hyeronimo, 145; Santa Sofia, 174; Santi Giovanni e Paolo, 137, 178, 180 n. 50; Servites, church of, 145; Zattere, 213, 214
—, army, *see* Ferrara, war of; Verona, Cittadella
—, cavalry, 61, 104-7; stradiots, 43, 49, 50, 66
—, *Collegio*, 16, 18, 44, 60, 69, 81, 91, 107, 134
—, Council of Ten, 30, 57, 64, 68-9, 81, 82, 106, 107, 134, 140, 142, 143, 153, 155, 156, 160, 162, 163, 202, 233

—, *ducali*, 18, 18 nn. 44, 45; 19, 20, 21, 23 n. 72, 25
—, factions, 160-1, 225
—, Great Council, 138, 150, 174
—, historians of, 233, 234; *see also* Brown, Horatio
—, navy, 29; defence of colonies, 40, 41-2, 55; river fleets, 42, 62, 63, 64, 65-6, 67, 70; in Second Turkish War, 43-5, 47-54; in War of Ferrara, 62-7 passim
—, *savi del Consiglio*, 69, 91
—, *savi di Terraferma*, 34, 60, 137
—, Senate, 14-25 passim, 57, 60, 61, 62, 68, 69, 71, 78, 82, 87, 101, 104, 137, 152-8 passim, 162, 163, 164, 168, 169, 171, 233
—, Signoria, 7, 17, 19, 76, 79, 88, 90, 92, 93, 159, 164, 172, 187, 190
—, *see also*: Agnello, B.; architecture; Este, Ercole d'; Ferrara; leagues; papacy; Paul II, pope; Turks; Verona
Venier, family, 213
—, Antonio, doge, 35 n. 17
—, Antonio di Andrea, *visdomino* of Ferrara, 94
—, Domenico, 132
—, Francesco, doge, 136, 139, 145
—, Marcantonio, procurator, 139
Veniexiana, La, 211, 212
Verci, G.B., 11
Verme, Alvise dal, 22, 23 n. 70
Verona, 12, 18, 102, 107, 108, 109, 163, 169, 203; Borgo di San Zeno, 11, 13, 23; Montagna del Carbone, 19; Quartiere Maggiore, 12
—, Council of Twelve, 16; Council of Fifty, 23; Verona and Venice, 14-5, 16, 17, 18, 22-3, 24-5, 26; *Figs. 1, 3, 5*
—, fortifications: Castel San Felice, 10, 11, 12, 22, 26; Castel San Pietro, 10, 11, 12, 17, 22; Castelvecchio (Castello di San Martino), 2, 10-11, 12, 17, 18, 19, 22, 24, 26
—, Cittadella: built by Visconti, 11-14; captains of, 20, 25; in contemporary sources, 24-5;

decline of, 25-6; lost and retaken (1439), 10, 22-3; manning of, 15, 17, 19, 20-22, 23; Venetian work on, 16-9 Porta Rofiolo, 13, 21, 22, 23; Porta San Antonio, 13; Rochetta della Brà, 12, 21, 22, 23, 24, 25; San Fermo in Braida, 13; Sant'Antonio a Corso, 21; Santa Croce *contrada*, 13, 25-6, 17 n. 40; Santa Trinità, abbey, 19, 20, 26; Torre della Paglia, 12, 24, 26; *Figs. 2, 4*
Vicenza, 24, 100, 102, 103, 114, 169; bishopric of, 151, 163; captured by Venice, 99, 101; *Consiglio Maggiore*, 100, 101
Villach (Austria), 120, 121
Villamarzana, 92
Villani, Giovanni, chronicler, 3, 4, 202
Villanova, 104
Visconti, family, 5, 13, 14,
—, Filippo Maria, duke of Milan, 5, 6, 7, 21
—, Luchino, *signore* of Milan, 5
—, Matteo I, *signore* of Milan, 5
Vitturi, Bartolomeo di Matteo, *visdomino* of Ferrara, 81, 96
Volano, 78
Von Harff, Arnold, 35, 37

Wootton, David, historian, 232
Wotton, Sir Henry, English ambassador to Venice, 231

Zagata, P., *Cronica della città di Verona* . . . , 11 n. 10, 13
Zanchani, Andrea, Venetian ambassador to Sublime Porte, 47
Zane, family, 150
—, Girolamo di Bernardo, *visdomino* of Ferrara, 94
—, Lorenzo, bishop of Spoleto, 162, 170 n. 126
Zanon, Augusto, porter, 224
Zantani, Antonio, rector, Modon, 50 nn. 77, 80, 82; 51, 52, 53, 54
Zante, 49, 50, 51, 53
Zavarise, Virgilio, chancellor of Verona, 23 n. 72
Zeno, family, 142, 150

—, Bachalario, 174
—, Caterina, dau. of Bachalario
—, Giacomo, bishop of Belluno and Feltre, 151, 154, 155, 157
—, Gianbattista, cardinal, 163, 172
—, Luca di Marco, *visdomino* of Ferrara, 94–5
—, Soradamor, dau. of Bachalario, m. Marin Contarini, 173, 174
Zigogna, Francesco, *provveditore generale* of the Morea, 51 n. 85
Zonchio, 40, 54; battles of, 29, 48, 50
Zorzi, Marco di Bertuccio, *visdomino* of Ferrara, 79, 98

List of Subscribers

Mrs C.P. Agelasto
Christopher Allmand
Professor Sydney Anglo
Giovanni Aquilecchia
C.A.J. Armstrong
Miss Jenny Arnott
Colin M. Bather
J.G. Bernasconi
C.F. Black
P. Boizot
Miss S.C.H. Bracken
Hans Brill
George Bull
Dr Edward Chaney
Sir Ashley and Lady Clarke
Dr Henry J. Cohn
R.B. Coyle
David Davies
Alistair Day
K.F. Day
Carlo Dionisotti
Anna Maria Edelstein
B.A. Gillman
John Gittens
Richard J. Goy
Professor R.A. Griffiths
J.R.S. Guinness
Mrs Randolph H. Guthrie Jr
John Hall

Dr Paul Hills
Dr Deborah Howard
Dr Peter Humfrey
Patricia H. Labalme
Professor John Larner
Mrs R.M. Letts
W. Lewington
Jacqueline Linsley
Nigel Llewellyn
O.M.T. Logan
Mrs Diana Macnaughton
R. Mallinson
Nicholas Mann
Professor L.R. Martines
Ms C.A. Moir
J.C. Morgan
Terence Mullaly
C.J. Nicholson
The Viscount Norwich
Mrs J.I. Olby
Dr Robert Oresko
Mrs A.J. Pattison
Dr J. Payan
J.W. Peat
Kenneth Powell
Ms Sarah Quill
Miss Rosemary Rendel
Dr E.C.M. Roaf
Sir Lewis Robertson

B.D. Rogles
Mrs V. Romieri
M.J. Rosenthal
Philip Rylands
Dr A.J. Sargent
Professor Juergen and Anne Schulz
Mrs D.R. Sheasby

C.E. Sheppard
John Vernon
Mrs Marina Wallace
Jeremy Warren
Evelyn Welch
Professor J.H. Whitfield
T.C.P. Zimmerman